ABOUT CROP

CROP, The Comparative Research Programme on Poverty, is a response from the academic community to the problem of poverty. The programme was initiated in 1992, and the CROP Secretariat was officially opened in June 1993 by the director-general of UNESCO, Dr Federico Mayor.

In recent years, poverty alleviation, reduction or even eradication and abolition of poverty has moved up the international agenda, and the CROP network is providing research-based information to policy-makers and others responsible for poverty reduction. Researchers from more than 100 countries have joined the CROP network, with more than half coming from so-called developing countries and countries in transition.

The major aim of CROP is to produce sound and reliable knowledge that can serve as a basis for poverty reduction. This is done by bringing together researchers for workshops, co-ordinating research projects and publications, and offering educational courses for the international community of policy-makers.

CROP is multi-disciplinary and works as an independent non-profit organization.

For more information you may contact:

CROP Secretariat
Fosswinckelsgate 7
N-5007 Bergen
NORWAY

tel: +47-5558-9739, fax: +47-5558-9745
e-mail: crop@uib.no
CROP on the Internet: http://www.crop.org

CROP is a programme under the International Social Science Council.

CROP PUBLICATIONS

Poverty: Research Projects, Institutes, Persons, Tinka Ewoldt-Leicher and Arnaud F. Marks (eds), Tilburg: Bergen and Amsterdam, 1995, 248 pp.

Urban Poverty: Characteristics, Causes and Consequences, David Satterthwaite (ed.), special issue of *Environment and Urbanization*, Volume 7, No. 1, April 1995, 283 pp.

Urban Poverty: From Understanding to Action, David Satterthwaite (ed.), special issue of *Environment and Urbanization*, Volume 7, No. 2, October 1995, 283 pp.

Women and Poverty – The Feminization of Poverty, Ingrid Eide (ed.), The Norwegian National Commission for UNESCO and CROP: Oslo and Bergen, 1995 (published in Norwegian only), 56 pp.

Poverty: A Global Review. Handbook on International Poverty Research, Else Øyen, S. M. Miller, Syed Abdus Samad (eds), Scandinavian University Press and UNESCO: Oslo and Paris, 1996, 620 pp.

Poverty and Participation in Civil Society, Yogesh Atal and Else Øyen (eds), UNESCO and Abhinav Publications: Paris and New Delhi, 1997, 152 pp.

Law, Power and Poverty, Asbjørn Kjønstad and John H. Veit Wilson (eds), CROP Publications: Bergen, 1997, 148 pp.

Poverty and Social Exclusion in the Mediterranean Area, Karima Korayem and Maria Petmesidou (eds), CROP Publications: Bergen, 1998, 286 pp.

Poverty and the Environment, Arild Angelsen and Matti Vainio (eds), CROP Publications: Bergen, 1998, 180 pp.

The International Glossary on Poverty, David Gordon and Paul Spicker (eds), CROP International Studies in Poverty Research, Zed Books: London, 1999, 162 pp.

Poverty and the Law, Asbjørn Kjønstad and Peter Robson (eds), Hart Publishing: Cambridge, 2001, 199 pp.

Poverty Reduction: What Role for the State in Today's Globalized Economy?, Francis Wilson, Nazneen Kanji and Einar Braathen (eds), CROP International Studies in Poverty Research, Zed Books: London, 2001, 372 pp.

The Poverty of Rights: Human Rights and the Eradication of Poverty, Willem van Genugten and Camilo Perez-Bustillo (eds), CROP International Studies in Poverty Research, Zed Books: London, 2001, 209 pp.

Best Practices in Poverty Reduction – An Analytical Framework, Else Øyen et al. (eds), CROP International Studies in Poverty Research, Zed Books: London, 2002, 144 pp.

LUCY WILLIAMS, ASBJØRN KJØNSTAD
& PETER ROBSON | editors

Law and Poverty: the Legal System and Poverty Reduction

CROP International Studies
in Poverty Research

Zed Books
LONDON · NEW YORK

Law and Poverty: the Legal System and Poverty Reduction was
first published by Zed Books Ltd, 7 Cynthia Street, London N1
9JF, UK and Room 400, 175 Fifth Avenue, New York, NY 10010,
USA in 2003.

www.zedbooks.co.uk

CROP International Studies in Poverty Research

Cover designed by Andrew Corbett
Set in Monotype Dante by Ewan Smith, London
Printed and bound in Malta by Gutenberg Ltd

Distributed in the USA exclusively by Palgrave, a division of St
Martin's Press, LLC, 175 Fifth Avenue, New York, NY 10010

A catalogue record for this book is available from the British Library.
Library of Congress cataloging-in-publication data: available

ISBN 1 84277 396 8 cased
ISBN 1 84277 397 6 limp

Contents

About the contributors

AMITA AGARWAL has been teaching political science for twenty years as a senior lecturer (equivalent to associate professor). She is also an honorary professor of human rights. Currently she is working on her post-doctoral research project from the South Asia Studies Center, University of Rajasthan, Jaipur, India. She has participated in several national and international conferences and has published books and many research papers. Her latest publications include a forthcoming book on human rights, *Human Rights for Survival of Civilization* (New Delhi: Kalinga) and *Indian Ocean and World Peace* (New Delhi: Kanishka, 2000). She is also an active member of several professional associations and is currently the State Chancellor of the Rajasthan chapter of the International Association of Educators for World Peace, which aims at enhancing peace and protecting human rights through education.

MOKBUL MORSHED AHMAD is an Assistant Professor in the Department of Geography and Environment, Dhaka University, Bangladesh. He teaches and researches mainly on economic geography, rural and regional development and NGOs/PVDOs. His most recent book, on NGO fieldworkers in Bangladesh, was published by Ashgate in 2002. Currently he is researching the religious NGOs in Bangladesh, looking at problems of funding and public acceptability.

GABRIEL AMITSIS, who has a PhD in Social Security Law, is a legal consultant in social insurance and welfare policy issues. He previously worked for six years as senior researcher in the Social Security Institute of Athens University. More recently, he has undertaken research and teaching at the Athens National School of Social Administration, the Greek Open University and the Technological Institute of Athens in areas relating to social security rights, national and international social assistance law and administrative law. His several publications include *The Legal Establishment of Subsistence Standards in the Greek and the International Order* (Athens: A.N. Sakoulas, 2001), *Administrative Principles of the Greek Social Welfare System* (Papazisis, Athens, 2001), 'Human Rights and Social Exclusion: The New European Agenda', in D. Pieters (ed.), *Confidence and Changes: Managing Social Protection in the New Millennium* (The Hague: Kluwer, 2001) and *The Greek Social Insurance System* (Athens: Ministry of Labour and Social Insurance, 2003).

AHMED AOUED is a former university researcher in human rights at the University of Oran, Algeria. He taught international development law and held the UNESCO Chair for Human Rights at the same university and attended several sessions of the Human Rights Commission in Geneva. He is now legal consultant and researcher for an international NGO in Geneva and has extensive publications in the area of human rights promotion and protection. He graduated from Glasgow University in 1980 (LLM) and 1992 (PhD).

ASBJØRN KJØNSTAD was born in Norway. He has been Professor Dr Juris at University of Oslo since 1978; Dean at the Faculty of Law, University of Oslo, 1986–88; vice-president of the European Institute of Social Security, 1993–97; visiting scholar at Boston University Law School and Boston College Law School, 1995–96; Juris Doctor Honoris Causa at Lund University, Sweden, May 1996; visiting professor at the University of Leuven, March and April 1997. He has written thirty-four books and more than 140 articles on social security law, medical law, welfare law, tort law and family law.

ANTONELLA MAMELI received her legal education at the University of Cagliari, Italy (Laurea in Giurisprudenza), and graduated from Yale Law School with a masters degree (LLM) and a doctorate (JSD). She is a member of the Italian Bar, the New York Bar and the Washington DC Bar and is now in private practice in Milan.

SUSAN NOTT is a senior lecturer in law at the Liverpool Law School, Liverpool University. She is an active member of Liverpool University's Feminist Legal Research Unit and, as such, has participated in a variety of research projects. These include research into the effectiveness of gender mainstreaming, the ability of women to gain access to healthcare and the legal situation of working women in the United Kingdom and the European Union. Her several publications include *All My Worldly Goods: A Feminist Perspective on the Legal Regulation of Wealth* (with Anne Morris, Dartmouth, 1995), *Making Women Count: Integrating Gender into Law and Policy-making* (edited with Fiona Beveridge and Kylie Stephen, Ashgate, 2000) and *Well Women: The Gendered Nature of Healthcare Provision* (edited with Anne Morris, Ashgate, 2002).

CAMILO PEREZ-BUSTILLO was the holder in 2002–03 of the W. Haywood Burns Memorial Chair in Civil Rights Law at the City University of New York (CUNY) School of Law. He is co-author and co-editor with Willem van Genugten of *The Poverty of Rights: Human Rights and the Eradication of Poverty* (London: Zed Books, CROP International Studies in Poverty Research, 2001). He taught and did research as an international human rights scholar and advocate based in Mexico from 1992 to 2002.

PETER ROBSON has an LLB from St Andrews, UK, and a PhD from Strathclyde, UK. He is a solicitor, and Professor of Social Welfare Law at the University of Strathclyde. He is also chair of the national housing charity SHELTER, a part-time judge in the Appeals Service dealing with disability appeals and child support appeals, and director of WESLO (a charitable housing company). He has lectured at the universities of Stirling, Glasgow, Heriot Watt and Strathclyde. His major interests are law and popular culture, housing law, social security law and clinical law. He was editor of *Scottish Housing Law News* from 1987 and joint editor of *Scottish Housing Law Reports*. He is joint author of *Homeless People and the Law* (Butterworths, 3rd edition, 1996) and *Residential Tenancies* (W. Green, 2nd edition, 1998) and joint editor and contributor to *Poverty and Law* (Hart, 2001) and *Health of Scottish Housing* (Ashgate, 2001). His most recent work in the *International Journal of Sociology of Law* is on 'Film Images of the Ethnic Minority Experience in the UK'.

DEBI S. SAINI, PhD (Delhi), is a senior faculty member at DCAC, University of Delhi. He was Professor of Human Resources Management at IILM, New Delhi (1996–99), and Professor of Labour Law at the Gandhi Labour Institute, Ahmedabad, India (1992–94). He has edited or authored six books in the area of labour relations; law, labour and society; and human resources management. He has also written a volume on *Social Security Law: India* which forms part of the *International Encyclopaedia of Laws* (General Editor: R. Blanpain) published by Kluwer Law International, The Hague. He has carried out assignments for the ILO and GTZ (Germany), among others. Dr Saini was founding editor of the journal *Management & Change* (1997–99). He has been a member of the editorial board of *Industrial Relations Journal*, Blackwell, Oxford (1997–2002). He recently drafted the All India Authority for Vocational Training (AIAVT) Bill that is expected to be introduced into the Indian Parliament for enactment soon.

KALINGA TUDOR SILVA holds a BA from the University of Peradeniya, Sri Lanka, and a PhD from Monash University in Australia. He has been Professor of Sociology at the University of Peradeniya since 1992. In 1992 he was the executive director of the Centre for Poverty Analysis in Colombo. From 2000 to 2002 he served as the secretary of the Asia–Pacific Network for Social Sciences in Health (APNET). His areas of research include the sociology of health, poverty and social inequality, ethnicity, social conflict and social development. His publications include *Watta-dwellers: A Sociological Study of Selected Urban Low-income Communities in Sri Lanka* (Lanham: University Press of America, 1991), *Towards a Healthy Society: Case Studies in Health Social Science Partnerships in Asia–Pacific Region* (Manila: Social Development Research Center, De La Salle University, 1996) and *Mobilisation of the Poor: A Means to Poverty Reduction?* (Stockholm: Sida).

PAUL SPICKER holds the Grampian Chair of Public Policy at the Robert Gordon University, Aberdeen, where he is Director of the Centre for Public Policy and Management. His research has included studies related to the care of old people, psychiatric patients, benefit delivery systems, housing policy, homelessness and local anti-poverty strategy; currently he is working on participative studies of the experiences and views of poor people. He has written widely in the field of social policy; his recent books include *Social Policy in a Changing Society* (with Maurice Mullard, London: Routledge, 1998), *The International Glossary of Poverty* (co-edited with David Gordon, London: Zed Books, CROP International Studies in Poverty Research, 1999) and *The Welfare State: A General Theory* (London: Sage, 2000).

LUCY WILLIAMS is Professor of Law at Northeastern University School of Law, Boston, and was the School's 1994–95 Public Interest Distinguished Professor. She has written and lectured widely in the area of welfare law and poverty. In August 1994 she was appointed by President Bill Clinton to the three-year Advisory Council on Unemployment Compensation, which evaluated all aspects of the unemployment compensation programme and made policy recommendations to the President and Congress. Prior to joining the faculty at Northeastern, she was an attorney at Massachusetts Law Reform Institute for thirteen years, where she specialized in employment and governmental benefits law.

Introduction

LUCY WILLIAMS

§ Much of the world is living in abject poverty and many individuals who are not living in poverty do not seem to care. The latter (this includes people from within a wide range of class and cultural perspectives) often articulates its political and personal apathy to those in poverty as a response to poor people's lack of initiative, indeed their personal fault. Of course, no one should canonize all poor people or exclude personal agency as a force in constructing one's experiences. Poor individuals, like all of us, have faults. But if academics and activists who work on behalf of the impoverished are to understand and be able persuasively to articulate the economic and personal situation of the poor, they must immerse themselves in the context and history of power relationships and income imbalances and the role of the legal system in establishing and maintaining inequitable societal structures.

Unlike what many people think, poverty is not a natural or pre-legal condition. Income distribution is not separate from the law. To believe that poverty is based only on individual failure ignores the legal structures that create and perpetuate income imbalances both internally to a nation-state and globally. In each country, advocates for redistribution must seriously critique their own country's legal systems to determine the ways in which the law constructs poverty internally and cross-border.

For example, in many Western developed countries, the accumulation of prevailing legal rules relating to property, contract, family and tort law provides a legal framework that contributes to developing and maintaining economic imbalances. Let me give one specific illustration: current US inheritance law, building on prior legal definitions of what is 'private property' and developed at a time when only moneyed white males could own property or had the right to vote, provided protections for wealthy individuals' economic interests. Through the law's definition of 'the ownership of property', the law privileged those with wealth, who could then maintain and pass on their assets to their heirs. Thus, the heirs of those originally able to own or purchase property were, likewise, economically privileged.

The ramifications of these common-law principles are evident in racial and gender income disparity today. The vast majority of women and people of colour in many Western developed nations do not have the resources, i.e. the assets, controlled by many white men. Thus, those with the major amount of assets can invest and continue to generate income for themselves and their families, income that is not based on their own waged work. Quite apart from a salaried income, they are able to provide their children with benefits (e.g. private, individualized and, frequently, superior academic experiences and extracurricular lessons or opportunities) that then often lead to privileged secondary education and access to higher paying jobs. The continuation of privileges, benefits and inheritance, in turn, creates ongoing 'entitlement', in both a legal and sociological sense. Their children have choices that those without resources simply do not have. They may choose to become philanthropists or use their propertied wealth to generate benefits for those who did not benefit from the common-law property construc- tions, but they have the *choice* of whether to do so, in part because of the legal definitions of property.

Ignoring this asset imbalance and the privilege that comes from 'asset advantage', mainstream legal discourse focuses on 'equal opportunity' within the waged workforce for those previously discriminated against because of disability, sexual orientation, gender or race. Those without assets are treated as if they were on an equal footing within the waged work setting. Once any person has been given an 'equal' opportunity to compete for a job, the appearance of imbalance is obscured. Thus, popular culture often ignores the role of legal institutions in reproducing hierarchy and thereby preventing the emergence of a racial/gender/ class-neutral world of 'equal opportunity'. But any discussion of 'equal rights' to employment opportunities and pay, while quite important to an anti-poverty strategy, is futile without a discussion of 'equal assets' and a re-examination of the traditional common law of property that perpetuates the asset, or 'opportunity', inequality.

As a scholar working in the United States, I would not presume to impose this analysis on radically different contexts, such as the situa- tion of non-Western developing nations. As the work collected here demonstrates, however, scholars from other countries and cultures have advanced parallel analyses of mechanisms through which the law estab- lishes and reinforces income and power imbalances, and indeed the identities of those who have or do not have the requisite educational or cultural background to accomplish jobs that society has structured.

In addition, contemporary developments in intellectual property and patent law contribute to maintaining an income and power imbalance between developed and developing countries, e.g. vis-à-vis access to pharmaceutical products and to technology in general. Developed countries uphold their laws as sacrosanct, resulting in profit to corporations in those countries, while indigenous populations lose the financial benefit from their significant contributions and people die from lack of easily accessible drugs. So the 'un-natural', legal definitions of who 'owns' property, and what 'property' is, become central to any global poverty analysis.

Yet, interestingly, when the judicial system interprets law in a way that reconfigures or reinterprets the traditional common-law notions, it is viewed as 'activist' – perhaps operating outside its legitimate role within the rule of law. Judicial decisions reinforcing the status quo (which has largely been maintained by judicial fiat) are not viewed in such a way. In other words, legal discourse does not view judicial opinions that enforce and maintain the current judicially created income and power configuration as 'activist', but rather as 'natural'.

Those of us who are struggling with cross-culture, cross-border alleviation of poverty must challenge ourselves to question each of our own countries' legal perceptions and expose how legal systems construct rather than combat poverty. We must approach the question of the causes of poverty from different perspectives, addressing the problem through disparate frameworks and lenses that, on occasion, appear to reflect conflicting philosophical/theoretical perspectives. In fact, reformist, parliamentarian, anarchist approaches need not be perceived as always representing diametrically oppositional positions, but rather can be theorized as a unity that allows those working in redistributive projects to understand the multiple ways in which to approach and envision anti-poverty initiatives. But in so doing, one cannot pretend to have a grand scheme, but rather to act on the basis of our best, considered judgment, and then regularly to reassess and criticize our actions in light of the results.

The papers in this book, presented and discussed at the Comparative Research on Poverty Workshop: Law and Poverty III, in Onati, Spain, in May 1999, provide a range of options for using law as a tool to struggle against, rather than sustain, poverty. They attempt to break open stereotypical ideas of poverty as a domestic issue – as opposed to a cross-border and global issue – and of poverty as natural, as opposed to being largely legally created. They reveal a number of ways in which the law is implicated in the construction of poverty and address various perspectives through which legal structures might be used to reconfigure income and power distributions in quite disparate cultures and across nation-state borders. They do not pretend to provide ultimate solutions, but rather to propose theoretical innovations that can serve as tools in the ongoing endeavour of addressing poverty.

The papers present divergent approaches for using the law to combat poverty. Some address very specific legal questions, whether within a statutory or constitutional framework or within a nation-state, regional or global context. Others look at delivery systems and address the shortcomings of implementation strategies and political actors. But the fact that an author focuses on an issue through a particular lens is not meant to exclude different approaches to the problem. The reader should not isolate articles as relevant only to a particular country or region. We believe that the papers presented at Law and Poverty III provide a range of approaches within a cross-cultural interchange.

The chapters in Part I address important ways in which poverty is legally constructed, often from a cross-cultural perspective. Ahmed Aoued focuses on the right to development as an important merger of economic and social rights that protect the survival and livelihood of people and communities and civil and political rights that are perceived as inherent to individuals. He challenges the dichotomy between economic and social rights versus civil and political rights, and argues that this bifurcation minimizes the central role of economic rights, particularly highlighting legal developments within the United Nations. Lucy A. Williams likewise challenges the artificial separation of legal arenas: immigration, social welfare benefits, low-wage work, and economic and financial integration. Considering the relationship between Mexico and the United States as a specific model through which to view integrated legal discourses, she connects disparate, indeed seemingly conflicting, areas of law to provide a cross-border understanding of the legal construction of poverty. Camilo Perez-Bustillo connects the global analysis of poverty to a critique of the neo-liberal economic agenda, focusing on political repression as a lens through which to understand poverty, marginalization and social exclusion. He urges that we address poverty in the context of a broader, global debate about the contemporary meaning of democracy.

Part II includes papers exploring the question of who should be responsible for addressing poverty. These start from a rejection of the traditional, sharp distinction between public and private. Should advocates for redistribution valorize a single site as the one from which to alleviate poverty, without recognizing the important connections and interconnections among social forces and various actors? Peter

Robson examines the shift in British views of responsibility for the poverty of single-parent families during the 1990s. In place of a route out of poverty through tax-financed, state benefits, he documents British policies that stress formal 'legal responsibility' for financial support within the 'private' sector of child support enforcement. Mokbul Morshed Ahmed adds to Robson's observations, but through a surprisingly different cultural lens. He criticizes the role of non-governmental organizations (NGOs) in Bangladesh as unresponsive to the poor people whom they should serve, posits that the NGOs' major allegiance is to their own Western-controlled funding sources, and argues for more accountability. From quite another perspective, Paul Spicker articulates the current version of the perennial debate regarding the personal fault of those in poverty. He takes on the predominant dialogue, arguing that social exclusion should not be equated with poverty. Indeed, poverty can refer to material circumstances, economic resources and/or social position. Exclusion is primarily understood in terms of social relationships. Rather, he argues that, to the extent that the concepts of poverty and exclusion are connected, inclusion in solidaristic social relationships is an important anti-poverty strategy. These chapters project a global anti-poverty discourse going beyond the conventional reliance on state-centred redistributive instruments to incorporate a recognition that anti-poverty strategies must equally address other social contexts that reinforce inequality.

Part III focuses on the role of legal entitlements in poverty alleviation and the judiciary's function in that process. Antonella Mameli's chapter analyses the role of the courts and of judicial review as a tool for combating poverty, juxtaposing the civil law system of Italy and the common-law system in the United States. She situates the perceived role of the judiciary within a historical context, discussing social antagonisms in each country and the means through which various social groups (in Italy, class-based, and in the USA, racially-based) have attempted to find a voice within the judicial system. Asbjørn Kjønstad provides a more concrete example of judicially-created entitlements, or lack thereof, within the Norwegian and European Union legal systems. He exposes the judiciary's juxtapositioning of, and often false distinction between, social insurance and social assistance, arguing for the development of a property right to social security. Gabriel Amitsis takes on the lack of an entitlement to subsistence benefits, i.e. a social safety-net, in Greece, arguing that legal mechanisms need to incorporate concepts of social citizenship, and conversely that concepts of social citizenship need to be strengthened by legal mechanisms. Specifically, he articulates how concepts of social citizenship in international documents can be melded with Greek constitutional and statutory law and deployed in the task of poverty alleviation.

Part IV sets forth a number of important legal initiatives that can be used to address specific aspects of poverty. Susan Nott advocates an approach she calls 'poverty proofing', i.e. an assessment of laws through a class lens, modelled on 'equality proofing', which views laws within a gender context. She cautions that, while all laws should be assessed for their potential impact on gender or class, such assessments must also recognize the differences within groups and not essentialize gender or class. While aware of numerous pitfalls in this process, she posits that poverty-impact assessments might raise awareness and consciousness of law as a factor in allocating income and assets. Kalinga Tudor Silva directly takes on the complex and difficult issues of alcohol and tobacco use in poor communities, focusing on Sri Lanka. But, quite unlike those who merely blame poor people who use alcohol or tobacco for their impoverished condition and who ignore the substantial issue of drug abuse within upper-class communities, he explores ways in which the law has contributed to differential treatment among users and to a class-based penal system. He then suggests alternative alcohol and tobacco legislation that might reduce poverty. Amita Agarwal focuses on the eradication of child labour as a means to reduce poverty, comparing provisions of the Indian constitution with international human rights initiatives. Her chapter should be read in conjunction with those of Aoued and Amitsis, all of which draw important lessons from human rights documents. Debi S. Saini presents a strong case for anti-poverty advocates, particularly in developing countries, to view labour laws (on the books and in implementation) as major tools for addressing poverty. He highlights the non-enforcement of key Indian constitutional and statutory provisions and documents the effect of non-enforcement on unions supported by a majority of the workers (as opposed to corrupt minority unions) that are attempting to provide a more equally balanced relationship between workers and management. He argues that the bureaucratic structure of labour law in India disempowers workers who are living in abject poverty in spite of the high-minded vision set forth in the Indian constitution, and he challenges activists to develop alternative strategies.

As a whole, the papers presented and the discussion at the Law and Poverty III workshop pushed us to develop broader theoretical frameworks in which to envision mechanisms to alleviate poverty. Key lessons of the conference are:

- While anti-poverty analysis has cultural and nation-state peculiarities that must be recognized and addressed (Agarwal, Ahmed), albeit with important lessons for other legal systems, it must increasingly be viewed through a global lens (Williams, Perez-Bustillo). This book particularly challenges anti-poverty advocates in the developed countries to address poverty globally.
- While poverty is certainly not an issue of only individual fault (Robson, Spicker), it has individual ramifications (Silva).
- Concepts of citizenship (and the class and gender implications of citizenship) need to be centrally incorporated into anti-poverty discourse (Amitsis, Aoued).
- Poverty is partially created and maintained by law, whether through statutory enactment, bureaucratic action or inaction, or judicial interpretation (Kjonstad, Saini); conversely, law can be a tool for redistribution (Mameli, Nott).

The editors hope that the papers presented at this workshop can move the discourse of redistribution beyond its current fixation on the nation-state and 'government' as the primary anti-poverty vehicle towards an understanding of the transnational dimensions of poverty and the need to rethink the public/private distinction as a means of addressing poverty.

PART I
Poverty as Legally Constructed

ONE | The right to development as a basic human right

AHMED AOUED

§ The question of the role of law in combating poverty is of prime concern, especially since 1997–2006 has been proclaimed the first United Nations Decade for the Eradication of Poverty.

An attempt is made in this chapter to project the right to development (RTD) as a central aspect of the bundle of rights that protect the survival and livelihood of people and communities (economic and social rights), and the rights that are inherent to individuals as such (civil and political rights). I would like to argue that the two sets of rights need to be viewed holistically and that a deeper understanding of their inherent linkage is necessary to strengthen the policy and legal intervention necessary to promote these essential survival and livelihood rights. I will also contend that, while great emphasis is still being placed on civil and political rights, little is being done to ensure the enjoyment of basic economic rights that are essential for human development, taking into account the legal development that had taken place within the United Nations (UN) system.

UNDERSTANDING THE SCOPE OF DEVELOPMENT/ RECONCEPTUALIZING THE RIGHT TO DEVELOPMENT

The right to development is a right of communities as well as individuals and is addressed in the Vienna Declaration of 1986.[1] It seeks to promote the full realization of all human rights – political, economic, social and cultural – so as to improve the potentialities of the overwhelming majority of humans. It also covers relations between states, so that responsibility for implementing this right is shared between citizens, states and the international community. For the less developed countries (LDCs), the notion of development derives from two distinct and complementary factors. One is the historical responsibility of the developed countries (DCs) for the present state of poverty and backwardness of the LDCs. Thus, practically all Third World demands formulated in various resolutions and other international documents, mainly during the 1970s, take as a basis this historical element.[2] From this history, the LDCs have developed the idea that in order to repair this past misfortune, rich countries must assist in the recovery of Third World economies. In other words, the DCs have the moral duty, and this is the second element, to participate in the development of the LDCs. To fulfil this moral duty, the LDCs proposed a right to development and have asked the DCs to recognize such a right.

One of the main objectives of the RTD is to combat poverty, an issue of primary importance since it touches on the very dignity of all human beings and limits considerably the enjoyment of other basic rights. While poverty is no longer associated solely with the countries of the South, southern countries still account for the majority of the world's poor. The extent of poverty worldwide is massive and the situation is getting worse. The latest estimate calculated that there are as many as 2 billion people living in extreme poverty, 90 per cent of them living in the LDCs, leading a miserable life with an income of less than a US dollar per capita per day. Africa is most affected by poverty, well ahead of Latin America where poverty is also increasing, both relatively and absolutely. It is clear that in most of these countries, many individuals suffer chronic shortages of housing, sanitation, education and access to potable water, fuel and food.

While the LDCs are struggling against poverty and backwardness to provide for the basic survival needs of their people, the developed world has been following a consumption pattern that cannot be described as 'sustainable', as illustrated by Table 1.1

Table 1.1 records only a limited number of commodities, yet it gives a rough idea of the inequalities in the levels of consumption between the developed and developing countries.

In a world where poverty and the marginalization of vulnerable groups are on the rise, it is important to stress the particular importance of the RTD. Particularly important is the need to focus on the structural causes that are leading to the impoverishment of many LDCs and to devise priorities to enable these countries to eradicate extreme poverty, while taking into account the degrading effects of such poverty on human personality.

The Vienna Declaration comments extensively on the importance of the RTD and recognizes and promotes the critical role of the international community in the realization of this right. It stresses the

TABLE 1.1 Consumption patterns

Commodity	Units of per capita consumption	Developed countries (24% of world population)		Developing countries (75% of world population)	
		% of world consumption	Per head	% of world consumption	Per head
Food					
Calories	kcal/day	34	3,395	66	2,389
Protein	gm/day	38	99	62	58
Fat	gm/day	53	127	47	40
Paper	kg/year	85	123	15	8
Steel	kg/year	79	455	21	43
Other metals	kg/year	86	26	14	2
Commercial energy	mtce/year	80	5.8	20	0.5

Source: UN Sub-Commission on Human Rights, 49th Session, 12 August 1997

linkage between the RTD, the prevalence of inadequate living conditions and the continued existence of widespread poverty. In the spirit
of the Vienna Declaration, development is not forcibly about economic
welfare only. It cannot solely be measured in terms of GNP growth,
the number of schools, hospitals or rate of inflation. The concept of
development goes beyond these purely materialistic considerations to
include much broader areas, such as culture, democracy and respect
for all human rights. As B. Stern (1983) put it: *'Developpement c'est
mettre l'homme debout.'* The Vienna Declaration stresses the idea that
gaining and securing the RTD can lead to the attainment of all other
rights and can promote individual dignity and self-confidence. It sus-
tains the view that appropriate living conditions promote physical and
mental health and provide people with psychological security, physical
ties with their community and culture, and a means of expressing their
individuality.

This trend has recently been reaffirmed by the UN Commission on
Human Rights which stated in an unpublished document (1998): 'All
persons in all countries are entitled to the realization of their economic,
social and cultural rights which are indispensable to their dignity and
the free development of their personality.'[3]

When the RTD is viewed as a human right, as international legal
developments in recent years have done, it necessarily implies, *inter alia*,

creating possibilities for the improvement of living conditions. This task calls for both a closer look at the human rights that are indivisible from the RTD and the identification of the particular causes of poverty that require increasing focus through the UN system. Particularly important is the fact that poverty has often been perceived as simply an economic issue, whereas it is equally important to view it from a human standpoint. In his report to the UN Commission on Human Rights (1997), the Special Rapporteur of the sub-commission on extreme poverty wrote: 'A person's living and working conditions had a direct effect on the quality of the work itself. It was thus essential to take every aspect of life and not merely the economic into account.'[4]

The number of state parties to the principal human rights instruments on development is considerably high, owing to the fact that there is a majority of LDCs in the UN General Assembly. However, the implementation of these instruments is hindered by a lack of interest from the DCs who ratify them without conviction or attach serious reservations that make their content meaningless. Statements and resolutions reaffirming international solidarity and official assistance as the basis for the enjoyment of the RTD cannot be seen as signs of progress, when the actions of the governments from which they emanated belied their words. Such an 'allegation' is confirmed by the claim often made by many Western leaders that the RTD is a collective right whose realization depends on economic resources not always available in many poor countries. This lack of political will of the DCs to accept the challenge posed by the emerging RTD is complicated further by the continuing debate over the controversial issue of the relation between this 'new' right and the Western concept of human rights. This relationship is an extremely important issue for the future of the RTD as one possible means to combat poverty.

THE INDIVISIBILITY AND INTERDEPENDENCE OF HUMAN RIGHTS AND THE RTD

The relationship between human rights and development was acknowledged, although vaguely, long ago in the Universal Declaration of Human Rights of 1948. Article 28 reads: 'Everyone is entitled to a social and international order in which the rights and freedoms set forth in this Declaration can be fully realized.' However, since it was generally accepted that the Declaration had no legally binding force, the UN General Assembly adopted two separate Covenants in 1966: the International Covenant on Economic, Social and Cultural Rights

(ICESCR) and the International Covenant on Civil and Political Rights (ICCPR). This distinction, inherent in the very names of the Covenants, is at the heart of the current debate between the South and the North about the indivisibility of human rights. Such a debate is not new and has its origins in the golden era of liberalism of the eighteenth and nineteenth centuries, which was dominated by liberals such as Thomas Jefferson who emphasized civil and political liberties (Kanyeihamba 1987).

Such a view is still valid in Western democracies, despite current developments that demonstrate that civil and political rights are inseparable from economic, social and cultural rights. As G. W. Kanyeihamba (1987: 221) wrote: 'Despite the dichotomy between civil and political rights on the one hand, and social, economic and cultural rights on the other, it is still the former which continue to be emphasized and preferred by the affluent nations of the world.' This distinction, however, has been formally rejected by the LDCs as exemplified in the Charter of the Rights of Man and People (the Charter) adopted in 1981 by the Organization of African Unity (OAU). Uniquely, the Charter covers economic, social and cultural rights as well as civil and political rights, thus emphasizing that the two categories of rights are indivisible and interdependent. These rights are considered by the Charter's drafters as the basis of all human rights.

The Vienna Declaration on the RTD went even further since the RTD was described as a human right; which means a universal and inalienable right that is inherent in all human individuals by virtue of their humanity alone, and as such should be respected, protected and promoted not only by states, but by the entire international community. Thus, since human rights are by definition 'moral claims', malnutrition, for example, is morally unacceptable because it is a flagrant breach of the most important right of all, the right to life. Without food a person loses first his dignity because he is unable to feed himself and his family, and then he loses his life because he is unable to feed his body. Both the right to life and the right to dignity are key concepts in all human rights instruments adopted by the international community, starting with the Universal Declaration of Human Rights in 1948. In this case, 'the right to food,' or, as it has been better expressed, the right to feed oneself, becomes critically linked to the RTD.

In 1993, the World Conference on Human Rights took a step further to include the RTD as a basic human right. The conference sustained the view that human rights, including individual or collective rights, are intrinsically linked to the full realization of the RTD. To separate these two sets of rights from the RTD, as some liberal doctrines have sought to do, undermines the principle of universality, indivisibility and interdependence of all human rights. Consequently, human rights, including the RTD, should be viewed only as indivisible and interdependent reflections of different aspects of the human person. The right to education, for example, is undoubtedly a civil and political right as well as an economic, social and cultural one. In the same line of thought, the right to organize trade unions and the right to peaceful gatherings belong to every individual and the community as a whole. The Vienna Declaration and Programme of Action (1993) reaffirmed the universality, indivisibility, interdependence and interrelatedness of all human rights and fundamental freedoms. It goes on to say: 'The international community must treat human rights globally and in fair and equal manner, on the same footing, and with the same emphasis.'

The same conclusions were confirmed and further elaborated on by the World Summit for Social Development (Copenhagen, 6–12 March 1995). The participants emphasized once again the principles of universality, indivisibility and interdependence of all human rights and committed themselves to create an economic, political, social, cultural and legal environment that will enable people to achieve social development. They also dedicated themselves to the goal of eradicating poverty in the world through decisive national action and international cooperation. A similar observation was made by the High Commissioner for Human Rights (1998) as he recalled that 'In accordance with the Universal Declaration of Human Rights, the ideal of free human beings enjoying freedom from fear and want can only be achieved if conditions are created whereby everyone may enjoy his economic, social and cultural rights, as well as his civil and political rights.'[5] That was a significant breakthrough; the RTD was no longer regarded as an automatic side-effect of economic growth, and the idea of human development starts gaining ground within the international community.

Theoretically, this recognition should have put an end to lengthy and fruitless discussions regarding the priority of one or another category of rights, since all human rights are equally important in ensuring human dignity and freedom. In practice, however, the distinction still persists in various international fora, obstructing considerably the progress of the RTD.

Addressing the 53rd Commission on Human Rights (1997), the US delegate pointed out that: 'It could no longer be argued that individual rights could not be realised until a country had developed, since only freedom not repression, could lead to sustainable development.'[6]

Although it may be said that there is indeed a strong correlation between development and freedom of civil and political institutions, it remains highly doubtful whether a democracy can triumph in a country where extreme poverty reigns. As the Russian delegate, at the same meeting of the Commission, replied, 'The right to work and to have adequate food was just as important for a democracy as the right to vote.'[7] He maintained that while it may be true to say that political democracy was the foundation for the enjoyment of human rights, democracy could not guarantee the same rights in the absence of social justice.

As this sterile debate goes on, the industrial world seems to be determined to promote individual human rights and fundamental freedoms, while poverty is increasing. Statistics show that one-fifth of the world's population lives in extreme poverty, while the richest 20 per cent receive nearly 83 per cent of worldwide income. As the world economy grows, the rich are getting richer and the poor poorer, primarily because of an unjust, unethical and inequitable international economic order.

THE EFFECT OF THE EXISTING UNJUST ECONOMIC ORDER ON THE IMPLEMENTATION OF THE RTD

Calls for a New International Economic Order in the 1970s failed and the North–South dialogue petered out in the 1980s, leaving the impression that the North has lost interest in developing the South (Stern 1983). The economic globalization currently taking place is the result of carefully planned legal and institutional changes embodied in a series of international agreements and controlled by international financial institutions. The planned globalization threatens the national sovereignty of many LDCs and the realization of the RTD by failing to alleviate poverty and thus jeopardizes the very foundations of a genuine human development.

When discussing development issues, members of the international community do not exhibit the expected level of common commitment to the realization of the RTD. The richest members have rarely focused on developing specific actions and programmes with human faces and instead rehash theoretical and political arguments. Human rights violations in the LDCs are the result of unfulfilled pledges by DCs, particularly their failure to devote 0.7 per cent of their GNP to official development assistance.

In the trade area, there is an increasing tendency for some groups or governments in developed countries to impose new trading conditions, for example, relating to environmental requirements or working conditions. While the reasons for doing this cross the political spectrum and are grounded in disparate and complex visions of redistribution, an isolation of these issues as trading conditions without a quid pro quo of increased economic benefit to the LCDs, often cancels out the main advantage of the LDCs namely, their labour-intensive, low-wage economies, thus contributing directly to widespread persistence of poverty in the LCDs.

Furthermore, the growing energy crisis in many parts of the world has also created unsustainable hardship for vulnerable segments of the population. During the past two decades or more, the energy crisis has deepened and the availability of essential natural resources has declined owing to the adoption of models of economic growth that are not necessarily compatible with the existing economic, political and social structures of the recipient countries. In addition to the inequities of development, many LCDs continue to be the hardest hit by price commodities, as has been pointed out in many reports of the UN specialized agencies. The absence of various bodies to look carefully at the impact of such transgressions on the LDCs' economies is exacerbating the situation further and constitutes a serious violation that affects access and entitlement to the RTD and has an impact upon a multitude of collateral human rights.

Economic globalization also poses a great challenge to the LDCs who fear instability, which in turn is bound to affect the human rights situation in those countries as a result of widespread poverty. The absence of minimum acceptable standards can lead to the individual being deprived of many basic rights, such as the right to sufficient food, health, education and housing. Unemployment, poverty and hunger are increasing rapidly with women and children as the chief victims. Massive cuts in healthcare, education and social services following World Bank and IMF programmes are causing instability, racism, refugee and migrant flows, illicit drug-trafficking, the rise of neo-facism and religious fundamentalism, ethnic conflicts, environmental degradation and even war (Serageldine 1990).

Far from enjoying the economic globalization, many countries are simply being sidelined by technological developments in communications, computers and biotechnology and further cannot escape the external debt burden that remains the most critical factor in perpetuating underdevelopment and poverty.

One of the major obstacles to the realization of the RTD is undoubtedly the issue of external debt that is strangling the economies of the debtor countries. Cancelling debt for some countries and easing the terms of repayment for others will certainly transform their financial situation.

Steps taken on the advice of international financial institutions to reduce LDCs' heavy debt burden have often proved ineffective, mainly because the multidimensional aspects of poverty have not been taken into account. Almost all LDCs have been in constant economic crisis for the past decade. Most of them have had to make sacrifices to avoid a payment crisis, and external debt still continues to be a major obstacle to their economic and social development. In heavily indebted Latin America, some 270 million persons or 62 per cent of the population live in poverty, 84 million of them in conditions of extreme poverty. Statistics show that a child dies of illness or hunger every minute in that part of the world, while 100 million have been abandoned and are living, eating and sleeping on the streets.[8]

It has been repeatedly voiced by LDC governments at different times and in different fora that priority should be given to addressing the problem of external debt, so as to reverse the flow of financial resources from the developing to the developed countries. At the end of 1991, Third World debt stood at US$1.351 billion, having doubled since 1981, and it has since risen to US$1.45 billion. The countries concerned were paying the industrialized countries more than US$50 million in interest each year. In terms of GDP per capita, the gap is widening between the North and the South. From US$5,700 in 1960, it grew to US$18, 677 in 1995. This means that less than 15 per cent of the world population have an average per capita GDP of US$19,665; while over 78 per cent of humans have barely an average per capita GDP of US$965, with the least developed countries among them registering a per capita GDP of US$238 in 1995, hardly one-ninetieth of the average per capita GDP of the developed world.[9]

Debt repayment has created a vicious circle: more than 40 per cent of LDCs' exports in 1988 were used for debt servicing and the countries concerned had to seek new loans which increased the debt and gave rise to further interest payments. External debt has thus become a modern form of slavery at the state level and contributes largely to the expansion of poverty.

The World Bank also bears part of the responsibility for the present state of bankrupt LDC economies. Its policy of structural adjustment programmes introduced in the early 1980s has proved its limits after two decades of experimentation, resulting in damaging effects on large segments of the LDCs' populations.[10] Structural adjustment policies and austerity are sometimes carried out at the expense of the well-being of individuals or population groups. From the RTD standpoint, investment in areas such as health, education, social programmes and housing is essential for the preservation of family ties, community values and national identity. This view is not shared by international financial agencies, particularly the Bretton Woods institutions, which subordinate individual well-being to the availability of resources while deliberately ignoring the individual human dimension as the central concern of any development effort.

In economic terms, financial gains are seen only as the driving force behind economic activity, but never as a means of realizing human rights, because international financial institutions do not consider the well-being of individuals and groups as an integral part of the development process.[11] Yet, many recent economic theories sustain the idea that it is essential to see social and economic policies as complementary aspects of the same process. As the Sub-Commission's Special Rapporteur on Human Rights and Extreme Poverty (1997) said in his report: 'The social devastation caused by purely macroeconomic policies could never be rectified by the later implementation of social policies.'[12] Being in a dominant position, international financial agencies are still adopting a very hard approach to economic problems, using strictly economic remedies in an attempt to enhance the development of deprived Southern countries. In seeking economic growth through liberalization, these agencies often implement development schemes that undermine or destroy traditional forms of sustainable economic self-sufficiency, while perpetuating poverty on a worldwide scale. This has, in some cases, had more impact on populations than war.

It is therefore important that the governments of the industrialized countries and international financial institutions take into account this aspect of human development in their assistance policies and become more aware of the impact of economic activity on fundamental human rights. It is equally important to strengthen the concept of the RTD in all the actions of international financial institutions and in the structural adjustment policies carried out with the participation of the Bretton Woods institutions. It is essential to move away from inflexible programmes that ignore the social and political differences between countries and move towards projects that take into account social considerations and the political feasibility of structural adjustment and investment programmes, realizing that growth does not automatically benefit the poor unless specific measures are taken to help the weakest and most vulnerable groups. As experience has shown, economic and social development is a crucial element in the promotion of human rights and democratic development. But economic development that does not enhance respect for human rights and democracy is a hollow victory at best. Addressing the 53rd Commission on Human Rights, the Algerian delegate remarked that the role of the UN was diminishing with respect to poverty and the involvement of the Bretton Woods institutions increasing. He urged that there should be adequate coordination between the IMF and the World Bank, on the one hand, and the Economic and Social Council (ECOSOC), on the other. The crucial importance of such coordination would be reinforced if the ECOSOC were replaced by an economic security council.[13]

Despite the side-effects of the globalization process, it would be naive to place the entire burden of underdevelopment and poverty on rich countries and international financial institutions. International efforts are undoubtedly indispensable for promoting economic development, but they must be preceded by self-initiated actions at the national level (Glan 1987). The failure by many LDC governments to adopt economic reforms and the failure to create acceptable living conditions has resulted in a situation where malnutrition, homelessness and un-employment are on the increase. At the root of the problem is a high level of government corruption that leads to foreign loans being swallowed up and more being needed. Income from natural resources has been required collateral for many LDCs. For example, in 1996, Mexico had to sacrifice two-thirds of its petroleum exports to the USA for the next ten years to repay its debt.[14] The economic crisis and the loss of economic sovereignty means for several LDCs a drastic fall in government expenditure, with resulting restrictions on health, education and housing. Only a tiny percentage of the budget is allocated to poverty programmes, while debt repayment costs up to 90 times the amount allocated to alleviate extreme poverty.

Such a state of anarchy is often aggravated by a lack of political reform within these countries to allow for more transparency and clarity in the management of the national economy. By excluding any effective participation of members of society in the relevant decision-making process as agents and beneficiaries of development, including a fair distribution of its benefits, authoritarian regimes are responsible for rising social discontent, which in turn constitutes a permanent source of political instability. Recent events worldwide have shown that if nations or their population groups were deprived of access to the basic needs required for equitable and integrated development, there would be a permanent danger of social uprising, which would inevitably lead to a set of human rights violations and power abuses. Equally disturbing for the development of many LDCs is the widespread phenomenon of wars, since many armed conflicts have arisen as a result of extreme poverty leading to general discrimination, massive repression of basic liberties and other forms of human rights abuses which gravely impede the realization of the RTD.

It appears from the foregoing that there is a strong link between extreme poverty and human rights violations and their effects on populations in terms of social and economic deterioration. Yet the UN's progress on the alleviation of poverty is lagging far behind the massive legislative work and the various instruments imagined to ensure the implementation of human rights worldwide and more particularly within the economically underprivileged nations.

THE IMBALANCE IN THE UN MECHANISMS DESIGNED TO ENSURE THE IMPLEMENTATION OF HUMAN RIGHTS AND TO PROMOTE THE RTD

There is no doubt that the United Nations has made a remarkable contribution to the promotion of human rights and to the advancement of respect for fundamental freedoms on a worldwide scale. However, the details of the UN action in the field of implementation and enforcement are different depending on the nature of the rights involved, whether individual political rights or collective economic rights. This duality of treatment is reflected in various international instruments and reinforced by state practice (Forte 1997). Thus, under the two Covenants there are two major ways of monitoring human rights implementation: the national and international reporting system on one hand, and the international complaint procedure on the other. Independently elected committees that operate within the UN Commission on Human Rights implement both methods. The committee established under the ICCPR (Art. 28) monitors the implementation of political and civil rights in a number of ways:

- It examines periodic reports from states parties to the Covenant on the measures they have adopted to give effect to the rights recognised in the Covenant (Art. 40).

- It can consider complaints of one state against another (Art. 41).
- It can receive, under the provisions of the Optional Protocol to the ICCPR, complaints from individuals alleging violations of their political or civil rights under the Covenant. The committee's 'views' are not legally binding on state parties, but states do comply for various reasons, including a genuine wish to fulfil the obligations of the ICCPR and a desire to enhance their international image.[5]

Another equally important mechanism for monitoring the application of human rights is the ECOSOC Resolution 1503 (XLVIII), which set up a complex confidential procedure whereby complaints which reveal 'a consistent pattern of gross and reliably attested violations of human rights and fundamental freedoms' could be examined. This machinery is open not only to victims of violations, but also to any person or group or non-governmental organization with a direct and reliable knowledge of the violations (Vojin 1997).

While the use of such mechanisms is constantly reviewed in the area of political and civil rights, their application in the area of economic and social rights still suffers from serious shortcomings, particularly because the reporting system was not introduced until 1985. The newly established committee scrutinizes reports on the progress made by states in achieving the observance of economic, social and cultural rights, which form the core of the RTD. The complaints procedure is still non-existent because of the opposition of the developed countries who are sceptical about the feasibility of monitoring the implementation of economic rights. Apart from this unique mechanism, no equivalent tool for monitoring exists in the sphere of economic rights as they are embodied in the RTD Declaration.

In addition to the above-mentioned mechanisms, the UN has developed, during the last decade, new techniques and procedures to deal with human rights violations in the area of political rights, which in essence do not derive their legitimacy from any particular human rights instrument. The new mechanisms commonly known as the Special Procedures of the Commission on Human Rights fall into two groups: those addressing human rights issues on a global basis by theme, and those that focus on the overall human rights situation in a specific country. The latter procedure is carried out by working groups entrusted with the task of reporting on allegations of human rights abuses in specific countries (Levin 1996). The former is carried out by Special Rapporteurs on specific phenomena such as torture, summary executions, disappearances, religious intolerance, and freedom of opinion and expression.[16] Both groups report to the UN Commission on Human Rights. In addition to the above mechanisms, there are additional initiatives that are directed at the promotion, protection and the implementation of the political rights of individuals.[17]

On the basis of such monitoring mechanisms, several countries were called upon to review their legislation and comply with internationally agreed-upon standard instruments (Vojin 1997: 178). This plurality of mechanisms is in effect a natural consequence of the dichotomy between political and civil rights on the one hand, and economic and social rights on the other, a dichotomy so dear to the liberal Western democracies. This duality is more visible at the national level, such as in the United States, which is totally opposed to the humanist approach to development advocated in the RTD documents (Denoon 1979).

Amazingly, there are still nations hostile to any inclusion of the right to develop, despite repeated appeals, and they have initiated serious revisions to various documents seeking to delete all reference to the RTD. Still more, the very same states opposed to the RTD have the audacity to clamour about human rights in other states and seek to pass resolutions censuring these states.

Thus, it has become current practice that when government leaders or NGO campaigners in the Western countries talk about human rights abuses and violations, the main emphasis is on civil and political rights. The cases of Salman Rushdie in the late 1980s and General Pinochet in the late 1990s, although fundamentally different, do show to what extent Western states are concerned with issues involving violations of (personal) political rights.

While these two cases have raised strong condemnations from the West, the West does not show similar concern about the millions of people dying from extreme poverty in the shanty towns of Calcutta, Khartoum or Bogota. During the annual session of the UN Commission on Human Rights in Geneva, it has now become a custom for NGOs such as Amnesty International, the International League for Human Rights, to mention only two, to regularly submit to the Commission documented cases of individuals being politically persecuted in their countries by their respective governments. They often try to lobby Western governments to take action and urge the Commission to pass resolutions condemning these countries or indeed to send Special Rapporteurs for an international investigation.

The intention here is neither to condemn Rushdie's freedom of expression nor to exonerate Pinochet from his crimes against humanity. All members of the international community, whether rich or poor, must unite to fight human rights abuses wherever they occur in the world. The aim is simply to highlight the reaction and efforts deployed worldwide by the Western countries to fight (political/civil) human rights abuses,[18] and to emphasize that such efforts are non-existent in the case of economic violations, made possible by the attitudes of the rich countries of the West as well as international organizations operating in the area of international trade and finance. Similarly, the Cuban embargo, the bombing of Iraq and the recent raids on Serbia 'to prevent a humanitarian catastrophe' are but other examples of the West's commitment and readiness to defend what it considers violations of human rights. Again, setting aside the question of the legitimacy of such actions, which is outside the scope of this chapter, the relevant question is: is the West ready to deploy the same efforts, energy and money to combat famine and extreme poverty to save millions of deprived people all over the world?

Contrasting this individualistic liberal approach with the LDCs' collective concept of human rights, Julius Nyerere, the first President of Tanzania, asserted:

> I agree that in the idealist sense of the word it is better that 99 guilty men should go free rather than one innocent man should be punished. But in the circumstances like ours ... conditions may well arise in which it is better that 99 innocent people should suffer temporary detention than that one possible traitor should wreck the nation. It would certainly be a complete madness to let 99 guilty men escape in order to avoid the risk of punishing one innocent person. Our ideals must guide us, not blind us. (Kanyeihamba 1987: 221)

These fundamentally opposed approaches in terms of priority in the treatment of human rights violations can be explained by two factors. First, the weakness of the UN system and, second, the attitude of rich nations which fail to recognize that economic, social and cultural rights are as important as civil and political rights. The UN system is yet unable to match the existing monitoring mechanisms in the area of political rights to the area of economic rights. The limited focus of rich nations prevents economic rights from being promoted or protected as well as other rights. This is due to the fact that the international community, and most notably the richest continent, is still far from agreeing on a strategy to create favourable conditions for the realization of the RTD. As they stand, the present international human rights instruments do not form a unified and effective system of norms, particularly with regard to monitoring mechanisms and obligations which are clearly biased towards enhancing and protecting political rights. This is well illustrated by the proliferation of various resolutions, working groups and human rights instruments which, incidentally, concentrate more on the civil and political arena than on the economic and social field. Consequently, the monitoring system has become more efficient in protecting the first set of rights than the second. This was implicitly recognized by the High Commissioner for Human Rights (1998) as he recalled that 'the realization of all human rights and fundamental freedoms, and particularly economic, social and cultural rights, is a dynamic process and that, as is evident in today's world, a great deal remains to be accomplished'.[19]

Furthermore, the effective functioning of human rights treaties and monitoring mechanisms relating to development requires not only the commitment of all state parties, but also a system of wide adherence and coordination by the UN bodies, particularly with a view to avoiding an imbalance in the treatment of some human rights at the expense of others.

Yet, in the Vienna Declaration it was made clear that the inherent, indispensable and permeable relationship between the full enjoyment of the RTD and certain civil and political rights will be compromised in the absence of mechanisms (measures) geared towards respecting, protecting and ensuring the RTD. Conversely, violations of many civil and political rights have a direct bearing upon the enjoyment of the RTD.

A great deal of the present stagnation, if not retardation, in the implementation of the Vienna Declaration on the RTD can be imputed to the lack of adequate mechanisms on the same pattern as that available in the area of political and civil rights. This is because the RTD has often been treated as a second-class right and attempts have often been made to limit its scope by those very states that are morally responsible for its implementation.

CONCLUSION

Poverty, which currently affects all countries of the South as well as countries of the North, constitutes, in terms of the law, a denial of human rights and social justice. In 1999, on the eve of the third millennium, the situation had, according to many available sources, not changed; if anything, it had worsened. The right to sustainable development was being flagrantly violated in dozens of countries by the unorthodox rules of an unjust economic world order. During the

1960s and through the 1980s, the UN and its agencies spoke about alleviating poverty in its simplest meaning. In the 1990s, it was a question of *extreme* poverty, with all the gravity that 'extreme' may imply. The 1998 World Bank report is a telling testimony to the continued threat facing millions of deprived people who are faced with the ravages of increasing poverty, lack of access to essential civil services and the concomitant increase in disease and epidemics resulting from unhygienic and life-threatening conditions.

The dialogue between the rich and the poor is a vital component in the realization of the RTD. The dialogue must eliminate obstacles to development. Focus must be on the elimination of the trans-boundary impact on human rights of state policies and the policies of international organizations, the creation of a fair international economic environment, and the strengthening of review mechanisms. Although the RTD has political, economic, social and other dimensions, it has yet to be incorporated into the programmes and activities of international organizations that must become more proactive.

Since the realization of the RTD is in principle a shared responsibility, there is no room for paternalistic considerations. The aim is to promote justice, dignity and peace by alleviating poverty, ensuring a minimum of basic needs and improving the living conditions of the underprivileged nations of the South and the individuals of the North. However, for that to be so, the international community must consider the well-being of individuals and groups as an integral part, not just a side-effect, of the development process. It is therefore important that governments of the industrialized countries and international financial institutions incorporate that idea into their assistance policies and become more aware of the impact of economic activity on fundamental human rights.

It is important that the position of the RTD in the UN bodies' agenda should be changed in order to bring about the human dimension of that right and not just the economic aspect.

The international community must review the impact of structural adjustment programmes and indebtedness on the RTD, taking into account the right of the LDCs to define for themselves what constitutes development. The realization of the RTD implies also the involvement of LDCs in the globalization process and the rehabilitation of such crucial agencies as UNCTAD, UNDP and FAO, which would be complemented by parallel action within the newly established WTO. It is equally important to encourage the formulation of programmes for poverty reduction, unite to put an end to armed conflicts worldwide that consume badly needed resources and prevail upon the rich nations to assist the poor ones to improve their living standards without setting undue conditions. These goals can be achieved only if a body is empowered to look carefully at the impact of the actions of the transnational companies as well as the policies of the international financial institutions on the economies of LDCs.

Progress towards the realization of the RTD as a concrete alternative for combating poverty relies finally on the moral and political commitment of Western countries and the measures taken to ensure the implementation of such a will. The argument that such a right was not enforceable was merely an indirect way of denying its existence. If the international community genuinely wishes to alleviate poverty, it should provide adequate monitoring mechanisms and consider a state's failure to fulfil its economic obligations as a serious violation of human rights. To that effect, it is essential for a complaint procedure to be established in the area of the RTD to balance that existing in the political sphere.

It is only then that development in its humanistic sense will not be a point of contention between the rich North and the poor South, but rather a point of convergence as have been political human rights thus far.

NOTES

1. Declaration on the Right to Development, General Assembly Resolution 41/128 of 4 December 1986. For an in-depth commentary on the Declaration, see *Report of the Global Consultation on the Right to Development* prepared by a UN Working Group (Geneva, January 1990) (New York: Centre for Human Rights, 1991).

2. Third World literature on development, abundant in the 1970s, considerably diminished in the late 1980s as any hope of establishing a New International Economic Order (NIEO) faded. For a compilation of instruments on the Law of Development, see Bulaj (1986) and Hayter (1981.)

3. UN High Commissioner for Human Rights, unpublished text, Commission on Human Rights Resolution 1998/33, 17 April 1998, Geneva.

4. UN Commission on Human Rights, 53rd session, 1997. Summary Record of the 13th Meeting. E/CN. 4/1997/SR.17, p. 10.

5. UN High Commissioner for Human Rights. Unpublished text, Commission on Human Rights Resolution 1998/33, Geneva.

6. UN Commission on Human Rights, 53rd session, 1997. Summary Record of the 13th Meeting. E/CN. 4/1997/SR.17, p. 11.

7. Ibid., p. 12.

8. UN Commission on Human Rights, 53rd session, 1997. Summary Record of the 15th Meeting. E/CN. 4/1997/SR.13, p. 10.

9. UN Sub-Commission on Human Rights, 49th session, 12 August 1997, Geneva.

10. For a critique of the World Bank structural adjustment lending, see Bello and Elison (1982).

11. Describing the role of the World Bank, Rotberg (1981) wrote: 'We are not a social agency committed to making transfer payments to solve the problems of misery or poverty.'

12. UN Commission on Human Rights, 53rd session, 1997. Summary Record of the 17th Meeting. E/CN. 4/1997/SR.17, p. 11.

13. Ibid., p. 9.

14. UN Commission on Human Rights, 53rd session, 1997. Summary Record of the 15th Meeting. E/CN. 4/1997/SR.15, p. 11. The danger of debt is well described by Payer (1975).

15. There are many examples of state parties complying with the views of the committee, e.g. Finland revised its Alien Act in order to make its law governing the detention of aliens compatible with the Covenant. In the case against the Netherlands, the committee found a violation with which the government of the Netherlands did not agree, but out of respect for the committee, it made an *ex gratia* payment to the complainant.

16. Other Special Procedures include: internally displaced persons, the sale of children, child prostitution and pornography, elimination of violence against women, contemporary forms of racism, racial discrimination and xenophobia.

17. The most common are the mandates requesting the UN Secretary General to prepare reports on various specific subjects. These may be either thematic or situation-based.

18. Visiting the refugee camps in Kosovo in June 1998, the British Foreign Minister Robin Cook said that what is happening in Kosovo is not just an internal affair.

19. UN High Commissioner for Human Rights. Unpublished text, Commission on Human Rights Resolution 1998/33, Geneva.

REFERENCES

Bello, W. K. and D. Elison (1982) *Development Debacle: The World Bank in the Philippines*, San Francisco: Institute of Food and Development Policy.

Bulaj, M. (1986) *Principles of International Development Law*, Dordrecht: Martinus Nijhoff.

Denoon, D. B. H. (1979) *The New International Economic Order: A US Response*, Baltimore, MD: Port City Press.

Forte, F. (1997) 'Human and Institutional Aspects in the Adjustment-Growth Programmes for Mediterranean Developing Countries', *Mediterranean Journal of Human Rights*, 1: 179-95.

Glan, P. (1987) *Development by People*, New York: Praeger.

Hayter, T. (1981) *The Creation of World Poverty. An Alternative View to the Brandt Report*, London: Pluto Press.

Kanyeihamba, G. W. (1987) 'Human Rights and Development with Special Reference to Africa', in F. Snyder and P. Slinn (eds), *International Law of Development: Comparative Perspectives*, Abingdon: Professional Books.

Levin, L. (1996) *Human Rights: Questions and Answers*, Paris: UNESCO.

Payer, C. (1975) *The Debt Trap*, New York: Monthly Review Press.

Rotberg, E. H. (1981) *The World Bank: A Financial Appraisal*, IBRD Pamphlets, Washington, DC: IBRD.

Serageldine, I. (1990) 'Tackling the Social Dimension of Adjustment', *Finance and Development*, 14: 18–20.

Stern, B. (1983) *Un Nouvel Ordre Economique International?*, Paris: Economica.

Vojin, D. (1997) 'The Procedure of Adopting the Decisions of the Human Rights Committee Relating to Communications Under the Optional Protocol to the International Covenant on Civil and Political Rights', *Mediterranean Journal of Human Rights*, 1: 167–9.

TWO | Cross-border reflections on poverty: lessons from the United States and Mexico

LUCY WILLIAMS

§ As the focus of United States' social welfare policy regarding lone- or single-parent families has shifted to time-limited benefits, no federal statutory entitlement,[1] and a quick and an assumed permanent transition into waged work, poverty academics, policy-makers and activists have increasingly understood the centrality of the connections between social welfare policy and low-wage labour in the US. However, they have focused less on the connection between these two fields and the areas of immigration and international economic organization. As a result, persons working in the cause of redistribution of income have often operated in analytical/theoretical vacuums. I posit that a specialized and isolated analysis often results in less than fully sophisticated political analyses and missed opportunities to develop effective poverty policies both within a domestic context and certainly within a globalized economy. This chapter provides some background that can set the stage for a more knowledgeable interchange among social welfare, low-wage work, immigration and global economic discourses, and begin to draw threads among these fields, particularly focusing on ways in which US policies connect to Mexico.

First I set out the reality of global inequality and the ways in which a failure to engage with global income and wealth disparity ignores critical issues within which any poverty analysis must be situated. I then look to the US and Mexico, countries with a 2,000-mile common border, as an example of the way in which multiple legal discourses should be analysed through a cross-border perspective. Initially, I explore two historical contexts: long-standing labour and immigration ties between the US and Mexico, and the creation of a false dichotomy within the US of those in waged work and single-parent families receiving social assistance benefits. I then focus on recent changes in US social welfare policy towards single mothers, many of whom are in low-wage work, and legal immigrants, the largest number of whom are from Mexico.

I juxtapose these two groups with the single mothers employed in the legally established Mexican 'maquiladoras' and the women and children-only villages in Mexico whose men are undocumented immigrants in the US. By exposing the artificiality of national borders vis-à-vis nationality and electoral voice, I pose the question of redistribution as a cross-border issue. Ultimately, my hope is that by bringing together seemingly disparate legal areas, scholars and activists can produce a more nuanced and comprehensive poverty strategy.

INEQUALITY THROUGH A GLOBAL PERSPECTIVE

Of course, extreme poverty exists in many countries of the world. But advocates and policy-makers often do not focus on international poverty when dealing with income imbalances within the US. Almost one-half of the world's population lives on less than US$2 a day and one-fifth live on less than US$1 a day.[2] Individuals in the twenty richest countries have an average income that is thirty-seven times that of the poorest twenty countries, and this gap has doubled in the past forty years.[3] This cannot be explained away through arguing that wealthier nations simply have higher standards of living.[4] Social indicators such as infant mortality and malnutrition demonstrate the serious ramifications of this great discrepancy in wealth. In rich countries less than one child in 100 does not reach his or her fifth birthday, while in the poorest countries as many as one-fifth of children do not. And while in rich countries fewer than 5 per cent of all children under five are malnourished, in poor countries as many as 50 per cent are.[5] Relying on such data, we could develop a strong argument that richer nations, which have often been instrumental in colonial exploitation, have a moral imperative to take responsibility for the extreme poverty in much of the world. Yet, quite apart from any ethical necessity, if legal academics and advocates take the national context for granted in developing redistributive policy, we are often, in ostrich-like fashion, hiding our heads in the sand in a time of increasing global economic integration.

Many, particularly in the labour and welfare areas, have understandably focused attention on their domestic scene in light of the crisis of declining union power and the intensity of assaults on the welfare state. However, in so doing, our rhetoric often reflects a nostalgia for isolationism. A nation-state focus rests on several increasingly problematical assumptions, including, for example (1) that nation-states can control the impact of capital flight and currency fluctuations; (2) that immigration can be regulated through border enforcement of legal prohibitions established by nation-states; and (3) that union density, even within a nation-state, will reach worker-majority levels and incorporate waged workers not currently included within any collective bargaining framework, so that vertical redistribution (from management to labour) through collective bargaining poses only limited risks of exacerbating horizontal inequalities (between higher paid unionized and non-unionized, low-wage workers).

Although perhaps some of these assumptions were plausible in the postwar years, social reality is rapidly pushing in a different direction. Labour and welfare law cannot be viewed as 'domestic issues' within any nation-state. In light of currently unfolding trends towards global economic integration, the concept of citizenship anchored solely in the nation-state is anachronistic. The expansion and liberalization of trade, mobility of capital and financing, the breakdown of the Bretton Woods mechanisms for currency control, the portability of many production techniques and equipment and the emergence of Third World manufacturing sharply call into question the assumption that employment and social policy can be made within a nation-state framework. All of this is in addition to the moral and political imperative for people in the developed world to accept responsibility for addressing the gross maldistribution of wealth and resources on a world scale.

Thus we cannot discuss redistribution within a domestic labour market as if the US had no links to the rest of the world. Economic life in the US involves massive cross-border capital and labour flows and integrated, cross-border production chains. Changes in, for example, labour and welfare laws in other countries often have important ramifications in the US (and vice-versa), whether in the form of human migration, capital migration or rising naturalizations (i.e. acquisition of US citizenship) by legal immigrants. More restrictive immigration policy, rather than reducing migration, may produce more undocumented immigrants, creating a quite different impact on US low-wage labour markets than that produced by legal immigration. Progressive lawyers attempting to develop new institutional mechanisms for redistribution must grapple carefully with the tension between capital mobility and restrictions on the free movement of persons.

The relationship between the US and Mexico highlights the implications of cross-border labour, welfare, immigration and trade interactions, particularly the impact of anti-NAFTA and anti-immigrant rhetoric on US welfare policy and naturalizations and the artificiality of borders vis-à-vis citizenship.

The Mexican/US border was largely open until 1965. There were no immigration quotas based on nationality as there were for most other countries, but there were certain categories of people who were excluded from admission to the US, such as prostitutes and, interestingly enough, 'contract laborers'.[6] However, this last exception was often ignored in practice.

Beginning in the Second World War, the Mexican/US governments implemented a 'guest-worker' programme, the Bracero Program,[7] under which Mexican men were transported into the US to do agricultural or field work, often in deplorable conditions. This programme was unilaterally terminated by the USA in 1964, in part because of US union opposition (the United Farm Workers under Cesar Chavez was organizing in California beginning in the early 1960s, and Bracero workers were often brought in to undermine strikes since they would be deported if they resisted crossing picket lines) and because of increased mechanization. Although officially defunct, the Bracero Program laid the groundwork for geographical patterns and social ties that later supported undocumented immigration.

One year later, in 1965, partially in response to the Mexican government's statements of their reliance on the Bracero Program for job-creation, the US and Mexico collaboratively created the Mexican Border Industrialization Program, or Maquila Program. This created a 20km strip in Mexico along the Mexican/US border to which US firms could import finished, ready-to-assemble components and raw materials and hire low-wage Mexicans to assemble the finished products. As long as the finished products were re-exported to the USA, the firms were not subject to Mexican import restrictions or duties and only paid a US tariff on the value added by the assembly in Mexico. The programme expanded rapidly, hiring a different population than that employed under the Bracero Program, i.e. primarily young single women, including single mothers (Pastor and Castañeda 1988: 289–90).[8]

That same year, Congress enacted immigration quotas for the Western hemisphere for the first time under the 1965 Amendments to the Immigration and Nationality Act.[9] While individual countries had no limits on the number of visas that would be granted, the law was later amended to establish an overall ceiling of 120,000 visas per year for the entire Western hemisphere.[10]

Thus, long before the North American Free Trade Agreement

(NAFTA)[11] was ratified in 1994, the two countries had strong labour market ties, albeit largely driven by US corporate interests. For many years, there had been mobility of labour from Mexico to the US, which had an impact on low-wage workers in both countries. It is within this historical context that the NAFTA and US immigration policy was and continues to be debated.

TRADITIONAL US SOCIAL WELFARE FOR POOR SINGLE MOTHERS

A critical parallel legal field that interacts with immigration and international trade law is that of social protection programmes in the US, particularly as they relate to expectations of participation in waged work. US social welfare policy, set against the backdrop of a rugged individualism concept, has always reflected an ambivalence about poverty, with certain groups (i.e. those defined as being in waged work) carved out for special treatment. As part of the Social Security Act enacted in 1935,[12] both Unemployment Insurance (UI) and a programme called Aid to Dependent Children, later Aid to Families with Dependent Children (AFDC), were established. The former was an acknowledgement that the US was not a full-employment society, and that there would always be both frictional and structural unemployment; the latter was designed to provide a less than subsistence amount for the children of single parents (predominantly women) and later the single parents themselves.[13]

However, the two programmes were always viewed very differently: UI was 'worthy' because it was tied to waged labour, and AFDC was 'the dole' because it was not tied to waged work, but to parenting. This bifurcation of social programmes allowed society to construct a false dichotomy between wage-workers and welfare recipients. People who advocated higher wages, better labour standards and more expansive unemployment insurance benefits as a social safety-net routinely distanced themselves from programmes like AFDC, that were needs-based programmes for which eligibility was not directly connected to waged work.

The method of data collection and presentation regarding the number and percentage of welfare recipients who were connected to waged work reinforced this dichotomy. If one used 'point in time' data, i.e. counting the percentage of those on a given day both receiving welfare and participating in waged work, there appeared to be very little overlap, as the data showed that only about 7 per cent of welfare recipients were also in paid labour.[14] But this type of data collection did not take into account the 'cyclical welfare/work population', the many who rotate between welfare and waged work on a regular basis.

Not until the 1990s (immediately preceding the passage of the Personal Responsibility and Work Opportunity Reconciliation Act of 1996)[15] did studies begin to record participation of welfare recipients in waged work over a longer period, usually two years, and to document how fluid these two groups, welfare recipients and wage-workers, are – a majority of women receiving welfare move in and out of low-wage work on a regular basis; they are part of the low-wage labour force. Producing a startlingly different result, one study found that of the 64 per cent of women on welfare for the first time who left the rolls within two years, almost a half left for work. But three-quarters of those who left welfare eventually returned, and 45 per cent returned within a year (LaDonna 1993). Another study found that 70 per cent of welfare recipients participated in some way in the labour force over a two-year period: 20 per cent combined work and welfare, 23 per cent worked intermittently and were on welfare between jobs, 7 per cent worked limited hours and looked for work, and 23 per cent unsuccessfully looked for work. The women in this study held an average of 1.7 jobs over the two-year period and spent an average of sixteen weeks looking for work (Spalter-Roth 1994). The problem, by and large, was not in a lack of work-effort, but in the conditions of low-wage labour markets in the United States.

The US legal rules concerning eligibility for benefits under the UI system reinforce the false dichotomy between wage-workers and welfare recipients. Although low-wage workers contribute to the UI benefit-pool in the sense that employers pass payroll taxes on to them in the form of lower wages, UI rules exclude many low-wage workers, particularly women and people of colour, from the definition of 'employee'.[16] Most of the single mothers who moved from AFDC to waged labour and then lost their jobs were ineligible for the 'worthy' UI programme because the legal eligibility factors excluded them from the definition of 'employees'.[17] Thus they returned to AFDC for their 'unemployment insurance' and were viewed as shiftless 'non-workers'.

THE RECENT SHIFT IN US SOCIAL WELFARE POLICY VIS-À-VIS LOW-WAGE LABOUR AND IMMIGRANTS

This brief history sets the critical context in which to understand the recent dismantling of social protection in the US. In 1996, the

Personal Responsibility and Work Opportunity Reconciliation Act (PRWORA)[18] rescinded the AFDC programme, and instead created Temporary Assistance to Needy Families (TANF) as a 'block grant'[19] with wide state discretion. Although there are few federal mandates in the new statute, two are central to the rhetoric of the new policy: (1) parents can receive TANF only for a maximum of five years in their lifetime,[20] and (2) states must have a fixed percentage of recipients in waged work and/or 'workfare' (i.e. working off their TANF grant)[21] at certain points in time.[22] Thus the focus moves away from income support for poor women and children, and on to short-term receipt of social welfare benefits with an assumed permanent transition into waged work.

This work requirement is and will continue to push millions of new people into low-wage labour markets with little social welfare protection.[23] Thus over 2 million single parents, mostly women, many with little education and low skill levels,[24] are relying on low-wage labour or some source of income other than TANF. Of the 2.3 million families still on the rolls,[25] many will reach the mandatory lifetime limit within the next few years and be terminated *regardless* of whether they had any reasonable opportunity to obtain paid labour or have any other source of income. Many poor mothers in the US who had previously moved in and out of low-wage work recycling on to AFDC as their 'unemployment insurance' can no longer do this due to the TANF time limits. They no longer have either AFDC or UI as a social safety-net; thus, many of them will be in a position in which they will have to accept paid labour with whatever conditions and wages they can get.[26] If they cannot find paid labour, they will be ineligible for further public assistance and therefore will be entirely dependent on private charity for survival.

While the statute contains language prohibiting states from displacing regular employees with mothers in workfare job slots, it eliminated language in the prior statute which protected regular employees against 'partial displacement'.[27] In other words, regularly paid employees can receive a reduction in their overtime hours or benefits, or can be cut from a full-time to a part-time job, and the work they had previously done for pay can be performed without pay by workfare workers. Employers can also fill established vacancies and openings created by attrition with workfare participants.[28] The impact of the full and partial job displacement that will be caused by workfare requirements on currently employed workers[29] is, of course, likely to increase substantially as the US moves into the predicted recession. Importantly, it is not inconsequential that most of those who will be displaced are unionized.[30]

At the same time as the US was rescinding its communal commitment to income support for single-parent families, social protection law was also altering the inclusion and identity of immigrants. The PRWORA rescinded the eligibility of legal immigrants, including low-wage workers, for virtually all social welfare programmes designed to assist the poor, including TANF, Food Stamps and Social Security Insurance (a programme for aged and disabled individuals who do not have a sufficient tie to waged work to qualify for regular Social Security benefits).[31] While some of the social protection benefits have been restored, the restorations are almost exclusively for immigrants who were in the US at the time the PRWORA passed in August 1996.[32] Therefore, the huge influx of legal immigrants who enter the country each year after 1996 are still ineligible for the majority of social protection programmes not connected to high wages or long-term labour-market participation.[33]

The question of the legality of statutes that exclude legal immigrants from social protection benefits is mired in the complex federalism system of the US. The Supreme Court has interpreted a number of constitutional provisions as establishing 'plenary power' in the federal legislative and executive branch over certain immigration issues.[34] Such plenary power constitutes a preemption of state power in the designated area, i.e. states are not allowed to legislate regarding immigration policies which have been vested in the federal government. In addition, '[t]he power of Congress to exclude aliens altogether from the United States or to prescribe the terms and conditions upon which they may come to this country'[35] is virtually unlimited, requiring judicial deference.

Vis-à-vis the PRWORA social protection immigrant exclusions, the judiciary has articulated this distinction most clearly in *Mathews v. Diaz*[36] and *Graham v. Richardson*.[37] In *Mathews*, the US Supreme Court upheld the exclusion of legal immigrants from a federal medical insurance programme until the immigrant had continuously resided in the US for five years and was admitted for permanent residence.[38] Yet only five years earlier, the Court had invalidated two states' (i.e. provincial) welfare laws that imposed durational residency requirements on all non-citizens, as violating the Equal Protection Clause of the Fourteenth Amendment of the United States Constitution.[39] The *Mathews* Court distinguished *Graham* by finding that 'the Fourteenth Amendment's limits on state powers are substantially different from the constitutional provisions applicable to the federal power over immigration and naturalization'.[40]

Thus the current US Supreme Court would likely rule that federal denials of social protection benefits, such as those contained in the PRWORA, are constitutional under Congress's plenary power, i.e. wide competence regarding immigration matters.

The connection between these immigrant provisions of the PRWORA and the NAFTA is critical to a cross-border poverty analysis. Mexicans are by far the largest group of legal immigrants who have chosen not to naturalize as US citizens (Pastor and Castañeda 1988: 323). Indeed, in spite of the long Mexico–US history of border exchange and guest-worker programmes, there has also been a societal perception that Mexicans did not have to assimilate because they were in the US only as 'temporary' workers.

Two years prior to the passage of the PRWORA, the US Congress ratified the NAFTA over the adamant opposition of virtually all US labour unions. One concession by Congress to US labour was the NAFTA–Trade Adjustment Assistance Programme that provided additional weeks of UI for retraining 'workers' (excluding workers not covered by UI laws, i.e. many welfare recipients) who lose their jobs due to increased imports or capital flight generated by the NAFTA.[41] The result of these complex and often isolated legal revisions is that US taxpayers are funding both the extended UI benefits and the retraining of 'workers' dislocated by US trade policy, at the same time as they are defunding many social welfare benefits to low-wage workers who are welfare recipients and legal, often Mexican, immigrants.[42]

INTERACTION BETWEEN TANF RECIPIENTS AND MEXICAN IMMIGRANTS IN LOW-WAGE LABOUR

These factors highlight a major tension between the expectation that the US low-wage labour force can and must absorb all welfare recipients, and the understanding of the close connection of the US with Mexican immigrants because of prior 'guest-worker' programmes, proximity, economic disparity, large common border and numbers of Mexicans already in the US. In particular, many in the US labour movement and many left and progressive academics and advocates have taken an anti-immigration position because of an assumption that immigration reduces the power of particularly unskilled low-wage US workers to negotiate higher wages and better working conditions.

Although studies on the impact of immigrants on the US economy and labour conditions reach widely divergent conclusions, often finding positive economic effects[43] and no negative effect on wages and labour conditions, the claim that immigration of unskilled workers reduces wages and conditions is still frequently touted as 'truth'.[44] Thus immigrants and prior TANF recipients are being rhetorically pitted against one another. For example, a US General Accounting Office study found no need for an immigrant guest farm-worker programme in part because welfare recipients affected by either the time limits or the work requirements of the PROWRA will provide a surplus supply.[45] When the US Immigration and Naturalization Service deported undocumented Mexican field-workers, growers were encouraged to hire welfare recipients (Simon 1998: A3). Of course, field-work is seasonal, so workers are laid off for four to six months at a stretch with no social protection benefits. And, although some social workers and growers note that field-work schedules vary depending on the weather and condition of the crop and that standard daytime child-care is not always adequate, the US Department of Labor takes the position that the child-care needs in farm occupations are no different from those in other industries.[46]

The cumulative effect of these policies creates racist hierarchies within racist hierarchies. The rhetoric of social assistance portrays US citizens receiving welfare as lazy women of colour. The PRWORA 'rehabilitated' them by removing any social safety-net after five years and exchanging dependence on AFDC or TANF for dependence on low-wage employers. These US citizens are, on occasion, perceived as in competition with legal immigrants, who have summarily lost eligibility for social assistance programmes, and undocumented immigrants – both groups that have sent significant remittances to impoverished families in their countries of origin.[47] Having convinced the US public that poverty is primarily a problem of work-effort, policy-makers have created a situation that worsens the plight of former welfare recipients and fails to recognize the presence and impact of cross-border poverty.

A number of other factors make the relationship between immigration policy, TANF and low-wage labour even more complex. Often policy-makers, scholars and activists across political persuasions have ignored the fact that, for certain industries, particularly those with high labour costs and geographical flexibility, capital is much more mobile across borders than humans. An anti-immigration policy which does not provide a supply of low-wage workers within our current economic structure may result in migration of certain job-sites entirely and, thus, even further diminution of US labour conditions.

The reverse of this equation is reflected in an implicit assumption when the NAFTA was ratified that the flow of goods and finances from Mexico to the US would be substituted for the flow of people, an assumption that required a pervasive economic development/job-creation programme in Mexico.[48] However, working at odds with such economic development in Mexico is the reduction (mandated by the International Monetary Fund structural macroeconomic adjustments) of agriculture subsidies which had benefited both large and small-scale farmers in rural areas. The resulting agricultural crisis has resulted in both farm foreclosures (with resulting dislocation) and reduced economic activity in urban areas situated near prosperous agricultural areas.[49]

Contrary to the assumption that NAFTA would reduce undocumented immigration, Census 2000 data indicate the opposite. The number of undocumented residents appears to be 9–11 million rather than the 6 million predicted.[50] Economists are crediting this increased immigrant population, many working in low-wage unskilled jobs, with reducing pressures for wage increases, thus fostering a 'full employment labor market environment without generating any additional wage inflationary pressures'.[51] Importantly, the majority of undocumented Mexican immigrants are men who leave behind their families, creating whole villages populated with only women, children and the elderly.[52]

Finally, immigrant workers are not necessarily substitutes who displace existing workers or increase labour supply to the point of reduced wages and labour conditions. Rather, a poverty/low-wage policy could be envisioned which juxtaposes each group of unskilled workers as complements (Heer 1996: 8–9). Under that analysis, we might argue for a pro-education and training policy for TANF mothers to move them into a position to complement rather than compete with unskilled immigrants.

THE POLITICAL FLUIDITY OF THE BORDER

Both US social protection reductions and political democratization in Mexico appear to be catapulting Mexicans living in the US into a central position that further explodes the concept of nation-state boundaries. In fact, the result of the welfare disqualifications of legal immigrants may be exactly the opposite of that intended by many of its proponents, i.e. to reduce the number of legal immigrants or to decrease the number of legal immigrants on the 'public dole'.

One major result of denying virtually all social assistance programmes to legal immigrants was a startling surge in United States naturalizations, particularly among Mexicans. The denial of benefits to legal immigrants, and other recent anti-immigrant political actions, resulted in a new consciousness among long-term legal Mexican immigrants that they must be a part of the electorate, i.e. that they must become naturalized US citizens who can vote.[53] Until 1994, the number of naturalizations by Mexicans legally residing in the US was fairly stable: there were 17,564 naturalizations in 1990; 22,066 in 1991; 12,880 in 1992; 23,630 in 1993 (US Dept. of Justice 1998: 180). In 1994, the year that Californians adopted Proposition 187 (barring undocumented immigrants from receiving publicly funded education and most social services and healthcare, and directing local law enforcement authorities, school administrators, social workers and healthcare aides to report suspected undocumented immigrants and, in some cases, legal immigrants),[54] the number of naturalizations surged to 46,186, and in 1995 to 79,614 (ibid.: 170). Most dramatically in 1996 (the year the PRWORA was being debated and enacted), Mexico was the leading country-of-birth of persons naturalizing, with 217,418 or 21 per cent of total naturalizations (ibid.).[55]

Once they become US citizens, Mexican-Americans have greatly expanded legal rights to bring family members into the US. Thus, the ironic end result of anti-immigrant politics may be that even greater numbers of Mexican immigrants will settle in the USA, naturalize and vote. Questions arise about the effect of this potential increase in family-member legal immigrants on the low-wage labour force, and the interplay between that population and the influx of welfare recipients possibly competing for the same jobs.

Juxtapose these developments to recent dramatic changes in Mexican laws relating to dual citizenship and the ability of non-residents to vote in Mexican elections. Mexican non-residents are now allowed to maintain dual nationality in Mexico and in the country of their residence, e.g. Mexican immigrants who are naturalized US citizens are now permitted to reclaim their Mexican nationality.[56] Mexico's constitution was modified to allow non-resident Mexican citizens to vote in Mexican elections without returning to Mexico. Although not yet implemented at the time of the 2000 elections (Smith 1999: A1)[57] (in which the Institutional Revolutionary Party [PRI] was defeated for the first time since 1920 by the National Action Party [PAN]), almost 10 million Mexicans more or less permanently residing in the USA could be eligible to vote in Mexican elections. They are expected to support either the PAN or the Party of the Democratic Revolution (PRD) (McDonnell 1999: A1), both of which are Mexican political parties advocating the democratization of labour unions in Mexico.[58]

Thus the huge increase in US naturalizations by Mexicans (in turn opening the door for further immigration by family members) and the breaking open, or democratization, of Mexican political parties and unions could have broad implications for social protection and low-wage labour in both the US and Mexico. The construction of dual nationality and dual voting privileges exposes the artificiality of protectionism and fixed borders which seems entrenched in social protection, low-wage labour and immigration discourse.

CONCLUSION

The myriad of issues discussed above are not designed to yield a single coherent poverty policy, but rather to challenge us to frame new questions about strategies to address poverty, wealth and inequality within an increasingly globalized economy:

Did the US labour anti-NAFTA position, albeit inadvertently, feed into a racist, anti-Mexican and anti-immigration policy, which then fuelled the anti-immigrant backlash in US welfare policy?

If one effect of social welfare cuts to US legal immigrants is a surge in naturalizations with a subsequent increased flow of family members migrating to the US, will this additional supply of wage-workers entice certain plants to remain in the US rather than relocate cross-border? How do these new immigrants correlate with those who would have obtained jobs if plants had moved to Mexico?

If immigration can expand or preserve certain industries in the USA, creating new jobs for complementary skill-holders, should an effective US poverty policy focus on increasing the human capital of US unskilled workers so that they might be able to take advantage of those new jobs? Could or should US progressives support such a policy with its implications for further constructing and supporting racial hierarchies?

What is the connection, within both a class and gender analysis, of the single mothers in the maquiladoras, the TANF mothers and the women-and-children-only towns? Men are involved in each setting in different ways, but there is little discussion among lawyers dealing with child support and those aware of the huge remittances being sent back to Mexico.

What do we expect regarding and whom do we value in waged work? Why are we so concerned about ensuring that US welfare recipients are in waged work, without acknowledging that many of them are and addressing both the ways in which low-income labour conditions and legal definitions construct their identities as non-workers? Conversely, why are we so derisive (within our rhetoric of 'rugged individualism') about undocumented immigrants in US waged labour who send critical remittances back to the women-and-children-only towns?

How do we begin to connect US social welfare cuts and IMF structural macroeconomic adjustment policies, and analyse their impact on low-wage labour markets cross-border?

Finally and most fundamentally, how do we develop a cross-border poverty redistributive strategy? An ongoing tension in the poverty debate is that between improving or maintaining living standards for low-wage workers and job creation for the unemployed poor. While often discussed as a policy question internal to a nation-state, the same issues are raised in cross-border poverty discourse. Where does a nation-state draw the line between its own citizens being in such poverty that it must protect their labour conditions through attempting to restrict migration of humans and its economy being solid enough and its citizens' living conditions sufficiently adequate that restrictive immigration may not be the priority? Can nations, in a time of the breakdown of borders through global economic integration, coherently establish that line? If a nation-state sets up an initial structure of attempted restrictive human mobility, will it ever reach a point of acknowledging that its internal poverty/unemployment is low enough that the country can focus on cross-border poverty? In other words, can an effective poverty policy be based on a protectionist position?

These are only initial questions and may not frame the most important interconnections. But if those committed to a redistributive poverty strategy do not struggle to engage in a complex cross-disciplinary, cross-border analysis of the interaction of low-wage labour, globalization, social welfare policy and immigration – if we do not begin to formulate the questions – we are missing an important opportunity to begin to provide answers that will contribute to the development of a more sophisticated and transformative redistributive policy.

NOTES

1. For a discussion of changes in the federal statutory entitlement, see Williams (1998).

2. Of the world's 6 billion people, 2.8 billion live on less than $2 per day and 1.2 billion live on less than $1 per day. Of these 43.5 per cent live in South Asia, 24.3 per cent live in Sub-Saharan Africa, 23.2 per cent in East Asia and the Pacific, 6.5 per cent in Latin America and the Caribbean, 2 per cent in Europe and Central Asia, and 0.5 per cent in the Middle East and North Africa. The number

of these poor has been decreasing in East Asia, but increasing in Latin America, South Asia, Sub-Saharan Africa and post-Soviet bloc European and Central Asian countries; World Bank, *World Development Report 2000–2001: Attacking Poverty* (2001), pp. 3–4, 21–3.

3. Ibid., p. 3.

4. Ibid., p. 24, Table 1.2 (relative income poverty by region).

5. Ibid., p. 3.

6. Act of 26 March 1910, ch. 128, 36 Stat. 263, 264 (repealed 1952).

7. Act of 29 April 1943, ch. 82, 57 Stat. 70 (eliminated 1964).

8. From 1974 to 1982, 87 per cent of the maquiladora workforce was female. As shifts in production occurred, requiring more managers to work with high technology equipment, more men were hired (La Botz 1992: 164). However, in 1990, of the 371,780 workers in 1,909 maquiladoras, 61 per cent or 226,483 were still women (163). Recent estimates indicate that there are between 4,000 and 4,500 maquiladoras operating in Mexico. Of the estimated one million plus employees in the maquila industry, women workers make up 56 per cent of the workforce, a declining percentage but an increase in overall numbers. *About the Maquiladora Industry*, at <http://www.mexicomaquila.com/mi.htm>. Pay is often less than $1 per hour, a far cry from the minimum wage in the US (Arriola 2000: 729, at 766–9, citing multiple sources). Although maquiladoras traditionally targeted women between the ages of fourteen and twenty-four and required routine pregnancy tests to avoid paying for legally mandated pregnancy benefits, many of the female workers are single parents (La Botz 1992: 176–7).

9. 8 USC §1151(a)(1965)(repealed 1976).

10. Ibid. (amended 1978).

11. 19 USC §3301 et seq. (1999).

12. Social Security Act of 1935, Pub.L.No. 74–271, 49 Stat. 620 (codified as amended in scattered sections of 42 USC).

13. Social Security Act Amendments of 1950, Pub.L.No. 81–734, §323, 64 Stat. 477, 551 (codified as amended at 42 USC §606).

14. Staff of House Committee on Ways and Means, 104th Congress, 2nd Session, Background Material and Data on Programs Within the Jurisdiction of the Committee on Ways and Means 474 (1996).

15. See discussion infra.

16. For example, UI coverage requires not just a connection to waged work, but a sufficient connection. States set a minimum amount that the employee must have earned within a designated period, disadvantaging low-waged and contingent workers. To meet monetary eligibility minimums, low-waged workers must work more hours than higher paid workers. (Advisory Council on Unemployment Compensation, *Report and Recommendations*, 17 [1995]). In nine states, a half-time, full-year (1,040 hours of work) worker who earns the minimum wage is ineligible for benefits, while the worker who earns $8 an hour for the same hours of work is eligible. Likewise, a two day a week, full-year worker earning the minimum wage would be ineligible in twenty-nine states, but the same worker earning $8 an hour would be eligible in all but two states.

17. For example, states often disqualify part-time workers or workers who have

been forced to leave their paid labour because of a breakdown in child-care or other family care-giving obligations. Spalter-Roth et al. (1994) found that only 11 per cent of those who combine paid work and welfare receive UI.

18. Pub. L. No. 104–93, 110 Stat. 2105, 42 USC §601 (1999).

19. Each state receives a fixed allocation of money to distribute largely within the discretion of the state; 42 USC §604(a)(1)(2000).

20. For example, states can decide which families will be eligible for benefits and the length of time families are allowed to receive grants, as long as the state does not allow families to receive benefits for more than five years throughout their lifetime; 42 USC §608(a)(7). A number of states have limited that time to two years; e.g. 1995 Mass. Acts c.5, §110(f) (limiting receipt to twenty-four months in any five-year period).

21. In addition, states may require mothers who have not found a private sector job within two months to work (usually in public sector employment), not for a paycheque, but in exchange for their welfare benefits; 42 USC §602 (a)(1)(B)(iv)(2000).

22. If states do not meet this requirement, they are fiscally penalized by the federal government; 42 USC §609(a)(3)(A)(Supp. 1999).

23. As of December 1999, the welfare, or TANF, national caseload had dropped by 49 per cent in the four years since the PRWORA had been passed, with very little follow-up of or explanation regarding those not in waged work. See, e.g., US Department of Health and Human Services, *Temporary Assistance for Needy Families (TANF), Third Annual Report to Congress* (August 2000). There were 2,264,314 fewer families and 6,370,360 fewer recipients on the welfare rolls.

24. In March 1999, an Educational Testing Service study found that without more education, two-thirds of welfare mothers lack the skills to advance economically, with a more severe impact on African-American and Hispanic women. However, many of the women could improve their prospects of moving into the middle class with minimal training; Carnevale and Desrochers (1999).

25. US Department of Health and Human Services, see note 23.

26. The impact of this waged work dependency is unclear and evolving. Early studies questioned whether low-wage labour markets could incorporate the numbers who are being dropped from the welfare rolls. And, of course, the geographical impact is disparate, since the areas with a higher number of welfare recipients do not necessarily correspond with the areas of high job growth. For example, between 1992 and 1996, as the United States' economy moved out of recession, New York City experienced a net gain of 88,000 jobs. If this rate of growth continued and every new job were given to a New York City welfare recipient, it would take twenty-one years for all 470,000 adults on welfare in New York City to gain employment; Finder (1996: A1). Other estimates indicate that the economy can create the number of jobs needed, not on short notice but only over the long term (Burtless 1994: 87). But even if the economy can absorb these workers over the long term, studies estimate that this huge influx of largely unskilled workers would depress wages, benefits and working conditions. The Economic Policy Institute has estimated that by moving nearly one million welfare recipients into the labour force, the time limits on receipt of social protection for this population will initiate an 11–12 per cent decline in real wages, but only for the bottom one-third of the

workforce; Mishel and Schmitt (1995). Recent studies, while noting that there is little current evidence of an effect on unemployment or wages, continue to predict substantial effects on low-income workers. Enchautegui 2001 (a 10 per cent increase in the number of wage-working welfare recipients will reduce the employment of low-skilled US-born men by 2 per cent and reduce their wages by 0.3 per cent; will reduce welfare recipient wages by 1.5 per cent; and in the long run, will reduce the wages of low-skilled women by 2.2 per cent); Hoynes 2000 (wages for female high school dropouts will be reduced by 5–14.5 per cent depending on elasticities of labour demand); Lerman and Ratcliffe 2000 (finding no current wage erosion, but recognizing that a serious recession would 'certainly weaken the wage and employment picture').

27. The prior statute was codified as 42 USC §684(c)(1)(1994), repealed by Pub. L. no. 104–93, 110 ArR.2167 (1996). The current statute is codified as 42 USC §607(f)(2)(Supp. 2000).

28. 42 USC §607(f)(1)(Supp. 2000).

29. One early study focused on New York City predicted that the likely result from placing 30,000 workfare participants in *public sector* slots would be to displace 20,000 other workers and reduce wages for the bottom one-third of the entire New York City workforce (*public and private*) by 9 per cent (Tilly 1996). Indeed, a recent study confirms that as the number of employees in New York's Department of Parks and Recreation has declined from 4,285 to 2,025 between 1991 and 2000, the number of full-time equivalent workfare workers increased from 182 to 2,237 ('Use of Work Experience Program Participants at the Department of Parks and Recreation', *Inside the Budget*, 72, 2 November 2000).

30. In addition to the impact on wages and displacement in low-wage labour markets in general in the US, working conditions may also be affected. For example, welfare recipients have been assigned to workfare jobs with no toilets or drinking water, jobs removing rotting and infected animal carcasses with no gloves, jobs requiring the use of acidic-spray cleaning fluid without safety equipment – in other words, jobs which violate existing health and safety laws and which existing wage-workers would refuse to take without improved conditions. See, e.g., *Capers v. Giuliani*, 677 NYS2d 353 (NY App. Div. 1998) (plaintiffs' affidavits in this case were printed in 'Welfare As They Know It', *Harper's Magazine*, 1 November 1997, at 24). Cf. the much discussed conditions of employment for single women in the maquiladoras (see, e.g., Arriola, supra note 8, pp. 765–94).

31. 8 USC, §1611(a)(1999).

32. E.g., 8 USC, §1611(b)(5)(2000) (restoring Supplemental Security Income and Medicaid eligibility to certain immigrants, termed 'not qualified' immigrants, who were receiving assistance on 22 August 1996); 8 USC, §1612(a)(2)(F)(2000) (restoring Supplemental Security Income and Food Stamps to 'qualified' blind or disabled immigrants residing in the USA on 22 August 1996).

33. In addition, there are other connections between migration and social protection benefits. For example, in 1997, certain legal residents were being stopped at the US border because the Immigration Service had received information from a state that the immigrant had received Medicaid, or healthcare, benefits. The immigrants were denied re-entry unless they agreed to reimburse the state for the past Medicaid received, although receipt of Medicaid does not create a legal

debt ('Settlement Reached in Medi-Cal "Debt"', *Immigrants Rights Update*, 16 September 1998, p. 8.

34. E.g., *Toll v. Moreno*, 458 US 1, 10 (1982) grounded its holding in the naturalization power, Art. I, § 8, Cl. 4, and the Commerce Clause, Art. I, § 8, Cl. 3, of the US Constitution. For a more complete discussion of the various powers underlying this doctrine and the various forms of legislation encompassed within the purview of federal plenary power, see Abriel (1995) (finding that the 'principal reasons advanced for federal preemption are the need for uniformity in immigration laws and the federal government's superior ability and authority to deal with foreign nations') (citations omitted).

35. *Lem Moon Sing v. United States*, 158 US 538, 547 (1895).

36. 426 US 67 (1976).

37. 403 US 365 (1971).

38. '[T]he fact that Congress has provided some welfare benefits for citizens does not require it to provide like benefits for *all aliens*. Neither the overnight visitor, the unfriendly agent of a hostile foreign power, the resident diplomat, nor the illegal entrant, can advance even a colorable constitutional claim to a share in the bounty that a conscientious sovereign makes available to its own citizens and *some* of its guests. The decision to share that bounty with our guests may take into account the character of the relationship between the alien and this country: Congress may decide that as the alien's tie grows stronger, so does the strength of his claim to an equal share of that munificence.' *Mathews*, 426 US at 80.

39. *Graham*, 403 US at 372. Interestingly, an important comparison can be made between this line of cases and federalism cases dealing with citizens. See, e.g., *Saenz v. Roe*, 67 USLW 4291 (1999).

40. *Mathews*, 426 US at 86–7.

41. 19 USC, § 2331 (2000).

42. See generally Johnson 1995 (describing the anti-Latin American, especially Mexican, immigrant sentiment regarding public benefits).

43. Note the recent studies crediting immigration with facilitating the US strong economy of the 1990s, supra note 51.

44. See, e.g., Mark Helm, 'Immigration Policy Hurting US Poor, Critics Claim', *Sun Sentinel* (Ft Lauderdale), 12 March 1999 (reporting that George Borjas, professor at Harvard University's Kennedy School of Government, testified before the House Subcommittee on Immigration and Claims that US low-skilled workers lose an average of $1,915 per year because of immigrant competition).

45. General Accounting Office, H-2A Agricultural Guestworker Program – 'Changes Could Improve Services to Employers and Better Protect Workers' (1998).

46. Ibid.

47. An estimated $6–10 billion in remittances is sent to families in Mexico each year, providing 'essential support for 1.1 million households in Mexico' according to the head of the Mexican National Population Council (CONAPO). Margaret Swedish, 'US–Mexico Border: Immigration Flow Likely to Remain Steady Despite Enforcement Measures', *Central America/Mexico Report* (May 2000), at <http://www.rtfcam.org/report/volume_20/No_2/article_2.htm>.

These remittances represent the second largest source of revenues in foreign currency, after tourism, and at least the third biggest legitimate force in the Mexican economy, after oil and tourism. Tim Weiner, 'Mexico Chief Pushes New Border Policy: Free and Easy Does It', *New York Times*, 14 December 2000, p. A12.

48. Arriola 2000: 805; Heppel and Torres (1996).

49. Ansley 1998; Sarah Anderson, John Cavanagh and David Ranney, 'NAFTA–Trinational Fiasco: Remember the Rosy Promises About Jobs, etc.? Here's a Reality Check', *The Nation* 263 (1996: 26).

50. D'Vera Cohn, 'Illegal Residents Exceed Estimate', *Washington Post*, 18 March 2001, p. A1. The initial count tallied 281.4 million US residents as opposed to the expected 275 million. The number of Hispanics, two-thirds of whom were Mexican, was 35.3 million rather than the estimated 32.5 million (ibid.); D. Vera Cohn and Darryl Fears, 'Hispanics Draw Even with Blacks in New Census', *Washington Post*, 7 March 2001, p. A1.

51. Andrew Sum et al., 'An Analysis of the Preliminary 2000 Census Estimates of the Resident Population of the U.S. and Their Implications for Demographic, Immigration, and Labor Market Analysis and Policymaking', Center for Labor Market Studies, Northeastern University, February 2001; Paul Magnusson, 'The Border is More Porous Than You Think', *Business Week*, 9 April 2001.

52. 'Migration Between Mexico & the United States', A Report of the Binational Study on Migration, 72 (1997); Ricardo Monreal, 'A Governor from a Hardscrabble State Who is Forging a New Style of Responsive Government', *Time*, 24 May 1999, p. 62; Eric Schlosser, 'In the Strawberry Fields: Migrant Workers and the California Strawberry Industry', *Atlantic Monthly*, November 1995, p. 80.

53. US Dept. of Justice (1998); Paul Van Slambrouck, 'Immigrants Shift Status: No Longer Sojourners', *Christian Science Monitor*, 21 September 1999, p. 1.

54. The core provisions of Proposition 187 were struck down by US District Judge Mariana Pfaelzer, and a subsequent settlement was mediated between the state and opponents of the initiative, in which Governor Gray Davis agreed to drop the state's appeal. See *League of United Latin American Citizens v. Wilson*, 908 F. Supp. 755 (CD Cal. 1995), modified by 997 F. Supp. 1244 (CD Cal. 1997), modified by no. 94-7569 MRP, 94-7652 MRP, 94-7570 MRP, 95-0187 MRP, 94-7571 MRP, 1998 WL 141325 (CD Cal. Mar. 13, 1998); Dave Lesher and Henry Weinstein, 'Prop. 187 Backers Accuse Davis of Ignoring Voters', *L.A. Times*, 30 July 1999, p. A1.

55. Of course, there were other legal changes which factored into this increase, most specifically the numbers of undocumented allowed to naturalize pursuant to the Immigration Reform and Control Act of 1986; 8 USC, §1101 nt. (1986). In subsequent years, the number has declined (134,494 in 1997 and 109,065 in 1998), but the percentage of persons from Mexico naturalizing has remained over 20 per cent of total naturalizations, and in fact has increased (22.5 per cent in 1996 and 23.6 per cent in 1997) (US Dept. of Justice 1998).

56. Constitucion Politica de los Estados Unidos Mexicanos, art. 37 (amended 1997). Note the nuances between nationality and citizenship that are beyond the scope of this chapter.

57. Although the Chamber of Deputies approved a package implementing this

election reform, the Senate (controlled by the PRI) allowed the measure to die in July 1999.

58. The Partido Revolucionario Institucional (Institutional Revolutionary Party or PRI), the political party that had been in power in Mexico since 1920, had held continuous office longer than any other party in the world. It has controlled the union structure by having an officially recognized union, the Confederacion de Trabajadores de Mexico (Confederation of Mexican Workers, or CTM). CTM leaders routinely were not democratically elected by membership, were bought off by the government and failed to represent their members to enforce what on the books is an excellent Mexican labour law (see generally La Botz 1992).

REFERENCES

Abriel, E. A. (1995) 'Rethinking Preemption for Purposes of Aliens and Public Benefits', *University of Los Angeles Law Review*, 42: 1597–607.

Altonji, J. and D. Card (1991) 'The Effects of Immigration on the Labor Market Outcomes of Less-Skilled Natives', in J. M. Abowd and R. B. Freeman (eds), *Immigration, Trade, and the Labor Market*, Chicago: University of Chicago Press.

Ansley, F. L. (1998) 'Rethinking Law in Globalization Labor Markets', *University of Pennsylvania Journal of Labor and Employment Law*, 1: 369–80.

Arriola, E. R. (2000) 'Voices from the Barbed Wires of Despair: Women in the Maquiladoras, Latina Critical Legal Theory and Gender at the US–Mexico Border', *DePaul Law Review*, 49.

Bean, F. D., R. O. de la Garza, B. R. Roberts and S. Weintraub (eds) (1997) *At the Crossroads: Mexican Migration and U.S. Policy*, New York: Rowman and Littlefield.

Beck, R. (1996) *The Case Against Immigration*, New York: W. W. Norton.

Borjas, G. J. (1990) *Friends or Strangers: The Impact of Immigrants on the U.S. Economy*, New York: Basic Books.

— (1994) 'The Economics of Immigration', *Journal of Economic Literature*, 32: 1667–717.

Borjas, G. J., R. B. Freeman and L. F. Katz (1992) 'On the Labor Market Effects of Immigration and Trade', in G. J. Borjas and R. B. Freeman (eds), *Immigration and the Work Force: Economic Consequences for the United States and Source Areas*, Chicago: University of Chicago Press.

Buchanan, R. (1995) 'Border Crossings: NAFTA, Regulatory Restructuring, and the Politics of Place', *Independent Journal of Global Legal Studies*, 2: 371–93.

Burtless, G. (1994) 'Employment Prospects of Welfare Recipients', in D. Smith Nightingale and R. H. Haveman (eds), *The Work Alternative: Welfare Reform and the Realities of the Job Market*.

Butcher, K. and D. Card (1991) 'Immigration and Wages: Evidence from the 1980s', *American Economic Review*, 81: 292–6.

Card, D. (1990) 'The Impact of the Mariel Boatlift', *Industrial and Labor Relations Review*, 43: 245–57.

Carnevale, A. and D. Desrochers (1999) *Getting Down to Business: Matching*

Welfare Recipients' Skills to Jobs That Train, Princeton, NJ: Educational Testing Service.

Edin, K. and L. Lein (1996) 'Work, Welfare, and Single Mothers' Economic Survival Strategies', *American Sociological Review*, 61: 253–66.

Ehrenberg, R. G. and R. S. Smith (1997) *Modern Labor Economics: Theory and Public Policy*, New York: Addison Wesley.

Enchautegui, M. E. (2001) *Will Welfare Reform Hurt Low-skilled Workers?*, Urban Institute Discussion Papers, Washington, DC: Urban Institute.

Filer, R. K. (1992) 'The Impact of Immigrant Arrivals on Migratory Patterns of Native Workers', in G. J. Borjas and R. B. Freeman (eds), *Immigration and the Work Force: Economic Consequences for the United States and Source Areas*, Chicago: University of Chicago Press.

Finder, A. (1996) 'Welfare Clients Outnumber Jobs They Might Fill', *New York Times*, 25 August, p. A1.

Friedberg, R. M. and J. Hunt (1995) 'The Impact of Immigrants on Host Country Wages, Employment and Growth', *Journal of Economic Perspectives*, 9: 23–44.

Friedmann, S., N. Lustig and A. Legovini (1995) 'Mexico: Social Spending and Food Subsidies During Adjustment in the 1980s', in N. Lustig (ed.), *Coping With Austerity*, Washington, DC: The Brookings Institution.

General Accounting Office (1998) *H-2A Agricultural Guestworker Program – Changes Could Improve Services to Employers and Better Protect Workers*, Washington, DC: General Accounting Office.

Goldfarb, R. S. (1996) 'Methodological Commentary-Investigating Immigrant-Black Labor Market Substitution: Reflections on the Case Study Approach', in H. O. Duleep and P. V. Wunnava (eds), *Immigrants and Immigration Policy: Individual Skills, Family Ties and Group Identities*, Greenwich, CT: Jai Press, Inc.

Goldin, A. H. (1990) 'Collective Bargaining In Mexico: Stifled by the Lack of Democracy in Trade Unions', *Comparative Labor Law Journal*, 11: 203–25.

Harris, K. (1993) 'Work and Welfare among Single Mothers in Poverty', *American Journal of Sociology*, 99: 317–52.

Heer, D. (1996) *Immigration in America's Future*, Boulder, CO: Westview Press.

Heppel, M. L. and L. R. Torres (1996) 'Mexican Immigration to the United States After NAFTA', *Fletcher F. World Affairs*, 20: 51–64.

Hoynes, H. W. (2000) 'Displacement and Wage Effects of Welfare Reform', in D. E. Card and R. M. Blank (eds), *Finding Jobs: Work and Welfare Reform*.

Huddle, Dr D. (1993) *The Net National Costs of Immigration in 1993*, Washington, DC: Carrying Capacity Network.

Jaeger, D. A. (1995) *Skill Differences and the Effect of Immigrants on the Wages of Natives*, Dissertation, University of Michigan.

Jencks, C. (1992) *Rethinking Social Policy: Race, Poverty, and the Underclass*, Cambridge, MA: Harvard University Press.

Johnson, K. R. (1995) 'Public Benefits and Immigration: The Intersection of Immigration Status, Ethnicity, Gender, and Class', *University of Los Angeles Law Review*, 42: 1509, 1519–28.

La Botz, D. (1992) *Mask of Democracy: Labor Suppression in Mexico Today*, Boston, MA: South End Press.

Lerman, R. I. and C. Ratcliffe (2000) *Did Metropolitan Areas Absorb Welfare Recipients Without Displacing Other Workers?*, Urban Institute Discussion Papers, no. A-45, Washington, DC: Urban Institute.

McDonnell, P. J. (1999) 'U.S. Votes Could Sway Mexico's Next Election', *Los Angeles Times*, 15 February 1999, p. A1.

Mischel, L. and J. Schmitt (1995) *Cutting Wages by Cutting Welfare: The Impact of Reform on the Low-Wage Labor Market*, Washington, DC: Economic Policy Institute.

Passel, J. and R. Clark (1994) 'How Much Do Immigrants Really Cost? A Reappraisal of Huddle's "The Costs of Immigration"', Washington, DC: Urban Institute.

Pastor, R. A. and J. G. Castañeda (1989) *Limits to Friendship: The United States and Mexico*, New York: Vintage Books.

Pavetti, L. (1993) *The Dynamics of Welfare and Work: Exploring the Process by Which Young Women Work Their Way off Welfare*, Cambridge, MA: Malcolm Wiener Center for Social Policy, Harvard University.

Pearce, D. M. (1993) Statement of the Women and Poverty Project, 'Wider Opportunities for Women', to the National Advisory Council on Unemployment Compensation.

Peters, S. (1990) 'Labor Law for the Maquiladoras: Choosing Between Workers' Rights and Foreign Investment', *Comparative Labor Law Journal*, 11: 226–48.

Siebert, C. D. and M. A. Zaidi (1996) 'Employment, Trade and Foreign Investment Effects of NAFTA', *Minnesota Journal of Global Trade*, 5: 333–55.

Simon, S. (1998) 'Growers Say U.S. Wrong, Labor is in Short Supply', *Los Angeles Times*, 5 January 1998, p. A3.

Smith, J. F. (1999) 'Vote Denied to Mexicans Living Abroad', *Los Angeles Times*, 2 July 1999, p. A1.

Sorensen, E. (1996) 'Measuring the Employment Effects of Immigrants with Different Legal Statuses on Native Workers', in H. O. Duleep and P. V. Wunnava (eds), *Immigrants and Immigration Policy: Individual Skills, Family Ties and Group Identities*, Greenwich, CT: Jai Press.

Spalter-Roth, R. (1994) *Making Work Pay: The Real Employment Opportunities of Single Mothers Participating in the AFDC Program*, Washington, DC: Institute for Women's Policy Research.

Spalter-Roth, R., H. Hartmann and B. Burr (1994) *Income Security: The Failure of Unemployment Insurance to Reach Working Mothers*, Washington, DC: Institute for Women's Policy Research.

Spalter-Roth, R., B. Burr, H. Martmann and L. Shaw (1995) *Welfare That Works: The Working Lives of AFDC Recipients*, Washington, DC: Institute for Women's Policy Research.

Spracker, S. M. and G. J. Mertz (1993) 'Labor Issues Under NAFTA: Options in the Wake of the Agreement', *The International Lawyer*, 27: 737–50.

Tilly, C. (1996) *Workfare's Impact on the New York City Labor Market: Lower Wages and Worker Displacement*, New York: Russell Sage Foundation.

Topel, R. H. (1994) 'Regional Trends in Wage Inequality', *American Economic Review*, 84: 17–22.

US Dept. of Justice, Immigration and Naturalization Service (1998) *1997 Statistical Yearbook of the Immigration and Naturalization Service*, 3, Washington, DC: US Dept. of Justice, Immigration and Naturalization Service.

Waldinger, R. (1996) 'Who Makes the Beds? Who Washes the Dishes? Black/ Immigrant Competition Reassessed', in H. O. Duleep and P. V. Wunnava (eds), *Immigrants and Immigration Policy: Individual Skills, Family Ties and Group Identities*, Greenwich, CT: Jai Press.

Williams, L. A. (1998) 'Welfare and Legal Entitlements: The Social Roots of Poverty', in D. Kairys (ed.), *Politics of Law: A Progressive Critique*, New York: Basic Books.

Yoon, Y.-H., R. Spalter-Roth and M. Baldwin (1995) *Unemployment Insurance: Barriers to Access for Women and Part-Time Workers*, Washington, DC: National Commission for Employment Policy.

THREE | Poverty as a violation of human rights: the Pinochet case and the emergence of a new paradigm

CAMILO PEREZ-BUSTILLO

Chile has moved farther, faster than any other nation in South America toward real free-market reform. The pay-off is evident to all: seven straight years of economic growth ... You deserve your reputation as an economic model for other countries in the region and the world. Your commitment to market-based solutions inspires the hemisphere. (President George Bush [Sr] in Chile, 6 December 1990 [cited in Collins and Lear 1995: 3])

§ Former Chilean dictator Augusto Pinochet was arrested while visiting London on 17 October 1998, on an Interpol warrant for his extradition pursuant to his indictment, by Spanish prosecuting Judge Baltasar Garzón, accusing him of various serious crimes under international law including genocide, state terrorism, homicide, torture, 'forced disappearances' and kidnappings directed at political opponents of his regime between 1973 and 1990. The case, originally brought as the result of joint efforts between Chilean victims of his rule and victims with Spanish nationality or dual citizenship, quickly ripened into a landmark test of evolving notions of 'universal jurisdiction' as to 'crimes against humanity'. Central legal questions focused on the extent, if any, to which former heads of state are entitled to immunity (and/or amnesty) for their conduct, as well as a test of 'competing sovereignties' among the interests of the United Kingdom, Spain and Chile, and those of human rights victims of the Pinochet regime throughout the world.

The essence of the case against Pinochet was upheld by two different panels of Law Lords in the UK in historic decisions, and, as a result, Garzón's extradition petition was authorized to proceed against him by British Home Secretary Jack Straw. But diplomatic pressures from both Spain and Chile eventually led to Pinochet's release by order of Straw and return to Chile in March 2000, ostensibly for reasons of serious illness. The international scandal generated by the case did serve, however, to spur the Chilean court system to both order the lifting of his supposed immunity from trial in his own country, and then to order his arrest, steps that would have been unimaginable prior to his detention in London. Both measures have since been suspended, once again for medical reasons, and the current stay in proceedings is under appeal before Chile's Supreme Court. The General remains under house arrest, with much of his previous political activism crippled, but has not yet been compelled to confront his accusers.

This chapter argues that the Pinochet case exemplifies broader dilemmas in contemporary international human rights law regarding the relationship between emerging standards of 'global justice', and persistent and deepening patterns of inequity and poverty throughout the world. The Pinochet case has been described by leading commentators as a triumph for the cause of international human rights, but it is also an important barometer of the limits and contradictions of this emerging framework of 'global justice' (see Falk 2000).

THE PINOCHET CASE AND ECONOMIC, SOCIAL AND CULTURAL RIGHTS

Since the adoption by the UN General Assembly of the International Covenants on Civil and Political Rights, and on Economic, Social and Cultural Rights, in 1966 (which did not enter into force until 1976), as detailed codifications of the rights contained in the more general Universal Declaration of Human Rights, adopted in 1948, internationally recognized rights have tended to be classified as either 'civil and political', or as 'economic, social, and cultural'.

The Vienna Declaration and Programme of Action of the 1993 World Conference on Human Rights sought to transcend the hitherto assumed dichotomy between these ostensibly competing sets of rights by declaring the overall framework of international human rights to be 'universal, indivisible and interdependent and interrelated' (para. 5), and further admonished that the 'international community must treat human rights globally in a fair and equal manner, on the same footing, and with the same emphasis' (ibid.). The Declaration further called for the examination of 'additional approaches' to 'strengthen the enjoyment of economic, social, and cultural rights' throughout the world, and called for a 'concerted effort to ensure recognition of economic, social, and cultural rights at the national, regional and international levels' (Klein Goldewijk and de Gaay Fortman 1999: xiii).

But in practice there is a persistent imbalance in international human rights enforcement and advocacy between 'civil and political' rights on the one hand, which tend to be privileged, and 'economic, social, and cultural' rights on the other, which tend to be relegated to secondary and sometimes marginal, aspirational importance. The overall dichotomy in modern international relations theory between the 'realist' and 'idealist' schools (Wilson v. Kissinger) is in this way replicated in the context of international human rights. This dichotomy is mirrored in the supposed contrast between civil and political rights characterized as 'negative', 'protective' and/or 'liberty'-based, and economic, social and cultural rights as 'positive', 'opportunity'-based and 'programmatic, to be realized gradually, and therefore not a matter of rights' (Asbjørn Eide, quoted in Klein Goldewijk and de Gaay Fortman 1999: 8). Economic, social and cultural rights have become the 'step-children' of the international human rights hierarchy, a second-class category of italicized 'rights' susceptible to 'progressive realization' (ibid.), which end up being conceived of as almost inherently utopian in nature. The imbalance between these two categories is thus both conceptual and structural.

Much of traditional and dominant international human rights scholarship is also littered with false assumptions about the supposed equivalence or interdependence between democracy and capitalism, and between capitalism and the satisfaction of economic, social and cultural rights; interestingly enough, however, contemporary 'neo-liberal' capitalism, the model pioneered by the Pinochet regime, in fact seems to *undermine* them.

According to Richard Falk, meaningful steps towards 'global justice' are blocked by the combined effects of 'two complementary logics' which 'underpin the current system of world order': 'statist logic' and 'market logic' (Falk 2000: 21). 'Statist logic' is derived from the Westphalian view (first authoritatively advanced by the Treaty of Westphalia in 1648, which ended the Thirty Years' War) of 'international society as constituted by territorial sovereign states' (e.g. traditional 'nation-states' as the fundamental legitimate protagonists in the context of both international relations and international law) (ibid.). The 'Realist' school of international relations is the principal contemporary ideological expression of this underlying 'statist logic'.

Meanwhile, in his view, 'market logic' is that which is derived 'from the moving forces of capital efficiency and minimal governmental regulation in an era of globalization' (Falk 2000: 21). As a result, 'increased opportunities for investment, growth, and trade are treated as the tests of a successful economic policy without raising questions about social harm' (ibid.).

The Pinochet case ran foul of both of these dominant logics. It was 'statist logic' that successfully drove the diplomatic pressures that resulted in his release and return to Chile with impunity; but it was 'market logic' which helped lay the basis for the conceptual narrowing of the case against him to international crimes grounded in issues of civil and political rights, and which ended up excluding violations of economic, social and cultural rights from the charges against him.

From Falk's perspective, 'neo-liberalism' is the contemporary, hegemonic version of 'market logic' in the era of globalization, characterized by 'liberalization of the economy, privatization of ownership, a minimal regulatory role for government, a stress on the most efficient return on capital, and a conviction that poverty, social distress, and even environmental deterioration are best addressed through the invisible hand of rapid economic growth and the beneficience of the private sector' (Falk 2000: 22).

Falk further argues that such 'market logic' has devastating consequences for the contemporary understanding of human rights. The result is that '[h]uman rights are understood to encompass exclusively the civil and political rights of the individual, with economic, social, and cultural rights being put aside. Indeed, the neoliberal repudiation of a socially activist government and of public-sector approaches to human well-being is an implicit rejection of many of the standards of human rights that are present in the Universal Declaration of Human Rights and the two Covenants' (Falk 2000: 47).

In this way, 'market logic' brings with it the spread of a 'neoliberal model of governance' (Falk 2000: 48) with its own stripped-down version of international human rights which ends up pitting civil and political rights on the one hand, and economic, social and cultural rights on the other, against each other:

[t]o the extent that the text of the Universal Declaration of Human Rights authoritatively identifies the scope of human rights, neoliberal ideology amounts to a drastic foreshortening with no legal or moral mandate. Human rights are narrowed to the point where only civil and political rights are affirmed. In the more general normative language of the day, 'individual freedom' and 'democracy' are asserted as beneficial, and indeed necessary, to the attainment of economic success via the market. By implication, moves to uphold social and economic rights by direct action are seen as generally dangerous to the maintenance of

civil and political rights because of their tendency to consolidate power in the state and to undermine individualism. (Falk 2000: 48)

The assumed dichotomy between the two fundamental categories of international human rights norms is especially problematic when it is applied in the context of regimes, such as that headed by Pinochet, where violations of economic, social and cultural rights are in fact grounded in, and made possible by, underlying violations of civil and political rights. My emphasis here is thus on Pinochet's Chile as a case study of a situation where the destruction of the civil and political rights of political organization, mobilization and participation were the necessary predicate for the dismantling of economic, social and cultural rights. Both sets of violations were inextricably intertwined and cannot be meaningfully distinguished. It could thus be argued that the rational integrity of contemporary international human rights understood as 'universal, indivisible, interdependent, and interrelated' demands that in a case such as that of Pinochet *both* kinds of violations ought to be addressed.

According to Chilean scholar Manuel Antonio Garreton, the Chilean military regime in fact expressly sought 'to eliminate collective identities, collective organization, and collective action' (Garreton 2001: 273), the ideological impulse which drove its targeting of victims as well as its approach to socioeconomic policy. In Tomas Moulian's (1997) view the Pinochet regime was thus nothing less than a military-led 'capitalist counter-revolution', an imposition of a literal 'dictatorship of the bourgeoisie' in Marx's original sense.

The heart of the case against Pinochet pursued by Judge Garzón was built on his dictatorship's systematic violation of civil and political rights (through genocide, torture, forced disappearances, kidnapping and murder of alleged political opponents of what Spanish judge Baltasar Garzón alleged to be a regime of state terror). The consideration of his case by the British Law Lords resulted in the case being focused on the issue of torture for purposes of extradition, with the genocide charge being dropped because of the lack of equivalence between British and Spanish law on this point.

My argument here as to the nature and scope of the crimes Pinochet is charged with is that the macroeconomic and social policies he pursued ('neo-liberal' and otherwise) resulted in the deliberate, massive violation of the internationally recognized economic, social and cultural rights of a majority of Chile's citizens. These violations are identifiable and quantifiable in terms of otherwise avoidable deaths and illness, and overall a significant decline in the quality of life for the whole country, with their harshest effects evident among its poorest and most marginalized sectors, e.g. its indigenous peoples. The point here is that these violations also amount to 'serious crimes' under international law that lay the basis for Pinochet's indictment and trial on the charge of 'social genocide' (explained in further detail below).

The failure to give adequate weight to the justiciability and enforcement of economic, social and cultural rights overall and in the specific context of the Pinochet case creates a vacuum in the normative system of international human rights which I have described elsewhere as a 'poverty of rights' that serves to increase the burdens of those trapped in the material expressions of increasing global poverty and inequality (Genugten and Perez-Bustillo 2001). Due justiciability and enforcement of economic, social and cultural rights, especially in complex contexts such as those of the Pinochet case, are necessary steps towards filling that destabilizing vacuum with what I have described as the mandates of the emerging framework of 'international poverty law'. This framework comprises a combination of rights accorded by concepts such as 'economic, social and cultural rights', the 'right to development' and 'sustainable development', the right to a 'New International Economic Order', and by the demands of the diverse movement for 'global justice' which has mobilized around demands to hold international financial institutions such as the IMF, World Bank and WTO accountable for their promotion of 'neo-liberal' policies which violate economic, social and cultural rights (and weaken the exercise of civil and political rights) for the same reasons alleged here in the context of the critique of the Pinochet regime.

This chapter argues that the Pinochet regime's acts against 'international poverty law' rights generally, and specifically against the economic, social and cultural rights of Chile's people, also merit prosecution and punishment as international crimes susceptible to universal jurisdiction. A specific basis for this argument in the context of the Pinochet case, in addition to the independent weight of economic, social and cultural rights in themselves as the subject of international recognition, is the Spanish High Court's determination in its review of the Pinochet prosecution that the acts of 'genocide' alleged in Judge Baltasar Garzón's indictment appropriately extend its scope from alleged crimes against discrete racial, ethnic or religious groups to crimes of a broader 'social' character.

Unfortunately, this historic recognition by the Spanish High Court ended up being purely academic in the context of the Pinochet case both circumstantially because of his release from detention and further proceedings in the United Kingdom and return to Chile, and for technical reasons because had Pinochet in fact been extradited to Spain for trial the Spanish courts would have been restricted to try him only for the extraditable crimes found by the House of Lords, and not by the Spanish High Court's interpretation of those charges. First British Home Secretary Jack Straw and then the second reviewing panel of Law Lords had decided that the charges of genocide originally formulated by Garzón (and upheld by the Spanish High Court) had to be dropped from Pinochet's extradition proceeding because of their lack of any equivalence under British law.

My argument here instead is that the Spanish High Court's approach to the question of 'genocide' in the Pinochet indictment ought to be taken one step further, as a basis for charging him with systematic violations of economic, social and cultural rights which rise to the level of a 'serious crime under international law' as understood by the Princeton Principles of Universal Jurisdiction, interpreted in light of Article 7 of the Rome Statute of the International Criminal Court.

Additional bases for pursuing the Pinochet regime's violations of economic, social and cultural rights (and those of similar regimes) can be found in the 1986 Limburg Principles on the Implementation of the International Covenant on Economic, Social, and Cultural Rights (echoed in part in the language quoted above from the 1993 Vienna Declaration), the 1997 Maastricht Guidelines on Violations of Economic, Social, and Cultural Rights, the evolving General Comments of the UN Committee on Economic, Social and Cultural Rights, and the findings of Special Rapporteurs on related topics. Such Principles, Guidelines and Comments are all essential elements of the emerging normative framework of 'international poverty law'. Both the Limburg Principles and Maastricht Guidelines stress the importance of standards of equivalence in the enforcement of civil and political, as well as economic, social and cultural rights. In the Limburg Principles (1986) (as later in the 1993 Vienna Declaration), the argument is that 'human rights and fundamental freedoms are indivisible and interdependent' and thus that *'equal attention and urgent consideration'* (emphasis added) should be given to the 'implementation, promotion, and protection' of both sets of rights (para. 3). In the Maastricht Guidelines (1997), this emphasis is further elaborated: '[I]t is now undisputed that all human rights are indivisible, interdependent, interrelated *and of equal importance for human dignity*. Therefore states *are as responsible for violations of economic, social, and cultural rights as they are for violations of civil and political rights*' (para. 4; emphasis added). No lesser standard should be applied to the issue of Pinochet's own culpability.

The Maastricht Guidelines further provide that

> [v]iolations of the Covenant occur when a State fails to satisfy what the Committee on Economic, Social, and Cultural Rights has referred to as 'a minimum core obligation to ensure the satisfaction of, at the very least, minimum essential levels of each of the rights' ... Thus a State Party in which any significant number of individuals is deprived of essential foodstuffs, of essential primary health care, of basic shelter and housing, or of the most basic forms of education, is prima facie, violating the Covenant. (para. 9)

The Guidelines also specify several additional different forms that violations of the Covenant may take, including:

a) The formal removal or suspension of legislation necessary for the continued enjoyment of an economic, social, or cultural right that is currently enjoyed [e.g. the Pinochet regime's repeal and 'reform' of pre-existent labour and social security legislation];

b) The active denial of such rights to particular individuals or groups, whether through legislation or enforced discrimination [the regime's singling-out of the country's indigenous Mapuche and Pehuenche population for especially harsh repression and reversals of their pre-existent rights];

c) The active support for measures adopted by third parties which are inconsistent with economic, social, and cultural rights [the regime's assumption of IMF and World Bank structural adjustment policies as its own];

d) The adoption of legislation or policies which are manifestly incompatible with pre-existing legal obligations relating to these rights, unless it is done with the purpose and effect of increasing equality and improving the realization of economic, social, and cultural rights for the most vulnerable groups [see above; results were increased *inequality* and poverty, deterioration of overall compliance and especially of conditions for the most vulnerable];

e) The adoption of any deliberately retrogressive measure that reduces the extent to which any such right is guaranteed (para. 9);

f) The calculated obstruction of, or halt to, the progressive realization of a right protected by the Covenant, unless the State is acting within a limitation permitted by the Covenant or it does so due to a lack of available resources or force majeure [neither of the latter arguments applies to the Chilean context; and the regime's own express adherence to neo-liberal ideology could be construed as precisely the kind of 'calculated obstruction' highlighted here];

g) The reduction or diversion of specific public expenditure, when such reduction or diversion results in the non-enjoyment of such rights and is not accompanied by adequate measures to ensure minimum subsistence rights for everyone [e.g. the effects of reducing overall health expenditures described below]. (para. 14)

Neo-liberal policies are especially vulnerable under closer scrutiny. In 1992, for example, Danilo Türk, the Special Rapporteur for Economic, Social and Cultural Rights, specifically stressed the 'implications of structural adjustment policies of the international financial institutions' (e.g. the IMF and World Bank) 'for rights protected by the International Covenant on Economic, Social, and Cultural Rights (Klein Goldewijk and de Baay Fortman 1999: 9). The Pinochet regime's socioeconomic policies were an early forerunner of such structural adjustment programmes, sharing all of their most essential features. International law scholar K. O. Rattray has similarly concluded that '[s]tructural adjustment programmes, the natural consequence of which is to cause deterioration in the standard of living of the vulnerable sectors of society, constitute a violation of the Covenant for which those [international financial] institutions are liable and accountable' (ibid., p. 12); in the context of the Pinochet case we need not go so far, since his regime pursued such policies at its own behest, voluntarily assuming them as its own.

THE ECONOMIC CHARACTERISTICS AND COSTS OF NEO-LIBERALISM IN CHILE

The case for Chile rests largely on the success of its protracted economic transformation. Over 25 years, Chile has converted its closed, state-run economy into a model of free trade, market-oriented capitalism. For many, Chile exemplifies the benefits of economic adjustment policy gone right, yet others note that problems of poverty and skewed income remain despite achievements in economic growth and stability. (Hornbeck 1995: 1)

According to one of Chile's leading critical sociologists, Tomas Moulian: '[w]hat we have in Chile is the marriage of a neoliberal economy with a neodemocracy, a simulated democracy. The end result is a neoliberal system defended now by its historic Socialist adversaries. Pinochet, for his part, is a symbol of this capitalist counterevolution, which profoundly changed our culture and even the capitalism we had before him' (Cooper 1998).[1]

> Moulian's thesis runs something like this: [t]he first two years of military rule merely reversed the Allende-era reforms, liberalized prices, lowered salaries, and subjected the working class to the now familiar nostrums of economic 'shock therapy'. The Chicago Boys period of 1975–81, shaped by Milton Friedman and Arnold Harberger, introduced structural 're-forms', increasing exports and creating new economic groups indebted to international banks. A draconian labor law clamped down on work-ers, and a wave of privatization (including Social Security) atrophied the state. That phase fizzled in 1982, leading to a mini-depression that liquidated national industry and drove half the population below the poverty level. (Cooper 1998: 9)

Nevertheless, according to Moulian, despite the 1982 economic collapse (very similar to that of Mexico between December 1994 and February 1995), 'a sense of direction was recovered immediately. A reordering, a re-privatization of everything, commenced under a neo-liberal pattern. The new economic groups which emerged were much stronger than the older ones. Not indebted to foreign capital, they were interwoven with it. And the tremendous pools of private money generated by the private pension funds were used to fuel these new groups. It was the workers' money that built such prosperity for the elite' (Cooper 1998: 9). All of this 'anticipated Reagan and Thatcher. Because of the neoliberal intellectual sway over the military, Chile started out early on the road that everybody now is on' (ibid.).

But what does all of this have to do with human rights and poverty? Moulian argues:

> In this sense the Chilean terror was rational. This whole model is frankly impossible without a dictatorship. Only the dictatorship could have disciplined the working class into submission while their salaries were lowered and their pensions used to accumulate wealth for others. Only a dictatorship can keep a country quiet while education, universi-ties, and health care are privatized, and while an absolute marketization of the labor force is imposed. Today, under this simulated democracy, the work force is too fragmented to recover and the population is dis-tracted by consumerism and disciplined by credit obligations. (Moulian in Cooper 1998)

In this way 'mass credit consumerism substitutes for development' (Cooper 1998: 8).

In seeking to apply Moulian's thesis to an analysis of the Pinochet case, it is critical to focus on the extent to which the debate over the merits and costs of Chile's economic 'model' must be extended to address these policies as part of an overall political process of 'capitalist counterrevolution' which instituted a 'neo-liberal system' in Chile with economic, political, social and cultural ramifications. The issues at stake go much beyond average GDP growth rates, unemployment or salary statistics, or degrees of opening of the Chilean economy. The prosecution of Pinochet for internationally cognizable crimes against humanity is also then implicitly an indictment of an overall political project.

But is there an adequate empirical basis for this argument? The first problem is deciding how to reconstruct the history of the Pinochet regime. Many of the apologists for its supposed macroeconomic successes have selectively focused only on certain periods of his rule between 1973 and 1990, and have failed to ground their analyses in a comparative framework looking at key indicators and how they shifted from the Allende period (1970–73) to the post-Pinochet governments of Patricio Aylwin and Eduardo Frei Ruiz-Tagle (1990 – to the present).[2]

The overall trends can be briefly summarized. If we focus on GDP growth, unemployment, inflation, Chile's trade balance, foreign debt and distribution of income, clear patterns emerge: '[A]verage economic growth ... was far from successful. During the two subperiods of the Pinochet regime [before and after each of the period's worst economic crises in 1975 and 1982 respectively] GDP grew by an annual average of 2.6 percent ... If one bears in mind annual population growth of 1.7 percent during the 1980's, per capita GDP growth was 0.9 percent yearly', hardly the stuff economic dreams or 'models' are made of (Souther 1998: 7, 17).

The average growth over the full period of Pinochet's dictatorship is lower than one might expect, in part because of negative growth of 13.3 per cent in 1975 and 13.4 per cent in 1982 (much more adverse results, by the way, than during comparatively grave economic crises as a result of the application of the same kind of neo-liberal policies in Mexico, 1994–95; Brazil, 1997–99; and most recently Argentina 2001–02). Chile's economic crises in 1975 and 1982 were in fact much worse than the economic crisis under Allende from which Pinochet had supposedly rescued the country and the economy. The single year of highest growth between 1970 and 1990 (an impressive 9.9 per cent) was during the last year of his rule. The next highest growth rate during this historical period is 9 per cent in 1971, ironically, if not tragically, the first complete year of Allende's presidency, and thanks to a very different kind of macroeconomic strategy. Growth soared again to 11 per cent in 1992, two years after Pinochet left the presidency. In sum, a comparative analysis of these growth rates shows that 'the boom periods barely made up for the periods of bust. Little real growth occurred' (Souther 1998: 1).

Tendencies in the unemployment rate are also instructive. Unemployment was 3.5 per cent in 1970 and only 3.3 per cent in 1973, the year of the coup. It has never dropped to such low levels again, coming closest at 4.6 per cent in 1993, three years after Pinochet left the presidency. It rose to double digits in 1975 (14.9 per cent officially, while analysts with a more critical perspective estimate an actual rate of some 33 per cent), and remained in double digits (never less than 10.4 per cent) from 1975 to 1985, dropping to 8.8 per cent (still more than 2.5 times the rate in 1973), only in 1986 (Hornbeck 1995: 3–4).

Inflation was already 34.9 per cent in 1970, and hyper-inflation kicked in during 1972, the beginning of the economic crisis during Allende's presidency which helped pave the way for the coup, hit 508 per cent in 1973, and was not brought under control again through the Pinochet period's initial phase of 'shock therapy' until 1977 (63.5 per cent). It remained in double digits throughout Pinochet's rule (except for a brief drop to 9.5 per cent in 1981, just before more than doubling the next year due to the second economic collapse during the dictatorship), and was never again less than 12.7 per cent (1988) until he left office. It then dropped steadily from 1990 (the last year partly under his rule) to a low of 7.2 per cent in 1996. Meanwhile the trade balance, as per cent of GDP, which was 1.9 per cent in 1970 and -1.3 per cent in 1973, went deeply into the red between 1977 and 1981, and did not recover fully under it hit 9 per cent in 1988, the year before Pinochet 'retired' (Hornbeck 1995: 3–4).

'To summarize, the first decade of authoritarian rule experienced certain short-lived policy achievements, but ultimately failed to bring about successful economic adjustment' (Souther 1998: 6) And at what cost? It is rarely remarked, for example, when speaking of the alleged Chilean 'model', that Pinochet's version of neo-liberal policies succeeded in achieving the highest per capita foreign debt in Latin America by 1985, when at $21 billion it came to exceed the size of the country's total GDP (ibid., pp. 10, 12), and involved the assumption by the government, and taxpayers, of unprecedented amounts of private debt ($7.7 billion) in order to rescue failed banks and large corporations that had initially benefited from the first round of 'shock therapy' and then collapsed when the bubble burst in 1982. According to Souther, during the first stages of the 'miracle', the 'Chicago Boys had privatized Chile's economic gains; during the crash, the socialization of the country's losses occurred' (ibid., p. 11). What emerged then was a state which was strongly intervention-ist in the service of private interests, but very weak in the service of the public interests that might have made a difference in the lives of the poor, amounting to a kind of 'socialism' for the rich and 'capitalism' for the poor typical of neo-liberal experiments.

By 1982

the miracle had cracked, undermined by a rigid application of monetarist dogma. Instead of withdrawing from the economy, the state had seized control of 70 per cent of the banks and a large chunk of the nation's private enterprise. Instead of stimulating competition, deregulation had led to a frenzy of speculation and a staggering foreign debt of over $20 billion. While helping to control inflation, the fixed exchange rate had dangerously overvalued the peso. And while making some industries more efficient, abrupt exposure to foreign goods had driven others into the ground, creating the highest urban unemployment on the continent. (Constable and Valenzuela 1991, quoted in Souther 1998: 12)

A crucial characteristic of the transitory imbalanced growth obtained by the initial 'shock therapy' stage of the overall neo-liberal 'stabilization' model was the concentration of benefits in a small handful of economic interest groups especially close to the Pinochet regime. According to Chilean economist Alexander Foxley: 'By 1980, five conglomerates, owned by the Cruzat and Vial groups, controlled more than half of the assets of Chile's 250 major private enterprises. By 1982 the banks owned by these groups controlled 60 per cent of all credit and 42 per cent of all banking capital' (quoted in Souther 1998: 14).

Another characteristic of the 'model' was direct transference of profits to the military itself. These came from an ironic source, CODELCO, the state copper company which had been nationalized by the Allende gov-ernment in one of its most important achievements, and which remained under government control throughout the Pinochet regime as a 'cash cow' consistently 'producing important fiscal revenues', with 10 per cent of these flowing 'directly to the military budget' (Souther 1998: 15).

The Pinochet regime also benefited from the support of multilateral aid which had been systematically cut off to the Allende government as part of the successful effort by the US government, in the words of Henry Kissinger, to 'make the [Chilean] economy scream' (quoted in Hitchens 2001). 'Encouraged by the junta's strong embrace of free market tenets, Western lending institutions that had shunned Allende turned on the spigot again. Foreign lenders agreed to refinance Chile's debt on unusually generous terms, and after U.S. aid was banned by Congress in 1976,[3] the pace of loans from the World Bank and the Inter-American Development Bank steadily increased. Between 1976 and 1986, these institutions made forty-six loans to Chile worth over $3.1 billion' (Constable and Valenzuela 1991: 172).

What were the consequences of all this for distribution of income and poverty? 'The distribution of income in Chile in 1988, after a decade of free market policies, was markedly regressive. Between 1978 and 1988, the richest 10 per cent of Chileans increased their share of the national income from 37 to 47 per cent, while the next 30 per cent of middle-income households saw their share shrink from 23 to 18 per cent. The income share of the poorest fifth of the population dropped from 5 to 4 per cent' (Collins and Lear 1995, quoted in Souther 1998: 19). Between 1980 and 1989, the wealthiest households in the top quintile 'increased their share of consumption from 44.5 per cent in 1970, and 51 per cent in 1980, to 54.6 per cent in 1989. During this time period, the poorest quintile saw its consumption drop by 3.2 per cent' (Souther 1998: 19–20, Table 9). 'Thus, during the Pinochet regime, free market policies produced uneven economic growth and further exacerbated the incidence of poverty' (ibid., p. 20). The proportion of indigent (extremely poor) Chileans in the Santiago metropolitan area increased from 8.4 per cent in 1970 to 11.7 per cent in 1980 and 14.9 per cent in 1989, while those classified as 'poor' increased from 20.1 per cent in 1970 to 24.3 per cent in 1980 and 26.3 per cent in 1989, resulting in a total increase in the poverty rate from 28.5 per cent in 1970, the first year of Popular Unity, to 41.2 per cent in 1989, the last year of the Pinochet dictatorship (ibid., p. 20, Table 10).

By 1985, according to a study by pro-regime economist Aristedes Torche, 'based on the ability to meet "basic needs" in food, health, and housing ... over 45 per cent of all Chileans remained poor and ... 25 per cent of those were "indigent"' (Constable and Valenzuela 1991: 232). A 1986 survey undertaken in two of Greater Santiago's poorest neighbourhoods found that 66 per cent and 74 per cent of the families surveyed respectively 'consumed less than the minimum calorie requirement for adequate nutrition' (ibid.).

Overall the national poverty rate increased from 17 per cent in 1973 to 45 per cent in 1990, while 'among the impoverished, the percentage forced to live in extreme poverty more than doubled' (Collins and Lear 1995: 243). Sharp decreases in poverty over the last decade have once again propelled Chile into the status of a 'model' for many analysts in terms of its current anti-poverty efforts, but it is rarely noted that this diminution has been achieved by *abandoning* key aspects of the socioeconomic policies pursued by the Pinochet regime, e.g. by combining targeting (a holdover from Pinochet's approach which has been much emulated elsewhere) with increased state spending on social programmes (by contrast with the Pinochet regime's penchant for *reducing* such expenditures).

Similar trends emerge in terms of the public health consequences of the regime's decision to privatize the social security system and publicly subsidized healthcare. Much has been made in this regard by some analysts of the sharp decrease in the infant mortality rate during the first years of the Pinochet regime, which is trumpeted as evidence of the success of this privatization effort. In fact, Souther demonstrates that infant mortality was sharply reduced from a rate of 65 per 1,000 in 1973 to 23 per 1,000 in 1984 precisely because the Pinochet regime *increased* state funding for preventative infant care at the same time that it *cut* funding for overall public health programming, thus targeting its efforts. Under Allende, all children under fifteen had qualified for a National Supplementary Feeding Programme of assistance to a broad category of impoverished infants and pregnant mothers. Pinochet restricted this programme to children under the age of six and to poor pregnant and nursing mothers (Souther 1998: 21). As a result, infant mortality initially went down but overall public health spending, and indicators, declined as well.

Meanwhile, by 1978 hospital beds per person had decreased by 17 per cent, and health services per person decreased 6 per cent from 1970 levels (Foxley 1984, quoted in Souther 1998: 21). According to the Inter-American Development Bank the number of hospital beds per 1,000 people dropped from 33.3 in 1983 to 2.6 in 1987 and 1.95 in 1990 (ibid.). By 1983 investment in public health facilities 'shrank to 11 percent of the level during the last year of the Allende administration', and the rate of infectious disease soared, with the incidence of typhoid due to contaminated water increasing from 102 per 100,000 in 1970 to a high of 215 per 100,000 in 1983, and that of Hepatitis A from 45 per 100,000 in 1975 to 105 per 100,000 in 1985.

According to Souther, these increases can be attributed directly to the Pinochet regime's drastic reduction in public investment on sanitation projects, as part of the overall retrenchment in public spending. At the same time as maintenance and sewage treatment declined, water rates were increased. 'Consequently, many Chileans in the poorer areas could not pay the new rates. In certain neighborhoods in Santiago, some 60 per cent of households had no running water' (Collins and Lear 1995: 122; Souther 1998: 23).

Interestingly, the increases in infectious disease rates were finally reversed, and sharp declines in the infant mortality rate were obtained by the same means: ultimate increases in government spending, mitigating the regime's rhetoric of strict dependence on free market mechanisms free from state intervention. In other words, the regime's own isolated successes in social policy came about precisely where its practice diverged from its dogma.

Major additional costs for the 'miracle' were disproportionately borne by organized workers, and by the working class in general. Real wages lost an average 37 per cent of their purchasing power during the regime, with the minimum wage falling to 55 per cent of its 1980 level by 1987 (Souther 1998: 12). Retrenchment in legal rights was an important element as well. One of Latin America's strongest and most politicized labour movements was virtually dismantled. 'After the coup, the administration suspended many of the rights of laborers, including the right to strike, collective bargaining, and the right to organize' (ibid.). In addition 'labor unions endured the brunt of some of the most severe repression during the 1973–1989 period' (ibid.).

The pre-Pinochet Labour Code was revised in 1979 and 'further limited workers' freedoms. A series of radical breaks with past policies gave employers the legal flexibility they deemed necessary for the modernization of the Chilean industry. Now the employers could fire workers, individually or en masse, at will' (Souther 1998: 19). Permissible subjects for collective bargaining were reduced strictly to the issue of wages, with other subjects 'such as the size of work crews, the technology used, or mechanisms for internal promotions' expressly excluded (ibid.). Clearly the Pinochet regime had its own variant of a 'rule of law' agenda with an explicit 'law reform' component.

As Orlando Caputo, one of Chile's best known critical economists, has summarized it, '[t]he Chilean system is easy to understand. Over the past twenty years $60 billion has been transferred from salaries to profits' (Cooper 1998: 4). 'These data illustrate that economic growth at least partly occurred at the expense of the labor force. The recovery did not produce an even distribution of economic progress. Clearly, one segment of the population was sacrificed' (Souther 1998: 13).

Another of the 'miracle"s most vaunted 'successes', the vast expansion of exports, especially of fruit products, epitomizes its overall effects.

Extraordinarily low wages, due to the abundance of economically desperate workers seeking employment after the collapse of the manufacturing sector, made the Chilean fruit exports cheaper in the international
market. Therefore, Chile could undersell its competitors, Australia
and New Zealand. With the boycott on South African products as a
result of the U.S. policy against apartheid, Chile's competition further
diminished. (Souther 1998: 25)

Thus Chile is a test case for analysing the full impact of neo-liberalism and structural adjustment in Latin America on human rights,
poverty and social justice – and on the democratic rule of law upon
which the latter depends – precisely because of the breadth of the claims
proffered by the apologists for its purported 'model'.

According to a 1998 *New York Times* editorial, Pinochet's coup 'began
Chile's transformation from a backwater banana republic to the economic star of Latin America' (Cooper 1998: 3). Chile, of course, never
was a 'banana republic' (a term strictly inapplicable even to historically
impoverished Honduras, the likeliest candidate for such an epithet), and
was in fact one of the region's most developed economies, with one of
the highest levels of education and social spending, long before the 1973
coup. It was also once one of Latin America's most stable democracies.
The supposed 'miracle' is in large part a massive international public
relations exercise attributing consistently high post-1986 growth rates
to pre-1986 policies, and suggesting directly or indirectly that there is a
correlation between this macroeconomic success and the authoritarianism of the Pinochet dictatorship. But even here the lessons may be more
ambiguous than is generally assumed.

Chilean economist Alexander Foxley notes that the central issue
confronting Pinochet was that the macroeconomic policies of developing
countries

> must conform to certain rules. These rules of 'sound economic manage
> ment' are perfectly codified by the international financial community,
> including the International Monetary Fund (IMF), large private inter
> national banks, and business groups. They consist of reducing the rate
> of expansion in money supply, eliminating the fiscal deficit, devaluing
> domestic currency, deregulating policies and private sector activities, and
> opening up the economy to free trade. Given such an explicit codifica
> tion of what constitutes sound policies, the restoration of confidence
> requires strictly abiding by them. In doing so, the economic policies
> acquire a distinct orthodox flavor. (quoted in Souther 1998: 1)

This is where Pinochet's own agenda for personalized power converged with broader currents. His regime provided a 'virtual laboratory for the testing of neoliberal doctrine from 1975 to 1990', with his dictatorial concentration of both political and economic power – and ultimately, social and cultural hegemony –'facilitating the quick and effective implementation of neoliberal policies by removing legal opposition and eliminating the means for public scrutiny, thereby greatly increasing the thoroughness of the experiment.'[4]

The gospel to be propagated, derived in large part from Adam Smith, Milton Friedman and Friedrich von Hayek, consisted fundamentally of three ideological paradigms: '1. The market as the framework of free and informed individual exchange; 2. The market as the paradigm of freedom or of a free and non-coercive social organization; 3. The market as the focus and the objective of economic scientific accumulation' (Valdés 1995, quoted in Souther 1998: 4). This is the essence of what Richard Falk has referred to as the 'market logic' which both deters the overall advance of 'global justice', and which impoverishes the notion and promise of international human rights as such, by reducing their sweep to a core of civil and political rights, and relegating economic, social and cultural rights to an aspirational periphery.

The critical focus here for forging the link between neo-liberalism, human rights, poverty and social justice is the implications of the above perspective for any meaningful framework of the rule of law. Pinochet's Chile did in fact promote an economic 'miracle', but only for the most wealthy and advantaged sectors of Chilean society (Souther 1998: 26). It is not possible for authentic democracy to flourish under such circumstances, if we assume that democracy is more than the formal trappings of traditional civil and political rights, and if we assume that democracy must in fact be radically extended from its narrowly political core to encompass economic, social and cultural rights and dimensions. It is within this context that Amartya Sen's understanding of poverty as fundamentally a deprivation of freedom becomes most compelling: Pinochet's Chile must then be understood as an exemplary synthesis of the process by which neo-liberal economic policies foster a new kind of poverty whose essence is the deprivation of citizenship.

The only viable way to sustain a political and economic project such as that promoted by the Pinochet regime is by sometimes generalized and sometimes selective recourse to terror and repression. Neo-liberalism is thus ultimately unsustainable within even a traditional liberal democratic framework to the extent that it fosters levels of poverty and inequality that undermine its own doctrinal and institutional premises. Pinochet's regime is then 'merely' an extreme expression of the fundamental incompatibility between generalized poverty, rampant inequality and any semblance of substantive democracy. If the universality, indivisibility and integral character of internationally recognized human rights standards mean anything, it must eventually mean that such policies and practices cannot stand the test of an authentic, radically democratic rule of law.

SOCIAL GENOCIDE AND OTHER SERIOUS CRIMES UNDER INTERNATIONAL LAW

The original indictment drawn up by Garzón against Pinochet accuses Pinochet of 'genocide', which according to the Rome Statute means 'killing … causing serious bodily harm … deliberately inflicting … conditions of life calculated to bring about … physical destruction in whole or in part. Imposing measures intended to prevent births … Forcibly transferring children of the group to another group' when 'committed with intent to destroy in whole or in part, a national, ethnical, racial, or religious group, as such' (Article 6). This is the same definition contained in the International Convention on the Prevention and Punishment of the Crime of Genocide adopted by the UN General Assembly in 1948, and in the Charters of the special tribunals for former Yugoslavia and Rwanda approved by the Security Council in 1993 (Resolution 827, 25 May 1993) and 1994 (Resolution 955, 8 November 1994) respectively.

It is worth noting here that there is an important historical and conceptual link between the adoption of the Genocide Convention and that of the Universal Declaration of Human Rights. The Genocide Convention was adopted by the General Assembly the day before the adoption of the Universal Declaration of Human Rights. Anglo-American notions of 'legislative intent' would suggest a direct, intended relationship here between the conceptualization of the acts proscribed by both instruments, against a common background of nascent postwar 'universalist' aspirations. Garzón's prosecutorial strategy reflects the convergence between these aims in the specific context of the Pinochet dictatorship.

This overlap should be extended in conceptual terms to the relationship between the acts proscribed by the Genocide Convention, and those which violate internationally recognized economic, social and cultural rights ('international poverty law'). In other words, the ultimately ideological divide between 'civil and political' rights on the one hand and 'economic, social and cultural' rights, on the other, according preferred status (and thus greater justiciability and enforceability) to the former than to the latter, which prevailed throughout the Cold War, and which still lingers today in a structural and conceptual imbalance between them, is also reflected in the tendency to conceive of 'genocide' in exclusively 'civil and political' terms, and not to recognize that the systematic violation of 'economic, social and cultural' rights could itself rise to genocidal levels under certain circumstances. My argument here then is that the gross and systematic character of the violation of economic, social and cultural rights during the Pinochet dictatorship had a genocidal character in this sense.

How can Pinochet's generalized acts of political repression be characterized as 'genocide'? First, they certainly included 'killing', 'causing serious bodily harm' and 'deliberately inflicting ... conditions of life calculated to bring about ... physical destruction in whole or in part'– but of whom, of which protected group?

According to the Spanish High Court which upheld the basis under Spanish criminal law for charging Pinochet with genocide, this generally recognized international crime has acquired a 'social' meaning beyond its original codification in the International Genocide Convention of 1948 (in turn based on the London Charter of the Nuremberg Tribunal). The Court notes in affirming the legal basis for Garzón's authority to proceed with the case that Pinochet's acts of political repression in Chile in fact served to differentiate the overall Chilean population into two groups: those who were to be repressed and those who were not. The sectors to be repressed were heterogenous in character, as specified below, but differentiated from all others by the decision to go after them. This decision had its most extreme, but typical, expression in the practice of forced disappearances, which amounted, according to the Spanish High Court, to their 'sudden expulsion from society forever'.[5]

Who were the victims in Pinochet's Chile? Overwhelmingly they were poor people and workers, and advocates on their behalf, members of organized left parties (especially Communist, Socialist, MAPU [Movement of Unitary Popular Action], MIR [Movement of the Revolutionary Left]), labour unions, peasants', women's and indigenous peoples' organizations, student movements and those linked to armed revolutionary movements. Pinochet's repression assumed that members of such groups were by definition enemies and opponents of his regime, and specifically of the 'neo-liberal' macroeconomic policies that it adopted and implemented. His 'genocide' was both 'ideological' and 'national' in character, for, in effect, it sought to annihilate an entire political spectrum from

Chile's public life by proscribing its organizations and systematically persecuting their members.

The Spanish High Court defines such practices as 'social genocide', which is carried out as a complement to the deliberate reduction of the living standards of the country's poorest and working people, as the result of intentionally redistributing wealth upwards and reconcentrating wealth in the most prosperous minority sectors. But the Spanish High Court failed to take the next necessary step in its own emerging logic. My argument here is that it was in fact the poor and working-class sectors of the country, the majority of Chile's population, who were the ultimate 'enemies' (and victims) of the regime.

In this way, the Spanish High Court insisted, genocide has come to mean actions of this kind undertaken concertedly against any 'national human group', and not more restrictively only those acts carried out against a 'group formed by persons who belong to the same nation'. Such a 'national human group' is, simply, 'a differentiated human group, characterized by some identifiable trait, that is part of a larger collective body'. A more restrictive definition of genocide would prevent its applicability to 'hateful actions such as the systematic elimination by those in power or by gangs of those diagnosed with AIDS ... or the elderly ... or foreign residents in a particular country', a result which the Court sought to forestall by applying a much broader 'social' definition to the genocide charges against Pinochet, a definition 'felt and understood by society, upon which its rejection and horror at such crimes is founded'.[6]

My argument here proposes to go at least one step further than that taken by the Spanish High Court. The forseeable consequences (quantifiable in terms of rates of poverty, inequality, unemployment, homelessness, hunger, illness, infant mortality, etc.) of pursuing neo-liberal (or other) economic policies such as those of the Pinochet regime should have subjected its chief architect to potential liability for 'social genocide' in a much broader sense.

According to Argentine/Mexican philosopher Enrique Dussel, the essence of the 'Ethics of Liberation'[7] is a principled emphasis on creating and maintaining the economic, political, social and cultural conditions and structures necessary for the preservation and reproduction of human life. It is also an ethics that legitimizes struggles and acts of resistance by the victims of a system that contravenes it, and that thereby seeks to provide a basis for such victims to become protagonists in the struggle for their own liberation from its effects. In this context the neo-liberal socioeconomic policies pursued by the Pinochet regime (and its peers elsewhere, e.g. Argentina) were literally 'genocidal' in their purposes and effects (intentionally destructive of the human life of specific, identifiable groups of 'victims', e.g. those who are poor, hungry, homeless, unemployed, ill, deprived of their children's company and potential assistance in old age). These victims are as much entitled to the recognition of their suffering, and to its relief and reparation, to the extent possible, as those victimized by the better-known abuses by such regimes of civil and political rights. Many victims in fact were affected by both kinds of violations.

When the British Home Secretary determined that Pinochet could not be extradited (and thus ultimately tried, at least in Spain) for genocide, it was not because his acts could not be charged or characterized as such – as Spain sought to – but rather for purely 'technical' reasons, which flow from a more restrictive interpretation of how to proceed in this matter in the British courts than that adopted in Spain. The Chilean courts may have the opportunity to undertake a broader approach, more consistent with emergent principles of international law.

Garzón's various indictments as they were revised and updated to address developments in the case essentially charged Pinochet with establishing an international criminal enterprise (known as 'Operación Condor', implemented in collaboration with allied military regimes in Paraguay, Uruguay, Bolivia, Brazil and Argentina), whose objectives were to conspire, develop and carry out a conspiracy made up of illegal detentions, kidnappings, torture, assasination of political opponents, the forced displacement of thousands of exiles and refugees, and the forced disappearances and murder of a selective nucleus of approximately 3,000 enemies of his and these other regimes.

The indictment estimates that as a result of this conspiracy some 500,000 people were detained (and virtually all submitted to some form of torture), more than 100,000 displaced from their countries of origin, and some 5,000 killed or disappeared (some 3,000 are listed by name). All of this was done, according to Garzón, in the service of specific economic and political objectives whose intentions this plan was intended to serve. The Spanish High Court described these objectives as the establishment of a new social order from which those human targets described above must be excluded as unfit. My argument here is that the same intention that was carried out by the regime *explicitly* as to those defined as its political enemies was applied at minimum *implicitly* to the victims of its socioeconomic policies.

The victims of the Pinochet regime's neo-liberal economic policies (and those of any similar regime) thus ought to be entitled to relief for 'crimes against humanity' cognizable under Article 7 of the Rome Statute of the International Criminal Court as acts of 'extermination' (b), 'persecution' (h), and/or for 'other inhumane acts of a similar character intentionally causing great suffering, or serious injury to body or to mental or physical health' (h), which were the foreseeable results of the application of such policies. In terms of acts of 'persecution', the argument would be that such policies in effect intentionally 'persecuted' poor and working people as groups who were 'identifiable' because of the deprivation of the economic, social and cultural rights to which they were entitled under international human rights law. These violations in effect sought to 'expel' the majority of Chile's poor and working people from the possibility of the enjoyment of their internationally recognized human rights, almost as assuredly as did their more selective physical extermination or exile.

The Chilean experience is an extreme illustration in this sense of Amartya Sen's insight that poverty is a deprivation of freedom in its most fundamental sense, understood in terms of a person, or a community's, ability to have control over their own circumstances. The material poverty induced by the Pinochet regime thus inflicted a commensurate 'poverty of rights' (the substantive deprivation of the supposed effects of one's formal recognition as a subject entitled to the protection of one's rights, characterized by Hannah Arendt as the most fundamental human right of all, the 'right to have rights'), which could be understood in light of Sen's insight as ultimately a violation of the poor's individual and collective rights to self-determination, and thus as equivalent to their deprivation of citizenship itself.[8]

CONCLUSION

My ultimate purpose here is to suggest some points of departure for an ongoing examination of the dynamics and challenges of cases and regimes such as that of General Pinochet, for an overall research and action agenda focused on exploring the relationship between human rights, poverty, social justice and the rule of law. The complex inter-twining of neo-liberalism, political repression, theoretical constructions of notions about poverty, marginalization and social exclusion must be disentangled, and situated amid broader debates about the contemporary meaning of democracy, international law – or of law at all – the role of the state, political culture and the deeper purposes of ethical social policy, ethical social science and ethical politics. But none of this can be ultimately justified unless we listen carefully to the voices of the victims (the tortured, raped and kidnapped, the poor, jobless, homeless and landless, the families of the murdered and disappeared).

To what extent is a Pinochet trial an adequate vehicle for such an effort? Mark Osiel has recently argued in his exploration of issues of law, truth and memory in the Nuremberg and Tokyo Trials, Eichmann and Barbie cases, and trials of the military junta commanders in Argentina, 'that the main mechanism of the criminal law, the trial, is probably not best suited to' the necessary task of establishing the 'public memory of past wrongdoing' that is a prerequisite to a successful transition to democracy (Osiel 1997). His concern, as framed by David Dyzenhaus, is that '"legal concepts and doctrines" often lose "their normal connection to the underlying moral and political issues at stake".' Osiel's solution is to 'widen the spatial and temporal frame of courtroom storytelling in ways that allow litigants to flesh out their competing interpretations of recent history, and to argue these before an attentive public. Only in this way can the debate within the courtroom be made to resonate with the public debate beyond the courtroom walls' (Dyzenhaus 1998: 181–2).

But perhaps it is Chilean writer Ariel Dorfman who has come up with the solution for Pinochet which is most just, most susceptible of restoring the balance lost from the Platonic perspective. For him, it is the relatives of the victims of the Pinochet regime who are a symbol of the Chile which does not function the right way, and who have demonstrated the limits of our transition to democracy.

> They represent in a deep sense, with all of the insurgent force of truth, each and every person who has been violated and wounded in our homeland. They are the conscience of Chile. Their suffering has conferred upon them a moral authority that must be taken into account before any decision is reached about Pinochet's ultimate destiny.
>
> Imagine how extraordinary it would be to have the future of our ex-dictator placed into the hands of his most essential victims. Think of the possibility that General Pinochet would be obliged to extend an invitation to the families of the disappeared to come to London, paying their way so that they could finally confront him for the first time in his life and in theirs. Think of the General trying to convince them that he has repented, that he is going to repair the harms he has visited upon them. Think of this man listening to them, one story after another and another, forced to watch their faces as they speak. Think of the moment when the General declares that he is going to spend the rest of his days helping them find the bodies of the disappeared. Think of

what it would mean for the General to plead with his most indomitable foes for their forgiveness. Imagine them granting him their mercy.

And then? And then, Dorfman says, 'let the victims decide'.[9] Imagine.

NOTES

1. Moulian's thesis is developed in great detail in his *Chile Actual: La anatomia de un mito* (1997).

2. See, generally, Hornbeck (1995) and Souther (1998).

3. Because of lack of cooperation by the Pinochet regime with investigations into the assassination of former Chilean Foreign Minister Orlando Letelier in a September 1976 car-bombing in Washington; at the time Letelier, a member of the Socialist Party and a former political prisoner during the first year of the regime, was Pinochet's most prominent and widely respected political opponent.

4. 'The right dictatorship at the ripest historical moment' (Souther 1998: 2).

5. Translation of the original text of the Spanish High Court decision, Rollo de Apelación 173/98, Sección Primera, Sumario 1/98, Juzgado Central de Instrucción Numero Seis, p. 8 (*El Pais Digital*, 6 November 1998).

6. Ibid.

7. Detailed in a book of the same name forthcoming from Duke University Press.

8. Interestingly, the Princeton Principles of Universal Jurisdiction recently drafted (2000–01) by a distinguished group of international law scholars include a list of 'Serious Crimes Under International Law' under Principle 2(1) – piracy, slavery, war crimes, crimes against peace, crimes against humanity, genocide and torture – with the express caveat that '[i]t should be carefully noted that the list of serious crimes is explicitly illustrative, not exhaustive. Principle 2(1) leaves open the possibility that, in the future, other crimes may be deemed of such a heinous nature as to warrant the application of universal jurisdiction' (Commentary on the Princeton Principles prepared by Steven W. Becker [see <http://www.princeton.edu/~lapa/unive_jur.pdf>], ibid., 48). Whether or not violations of internationally recognized economic, social and cultural rights might constitute crimes recognizable under Principle 2(1), drafted in large part in the light of what it describes as the Rome Statute's 'authoritative' list in Article 7, once they exceed some given threshold, is not discussed in the Commentary.

9. Ariel Dorfman, 'Que decidan las victimas', *El Pais Digital*, 2 December 1998.

REFERENCES

Collins, J. and J. Lear (1995) *Chile's Free-Market Miracle: A Second Look*, Oakland, CA: Institute for Food and Development Policy, Food First.

Constable, P. and A. Valenzuela (1991) *A Nation of Enemies: Chile under Pinochet*, New York: W. W. Norton.

Cooper, M. (1998) 'Chile: Twenty-Five Years after Allende', *The Nation*, 23 March 1998.

Dyzenhaus, D. (1998) *Judging the Judges, Judging Ourselves: Truth, Reconciliation and the Apartheid Legal Order*, Oxford: Hart Publishing.

Eide, A. (1998) 'Economic, Social and Cultural Rights as Human Rights', in A. Eide, C. Krause and A. Rosas (eds), *Economic, Social and Cultural Rights*, Boston, Dordrecht and London: Nijhoff/Kluwer.

Falk, R. A. (2000) *Human Rights Horizon: The Pursuit of Justice in a Globalizing World*, New York: Routledge.

Foxley, A. (1984) 'Vulnerable Groups in Recessionary Situations: The Case of Children and the Young in Chile', *World Development*, 12(3).

Garreton, M. A. (2001) 'Popular Mobilization and the Military Regime in Chile: The Complexities of the Invisible Transition', in S. Eckstein (ed.), *Power and Popular Protest: Latin American Social Movements*, Berkeley: University of California Press.

Genugten, W. van and C. Perez Bustillo (eds) (2001) *The Poverty of Rights: Human Rights and the Eradication of Poverty*, CROP International Studies in Poverty Research, London: Zed Books.

Hitchens, C. (2001) *The Trial of Henry Kissinger*, New York: Verso.

Hornbeck, J. F. (1995) *Chilean Trade and Economic Reform: Implications for NAFTA Accession*, Major Studies and Issues Briefs of the Congressional Research Service, Washington, DC: Library of Congress.

Klein Goldewijk, B. and B. de Gaay Fortman (1999) *Where Needs Meet Rights: Economic, Social and Cultural Rights in a New Perspective*, Risk Book Series, Geneva: World Council of Churches (WCC) Publications.

Moulian, T. (1997) *Chile Actual: La anatomia de un mito*, Santiago: ARCIS Universidad, LOM Ediciones.

Osiel, M. (1997) *Mass Atrocity, Collective Memory and the Law*, New Brunswick, NJ: Transaction Publishers.

Souther, S. (1998) 'An Analysis of Chilean Economic and Socioeconomic Policy: 1975–1989', University of Colorado at Boulder: <http://csf. colorado.edu/students/souther.sherman>.

Valdés, J.G. (1995) *Pinochet's Economists: The Chicago School in Chile*, New York: Cambridge University Press.

PART II

Responsibility for Alleviating Poverty

FOUR | The politics of child support

PETER ROBSON

INTRODUCTION

Overview

The traditional discretionary role of the British courts in relation to aliment was drastically altered by legislation passed in 1991. Hitherto, judges had had the power to decide what level of financial support they considered appropriate and fair, unrestricted by any guidelines. From 1 April 1993, maintenance of children became almost exclusively the province of an autonomous government body, the Child Support Agency (CSA), implementing the controversial Child Support Act 1991 throughout Britain. This Act provides that the maintenance due to a child be determined by applying a complex set of formulae, treating like cases exactly the same and involving minimal discretion.

The long-term future of the rigid formula approach is uncertain as of June 1999,[1] after a series of problems in implementing the legislation and a Green Paper in the summer of 1998 promising radical simplification. The government suggested in January 1999 that it was 'working towards implementing a simple, straightforward child maintenance service, which is both efficient and fair, and which parents can trust'. The Social Security Secretary, however, did point out that 'the radical changes proposed ... cannot be implemented overnight'. In the meantime, there has been encouragement, although not yet compulsion, to involve lone parents in the world of waged work. Interviews have been arranged and help and advice on job search, training, child-care, benefits and financial support have been offered to lone parents whose youngest child is aged over five years and three months.[2] Jobs have been obtained by some 7 per cent of the 88,000 lone parents to whom letters were sent.[3] In addition, the way in which assessments from self-employed parents are calculated has changed since October 1999.[4] Finally, 20 per cent of the workload of the CSA is being removed by eliminating the requirement that low-earning parents cooperate with the Agency.[5]

Background of the scheme

Child support policies relating to families headed by lone parents have developed as the number of such families has risen in Great Britain from under 8 per cent in 1971 to 23 per cent in 1994.[6] There appear to have been two distinct but related policies behind the reforms of the 1990s. First, there was a recognition of the ineffectiveness of the existing court-centred system of assessment and collection. The number of parents receiving maintenance fell from 50 per cent in 1980 to 25 per cent in 1989.[7] Second, there was a strong desire to shift the burden of support from the community in general to the absent parent and save on public expenditure. The number of lone parents forced to rely on the fixed state income support rose from 37 per cent in 1971 to 59 per cent in 1986,[8] and to 70 per cent in 1989.[9] This means-tested benefit ensures that no one falls below the poverty line in Britain and is payable to those whose resources, income and capital are below a certain level.[10]

A considerable number of studies into the lives of those in households headed by a lone parent have been carried out since 1976. The focus has varied from how mothers coped bringing up children on their own[11] to the impact of measures to assist low-income families.[12] Research has suggested that financial support policies for children through a benefits system in the era of the welfare state have been concerned with maintaining a differential between wages and benefits as well as restraining public expenditure.[13] Studies have shed light on life on benefits in general[14] and the difficulties for lone parent families in particular. As for child support payments, the pattern of receipt seemed to follow the course of contact with children by the absent parent. Maintenance lessened soon after separation and dwindled over the next fifteen months.[15] Custodial parents in waged-work were more likely to be in receipt of maintenance, as they had better qualifications and greater abilities to pursue maintenance claims.[16] The role of child maintenance from ex-partners did not figure in lone parents' decisions about returning to work. Reliable child-care and good wages were seen as most important.[17] But the research was focused on the overall nature of support for children and the differential impact of lone parenting.[18] The issue of the source of child maintenance did not figure extensively in this work.[19]

There was no direct investigation into how the public perceived the extent to which lone parents had a legitimate claim to collective support. The thrust of the Child Support Act 1991, however, reflects a shift of approach from the concerns of the research with the problems of lone parent families. The legislation proceeds from the assumption that such families are problematic and that collective support is to be residual rather than central.

The background to the British approach was discussed by various writers prior to the introduction of the legislation.[20] Maclean suggested that a combination of economic pressure and impatience with what the Conservatives perceived as a 'nanny state culture of dependency' helped create a political climate in which maintenance recovery arrangements were deemed worthy of strengthening.[21] The problem was exacerbated by court decisions such as *Delaney* v. *Delaney*[22] in which the judge reduced a maintenance award in order to enable an absent father and his new partner to get started on their new life, leaving the first family relying on means-tested state benefits for those below the poverty line.

Maclean also suggested that, with the loss of legal aid in divorce settlements, the continuation of court-based maintenance payments would have become 'problematic'.[23] Jacobs and Douglas took the view that the 1991 Act formed the third plank in the Thatcher government's programme to stress the importance of parental responsibilities. They referred to the introduction in England and Wales of the Children Act 1989 with its concept of parental responsibility and the Criminal Justice Act 1991 with its emphasis on parental responsibility for the delinquent behaviour of their children.[24] In Scotland, the Children (Scotland) Act 1995 likewise placed an emphasis on parental responsibilities as the foundation of parental rights.[25] The Scottish legislation, however, did not slavishly mirror that in England and Wales. The extensive reforms of the Scottish criminal justice system in Scotland during the 1990s, for instance, did not include any equivalent to the parental responsibility sections of the Criminal Justice Act.

THE CHILD SUPPORT ACT 1991

Whatever governmental motives may have been, the resulting legislation was complex and inaccessible. Critical debate was inhibited by the general nature of the Act, with extensive reference to regulations for substantive details of how the system would work.[26] The original Child Support Bill published on 14 February 1991 contained over 100 regulation-making powers. The bill was passed virtually unchanged by July 1991 and received the Royal Assent to become law on 25 July 1991. The one area of extensive debate was the proposal to restrict benefits paid to those women who did not wish to reveal the identity of the father of any children for whom they were claiming. This concern was not surprising since, by 1991, 75 per cent of single parents were on income support. The debates in the Commons and Lords centred on this issue.[27] A compromise was reached whereby the legislation retained the reduced benefit direction. During the passage of the legislation, an exemption was added from the requirement to cooperate with child support enforcement if an application for maintenance from the absent parent would put the parent or any child living with her at 'risk of harm or undue distress'.[28] In addition, the legislation included a provision that the welfare of children should be taken into account when discretionary decisions, such as reducing benefits, were being made.[29]

The transition to the new system was facilitated by the setting up of a Child Support Unit in April 1992 to improve the service to customers of the Department of Social Security (DSS) Benefits Agency.[30] The legislation itself was launched on 5 April 1993 without the benefit of any actual pilot studies being carried out as to possible teething troubles. The key regulations were introduced in July 1992 leaving a short familiarization period for what are immensely complex issues.[31] This chapter provides an outline of the operation of the system that was introduced in 1993. The basic structure – support derived from applying a fixed formula – remains intact.

Alternative approaches

There are several models of a formula-based system. The system that the Australian Child Support Agency[32] operates involves a straight percentage, as does that of the New Zealand Child Support Agency.[33] The antipodean formulae take the gross income of the absent parent, usually based on the previous full tax year's income, and deduct a figure for exempt income based on current family commitments. A percentage of the remaining figure is then calculated based on the number of children for whom child support is being assessed.[34] This system is also found in Wisconsin, the US state often touted as a model for experiments in reducing welfare.[35]

Other common law jurisdictions operate court-based discretionary models for assessing the appropriate sum that an absent parent is required to pay. The problem of enforcing such court orders continues to burden custodial parents and official statistics suggest that this method of approach does not necessarily lead to higher numbers of absent parents paying.[36] There are individual systems of state support and sanction in the United States.[37] The disincentives for non-payers include in certain states loss of driving licences[38] as well as negative publicity on the television about 'deadbeat dads'.[39] Collection devices have included using marriage licence statutes,[40] linking support rights with inheritance,[41] and allowing mothers on welfare to keep all their child support payments from the father.[42] In addition to state and county enforcement bodies,[43] there is a Federal Office of Child Support Enforcement.[44] There are also a significant number of private agencies that engage to recover child support and arrange for increases. They do this by charging a percentage of the sums recovered.[45]

The issue of child support has been raised in the context of changes in divorce laws in the 1990s across a range of Western states including France,[46] Sweden,[47] and Canada.[48] In Norway the *bidragsfogd* has, reportedly, impressive performance figures. It obtains payments from 90 per cent of the men liable to make child support payments and recoups some 80 per cent of the interim payments made by the state to families where there is an absent parent.[49]

Obligation to cooperate

As indicated above, one of the concerns of the British government expressed in the 1990 White Paper was the cost to the community of single parents living on income support.[50] With the exception of risk and harm noted previously, the legislation obligates parents with care who are receiving income support, family credit or any prescribed benefit to authorize the Secretary of State to recover maintenance from the absent parent.[51] In order to make the recovery likely, the parent with care can be asked to provide information to facilitate the tracing of the absent parent. The principal issue that has emerged is whether the parent with care has grounds for suspecting that there are fears for her own or her children's safety in the event that the absent parent is contacted by the CSA. The courts in England have made it clear that when deciding the question of the welfare of the child there is no obligation on the CSA to make enquiries of the absent parent.[52] As for the general question of the relationship between the social security and child support systems, the Court of Appeal has indicated that the claim that parents with care may not be entitled to income support was not the crucial issue. Section 6 grants the Secretary of State authority to act based on what was 'actually' paid, rather than what was 'lawfully' paid by way of the relevant social security benefits.[53]

Reduced benefit direction Where the parent with care fails to cooperate with the CSA, a written notice may be served requiring either compliance or reasons to be given for failing to do so.[54] The

Child Support Officer (CSO) must, at the end of the specified six-week period, consider any reasons given. The CSO may act after two weeks if there is no response from the parent with care. If the CSO determines that there are no reasonable grounds for non-cooperation, then a reduced benefit direction may be given.[55] This reduces the amount of benefit payable by a specific percentage. Originally this was set at 20 per cent for the first six months and then 10 per cent for the next twelve months,[56] for a fixed maximum period of eighteen months.[57] In October 1996, this reduction was extended to an indefinite period at a higher level of 40 per cent.[58]

In terms of determining whether there is good cause for a parent with care to refuse to cooperate, Commissioners' decisions have discussed the meaning of a risk of harm or undue distress. The test is not whether it is certain or definite that the harm or undue distress *will* occur but whether this *might* occur.[59] The correct test involves whether 'there is a realistic possibility' of harm or undue distress being suffered. The risk does not have to be 'substantial', but must be real rather than imagined. 'Distress' must, however, be 'undue'. Guidance from the Secretary of State suggests that good cause does not exist based solely on a custodial parent's concern over the withdrawal of informal financial assistance nor fear that the absent parent will want contact with the child. Nor is good cause met by the distress to an absent parent who might not want a new partner to know of the child.[60]

In the first year good cause was raised in some 8 per cent of cases where application forms were issued.[61] The number of good cause requests rose from 65,000 to 190,000 between 1993/94 and 1996/97 and the acceptance rate fell from 49 per cent to under 20 per cent. Benefit penalties were imposed in only about one-third of cases where good cause was refused partly because of the welfare of the child consideration.[62] Nevertheless, the number of reduced benefit directions has been considerable: 18,000 were issued in the first two years of the Act's operation, between 50,000[63] and 65,000[64] in the first four years, and 27,478 in 1995/96.

The numbers of parents with care who have accepted, or at least not appealed, a reduced benefit direction increased from 4.3 per cent in 1994/95 to 9 per cent in 1995/96.[65] Large numbers of parents with care were seen as being able to opt out of the child support scheme. Governmental concern was expressed at the number of situations where it was suspected there had been collusion between the parent with care and the absent parent so that women were refusing to cooperate and shifting the burden of child support from their ex-partners on to the community for no good reason. This was looked into in an in-house report by the Department of Social Security[66] and by the Social Security Committee.[67] The latter recommended that the changes to the regulations extending the benefit penalty should be supplemented by regular interviews and a consideration of whether fraud investigations should commence. Central government regulations extended the benefit penalty to 40 per cent in line with the penalty imposed for failing actively to seek work. The father makes up the shortfall by making 'under-the-counter' direct payments and saves money while guaranteeing that the children, rather than the tax authorities, get the benefit.

Departures from the formula

The other area where there had been complaints from users of the Child Support system was in the apparent ability of some absent parents and, to a lesser extent, some parents with care to live a comfortable life. Following consideration of the problems encountered both by custodial and absent parents with the inflexible formula approach adopted in the 1991 Act, a major break with the formula approach was introduced by the Child Support Act 1995.[68] The 'departures directions' contained in that Act provided an element of flexibility and an opportunity for consideration of individual circumstances. There are two aspects to the concept of 'departures'. First, it permits individuals with certain special expenses to have allowances made for these. Second, it allows evidence to be introduced indicating that the declared income of a person is incorrect. A pilot system was tested during 1996.

The current departures system came into effect in December 1996.[69] Certain special expenses not taken into account in the standard assessment may now be taken into account, such as travelling costs.[70] The other areas where there had been complaints from users of the Child Support system was in the apparent ability of some absent parents and, to a lesser extent, some parents with care to live a comfortable life with very low declared income. The departure direction allows the CSO to depart from the formula where the parent's overall lifestyle requires a substantially higher income than the amount on which the maintenance assessment is based.[71] There may still be situations where the income and the lifestyle are incompatible but where there can be no departure direction as the lifestyle is paid for either out of capital or by the new partner. There may, however, be an increase in the assessment where the CSO determines that it is appropriate for the partner to contribute to the housing costs.[72] Related to this issue is the suspicion that a parent may be under-using assets which could produce income or which could reasonably be sold.[73] Provided that there is a minimum of £10,000 involved there may be a direction that such assets be regarded as having a notional income.

There may also be departures where a parent has unreasonably diverted income such as by paying a partner a salary but receiving nothing directly.[74] In addition, where either parent is exempt from the ceiling on housing costs, departure may be applied where the housing costs are unreasonably high.[75] Finally, where travel costs allowed under the formula are unreasonably high, then there may be departure from the formula figure.[76]

Simplifying the formula

In the general election of 1997, no political party was committed to the retention of the CSA and its abolition was widely predicted. The problem of an alternative, however, was also evident. The previous court-centred system was arbitrary and dependent on the whims of a range of different sheriffs and judges with divergent views on what level of financial support was appropriate in different circumstances. The discretion of the predecessor of the CSO, the liable relative officer, where benefit claimants were involved also had not produced a consistent approach to child support recovery. As is noted below, child support legislation depends for its effectiveness on how it is perceived within the community. Child support ran the risk of becoming the poll tax of the 1990s. The Green Paper published in July 1998, *Children First: A New Approach to Child Support*,[77] describes the 1993 scheme as 'a mess'[78] and recommends that the child maintenance system be much simpler. Its recommendations to this end were largely adopted.

Monitoring the performance of the Child Support Agency

Any discussion of the changes and developments in the Child Support Act 1991 needs to take account of the plethora of administrative problems. Those implementing the Act encountered these right from the beginning of the operation of the legislation in April 1993, and they were particularly serious in the first year.[79] There was a shortfall in the expected saving of some £112 million.[80] Only 14 per cent of monitored assessments were correct in the first year of the CSA.[81] This rose to 29 per cent in the second year.[82] Administrative problems bedevilled the operation throughout its first five years.[83]

In October 1993, the Social Security Committee raised a series of minor issues[84] and made various recommendations.[85] Based on these, the government made minor changes in the operation of the formula.[86] In October 1994, the committee made an additional twenty-three recommendations.[87] A number of these were put into effect, the most significant being the treatment of capital agreements made prior to the introduction of the 1991 Act.[88] The Social Security Committee continued to monitor the performance of the Agency during 1995.[89] The issue of the benefit penalty was looked at in 1995 and the Social Security Committee's views were sought on the question of the duration and level of benefit penalty for failure to cooperate.[90] The committee supported the draft changes which the government had produced extending the length and depth of the penalty.[91]

During the rest of the 1990s things did not improve appreciably and the reports of the House of Commons Social Security Committee[92] recorded a range of administrative problems. The first report[93] noted that performance had not always measured up to the high standards the Agency had set out to achieve.

The Ombudsman[94] for his part was highly critical, pointing out that maladministration leading to injustice was likely to arise when a new administrative task was not tested first by a pilot project. In his January 1995 report, the Ombudsman looked at the structural problems of the CSA, drawing on a representative sample of cases remitted to him by MPs. The kinds of issues identified were delays, erroneous requests and misidentifications, as well as general errors in administration.[95] The National Audit Office joined the chorus of critics.[96] The Child Support Agency had four chief executives during its first five years. It is little wonder that staff, after five years of operating this system, were reported as feeling unable to cope with the pressure.[97]

Assessing Child Support

One goal of the government was that the Child Support Act should encourage parents back to work by making dependence on income support less attractive. Studies carried out prior to the 1991 Act found a reasonable degree of satisfaction with those claimants using the DSS services to assess and collect child maintenance.[98] This hope was not borne out by early studies into the operation of the legislation,[99] suggesting that the Act did not provide adequate policies to achieve its goals. It reduced women's access to the social security safety-net and transferred women's dependence to both the labour market and men. There were, however, no corresponding policies to strengthen the capacity of the labour market to deal with women's work needs. Nor, tellingly, was any work done to increase the willingness or ability of men to provide financial support.[100] The Liverpool study suggested that there was also little support for the Act among parents with care. Its implementation was perceived as coercive and intrusive. For low-income parents with care, there was little incentive to cooperate with the Child Support Agency.[101] Initial national research suggested that the scheme had limited financial impact on the vast majority of women: 72 per cent were no better or worse off; 8 per cent were worse off and 20 per cent better off. The impact on men was somewhat different: 47 per cent were the same, with 5 per cent better off and 48 per cent worse off. The impact on the community was that in 51 per cent of cases the result was the same to the Treasury: 37 per cent resulted in a saving to the public purse and 12 per cent involved extra expenditure.[102]

The concentration on the reduction of the social security bill by targeting parents with care on benefit, and thus in poverty, seems to have compromised the legislation's other objectives.[103] These included the arbitrary use of discretion to determine maintenance awards, the absence of regular systematic increases in maintenance payments and the apparent ease of avoiding complying with court orders.[104] The DSS had suggested in 1990 that the pre-Child Support Act system of maintenance was 'unnecessarily fragmented, uncertain in its results, slow and ineffective'.[105] The concern to reduce public expenditure undermined potential popular support,[106] more frequently encountered in other legal systems.[107] By contrast, the political and media campaign against the legislation during the 1990s did not feature the voices of low-income parents. Rather it was dominated by what Richard Collier described as 'middle-class male angst'[108] as men complained about the sudden shift to being required to make a contribution to their children's upkeep more in tune with the actual costs of such care than what courts had previously awarded. In practice, the lack of investigative powers in the CSA combined with its actual performance and policy towards enforcement has led it to be dubbed a toothless dragon – or vegetarian tiger.[109] A related structural problem implicit in the formula approach was the assumption it made about the nature of the population: static, enjoying fixed employment and non-fluid relationships.[110] These may be the aspirations of those concerned with 'traditional family values'. They do not correspond with the lives that people actually led in the documented research.

The problems that have been encountered both by absent parents and parents with care have led to a situation where those who can avoid the CSA do so, just as the courts were avoided before the 1991 Act. Researchers have noted the prevalence of private agreements struck between absent and caring parents. Whereas, according to the Nuffield study, 'parents used to bargain in the shadow of the courts, many now bargain in the shadow of the CSA'. [111] The major change has been the weakening of the bargaining position of men, since absent parents have more to fear from the levels of maintenance set (if not actually enforced) by the CSA. The result has been that the CSA has shifted the focus away from society having a primary concern with children's welfare. This rests clearly with parents and to that extent it can be said that responsibility for maintaining children has been privatized. [112]

The most recent data consulted on the impact of the legislation suggest that caring parents' current source of income has altered over the years. [113] For those who have full maintenance assessments – some 787,000 parents – their sources of income are as follows: 45 per cent income support/income-based jobseeker's allowance, [114] 21 per cent receiving Family Credit [115] and 35 per cent not receiving any of these benefits. The amount being received fell, however, from around £24 to £20 between May 1995 and November 1998.

Towards a new future

Extreme consequences have stemmed from the work of the CSA. In the early days the tabloid newspapers documented a series of suicides and attempted suicides that were claimed to be the result of stress caused by the operation of the formula and the heavy-handed approach of the Agency. [116] One conviction was reported in mid-1998 where a woman hired a contract killer to do away with her husband. She feared the CSA would threaten her lifestyle and result in her losing her Mercedes. [117]

Pressure groups, such as the National Association of Citizens Advice Bureaux, [118] the Child Poverty Action Group, [119] the National Council for One Parent Families [120] and a range of major children's charities, have campaigned and commented on the impact of the legislation on low-income groups and families. [121] They have carried out work on the Child Support Act as it affects their client groups. In addition, a range of organizations has emerged with a particular perspective on the Child Support legislation. These include groups whose aim has been to repeal the legislation – Network Against the Child Support Act and the Campaign Against the Child Support Act and the National Campaign for Fair Maintenance, as well as groups, such as Legal Action for Women, concerned that the legislation operates inequitably in a range of different ways. [122]

The concern with the operation of the formula and the performance of the CSA bore fruit in the publication of a consultation paper, *Children First*, in July 1998. [123] The National Association for Child Support Action expressed concern that the simple formula approach had the potential to 'allow ministers to pitch figures sufficiently low to defuse opposition, while designing in the opportunity to increase levels with impunity in the years ahead'.[124]

A range of alternative options has also been suggested which address the issue of embedding child support more firmly within the national culture by ensuring that increases in payments go to the children rather than in Treasury savings.[125] The same imperative of saving the costs of welfare was the stimulus for the US policy[126] and was suggested as the main goal in Britain too.[127] US research also noted that where women have a strong political base, the bureaucracy responds to this and increases enforcement.[128] For example, in 1974 the equivalent federal legislation in the USA was highly contentious and passed Congress by only one vote. When the legislation came up for renewal ten years later, the vote was unanimous.[129]

In policy terms, some are concerned that support for lone-parent families is in danger of being separated from issues relating to support for all families with children, and urge the integration of policy regarding income support, housing and child-care.[130] Others criticize the Child Support Act for casting women in their traditionally dependent role[131] and seeking to reproduce traditional family and gender relationships.[132] The difference in the way financial issues are seen by both parties has also been the subject of analysis.[133] A more child-centred approach would involve a guaranteed minimum income for single parents linked with a tax on absent parents based on their incomes and liabilities.[134]

Rescuing Child Support?

The outcome of the government's consultations was the Child Support, Pensions and Social Security Act 2000. It introduced changes in three distinct areas. Part I of the Act deals with Child Support and concerns us. It received the Royal Assent on 28 July 2000 and comes into effect by statutory instrument. Draft reform plans were indicated in a consultation document, *Children First* (Cm 3992, July 1998), and finally set out in the White Paper, *Children's Rights and Parents' Responsibilities* (Cm 4349, published July 1999). The principal issues for reform were:

- simplification of the child support liability assessment using a percentage of the non-resident's net income in place of the fixed formula
- introduction of a child maintenance premium in income support and income-based Jobseeker's Allowance to enable families on these

means-tested benefits to keep up to £10 a week of their maintenance in place of the loss of benefit £ for £
- sanctions strengthening and improved compliance
- improvement of CSA service levels

Maintenance liability calculations There are to be four rates:
- *Basic rate*, depending on the number of children[135]
  One child: 15 per cent of non-resident parent's income
  Two children: 20 per cent of NRP income
  Three children: 25 per cent of NRP income
- *Reduced rate*, payable where the NRP's net weekly income is between £100 and £200 at a rate prescribed by regulations. [136] Liability will increase in proportion to the amount by which the net income exceeds £100.
- *Flat rate*, where net income of the NRP is £100 or less or the NRP is in receipt of a prescribed benefit, pension or allowance.[137] Also applicable where the partner is in receipt of such benefits. This will apply to means-tested benefits like income support and income-based JSA. The amounts will be lower for those on the prescribed benefit.
- *Nil rate*, if the NRP has weekly income of below £5 or is in a prescribed category including full time students in further education and prisoners.

Apportionment Where there is more than one person with care and more than one qualifying child the liability of the NRP will be apportioned in accordance with the number of qualifying children. For example, for four children, three with one partner and one with another, money will be divided 75 per cent and 25 per cent.

Shared care[138] There are provisions for shared care where maintenance is paid at the basic or reduced rate. Where the NRP shares care, the

Nights per year	Reduction
52 to 103	one-seventh
104 to 155	two-sevenths
156 to 174	three-sevenths
175 or more	one-half

amount he would otherwise pay is reduced depending on the amount of overnight care provided.

Shared care – flat rate If there is a flat rate liability for the NRP because he is in receipt of a prescribed social security benefit and if there is shared care for at least fifty-two nights in the year, the liability is reduced to nil.[139]

Regulations about shared care[140] Regulations will define what nights count for the purpose of shared care and the use of periods other than twelve months to determine the reductions under the 2000 legislation.

Net weekly income[141] In calculating net weekly income, certain matters will be taken into account: income tax, National Insurance contributions and approved pension scheme payments.

Reform of applications by persons on benefit Parents with care on income support, income-based JSA or other prescribed benefits will be treated as having applied for child support. They must specifically request the Secretary of State not to recover child support maintenance.[142] The good cause defence remains as well as the rate of penalty – 40 per cent of the adult personal allowance.

Default maintenance decisions[143] When a final maintenance calculation cannot be made through insufficiency of details and the need to verify information, the new Act provides for a maintenance calculation at a default rate. These are being set at 15 per cent, 20 per cent or 25 per cent of average NRP's weekly earnings according to the number of qualifying children. At the time of writing this average figure is around £200. It is intended that there will be recalculation only if the full rate is higher than the default maintenance where NRPs are not cooperating.

Departure from the usual rules for calculating maintenance[144] Where the child support rates do not reflect the NRP's ability to pay, there can be variation of the rates payable in exceptional cases. The intention of the government is to define the acceptable exceptions with precision. There is an overall requirement that existing payments must be made regularly[145] and that maintenance liability will be varied only if it is just and equitable so to do.[146] In deciding the question of whether variation would be just and equitable, the Secretary of State must consider the welfare of any child likely to be affected, as well as taking into account factors prescribed by regulation.[147] This procedure will involve a preliminary sift and rejection by the Secretary of State of applications where there are either no grounds to allow a variation, insufficient information or any other prescribed circumstances.[148]

Cases for variation In addition to special expenses, specified in regulations, and property and capital transfers, the Act provides for further special cases. Examples of these are given in Schedule 4B[149] and include:

- where the NRP has assets that exceed a prescribed value (£65,000) other than his normal place of residence
- where the NRP enjoys a lifestyle which is inconsistent with the income used to determine the rate of liability
- where the NRP is in receipt of income to which the Secretary of State would not otherwise have had regard – at least £100 on top of prescribed social security benefit or war pension – or has a nil rate of liability
- where the NRP has unreasonably reduced the amount of income to which the Secretary of State has had regard in the calculation of maintenance liability

There is a limit on the amount of special expenses that may be taken into account for the purposes of variation.[150] There is to be a minimum amount required to bring the variation provisions into play, depending on the NRP's net weekly income.

False information[151] In lieu of the ineffective sanction of punitive interim maintenance assessments for uncooperative NRPs, there are now fines of up to £1,000 for anyone who makes false statements or refuses to supply information.[152] It is a defence that the person charged can establish that he had a reasonable excuse for failing to comply.[153]

Inspectors[154] There is now provision for inspectors to be appointed for fixed periods rather than just on an ad hoc basis as under the original legislation. The premises which are liable to inspection are widened to include premises at which an NRP is or has been employed, premises where the NRP carries out a trade, profession, vocation or business as well as premises at which there is information held by someone

(A) whom the inspector has reasonable grounds for suspecting has information about an NRP acquired in the course of A's own trade, profession, vocation or business.[155] The meaning of 'premises' includes movable structures and vehicles, vessels, aircraft and hovercraft as well as offshore oil installations and 'places of all other descriptions whether or not occupied as land or otherwise'.[156]

Disqualification from driving[157]   There is now provision for the loss of a driving licence for a specified period of up to two years where the court is of the opinion that there has been wilful refusal or culpable neglect on the part of the liable person.[158] This order may be given on a suspended basis for such period and on such conditions as are thought just. Where considering both a civil imprisonment and a driving ban the court must in the presence of the liable person inquire as to whether he needs a driving licence to earn his living, his means and whether there has indeed been wilful refusal or culpable neglect.[159]

Commitment to prison[160]   Where the sheriff is satisfied that there has been wilful refusal or culpable neglect by the liable person in paying, the non-resident parent may be imprisoned for a six-week maximum period,[161] provided he is not under the age of eighteen.[162]

Financial penalties[163]   As an alternative to the abandoned sanction of interest charges and the alternative of 'additional sums', discretionary financial penalties are introduced of up to 25 per cent of the amount owed.[164]

Voluntary payments[165]   Until now voluntary payments had no recognized status and were not necessarily counted against arrears. These payments are now defined.

Epilogue

What the detailed effect of these changes is likely to be can only be guessed at the time of writing since the reforms did not come into effect until 2002. Certainly, drawing on historical and comparative evidence, the impact of future child support would seem to depend on a number of factors, both local and global. Does the breakthrough of women in politics in Britain's election of May 1997 represent a critical mass that will provide an effective counterweight to the male perspective on providing adequate financial support to children? Given a series of governments with a shared strategy of withdrawal of the state from key areas of social welfare in favour of market solutions, is the future of children in poverty anything but bleak? In the longer term, how will patterns of work affect the nature and levels of support that globalizing business and the community judge reasonable to provide for an increasingly female workforce?

NOTES

This chapter is based on research for the author's chapter in K. McK. Norrie and A. Wilkinson (eds), *Parent and Child*, 2nd edn (1999).

1. 30 November 1998 was the final date for comments on the Green Paper of July 1998 and the government's proposals attracted minimal attention. The new legislation had not been brought into effect by August 2003.

2. New Deal for Lone Parents, December results published 4 February 1999, <http://www.dss.gov.uk/hq/press/press299/026.htm>.

3. Ibid.

4. New Child Support Rules for Self-Employed Parents, 8 March 1999. The Inland Revenue will be able to provide earnings information where the parent fails to supply the necessary information, <http://www.dss.gov.uk/hq/press/press399/053.htm>.

5. 'CSA to lose lone parents on low pay', *Guardian*, 8 March 1999, p. 10.

6. General Household Survey, Office for National Statistics, *Social Trends 27* (1997), fig. 2.9.

7. *Children Come First* (Cm 1264, 1990).

8. Jonathan Bradshaw and Jane Millar, *Lone Parent Families in the UK*, DSS Research Report No. 6, 1991, Chapter 6.

9. Ibid.

10. For details see *National Welfare Benefits Handbook* CPAG Guide. It was known as 'supplementary benefit' until 1986.

11. Angela Hopkinson, *Single Mothers: The First Year, A Scottish Study of Mothers Bringing Up Their Children On Their Own*, Scottish Council for Single Parents, 1984.

12. Martin Evans, *Giving Credit Where it's Due? The Success of Family Credit Reassessed*, LSE, 1996; research period covered preceded the introduction of the Child Support Act.

13. Joan C. Brown, *Children in Social Security*, Policy Studies Institute, 1984.

14. Roy Sainsbury, Sandra Hutton and John Ditch, *Changing Lives and the Role of Income Support*, DSS Research Report No. 45, 1996; research period covered preceded the introduction of the Child Support Act.

15. Anna Leeming, Judith Unell and Robert Walker, *Lone Mothers*, DSS Research Report No. 30, 1994, Chapter 7; research period covered preceded the introduction of the Child Support Act.

16. Stephen McKay and Alan Marsh, *Lone Parents and Work*, DSS Research

Report No. 25, 1994; research period covered preceded the introduction of the Child Support Act.

17. Reuben Ford, Alan Marsh and Stephen McKay, *Changes in Lone Parenthood 1989–1993*, DSS Research Report No. 40, 1995.

18. Bradshaw and Millar, *Lone Parent Families in the UK*.

19. Jonathan Bradshaw, John Ditch, Hilary Holmes and Peter Whiteford, *Support for Children – a Comparison of Arrangements in Fifteen Countries*, DSS Research Report No. 21, 1993; Jo Roll, *Lone Parent Families in the European Community*, European Family and Social Policy Unit, 1992.

20. M. Maclean and J. Eekelaar, 'Child Support: The British Solution', *International Journal of Law and the Family*, Vol. 7, 1993, p. 205; see also G. Barton and G. Douglas, *Law and Parenthood*, Butterworths, London, 1995, Chapter 9.

21. Mavis Maclean, 'The Origins of Child Support in Britain and the Case for a Strong Child Support System', in R. Ford and J. Millar (eds), *Private Lives and Public Responses*, Policy Studies Institute, 1998.

22. [1990] 2 Fam 457.

23. Maclean, 'The Origins of Child Support in Britain and the Case for a Strong Child Support System'.

24. *Child Support: The Legislation*, Sweet & Maxwell, 1993.

25. Andrew Lockyer and Frederick Stone, *Juvenile Justice in Scotland*, T & T Clark, Edinburgh, 1998, pp. 107 ff.

26. Wilson, 'The Bairns of Falkirk: The Child Support Act 1991', 1991 SLT (News), p. 417.

27. House of Lords, Official Report, 25 February 1991, col. 817 for a critical perspective per Lord Simon.

28. Section 6(2).

29. Section 2.

30. Mark Speed, Christine Roberts and Kai Rudat, *Child Support Unit National Client Survey 1992*, DSS Research Report No. 14, 1993.

31. It is not intended in a work of this kind to deal with all the immensely complex calculation issues raised by the 1991 Act. For such a treatment see Butterworth's *Scottish Family Law Service* and *Child Support Handbook* (CPAG).

32. HC 470 (1994), *The Operation of the Child Support Act: Proposals for Change*, House of Commons Social Security Committee, Fifth Report 1993–94, London: HMSO, p. 81; S. Parker, 'Child Support in Australia: Children's Rights or Public Interest?' *International Journal of Law and the Family*, 5, 1991, p. 24; M. Harrison, 'The reformed Australian child support: an international policy comment', *Journal of Family Issues*, 12, 1991, p. 430.

33. M. Henaghan and B. Atkin, *Family Law Policy in New Zealand*, 1992.

34. Loc. cit. at para 57 – Australia – 1 child 18 per cent; 2 – 27 per cent; 3 – 32 per cent; 4 – 34 per cent; 5+ – 36 per cent; New Zealand 1 – 18 per cent; 2 – 24 per cent; 3 – 27 per cent; 4 + – 30 per cent.

35. Discussed in G. Davis, N. Wikeley, R. Young, J. Barron and J. Bedward, *Report of a Study of the Child Support Agency*, Nuffield Foundation, 1997, p. 6.

36. J. Pearson, 'Legislating Adequacy: The Impact of Child Support Guidelines', *Law and Society Review*, 23, 1989, p. 569.

37. S. Abel and E. Sussman, 'Child Support Guidelines: A Comparison of New York, New Jersey and Connecticut: A Synopsis', *Family and Conciliation Courts Review*, 33, 1995, p. 426; J. Pearson, 'Child Support in the United States: The Experience in Colorado', *International Journal of Law and Family*, 6, 1991, p. 321.

38. M. Ray, 'Child Support: Class Biases, State Interests and the Judicial Response', paper delivered at the Law and Society Annual Meeting, June 1994.

39. Ibid.

40. M. Rogers, 'Use of the Texas Marriage Licence Statutes as a Child Support Collection Device does not Violate Equal Protection', *Baylor Law Review*, 48, 1996, p. 1153.

41. P. Monopoli, '"Deadbeat dads": Should Support and Inheritance be Linked?', *University of Miami Law Review*, 257, 1994.

42. 'Where Wisconsin goes, can the world follow?', *The Economist*, 1 November 1997, p. 25.

43. Such as Marion County Prosecutor's Office Child Support Division, Indianapolis, Indiana, charging a one-off $25 dollar fee for non-welfare clients.

44. R. Landers, 'Prosecutorial Limits on Overlapping Federal and State Jurisdiction', *Annals of the American Academy of Political and Social Science*, Vol. 543, 1996, p. 64.

45. The organizations have official-sounding names and include the Child Support Assistance Network, the Child Support Network and the National Child Support Network.

46. M. Fine and D. Fine, 'An Examination and Evaluation of Recent Changes in Divorce Laws in Five Western Countries: The Critical Role of Values', *Journal of Marriage and the Family*, 56, 1994, p. 249.

47. Ibid.

48. E. Zweibel, 'Child Support Policy and Child Support Guidelines: Broadening the Agenda', *Canadian Journal of Women and the Law*, 6, 1993, p. 371.

49. 'MR = AG – CB: the algebra of care', *Guardian*, 15 May 1998.

50. *Children Come First* (Cm 1264, 1990).

51. Section 6(1).

52. *R* v. *Secretary of State for Social Security ex p Lloyd* [1995] 1 FLR 856 (QBD).

53. *Secretary of State for Social Security* v. *Harmon*, *The Times*, 10 June 1998.

54. Section 46(3).

55. Section 46(5).

56. CS (MAP) reg 36.

57. Ibid.

58. CS (MAP) reg 36 (as amended).

59. CCS/1037/1995 (starred 10/96).

60. But see CCS/12609/1996 (starred 78/96) – good cause where daughter knew her father but not that he had another family.

61. HC 440 (1996), *Child Support: Good Cause and the Benefit Penalty*, Social Security Committee, Fourth Report, Session 1995–96, London: HMSO, p. vii.

62. E. Knights, C. Blackwell, S. Cox and A. Garnham, *A Child Support Handbook*, CPAG (6th edn), 1998, p. 93.

63. HC 440, *Child Support: Good Cause and the Benefit Penalty*, p. vii.

64. E. Knights, *A Child Support Handbook*, p. 93.

65. Ibid.

66. *The Requirement to Co-operate: A Report on the Operation of the 'Good Cause' Provisions*, DSS, April 1996.

67. HC 440, *Child Support: Good Cause and the Benefit Penalty*.

68. *Improving Child Support*, Cm 2745 (1994).

69. *Child Support Departure Direction and Consequential Amendments Regulations 1996* (SI 1996 No. 2907).

70. Six kinds of costs are specified in the regulations: (1) costs incurred in travelling to work, (2) costs incurred in maintaining contact with a child or children covered by the maintenance assessment, (3) costs attributable to a long-term illness or disability of the applicant or dependant of the applicant, (4) debts incurred before the absent parent became an absent parent where these debts were for the joint benefit of both parents or for the benefit of the child involved, (5) pre-1993 financial arrangements from which it is impossible for the parent concerned to withdraw or from which it would be unreasonable to expect the parent to withdraw, and (6) costs incurred by a parent in supporting a child who is not his child but who is part of his family.

71. DDCA reg 25.

72. DDCA reg 25(3).

73. DDCA reg 23(2)(a).

74. DDCA reg 24.

75. DDCA reg 26.

76. DDCA reg 27.

77. Cmd 3992 1998 – the comment period lasted until 30 November.

78. Foreword by Prime Minister Blair, p 1.

79. HC 983 (1993), *The Operation of the Child Support Act*, Social Security Committee First Report, Session 1992-93, London: HMSO.

80. HC 470, *The Operation of the Child Support Act: Proposals for Change*.

81. *Annual Report of the Chief Support Officer 1993–94*, London: HMSO, 1994.

82. *Annual Report of the Chief Support Officer 1994–95*, London: HMSO, 1995.

83. G. Davis, N. Wikeley and R. Young with J. Barron and J. Bedward, *Child Support in Action*, Oxford: Hart, 1998, Chapter 4.

84. *First Report of the Social Security Committee, 1993-94*, Cm 2469, HMSO, February 1994.

85. (i) the £8 element in the protected income be increased to either £20, £30 or even £40 to allow paid absent parents to work, to increase incentives to work and not to be restricted to particular categories of expenses; (ii) payments of assessments should be phased in over a period of up to two years; (iii) allowance to be made

EDITIONS LE PRINTEMPS LTEE

4, Route du Club Vacaos,
Ile Maurice.
Tel: 6961017 - 6862647
Fax: 6867302

1er Etage
Mamode Ally Court
Desforges Street, Port-Louis.
Tel./Fax: 2403578

VAT Reg. No. VAT 20086379

N° 62597 **SALES INVOICE** CASH/CREDIT

Name of Customer: VIMLA LUTCHMUN Date: 30/09/04

Address U.O.M Reduit Tel No.

Qty	Details	Rs	Cs	Rs	Cs
1	Law and Poverty - the legal system and Poverty reduction Author :- Williams/ Kjonstad / Robson			299	

B.L.P LTEE
PAID
DATE:
CASH/CHEQUE No.:
AMOUNT. 299

already paid

| | | Total | 299 | |

Delivered by

Checked by

Customer's Sig

Terms of Payment

Printed by: A. B. PRINTING, VACOAS Tel: 6962183

for stepchildren in calculation of exempt income; (iv) consideration to be given to reduction of care element in maintenance requirement once children reached age of 11; (v) there was no sensible way of calculating current values of past capital settlements in order to take account of them in the formula; (vi) if absent parents return the ME forms within two weeks of issue liability for maintenance should begin from the date of assessment; (vii) amendments to the citizens' charter for the Agency should include a 28-day appeal period.

86. HC 69 (1993), *The Operation of the Child Support Act*, House of Commons Social Security Committee First Report 1993–94, London: HMSO.

87. HC 470, *The Operation of the Child Support Act: Proposals for Change*, p. 81.

88. Ibid.

89. HC 303 (1994–95), *The Operation of the Child Support Act*, London: HMSO.

90. HC 440, *Child Support: Good Cause and the Benefit Penalty*.

91. Ibid., p. v.

92. HC 50, *The Performance and Operation of the Child Support Agency*, House of Commons Social Security Committee, Second Report 1995–96, London: HMSO.

93. CSA, *The First Two Years*.

94. Parliamentary Commissioner for Administration (1995), *Investigation of Complaints against the Child Support Agency*, Third Report, Session 1994–95, London: HMSO.

95. Ibid.

96. NAO (1995), Child Support Agency Memorandum by the Comptroller and Auditor General to the House of Commons Public Accounts Committee, within Committee of Public Accounts First Report on the Child Support Agency (HC 31, 1995).

97. Davis et al., *Report of a Study of the Child Support Agency*, p. 50.

98. Speed et al., *Child Support Unit National Client Survey 1992*.

99. P. Daniel and E. Burgess, *The Child Support Act: The Voice of Low Income Parents with Care*, London: Social Responsibility Department, Diocese of Southwark, 1994; K. Clarke, G. Craig, C. Glendinning and M. Thompson, *Children Come First? The Child Support Act and Lone Parent Families*, London: Barnardo's, Children's Society, NCH, NSPCC, SCF, 1994; National Council for One Parent Families, *The Child Support Agency's First Year: The Lone Parent Case*, London: NCOPF, 1994; National Association of Citizens Advice Bureaux, *Child Support: One Year On*, London: NACAB, 1994.

100. D. Abbott, 'The Child Support Act 1991: The Lives of Parents with Care Living in Liverpool', *Journal of Social Welfare and Family Law*, 18, 1996, p. 21.

101. Ibid., p. 33; see also E. Kempson, A. Bryson and K. Rowlingson, *Hard Times? How Poor Families Make Ends Meet*, London: Policy Studies Institute, 1994.

102. Davis et al., *Child Support in Action*.

103. C. Glendinning, K. Clarke and G. Craig, 'Implementing the Child Support Act', *Journal of Social Welfare and Family Law*, 18, 1996, p. 273.

104. Ibid., p. 275.

105. *Children Come First*, Cm. 1264, Vols I and II, London, HMSO, Vol. I, para 1.

106. Glendinning et al., 'Implementing the Child Support Act'.

107. See above, cf. notes 36–41.

108. R. Collier, 'The Campaign Against the Child Support Act: "Errant Fathers" and "Family Men"', *Family Law*, 384, 1994.

109. Davis et al., *Report of a Study of the Child Support Agency*, p. 64.

110. Ibid., p. 95.

111. Ibid., p. 69.

112. Ibid., p. 95.

113. Child Support Agency Quarterly Summary of Statistics for November 1998 published 11 February 1999 <http://www.dss.gov.uk/hq/press/press299/032.htm>.

114. Means-tested benefit for those not involved in waged work.

115. Means-tested benefit for those in low-paid waged work.

116. Collier, 'The Campaign Against the Child Support Act: "Errant Fathers" and "Family Men"'.

117. *Express*, Tuesday, 30 June 1998, 'Ex-wife hired hitman to keep up life of luxury' – the wife was sentenced to three and half years for soliciting to murder.

118. NACAB, *Child Support: One Year On*.

119. CPAG, *Putting the Treasury First*, 1994.

120. NCOPF, *The Child Support Agency's First Year: The Lone Parent Case*.

121. K. Clarke, C. Glendinning and G. Craig, *Losing Support: Children and the Child Support Act*, Barnardo's, The Children's Society, NCH Action for Children, National Society for the Prevention of Cruelty to Children, Save the Children, 1994.

122. All gave evidence prior to the publication of the Green Paper, *Improving Child Support*. See also Julia Brosnan, 'Men behaving sadly', *New Statesman and Society*, Vol. 8, 4 August 1995, p. 16 on the formation of the Cheltenham Group to have the Child Support Act repealed.

123. Cmd 3992, 1998.

124. *Nacsa News*, Issue 2, 1998, Milton Keynes.

125. K. Clarke, C. Glendinning and G. Craig, 'Supporting Children? The Impact of the Child Support Act on Lone Mothers and Children', in Ford and Millar (eds), *Private Lives and Public Responses*.

126. J. Josephson, 'Public Policy as if Women Mattered: Improving the Child Support System for Women on AFDC', *Women and Politics*, Vol. 17, 1997, p. 1.

127. P. Bingley, G. Lanot and E. Symons, 'The Child Support Reform and the Labor Supply of Lone Mothers in the United Kingdom', *Journal Human Resources*, 30, 1995, p. 256.

128. L. Keiser, 'The Influence of Women's Political Power on Bureaucratic Output: the Case of Child Support Enforcement', *British Journal of Political Science*, 27, 1997, p. 136.

129. 'MR = AG – CB: the algebra of care', *Guardian*, 15 May 1998.

130. J. Millar and R. Ford, 'Lone Parenthood and Future Policy', in Ford and Millar (eds), *Private Lives and Public Responses*.

131. S. Millns, 'Legislative Constructions of Motherhood', *Parliamentary Affairs*, 49, 1996, p. 161.

132. J. Millar, 'State, Family and Personal Responsibility: the Changing Balance for Lone Mothers in the United Kingdom', *Feminist Review*, 24, 1994; L. Harding, *Family, State and Social Policy*, Macmillan, Basingstoke, 1996.

133. B. Simpson, 'On Gifts, Payments and Disputes: Divorces and Changing Family Structures in Contemporary Britain', *Journal of the Royal Anthropological Institute*, 3, 1997, p. 731.

134. Davis et al., *Report of a Study of the Child Support Agency*, p. 95.

135. Schedule 1 Part I para 2.

136. Schedule 1 Part I para 3.

137. Schedule 1 Part I para 4.

138. Schedule 1 Part I para 7.

139. Schedule 1 Part I para 8.

140. Schedule 1 Part I para 9.

141. Schedule 1 Part I para 10.

142. CSPSSA 2000 Section 3.

143. CSPSSA 2000 Section 4.

144. CSPSSA 2000 Section 5.

145. CSPSSA 2000 Section 5 inserting Section 28C into the Child Support Act 1991.

146. Section 28F(1)(b) (as inserted).

147. Section 28F(2)(a) and (b) (as inserted).

148. Section 28B(2)(a), (b) and (c) (as inserted).

149. Paragraph 4(2) (as inserted by Schedule 2).

150. Paragraph 5(4) and (5) (as inserted by Schedule 2).

151. CSPSSA 2000 section 13 (inserting Section 14A into the Child Support Act 1991).

152. Section 14A(2) and (5).

153. Section 14A(4).

154. CSPSSA 2000 Section 14 (inserting Section 15 into the Child Support Act 1991).

155. Section 15(4A) (as inserted).

156. Section 15(11) (as inserted).

157. CSPSSA 2000 section 16 (inserting Sections 39A and 40B into the Child Support Act 1991).

158. Section 40B(1) (as inserted).

159. Section 39A(3) (as inserted).

160. Section 40A(as inserted).

161. Section 40A(5) (as inserted).

162. Section 40A(3) (as inserted).

163. CSPSSA 2000 Section 18 (inserting Section 41A into the Child Support Act 1991).

164. Section 41A(2) (as inserted).

165. CSPSSA 2000 Section 20 (inserting Section 28J into the Child Support Act 1991).

FIVE | The state, laws and NGOs in Bangladesh

MOKBUL MORSHED AHMAD

§ This chapter first outlines the overall situation of non-government organizations (NGOs)[1] in Bangladesh, then sets out the legal issues in detail and finally makes proposals for improvements. State–NGO relations in Bangladesh have moved through stages of indifference and ambivalence (White 1999; cf. Sen 1999 on India). In other parts of the Muslim world, the state has in general been sceptical or strict towards NGOs, human rights and community groups (Huband et al. 1999; Huband 1999; Galpin 1999). When the government of Bangladesh tried to control the activities of NGOs, the donors[2] put pressure on the state. The government then responded by imposing more paperwork on the NGOs, thus increasing their transaction costs. The state has failed to make NGOs more transparent, functionally or financially. So NGOs can easily violate laws both because of the weakness of the state and because their own strength over time has been fortified by the donors. This is a complex area, weighing the cultural, often gendered, concerns of the state against NGOs, whose interests are not necessarily those of local grassroots organizations, but of external donors.

NGOS IN BANGLADESH

Since the independence of Bangladesh in 1971, the state has largely failed to assist the poor or reduce poverty, while NGOs have grown dramatically, ostensibly to fill this gap. The Association of Development Agencies in Bangladesh (ADAB) had a total membership of 886 NGOs/PVDOs (Private Voluntary Development Organizations) in December 1997, of which 231 were central and 655 chapter (local) members (ADAB 1998); the ADAB *Directory* lists 1,007 NGOs, including 376 non-member NGOs. The NGO Affairs Bureau of the Government of Bangladesh (GOB), which has to approve all foreign grants to NGOs working in Bangladesh, released grants worth about

US$250 million in the financial year (FY) 1996/97 to 1,132 NGOs, of which 997 are local and 135 are foreign (NGO Affairs Bureau 1998). NGOs have mainly functioned to service the needs of the landless, usually assisted by foreign donor funding as a counterpoint to the state's efforts (Lewis 1993).

Some NGOs have shown success in providing services such as education, health and microfinance to their clients and promoting human rights, particularly women's rights. This has been accompanied by a backlash from the local elite, religious leaders and organizations (Rafi and Chowdhury 2000; Shehabuddin 1999).

But NGOs in Bangladesh have not originated from grassroot organizations (GROs) in civil society; rather, it is NGO workers who set up groups, which clients then join to get microcredit and other services. Most Bangladeshi NGOs are totally dependent upon foreign funds. The volume of foreign funds to NGOs in Bangladesh has been increasing over the years and stood at just under 18 per cent of all foreign 'aid' to the country in FY 1995/96. Donors increased their funding from 464 NGO projects in 1990/91 to 746 in 1996/97, a 60 per cent increase in six years; the total amount disbursed showed a 143 per cent increase over the period (NGO Affairs Bureau 1998). However, the disbursement of funds to NGOs is highly skewed. The top fifteen NGOs accounted for 84 per cent of all allocation to NGOs in 1991/92, and 70 per cent in 1992/93 (Hashemi 1995). NGO dependence on donor grants has kept the whole operation highly subsidized by foreign capital. For example, the annual working costs of BRAC's (Bangladesh Rural Advancement Committee, one of the largest NGOs in Bangladesh) branch-level units are still more than three times their locally generated income (Montgomery et al. 1996).

THE STATE AND THE LAW

Legal status of NGOs, past and present

Since 1860, the state has attempted to regulate NGOs.[3] The most significant steps of the Ershad government regarding NGOs were the abolition of the NGO Standing Committee, the creation of the NGO Affairs Bureau (NAB) and the appointment of an Adviser for NGO Affairs with ministerial status (White 1999). The NAB started functioning effectively from 1 March 1990. It was headed by a Director General and became the contact point between the state and various foreign and local NGOs receiving foreign donations. As all NGO activities came under the purview of the 'President's Secretariat Public

Division', NGOs were supposed to be regulated by the NAB instead of the Department of Social Welfare. Within a short period of time, the Bureau had shown promise by its quick clearance of NGO applications, discussed below. However, the procedures still remain complex and need further improvement.

Specifically, the state in Bangladesh requires each NGO to register formally with NAB, and to renew this registration every five years. Each project must be approved in advance by the NAB, as must all foreign funding. Each NGO must receive all funding through a single, specific bank account, and the bank must submit full reports to the central bank, which then reports to the NAB and to the Economic Relations Division (ERD) of the Finance Ministry. The NAB also regulates the use of foreign consultants. For projects and programmes of disaster-relief, requirements are similar but the NAB must decide more rapidly. Each NGO must submit annual auditor's reports to the NAB, having appointed its auditors from the list approved by the NAB. Penalties for false statements, failure to submit declarations or other contraventions of the law include heavy fines payable by the NGO and/or imprisonment of NGO directors. The transaction costs for NGOs in securing permissions and approvals are very high, in both avoidable delays and unnecessary paperwork. Far too much unnecessary information is required, usually in multiple copies.

State regulations define the term 'voluntary activity' as an activity undertaken, with partial or complete support from external sources, by any person or organization to render voluntary services pertaining to agricultural, relief, missionary, educational, cultural, vocational, social welfare and other developmental activities in the country. Although the definition seems to cover almost all kinds of voluntary activities, the state retains the right to include or exclude any activity as 'voluntary'.[4] The state apparently intended to widen the scope of the definition in order to prevent both the donors and recipients from making or receiving grants/donations in contravention of official ordinances.[5]

Ordinances/regulations/circulars vest the NAB with all its responsibilities regarding coordination, regulation and monitoring of foreign and foreign-assisted non-government voluntary organizations and individuals working in Bangladesh.[6] While considering the application for registration, the NAB is required to seek approval from the Home Ministry.[7]

Projects may be for one or several years. NGOs can submit a five-year project proposal, commensurate with an identified priority area of the five-year plan of the state. The NAB arranges approval and release of the funds on a priority basis for such projects. The targets specified in the project proposal, however, must be achieved within the stipulated period. Usually funds for the following year can be released for the project if its implementation strategy and achievement of target for the year are considered to be satisfactory by the Bureau (Circular: Section 7 [h]: 1993).

Existing NGO regulations make an exception for projects for assistance to disaster-affected areas. For disaster rehabilitation pro-grammes, NGOs have to submit their project proposal with requisite details on a prescribed proforma FD-6 (Circular: Section 7.1[a]: 1993). The NAB communicates its decisions with 21 days from the day of the receipt of the project proposal and forwards it to the relevant ministry for its opinion. The ministry must send its decision to the NAB within fourteen days (Circular: Section 7.1[b]: 1993).

The state and its machinery have from time to time introduced several rules and procedures, but, due to their complexity and the weakness of the state, NGOs can easily evade them. The rules for receipt and use of foreign donations[8] and the banking transactions of NGOs[9] are interesting examples:

Submission of annual reports: NGOs are required to prepare annual reports on their activities within three months of the end of the financial year and send copies to the NAB, ERD, the relevant ministry, Divisional Commissioner(s), Deputy Commissioners and the Bangladesh Bank.

Power of inspection: The state may, at any time, inspect the accounts and other documents of NGOs. The state may require the NGO to submit a declaration as notified in the official gazette (Ordinance XLVI: Section 4[1]: 1978). Failure to produce any accounts or other docu-ments or failure to furnish any statement or information by the NGO is a contravention of state regulations (Ordinance XLVI: Section 4[3]: 1978). The NAB has the responsibility and power to audit and inspect the accounts of NGOs (Circular: Section 10[a]: 1993). The accounts of any NGO must be audited by the person/s appointed by the relevant NGO or persons enlisted/approved by the NAB. Audit reports must be submit-ted to the NAB within two months of the end of the financial year.

The above description gives a picture of the manner/procedure regarding the way the state of Bangladesh regulates those NGOs that finance charitable work through foreign donations. The donor agencies led by the World Bank (WB) have strongly supported the formulation of the state's policy on NGOs, particularly in the direction of streamlining the administrative and legal framework within which NGOs operate, to increase their effectiveness (Zaren 1996).

NGOs in Bangladesh have increasingly become subject to question and criticism from the government, political parties, intellectuals and the public in general. Recently there have been allegations of misuse of funds, gender discrimination and nepotism lodged against GSS (Gano Shahajyo Sangstha), a large NGO. State and private donor investigations found that the rural female workers of GSS were compelled to go on maternity leave without pay. They also found that GSS bought lands worth millions of Taka[10] to build its headquarters in Dhaka. Based on this information, the donors also stopped funding the GSS (Kabir 1999; NFB 1999c).

During the long process of NGO development in Bangladesh, many NGOs have certainly enriched themselves with structures and buildings, while empowerment of the poor, beyond better services, has been rather limited. Recently, NGO activities and expenditures came under fire in the national Parliament and other fora (*Daily Star*, 1999b; NFB 1999d). One Member of Parliament alleged that some NGOs raised money on false promises of jobs and credit, but instead misappropriated it. Another MP claimed that some NGOs make loans at the high rate of 14 per cent and resort to 'inhuman torture' on debtors who fail to repay on time (NFB 1999a). The relevant minister gave a face-saving answer to all these allegations but in reality there is poor control by the state over NGOs in Bangladesh. This was reiterated by the head of NAB on another occasion (NFB 1999b).

It is possible for any powerful NGO deliberately to manipulate the Home Ministry or any relevant ministry when it has not delivered an opinion within the stipulated time (as mentioned in Circular 1993) so that the application may be passed without any objection.

According to law,[11] no person or organization may receive or spend foreign loans/grants without prior state approval. The NAB Report submitted to the Prime Minister's Secretariat in 1992 stated that various NGOs had disbursed 1.5 billion Taka without prior state permission in the financial year 1990/91. Quite often, large amounts of money come into the country illegally. The Salvation Army received 12.5 million Taka without state approval (Report of the NAB for the Prime Minister 1992); similarly, 'Sheba Shongho' spent 13.5 million Taka without state approval, and the 'Finnish Free Mission' also violated state instructions (Report-1, 18 August 1992; as reported in *Bhorer Kagoj* [Bangladeshi daily newspaper], 29 October 1992.)

The Report of the NAB for the Prime Minister (1992) found that senior officials of some NGOs quite often travel abroad and, without state approval, obtain foreign donations. According to the Report, the accounts provided by the NGOs may fail to match those provided by the Bangladesh Bank although, according to law,[12] if any organization wants to carry out a charitable programme, it should receive any foreign currency through an approved bank in Bangladesh. This restriction was imposed to give the state a true picture of the total amount of foreign currency in the hands of NGOs. Yet, according to another Act,[13] an organization or person can bring any amount of foreign currency into Bangladesh. Therefore, as a result of this dual system, no one is able to know the total amount of foreign currency actually received by any NGO.

According to a nineteenth-century Act,[14] voluntary societies cannot undertake business-oriented projects. The same Act also provides that, upon the dissolution of the society and payment of all its debts and liabilities, no property whatsoever shall be paid to or distributed among the members of the society but should be vested in a managing committee. In a 1961 Ordinance there is a provision for gaining profit in order to create job opportunities. Both the Act and the Ordinance apply to the same cases. As a consequence, some NGOs are flourishing simultaneously as service-oriented organizations and as profit-oriented business organizations. The state is also being deprived of taxes by NGOs taking advantage of loopholes in the regulations. Some senior officials of certain NGOs have used loopholes to become affluent.[15]

BRAC is currently alleged to be running successful businesses like a commercial organization, contrary to its charitable status. BRAC's cold storage, press, a marketing organization named 'Aarong', a real estate company, and a restaurant are highly profitable. Recently BRAC has received state approval to open a commercial bank for microlending (*Financial Times*, 11 December 1998). BRAC provides no accounts of its commercial organizations' income or expenditure to any state department. White (1999) points out that BRAC generates 31 per cent of its income from its business sources. As BRAC is not registered under the Ordinance of 1961, if it dissolves then all its property will be vested in the managing committee. BRAC possesses more than fifty modern automobiles (Zarren 1996).

The Report of the NAB for the Prime Minister (1992) levels a complaint against PROSHIKA, another large NGO. Although PROSHIKA is registered under the 1961 Ordinance, it none the less has developed a transport company of twenty-eight buses at a cost of 30 million Taka. At a cost of 15 million Taka, PROSHIKA has also established a press and a garment industry and is investing 5 million Taka in a video library. Recently it has started an Internet and software business.

In some cases, service-oriented NGO projects are basically market-oriented, with the objective of earning profits through long-term capital investment. BRAC's cold storage project (costing 70 million Taka) and Savar Ganosastha Kendro's (GK, another large NGO) highly profitable clinic, university and medicine businesses are striking examples. Allegations have also been made against GSS, another large NGO which used donors' funds to open a printing press and media business without being audited and taxed as per rules of the state. The Report also pointed out that profits from these commercial ventures of NGOs are not taxed and not always used for their clients, since NGOs depend on donors for their 'development' projects (Kabir 1999).

Report of the NAB for the Prime Minister (1992) states that ADAB's dishonesty is evident as it has several bank accounts. The holding of several bank accounts is a violation of a state rule, which requires that NGOs receive foreign donations through a single bank account (Regulation Rules: Section 4[4]: 1978). The power to appoint any state-registered firm as an auditor is currently vested in the NGOs themselves; it is alleged that this has resulted in auditors giving favourable reports on their clients. The NAB is further reported to have two audit supervisors but not a single auditor, so that the state is unable to obtain a clear picture of the actual status of NGOs in the country. Due to poor capacity of NAB, only a random sample of audit reports are examined, so most NGOs are not reviewed.

After audit and inspection, if a complaint is lodged against an NGO, virtually no appropriate action is taken. Usually a note is passed to the NGO to correct the error, which is a trivial remedial measure. Due to the strong support of donors for NGOs, in the recent past the state has had to scrap its own desire to withdraw the registration of a number of NGOs and even had to change the head of the NAB when that individual appeared to take a tough line with NGOs that had indulged in irregularities (Hashemi 1995). When the NAB cancelled the registration of three NGOs for financial irregularities, the head of a diplomatic mission in Dhaka personally intervened, brought the issue to the attention of the Prime Minister's office and got the cancellation order withdrawn. This action created great dissatisfaction among the officials of the Bureau (Hashemi 1995).

As NGOs are heavily dependent on foreign resources, the flow of money from the outside, in the absence of accountability, can make the NGOs corrupt, controversial and autocratic (Zarren 1996). Despite the negative effects, ironically real in many cases, NGOs are accountable to the donor countries rather than the state of Bangladesh (Islam 1995).

In reality, the state is unable to control NGOs. The NGOs often work against the directions and decisions of the state. Weak administration on the one hand and strong national and international backing on the other encourage some NGOs to defy the state and to work according to their own whims. In the recent past, the registration of ADAB was cancelled by the NAB but reinstated within a few hours. A powerful international lobby naturally achieved this. There is a tug of war between the NAB and the Social Welfare Directorate which gives the NGOs opportunities to break the rules (*Daily Inquilab*, 23 September 1992; *Daily Sangbad*, 6 January 1993).

RECOMMENDATIONS

The following recommendations would improve the existing legal status of NGOs in Bangladesh by reducing bureaucracy, removing legal contradictions and making NGOs more accountable and transparent.

State Rules, Acts and Ordinances should be replaced or modified to reflect the current critical atmosphere.[16] The state should remove all administrative and procedural bottlenecks created through promulgation of various Ordinances and streamline the existing working procedures, enabling NGOs to complete all formalities within the shortest time possible. The state should evaluate the strength and weakness of current measures for regulating NGOs and ensure promulgation of flexible and effective rules and regulations.

Improving NGO efficiency

It takes more than two months to prepare renewal papers for an NGO registration, which, in any event, are not thoroughly scrutinized. Because the state has the authority to cancel the registration of any NGO or stop its activities and inform the donor, in any case of serious allegations, once a NGO is registered, renewal procedures should be simplified.

Some of the foreign donation (FD) forms and procedures followed by the NAB are complex and cumbersome. The application forms and procedures should be simplified through discussion between the GOB and NGOs. With regard to registration, the Home Ministry should grant approval or disapproval within sixty days of receiving the application from the NAB. An application for the appointment of expatriates or extension of tenure should be decided within twenty-five days. The NAB should send reminders to the National Security Intelligence (NSI).

Appropriate action should be taken by the administrative ministries, divisions and departments to give their advice to the NAB within twenty-one days with regard to approval of NGO projects.

To enable NGOs to prepare budgets and implement projects within the time limit of a financial year, if the report about a particular NGO is satisfactory, then the NGO could be given clearance for other projects in the same year without further investigation by the NAB.

The existing procedure that requires projects and clearance of funds to be annually approved by the state should be changed. NGOs which have approval for a project should be able to use foreign funds until the project is completed, without annual renewal. Since the funds must be received through specific NGO bank accounts, the state will be able to monitor the flow of foreign funds to the NGO sector and to each NGO. It will be the business of NAB officials to check whether an NGO has several bank accounts.

The National Security Intelligence (NSI) should be aware of each NGO's activities so that it is ready to comment on an application without further inquiry. If the NGO has done anything highly objectionable during the last thirty years since Bangladesh became independent, it should be closed and the relevant donor informed.

For NAB approval of projects, NGOs should be required to submit the names of its board members and/or executive committee and the number of staff positions in each category. Staff names, however, should not be required.

Improving the law

According to a circular of 1993,[17] 'No such project would be approved if it offends the feelings of the people of any religion, has adverse effects on the culture and values of the country or if the project is based on a political programme.' Nearly 90 per cent of the laws in Bangladesh are secular. But approximately 87 per cent of the population is Muslim (BBS 1998) and Islam is the state religion in Bangladesh. Therefore, there are legal problems in Bangladesh arising from unresolved conflicts in the law. While women's independence and empowerment programmes are against the beliefs of many strict Muslims, 'gender development' is now a leading concern of Western donors. So, a specific political party could firmly resist women's development and NGOs would have to end women's development programmes (Chazan 1998). This would be an unethical as well as undesirable result.

For example, recently unrest started when Islamic teachers and students organized a general strike in a north-eastern town of Bangladesh and demonstrators attacked a rally of NGO women clients and set fire to the offices of several NGOs. Several individuals were injured. The rally had been organized by NGOs that had lent money to millions of poor Bangladeshi women to start small shops or businesses such as poultry breeding and weaving. Several thousand women who benefited from such loans took part in the rally. Islamic groups said they objected to women taking part in celebrations to commemorate the 1971 victory over Pakistan that led to the independence of Bangladesh. But NGOs said that the fundamentalists had objected to Muslim women going out to work. Human rights groups urged the state to take action against Islamic fundamentalists who attacked women taking part in a rally to commemorate the country's independence struggle (Chazan 1998). Another similar conflict erupted in Faridpur, a district town in central Bangladesh (*Daily Star* 1999a). Given the unrest, the state should take a stronger role in regulating NGOs. Without defining what kinds of programme would affect native culture or offend people of any religion, it should ensure that NGOs are connected to grassroots organizations and accountable when representing their interests.

There is supposed to be an investigation[18] as to whether an NGO is involved in any political or anti-cultural activity under the guise of a development programme. Currently, CARITAS is involved in consciousness-raising by making people aware of their rights, teaching them to be independent and morally strong, thereby empowering people at the grassroots level. This is not a crime; few people see empowering individuals as an anti-state activity. This section of the circular should therefore be modified.

Indeed, it is very difficult to draw the line between freedom of NGOs to raise important class/race/gender issues that may be unpopular with some governments and NGOs that are not responsive to local needs. The success of NGOs lies within their capacity to make changes in the lives of their clients; so making structural changes may be risky but should be an important agenda for the NGOs. At the same time the role of Northern NGOs should be to help their Southern partners and make their voices heard by the Northern people and policy-makers. This may change the attitudes and policies of the donors. This is an important role for Northern NGOs, which should be taken seriously.

Holding NGOs accountable

The state audit system is ineffective. A mechanism must be developed under which the state officials involved in the development process make regular field visits to NGO programmes. Such state officials should also conduct impact evaluations upon the completion of a project to enhance the state's understanding of the programme dynamics and the operation of NGOs.

Commercial activities of NGOs should be duly taxed and profits from them should be used for development work. The law should be changed accordingly and NAB should make sure that it is implemented properly. In conformity with law, immediate legal action ought to be taken against the officials of several NGOs who are involved in misappropriation, embezzlement or accused of misconduct, irregularity or law-breaking.

Theoretically, the state is accountable to Parliament and ultimately to the public for its activities and programmes, but NGOs remain unaccountable. This is unacceptable. NGOs must be regulated by Parliament, at least in terms of accountability and transparency. If the government can remain above narrow party interests and if the opposition party can remain strong and responsible, then an effective parliamentary committee could be created to scrutinize and evaluate the activities and programmes of the NGOs.

CONCLUSION

In Bangladesh, NGOs play a pivotal and pragmatic role when the state does not reach the poor and meet their needs. Despite their numbers, NGOs have brought little change in levels of poverty. Even the largest NGOs in Bangladesh taken together cover only a fraction of the population: perhaps only 10–20 per cent of landless households (Hashemi 1995). This highlights the need to reach more poor people to increase provision of services, given the limitations of the state and the laws. So, alleviation of the poverty of the masses should be at the top of the agenda of the NGOs, state and donors in Bangladesh.

However, the NGOs' umbrella body (which is required to elect its executive committee) is not broad-based. Elections to the executive committee are often not properly held and its membership is often confined to friends and relatives. This surely frustrates the potential of NGOs as democratic voluntary organizations. Nevertheless, NGOs cannot function in isolation from the mainstream of political, economic and social life in this country. They must conform to certain standards, adhere to state regulations and have their work coordinated at the state level. NGOs can only complement the state's activity. Under the current system, the state cannot ask NGOs to become more transparent and accountable or to cooperate more with the state due to donor pressure. The government in Bangladesh is very weak (Wood 1997). Instead, the state creates undue hindrances which only increase the transaction costs of NGOs without encouraging or forcing the NGOs to respond more to the needs of the poor. But still NGOs need to be transparent to their clients, donors and the state both functionally and financially if they really want to represent the interests of the poor or at least provide services to them.

NOTES

1. NGOs are non-profit development organizations or NGDOs. Most NGOs in Bangladesh are foreign-aided development organizations. Although NGO activities are described as 'voluntary' in this chapter, this has been due to the official documents and laws which include all voluntary or non-profit work. Salamon and Anheier (1997) tried to define non-profit organisations as:

a) Organized, i.e. institutionalized to some extent; b) private, i.e. institutionally separate from the state; c) non-profit-distributing, i.e. not returning any profits generated to their owners or directors; d) self-governing, i.e. equipped to control their own activities; e) voluntary, i.e. involving some meaningful degree of voluntary participation, either in the actual conduct of the agency's activities or in the management of its affairs.

The World Bank usually refers to NGOs as any group or institution that is independent from government, and that has humanitarian or cooperative, rather than commercial, objectives. Specifically, the Bank focuses on NGOs that work in the areas of development, relief or environmental protection, or that represent poor or vulnerable people (World Bank 1996). This definition of NGO has been used in this chapter.

2. The official donors are DFID (Department for International Development), NORAD (Norwegian Agency for International Development), CIDA (Canadian Agency for International Development) and SIDA (Swedish Agency for International Development). Other donors include Oxfam, CUSO (Canadian University Services Organization) and ActionAid.

3. In 1860, the then Provincial Government of Bengal promulgated the Societies Registration Act no. XXI to improve the legal position of societies for the promotion of literature, science or the fine arts, for diffusion of knowledge or for charitable purposes. The First Ordinance no. XLVI of 1961 was promulgated on 2 December 1961 by the Martial Law Administration of President Ayub Khan. It made registration mandatory for all NGOs working in what was then East Pakistan and made the Director of Social Welfare responsible for ensuring registration. The Foreign Donations (Voluntary Activities) Regulation Ordinance 1978 was promulgated on 15 November 1978 by President Ziaur Rahman to regulate the receipts and expenditure of foreign donations for voluntary activities. The Foreign Donations (Voluntary Activities) Regulation Rules were promulgated on 12 December 1978, requiring all NGOs intending to receive foreign funds to be

registered under specified prescribed rules. The Ershad government promulgated the Foreign Contributions (Regulations) Ordinance 1982 on 6 September which reiterated that no individual representing NGOs or the organizations themselves would be allowed to give or receive any foreign contribution without prior permission from the state. The government amended the Foreign Donations (Voluntary Activities) Regulation Rules 1978 on 14 May 1990.

4. The Foreign Donations (Voluntary Activities) Regulation Ordinance 1978 (hereafter FDRO, 1978), for example, defined 'foreign donations' as donations, contributions or grants of any kind made for any voluntary activity in Bangladesh by any foreign government or organization or a citizen of a foreign state, or by any Bangladeshi citizen living or working abroad (Ordinance XLVI: 1978). The Foreign Contributions Regulation/Ordinance 1982 (hereafter FCO, 1982) replaced the term itself by 'foreign contribution', defined as any donation, grant or assistance made by any government, organization or citizen of a foreign state (Ordinance XXXI: Section 3: 1982). According to FCO, 1982, any foreign payment, in cash or kind, even a ticket for a journey abroad, has to be considered as a foreign contribution.

5. The ordinances and regulations are:
a) The Foreign Donations (Voluntary Activities) Regulation Ordinance 1978: Ordinance no. XLVI of 1978.
b) The Foreign Donations (Voluntary Activities) Regulation Rules 1978: no. SRO 329–l/78.
c) The Foreign Contributions (Regulation) Ordinance 1982: Ordinance no. XXXI of 1982.
d) Working procedure for Foreign and Foreign-assisted Bangladeshi Non-Government Voluntary Organizations (NGOs) A Circular: 22.43.3.1.0.46.93–478, dated 27 July 1993.

6. The Responsibilities are:
a) Arranging 'one-stop service' for NGO registration and processing of project proposals; NGOs are not required to go to any other office or authority for these purposes (Circular: Section 2: 1993).
b) Approving project proposals submitted by NGOs, releasing project funds and approving appointments of expatriate officials/consultants and their tenure of services (Circular: Section 2: 1993).
c) Scrutinizing and evaluating reports and statements submitted by NGOs.
d) Coordinating, monitoring, inspecting and evaluating NGO programmes and auditing their income and expenditure of accounts.
e) Collecting fees/charges fixed by the government.
f) Examining and taking necessary action on the basis of reports on NGO programmes.
g) Enlisting Chartered Accounts for auditing NGO accounts.
h) Approving receipts of 'one-time contribution' by NGOs. Such contribution is made for buying equipment or for construction of a house/building (Circular: Section 2: 1993).

NAB is also responsible for maintaining communication with concerned ministries/agencies on subjects related to operations of NGOs in the country and for obtaining views/opinions from these agencies when required. Government Ordinance/Regulations require necessary assistance and cooperation from concerned ministries/divisions, other subordinate departments/directories, Divisional Commissioners and Deputy Commissioners for the smooth discharge of the stipulated responsibilities of NAB. The Ordinances/Regulations also require that different ministries/divisions of the government and their subordinate offices will consult NAB prior to entering any Agreement/Memorandum of Understanding (MOU) with foreign and foreign-assisted Bangladeshi NGOs. Before signing such Agreements/MOUs, the concerned NGO must be registered under section 3(2) of the Foreign Donations (Voluntary Activities) Regulation Ordinance 1978 (Circular: Section 4: 1993). Such agreements (MOU) are usually signed between an NGO and the government for programmes like running a certain number of schools on behalf of the government or a collaborative programme such as the Expanded Immunization Programme.

7. The Home Ministry is required to give its decision within sixty days of receipt of the letter from the NAB. In considering the application, the Home Ministry is expected to look into the following matters:

a) Whether the organization or person(s) involved is/are involved in anti-state/ anti-social activities and whether the person(s) concerned had been convicted for these or any other immoral act.

b) Identities of the members of the executive committee of the organization, their relationship and social status.

c) Previous experience of the organization in social welfare activities.

d) Whether the organization has its own office (Circular: Section 6.1(d): 1993).

If the NAB does not receive the Home Ministry's decision within the specified time, the NAB is required to send a written reminder to the Home Ministry after thirty days (Circular: Section 6.1[d]: 1993). It will then be presumed that the Ministry does not have any objection to the application for registration of the NGO concerned. The NAB is required by law to issue the letter of registration within ninety days of receipt of the application. The registration remains valid for five years unless cancelled by the state (Circular: Section 6.1[d]: 1993). The state retains the right to cancel the registration of an NGO. Registration can be renewed for five years provided NAB is satisfied with the performance of the NGO. The constitution of the NGO, names and addresses of the members of the executive committee, minutes of the annual general meetings of the NGO and the fee for renewal or registration should accompany renewal applications.

While scrutinizing it, the NAB has to consider whether a project contributes to socioeconomic development, without duplicating existing state and non-government programmes (Circular: Section 7[1]: 1993). After scrutiny, the NAB forwards the proposal to the relevant ministry, which has to reply within twenty-one days. If it does not, the NAB can assume that the ministry has no objection to the project (Circular: Section 7[d]: 1993). However, if the ministry has an objection to the project or recommends modification of the project, the arguments will have to be communicated to the NAB in detail. If it finds the objection/modification unacceptable, the NAB may approve the project after obtaining clearance from the Prime Minister's Office (Circular: Section 7[e]: 1993). The NAB, if necessary, can approve the project proposal after making changes and modifications. But in such a case the opinions and limitations of donor agency/agencies and relevant NGOs should be considered (Circular: Section 7[f]: 1993). The NAB is required to communicate its decision within forty-five days of receiving the project proposal with the requisite details (Circular: Section 7[g]: 1993).

8. Any person or organization registered as an NGO may receive or operate any foreign donation only with prior approval or permission of the state (Regulation Rules: Section 4[1]: 1978). To receive/utilize foreign donations for approved projects NGOs must submit the application (through FD-2 form in triplicate) to the Director General of the NAB. The NAB issues the order to release foreign funds after consideration of the activities and budget of the NGO's approved projects, the progress and implementation of on-going projects and documents relating to receipt of foreign funds. The NAB sends copies of the order to the ERD, Bangladesh Bank (the central bank), relevant ministries, Divisional Commissioner(s) and donor agencies for information and necessary action. In the case of an approved project, to receive further instalments of a foreign donation the NGO has to submit an application using form FD-2 in triplicate. Subsequently, statements of foreign donations received and spent in the previous year must be submitted on form FD-3 in triplicate. The bureau communicates its decision within fourteen days of receipt of the application, after examining the annual progress report on the project.

Applications to appoint/extend the tenure of expatriates in approved projects must be submitted by the relevant NGO to the NAB for approval on form FD-9. The NAB will ask the Home Ministry to comment within twenty-five days. Each proposal for the appointment of expatriate personnel must be within the person-months approved by the NAB. Statements of their emoluments (even if received from outside Bangladesh) must be submitted to the NAB every year.

9. To facilitate easy accounting, all persons or organizations registered as NGOs must receive all funds in foreign exchange through a single specified account opened in any scheduled Bank of Bangladesh which must submit statements of such funds to the central bank, i.e. the Bangladesh Bank (Regulation Rules: Section 4[4]: 1978). The scheduled banks maintaining such accounts (in both foreign currency and Bangladeshi Taka) are now required to submit a statement on foreign funds to the Bangladesh Bank and the Director General of NAB every six months (Circular: Section 5[h]: 1993). At present the Bangladesh Bank is supposed in its turn to submit statements to the ERD as well as to the Director General of NAB. All NGO payments exceeding 10,000 Taka have to be made by cheque and all salaries and allowances must be paid through bank accounts (Circular: Section 5[I]: 1993).

10. 1 US$ = 56 Taka in September 2000.

11. The Foreign Donation (Voluntary Activities) Regulation Ordinance 1978 Section 3(1) and Section 3(3) and the Foreign Contribution (Regulation) Ordinance 1982, Section 4(1).

12. The Foreign Donation Regulation Act 1978.

13. The Exchange Control Regulation Act 1947.

14. The Societies Registration Act 1860.

15. The Government's Audit Report, 1992.

16. Some sections of the Ordinance of 1961 may be incorporated in the Ordinance of 1978.

17. The Bengali version of circular 1993, 'Paripatra' (Section 6 [KA]).

18. According to the English version of the 'Paripatra' (Section 7.1–3).

REFERENCES

ADAB (Association of Development Agencies in Bangladesh) (1998) *Directory of PVDOs/NGDOs in Bangladesh (Ready Reference)*, Dhaka: ADAB.

BBS (1998) *Statistical Pocketbook of Bangladesh*, Dhaka: BBS.

Chazan, D. (1998) 'Aid Offices Set on Fire in Bangladesh', *Financial Times*, 9 December 1998.

Daily Star (1999a) 'Tension Prevails at Faridpur Over ADAB Conference', *Daily Star*, 6 March 1999.

— (1999b) 'Kibria on Microfinance Institutions: Time Has come for Regulating Their Lending Activities', *Daily Star*, 7 May 1999.

Ebdon, R. (1995) 'NGO Expansion and the Fight to Reach the Poor: Gender Implications of NGO Scaling-up in Bangladesh', *IDS Bulletin*, 26 (3): 49–55.

Galpin, R. (1999) 'Pakistan Tightens Screw on Opposition', *Guardian*, 15 May 1999.

Hashemi, S. M. (1995) 'NGO Accountability in Bangladesh: Beneficiaries, Donors and State', in M. Edwards and D. Hulme (eds), *Non-governmental Organisations – Performance and Accountability Beyond the Magic Bullet*, London: Earthscan.

Huband, M. (1999) 'Top Egypt Academics Repudiate Draft Law', *Financial Times*, 25 May 1999.

Huband, M. et al. (1999) 'Middle Eastern NGOs Strain at the Bonds of Authoritarian Government', *Financial Times*, 10 June 1999.

Islam, M. A. (1995) 'Editorial', *Independent* , 14 June 1995.

Kabir, N. (1999) 'In a Mess: One of the Better-known NGOs Faces Charges of Irregularities', *Daily Star*, 25 May 1999.

Lewis, D. J. (1993) 'NGO–Government Interaction in Bangladesh', in J. Farrington and D. J. Lewis (eds), *Non-Governmental Organisations and the State in Asia: Rethinking Roles in Sustainable Agricultural Development*, London: Routledge.

Montgomery, R. et al. (1996) 'Credit for the Poor in Bangladesh – the BRAC Rural Development Programme and the Government Thana Resource Development and Employment Programme', in D. Hulme and P. Mosley (eds), *Finance Against Poverty*, Vol. 2, London: Routledge.

NFB (News from Bangladesh) (1999a) 'NGO Activities Come Under Fire in JS', *NFB* (daily interactive edn), 5 February 1999.

— (1999b) 'Government Won't Control NGO Activities, Says DG', *NFB* (daily interactive edn), 3 March 1999.

— (1999c) 'Donors Block Tk. 1.5b Fund for GSS', *NFB* (daily interactive edn), 7 May 1999.

— (1999d) 'PKSF's Call to Hold NGOs in Leash', *NFB* (daily interactive edn), 10 May 1999.

NGO Affairs Bureau (1998) *Flow of Foreign Grant Fund Through NGO Affairs Bureau at a Glance*, Dhaka: NGO Affairs Bureau, PM's Office/GOB.

Rafi, M. and A. M. R. Chowdhury (2000) 'Human Rights and Religious Backlash: the Experiences of a Bangladeshi NGO', *Development in Practice*, 10 (1): 19–30.

Report of the NAB for the Prime Minister (1992) 'There are Several Complaints of Irregularity and Corruption against the NGOs', *Bhorer Kagoj* (daily newspaper in Bangla), 29 July 1992.

Reza, H. (1992) 'Main Report, NGO: New Challenge for the State and Government', *Kagoj* (weekly magazine in Bangla), 31 August 1992.

Salamon, L. M. and H. K. Anheier (1997) 'Toward a Common Definition', in L. M. Salamon and H. K. Anheier (eds), *Defining the Nonprofit Sector: A Cross-national Analysis*, Manchester: Manchester University Press.

Sen, S. (1999) 'Some Aspects of State–NGO Relations in India in the Post-Independence Era', *Development and Change*, 30: 327–55.

Shehabuddin, E. (1999) 'Contesting the Illicit: Gender and the Politics of Fatwas in Bangladesh', *Signs*, 24 (4): 1011-44.

Task-Force Report (1992) *Report of the Task-Forces on Bangladesh Development Strategies for the 1990s: Managing the Development Process*, 2 vols, Dhaka: University Press Limited.

White, S. (1999) 'NGOs, Civil Society, and the State in Bangladesh: The Politics of Representing the Poor', *Development and Change*, 30: 307–26.

Wood, G. D. (1997) 'States Without Citizens: The Problem of the Franchise State', in M. Edwards and D. Hulme (eds), *NGOs, States and Donors – Too Close for Comfort?*, London: Macmillan.

World Bank (1996) *The World Bank's Partnership with Nongovernmental Organisations*. Washington, DC: Participation and NGO Group, Poverty and Social Policy Department/The World Bank.

Zarren, F. (1996) 'The Legal Status of NGOs in Bangladesh: A Critical Assessment', *Social Science Review*, XIII (2): 67–90.

six | Exclusion and rights

PAUL SPICKER

§ Exclusion is not poverty. Although the two concepts are often closely identified, the idea of exclusion stems from different sources. Poverty is a word with many meanings: it can refer to material circumstances, economic resources and social position. Exclusion is primarily understood in terms of social relationships: people are excluded when they are not part of the networks of relationships which make up a society. In this chapter, I want to consider the relationship of this model to the idea of rights.

THE IDEA OF EXCLUSION

The idea of exclusion has come to the European Union from France. René Lenoir's book *Les exclus: un français sur dix* (1974) was written at a time when poverty scarcely formed part of the debate in France. In the absence of that debate, the idea of exclusion provided an alternative conceptual framework, addressing related moral concerns in the context of a very different social model. The guiding principle of social protection was the Catholic principle of solidarity, or mutual obligation, which is described in the Code de Sécurité Sociale as the central principle of social security in France (Dupeyroux 1998: 290). Between the end of the war and the 1970s, the scope of the French social security system was progressively extended until, following reforms in the early 1970s, virtually all employees might be said to be covered. But Lenoir's book drew attention to those outside the labour market who were not covered by France's complex patchwork of social insurance. The first attempts to 'insert', or include, the excluded were made in the mid-1970s, and from that time onwards 'solidarity' came increasingly to mean not just covering people through mutual insurance but redistribution to those who would not otherwise be covered. The movement towards 'insertion' culminated in the introduction, late in 1988, of the Revenu Minimum d'Insertion (RMI), a basic income-tested benefit available on condition of an agreement to an individual programme for social inclusion.

This model has been influential in Europe in two ways. First, the RMI has offered an important approach in its own right, offering a pattern for benefit receipt which has also been adopted in Belgium and northern Spain; other initiatives in Britain (the 'Jobseekers' Agreement) and Denmark might be thought to reflect similar influences. Second, and more important, 'exclusion' has provided a conceptual basis for the development of policy in the European Union. The idea of exclusion was adopted, quite explicitly, as an alternative to poverty because of the difficulty of obtaining agreement on anti-poverty policy (Tiemann 1993), and powers to combat exclusion were agreed first in the Social Protocol to Maastricht and subsequently in the Amsterdam Treaty.

In much of the European Union, the idea of exclusion is still viewed with some perplexity, and interpretations of the idea tend to reflect the politics and ideology prevalent in the member-states. Ideas have a force of their own, however, and exclusion has potential implications quite distinct from the idea of poverty.

Exclusion is, at first sight, a concept of staggering generality.

> Social exclusion affects individuals, groups of people and geographical areas. Social exclusion can be seen, not just in levels of income, but also matters such as health, education, access to services, housing and debt. Phenomena which result from social exclusion therefore include:
>
> - the resurgence of homelessness
> - urban crises
> - ethnic tension
> - rising long term unemployment
> - persistent high levels of poverty. (Tiemann 1993)

This is supposed to be broader than poverty, and Palier and Bonoli comment that the idea covers a wide range of problems: 'poverty, long-term unemployment, public housing, urban problems, various handicaps, AIDS, racism, immigration etc.' (Palier and Bonoli 1995: 682). But, for many people, exclusion means something very similar to poverty. That view is reinforced by some of the documents coming out of the European Commission:

> When we talk about social exclusion we are acknowledging that the problem is no longer simply one of inequity between the top and bottom of the social scale (up/down) but also one of the distance within society between those who are active members and those who

are forced towards the fringes (in/out). We are also highlighting the effects of the way society is developing and the concomitant risk of social disintegration and, finally, we are affirming that, for both the persons concerned and the society itself, this is a process of change and not a set of fixed and static situations. (Commission of the European Communities 1993: 43)

These points have all been made about poverty. The first point is central to Peter Townsend's analysis of poverty in the seminal book *Poverty in the United Kingdom* (1979); indeed, Townsend refers to poor people as being 'excluded' on the first page of the main text:

Individuals, families and groups in the population can be said to be in poverty when they lack the resources to obtain the types of diet, participate in the activities and have the living conditions and amenities which are customary, or at least widely encouraged or approved, in the societies to which they belong. Their resources are so seriously below those commanded by the average individual or family that they are, in effect, excluded from ordinary living patterns, customs and activities. (Townsend 1979: 31)

The point about social disintegration is a regular aspect of studies of the 'underclass' (Morris 1994), while studies of the dynamic nature of poverty have been a part of the literature for years (Kolvin et al. 1990 – a longitudinal study based on poor families begun in 1950).

There is certainly a substantial overlap between the ideas of exclusion and poverty, and in recent years the overlap has been reinforced by increasing concern with the relational aspects of poverty. The concepts are, however, discrete, and there are aspects of each idea which are not taken into account by the other.

The idea of exclusion begins with the idea of solidarity. Society is composed of a complex system of solidaristic social networks, such as the family, employment and community. People are included by virtue of a web of overlapping relationships which bring them into contact with other people, binding people with mutual obligations. One can imagine, Alfarandi writes, 'a system of concentric circles of solidarity, wider and wider, which goes from the nuclear family to the international community' (Alfarandi 1989: 73). People are marginal when they are linked only peripherally to these networks; they are excluded when they are not part of them at all. The archetypal excluded person is the single homeless person. There are few people who have no social ties at all, but some groups – such as homeless psychiatric patients – may have very limited ties, breaking off even from the residual links with their families.

By this model, a person might be poor without being excluded. Poverty is understood in many ways, but whether it is taken to refer to material need, standard of living, lack of resources or relative deprivation, the problems it poses for participation in society tend to imply restriction rather than strict exclusion. Long-term unemployed people, often represented as characteristic of socially excluded people, are still likely to retain a string of social contacts, including contacts with family and community as well as a range of social activities. And it is possible to imagine circumstances in which people might be poor without being excluded in any meaningful sense: life in the barrios of South America is a life of poverty, but it is not, for most, life without a family, a community or other networks of social support.

Conversely, people might be excluded without being poor. Resources are necessary for participation in society, but they are not sufficient. Many people are in circumstances where they are likely to be socially rejected – for example, people with disabilities, AIDS or mental illness. Old people with senile dementia can present an extreme example of exclusion, suffering a form of 'social death' before their physical death; they undergo a period of progressive removal from society, in which they become 'non-persons'. They may, of course, be poor as well, but the process affects the formerly rich and powerful (like Ronald Reagan) as well as the poorest.

One of the central difficulties of distinguishing poverty from exclusion is that 'poverty' means so many things. Among the many definitions are some which are difficult to distinguish from exclusion. The first is the definition of poverty in terms of the inability to participate in society, an idea which may well have been influenced by debates on exclusion. The second is the idea of poverty as a lack of entitlement. Drèze and Sen (1989) argue that poverty has to be seen primarily as a lack of command over resources, and so of rights to goods and services which already exist. A third is Wresinski's identification of poverty with 'lack of basic security': 'the absence of one or more factors that enable individuals and families to assume basic responsibilities and to enjoy fundamental rights in which people lack resources and rights' (cited in Duffy 1995).

I have argued that poverty and exclusion are conceptually distinct, but there is an important reservation to make about that position. The complexity of poverty definitions means not simply that the definitions tend at times to overlap, but that the debate about poverty is often indistinguishable from the issue of exclusion: poverty is being discussed as if it means exclusion, and exclusion is being discussed as if it means poverty. Although each has its own distinct and unrelated issues, I think the close identification of the two is unavoidable. Poverty often has important relational elements; exclusion often has a significant material base. This implies that effective action against poverty must also respond to the problems of exclusion.

RESPONDING TO EXCLUSION

The real distinction between poverty and exclusion lies in the prescriptions which the different models have for practice. Poverty is avoided primarily by meeting need, or by improving resources. Exclusion, by contrast, can be avoided only by social means – through the inclusion of people in solidaristic social networks. There are three basic options for responses – three routes to social inclusion. The first is prevention: attempting to ensure that people are part of social networks at the outset. Programmes promoting work, family and community can be seen as a means of achieving that. The second is the extension of solidarity: the attempt to develop social protection, going further than networks of family or occupation might allow. The third is 'insertion': the attempt to include, or re-include, excluded people through special mechanisms. This is the model of the RMI in France (Thévenet 1989; Mlekuz 1996).

The RMI offers the best evidence for the distinct nature of the response to exclusion. 'Insertion' is intended to draw people who are excluded or marginal into defined relationships with the rest of society. The individual claimant has to make a contract of insertion, which is drawn up after negotiation with a social worker, and submitted for approval by a local Commission of Insertion (CLI). The Commission, in turn, has responsibility for developing opportunities for inclusion, through negotiation with other agencies and the purchase of services. The content of contracts varies: in many authorities, the emphasis falls primarily on employment, but in others the emphasis has fallen on social integration, including contracts concerned with motivation, behaviour, family relationships and health (Euvrard and Paugam 1991). The idea of the contract, at first sight, has elements of 'workfare', the American system which makes benefit receipt conditional on work (see, e.g., Ogborn 1988; King 1995). Like workfare, there is a strong emphasis on the role of employment, and like workfare there are penalties for non-compliance (Bichot 1992). At the same time, there are significant differences. On the one hand, there is the commitment of the person to integrate; on the other, there is the commitment of social organizations to create the structures and opportunities which are necessary for the person to do so (see Spicker 1995: 8–14).

This approach has been widely imitated. Versions of the RMI have been introduced in Portugal (Coutinho 1998), northern Spain (Ayala 1994) and Italy (MISEP 1998: 23–4). It is difficult here for me to resist a digression. The French approach to 'insertion' particularly interested me, and it is the origin of a programme I have been helping to develop in Dundee. In 1999, the Scottish Executive invited bids for Social Inclusion Partnerships, or SIPs. In most cases in Scotland, this term has simply been seen as an extension of the old Urban Programme (which is the source of funding), and most of the policies it relates to are area-based. The SIP in Dundee proposed a city-wide programme for young people aged eleven to eighteen from deprived backgrounds. First, the SIP was to take responsibility for developing opportunities for inclusion, negotiating with a range of providers and commissioning services where appropriate. Second, the SIP was to make agreements with the young people themselves, making the service provided conditional on the cooperation of the young person. Agreements would attempt to balance obligations (such as school attendance or non-offending) and benefits (to be negotiated according to the preferences and wishes of the young person – a course in music or art, learning to drive, an outward bound adventure). The effect of non-compliance would be to end the contract – which means that the young person would not benefit – but no penalty will be attached. The aim, in other words, was to apply the positive aspects of the French system, without imposing the negative ones. The Scottish Executive is treating the project as a pilot, and has said that if the evaluation is successful the scheme will be considered for national use. However else the approach may be described, it is very different from a conventional anti-poverty strategy.

RIGHTS: CIVIL, ECONOMIC AND SOCIAL

T. H. Marshall (1981) saw the development of rights as falling into three main stages: first civil rights, then economic rights, then social ones. Civil rights include the principal political rights, and rules governing public behaviour. Economic rights cover the rights which result from engagement in the economic process – rights covering contracts, ownership, the distribution of goods and command over resources. Social rights include both collective action, such as the rights of trades unions, and rights to welfare.

The application of Marshall's model to poverty is fairly direct, because the development of the English welfare state that Marshall was concerned with was intimately linked with the Poor Laws. In Marshall's view, civil rights developed in the eighteenth century, economic rights in the nineteenth and social rights in the twentieth. The pattern is not as straightforward as Marshall paints it; many economic rights, including the ability to sell land, were forged in England in the sixteenth century. The link is even less clear in other countries; Scotland had universal basic education, an important social right, from 1691. If we leave aside the specifics, though, there is a substantial argument at the root of it: that the process of gaining rights is a gradual one, and each set of new rights has been the foundation for the next. In Britain, and in Marshall's argument, the root of the development of such rights has been the legal process. Law establishes the conditions and framework under which people relate to each other, and makes it possible to develop further, subsequent claims of right. This has been the dominant model in the UK and USA, and it culminates in the International Declaration of Human Rights by the UN.

There are, though, two other contending processes through which rights might be developed, and neither of them is traditionally thought of as dependent on a foundation of legal rights. Economic development tends, in general, to lead to increasing numbers of people gaining rights, because the effect of engaging in the economic process is to develop relationships – for example, by earning and spending money – which serves to maintain not only the worker and the worker's dependants but those who are able to provide services to the workers. The economic argument is not simply about wealth or resources; it is also about inclusion, and economic development may lead directly to social inclusion through incorporation in the formal economy. This argument has to be treated with some caution: it is the source of several very questionable propositions – arguments that 'a rising tide raises all boats', the 'trickle down' effect or the demand for 'structural adjustment' in malfunctioning economies. But it is still powerful, because it is largely true.

The development of social rights may also, in practice, derive not from legal or political intervention, but from collective mutual action. This has been one of the principal sources of the development of social protection in Europe; the 'welfare states' in northern Europe have developed principally by adapting mechanisms developed through independent mutuals. Although social insurance schemes are often compulsory, it is important to avoid the fallacious assumption that they are state-based agencies imposed by legislative fiat. Until very recently there was no direct requirement to join the systems protecting people from unemployment and sickness in Denmark, Sweden and Finland. Compulsion was considered unnecessary. (Compulsory contributions were finally introduced as a means of raising revenue to cope with the economic downturn of the 1990s [Ploug and Kvist 1994] – in other words, as a form of taxation.)

There is, of course, a connection between all these categories. Political rights have often followed economic rights. People do not gain economic rights simply through engagement in the economic sphere; they gain them through political action. People do not gain social rights simply through cooperative behaviour; economic and political rights have also been fundamental. Civil, economic and social rights are so far intertwined in practice that it is difficult to identify any one of them as 'prior' to others, either historically or lexically. This also means that we should be suspicious of any claim that the development of legal rights is a precondition for economic or social protection, though it may be an essential adjunct. Drèze and Sen (1989), considering the cause of famines, are primarily concerned with economic rights; people do not lack resources because they were not given them, but because they did not gain them in the process of development. Drèze and Sen see the principal form of redress for people without rights as lying, not in economic processes, but in political ones. The effect of giving people political rights is also to give them the ability to address their problems; and they argue, strikingly, that there has never been a famine in a democracy.

THE RIGHTS OF THE EXCLUDED

Rights are rules governing social relationships. They are primarily concerned with behaviour, and the way in which people relate to each other. This means that they are often closely identified with social obligations; Benn and Peters (1959: ch. 4), for example, argue that all rights are correlated to duties. This is a mistake, because there are different forms of rights, and some (liberties, privileges and immunities) do not imply duties on other people. However, 'claim rights', which allow people to enforce claims against others, do. Exclusion is defined, to a large extent, in terms of the obligations people have to each other, and in so far as these obligations are correlative with rights, it is with claim rights.

At the same time, people may have rights in some respects and not others. They may be included politically, but not economically or socially. It follows that exclusion may occur even in cases where someone holds rights. It does not follow that someone who is socially protected also has civil rights – the circumstances of detained mental patients are illustrative – or that someone with political and economic rights has social rights. Debates on exclusion have tended to focus specifically on social rights, because the issue was initially raised in relation to people who were not entitled to social protection, but they should not be confined to those rights.

Civil rights

The most obvious case of exclusion from civil rights, though not necessarily the worst, is that of people excluded from citizenship because they are foreign nationals. To be 'without papers' in France is to be denied every form of economic and social protection. But there are other, often quite extreme, cases. There are prisoners, one of the only circumstances in the modern world in which forced labour, or slavery, is considered compatible with human rights. There are people with severe dementia, who are often treated as socially dead, with all rights extinguished. And there are people with severe mental and physical disabilities, often described as 'human vegetables' (Feinberg 1980). I have argued elsewhere for rights and citizenship in these cases, on three grounds: first, that this is not an accurate reflection of these people's competence and feelings, second that their rights cannot be questioned without questioning the presumption of rights for others, and third that it is only through rights that people can be protected (Spicker 1990).

Economic rights

There is a central weakness in economic rights as they are presently understood: there is no presumption of inclusion, and there are no obligations which can help to guarantee inclusion. The 'right to work' remains, like the idea of natural rights, 'nonsense on stilts'. The development of a market economy does not guarantee extended economic rights; in many cases, notably in Eastern Europe, it may imply a contraction.

Exclusion has often, in the European Union, been identified with exclusion from the labour market, and in particular with the condition of long-term unemployed people. The White Paper on Social Policy, for example, makes its objective 'the social integration of those who cannot join the labour market' (Commission of the European Communities 1994: 38). One of the central weaknesses of the French RMI has been its heavy emphasis on employment issues, often ignoring other routes to social inclusion. But there are other routes to economic inclusion – most obviously, the maintenance of an adequate income through systems of social protection; the reason why so few people with children have to claim the RMI is that family benefits in France provide a superior alternative income. The problem of exclusion for some poor people has been precisely the problem of those who have neither social protection nor employment.

Social rights

It is in relation to social rights that the arguments about exclusion were made. One significant implication of the idea of 'solidarity' is that the solidarity which is shown in the provision of social protection does not have to be shown by the government. This approach was seized on by the European Commission because it gave a flexible standard towards which to work. People are 'included' if they are covered in any way at all, and 'excluded' only if they are not. The aims of the Commission are, then, progressively to extend the boundaries of solidarity, and to include those people who are not otherwise included (Chassard and Quintin 1992).

This is only a partial view of social rights, however. Even if people are fully protected socially, they are not necessarily accepted or able to participate in society. The idea of 'stigma', which has been dominant in the discourse of social policy of the United Kingdom for well over a century, points to the potential of people to be socially rejected even though they are protected (Spicker 1984) – and even, in many cases, rejected *because* they are protected. 'All social services', Pinker (1971)

TABLE 6.1 Responding to economic, social and political exclusion

Form of exclusion	Responses		
	Prevention of exclusion	*Extension of solidarity*	*Insertion*
Economic	Economic development; employment; social protection	Social protection through non-contributory services	Job creation; conditional benefits (RMI)
Political	Citizenship	Participation	Empowerment
Social	Providing social services and facilities	Community development; anti-discrimination laws	Social work; anti-poverty measures

argues, 'are systems of exchange': many involve an exchange of status, and the acceptance of degradation, as a condition of service receipt.

Exclusion and rights

There are three basic patterns of response to exclusion, and three fields of operation: economic, social and political. This suggests a matrix of the kind considered in Table 6.1. The measures mentioned in the table are indicative, not exhaustive. In important respects, too, they are overlapping. There is an overlap, first, between the interconnected categories of economic, social and political rights, and second, between the classes of response which are available: a single measure, like the introduction of a basic pension for old people, can have an effect in several cells of the matrix simultaneously. Most of the measures are complementary, rather than distinct.

THE ROLE OF THE LAW

This book is concerned with the role of law in alleviating poverty, but I have been considering rights in a much broader context. Legal protection is only a part of the picture. In relation to political rights, the role of the law is strong: it is directly concerned with citizenship and empowerment, both creating the framework for inclusion and setting the terms on which it takes place. In relation to social rights, the role of the law is less central; law determines some important preconditions for exclusion, but it is not sufficient in itself. The role is arguably weakest in relation to economic rights: the law can provide the framework for these rights, but the issues are substantive economic ones. There is, I think, a reason for this. Law establishes the context in which relationships develop, and the rules by which they do so; it is necessary for the development of many relationships, but it is not sufficient to create them. In political action, the legal context substantially defines the relationships; in economics, it is not enough. That is one of the main reasons for the strength of legal direction in the development of political rights, and the weakness of law in developing economic relationships.

These limitations have important implications for any strategy to deal with exclusion. There is something vaguely absurd about the idea of a law announcing, 'you're included', like Peter Pan sprinkling fairy dust over children so that they can fly. People cannot be included by a declaration of rights, like the laws in some countries which announce that old people should be respected (International Council on Social Welfare 1969: 430); social relationships call for more than words.

What is likely to happen, rather, is that, in so far as relationships are affected by the legal framework, some people will be included and others will not. In a previous article in this series, I examined some potential contradictions between claims for legal rights and social inclusion (Spicker 2001). Improving people's economic or political status can lead to greater inclusion, but equally this can be exclusive; much depends on how the rights are defined. Although substantive rights to resources, such as income or housing, are fundamental to participation in society, they also have the potential to be profoundly stigmatizing. The potential of legal rights for inclusion is, then, ambiguous. This is an important constraint on the development of universal rights. A successful declaration of rights fosters greater inclusion, but any gains and losses are relative, not absolute. The process of including people is one in which boundaries are redefined and pushed back; but the boundaries remain, and there is no way such a development can become truly universal. The debate becomes, then, an issue of the expansion of solidarity – or increasing relatively the degree of inclusion – rather than true universalism.

REFERENCES

Alfarandi, E. (1989) *Action et aide sociales*, 4th edn, Paris: Dalloz.

Ayala, L. (1994) 'Social Needs, Inequality and the Welfare State in Spain', *Journal of European Social Policy*, 4 (3): 159–79.

Benn, S. I. and R. S. Peters (1959) *Social Principles and the Democratic State*, London: Allen and Unwin.

Bichot, J. (1992) *Economie de la protection sociale*, Paris: Armand Colin.

Chassard, Y. and O. Quintin (1992) 'Social Protection in the European Community: Towards a Convergence of Policies', paper presented to the International Conference on Social Security 50 Years after Beveridge, University of York.

Commission of the European Communities (1993) 'Medium-term Action Programme to Control Exclusion and Promote Solidarity', COM(93), 435.

— (1994) 'European Social Policy – A Way Forward for the Union', COM(94), 333 final, 27 July, vol. 1, p. 38.

Coutinho, M. (1998) 'Guaranteed Minimum Income in Portugal and Social Projects', *Social Services Research*, 2: 1–10.

Drèze, J. and A. Sen (1989) *Hunger and Public Action*, Oxford: Clarendon Press.

Duffy, K. (1995) *Social Exclusion and Human Dignity in Europe*, CDPS(95) 1 Rev., Strasbourg: Council of Europe.

Dupeyroux, J.-J. (1998) *Droit de la Sécurité Sociale*, Paris: Dalloz.

Euvrard, F. and S. Paugam (1991) *Atouts et difficultés des allocataires du Revenu Minimum d'Insertion*, Paris: La Documentation française.

Feinberg, J. (1980) *Rights, Justice and the Bounds of Liberty*, Princeton, NJ: Princeton University Press.

International Council on Social Welfare (1969) *Social Welfare and Human Rights*, New York: Columbia University Press.

King, D. S. (1995) *Actively Seeking Work?*, Chicago: University of Chicago Press.

Kolvin, I., F. Miller, D. Scott, S. Gatzanis and M. Fleeting (1990) *Continuities of Deprivation?*, Aldershot: Avebury.

Lenoir, R. (1974) *Les exclus: un français sur dix*, Paris: Editions du Seuil.

Marshall, T. H. (1981) *The Right to Welfare*, London: Heinemann.

MISEP (European Commission Employment Observatory) (1998) *Policies*, 64 (Winter).

Mlekuz, N. (ed.) (1996) *A quoi sert le RMI?*, Condé sur Noreau: Corlet.

Morris, L. (1994) *Dangerous Classes*, London: Routledge.

Ogborn, K. (1988) 'Workfare in America: An Initial Guide to the Debate', *Social Security Review* (Australia), 6.

Palier, B. and G. Bonoli (1995) 'Entre Bismarck et Beveridge', *Revue Française de Science Politique*, 45 (4).

Pinker, R. (1971) *Social Theory and Social Policy*, London: Heinemann.

Ploug, N. and J. Kvist (eds) (1994) *Recent Trends in Cash Benefits in Europe*, Copenhagen: Danish National Institute of Social Research.

Spicker, P. (1984) *Stigma and Social Welfare*, Beckenham: Croom Helm.

— (1990) 'Mental Handicap and Citizenship', *Journal of Applied Philosophy*, 7 (2): 139–51.

— (1995) 'Inserting the Excluded: The Impact of the Revenu Minimum d'Insertion on Poverty in France', *Social Work in Europe*, 22: 8–14.

— (2001) 'The Rights of the Poor', in P. Robson and A. Kjønstad (eds) *Poverty and the Law*, Oxford: Hart Publishing, pp. 3–14

Thévenet, A. (1989) *RMI Théorie et pratique*, Paris: Centurion.

Tiemann, S. (1993) 'Opinion on Social Exclusion', OJ 93/C 352/13.

Townsend, P. (1979) *Poverty in the United Kingdom*, London: Penguin Books.

PART III

The Establishment of Legal Entitlements

SEVEN | Judicial review, social antagonism and the use of litigation as a tool for combating poverty

ANTONELLA MAMELI

§ Traditionally, the role of litigation as a tool for combating poverty and obtaining social change and legal reform has varied considerably in civil law and common law countries. The roots of these differences have been connected to the importance of judicial review, to the future potential influence of successful cases in common law and to the role of the judiciary in each legal setting. However, the perceived characterization of a civil law system as lacking the binding character of judicial precedents is becoming less and less apparent. Similarly, a description of the common law systems as characterized by an opposition between judicial and legislative sources of law-making, and the evaluation of their respective relevance within the legal system, is not accurate. A comparative analysis of two systems, focusing on two countries, Italy and the United States, shows that issues of access to justice cannot be separated from the system of social relationships developed in a specific legal system. The legal element cannot be detached from the social history of a country.

As a consequence, any evaluation of the use of litigation as a tool for combating poverty must take into account two elements: a 'legal' one, i.e. the role of judicial review and the judiciary in a specific country, and a 'social' element, i.e. the social structure and the mechanisms of social antagonism developed within that historical tradition – the conflicts among social groups or classes of that particular society. Of course, these elements are not distinct; what is articulated as the 'legal' and the 'social' incorporate and build on each other. Yet reconstructing, using a comparative perspective, the differential access of diverse social groups to litigation shows the processes of discrimination and exclusion of these particular societies and the different ways in which the two systems control conflicts.

Italy: a civil law system

In civil law systems such as Italy, the articulated primacy of the legislature has a historical justification. The use of courts to achieve concrete legal changes is not considered part of the civil law tradition. Dating at least back to the French Revolution,[1] with its insistence that law be made only by representatives of the legislature, judges have not been viewed as playing a creative role within this tradition. According to certain revolutionary theories, the judiciary should have no interpretative function and should refer problems of statutory interpretation to the legislature. Civil law judges should not even interpret incomplete or unclear statutes. These theories also assumed that systematic legislation would be clear and complete, so that the function of the judge was merely to be the mouthpiece of the law. Judges were viewed as part of the state bureaucracy, and distrusted by rising social movements, such as the labour movement. The judiciary thus was not perceived and did not perceive itself as playing an important role in shaping civil liberties. Social movements became the source of pressure for societal change.

The revolutionary bourgeoisie, the dominant class during the eighteenth and nineteenth centuries, made a fundamental contribution towards the assertion of civil liberties and equal protection guarantees. Additionally, from the second half of the nineteenth century, the rising working class provided the impetus for attaining new civil liberties, in particular for the associative liberties thwarted at first by the liberal state.[2]

In monoclass states, like Italy during the nineteenth century (a time in which the bourgeoisie constituted the only class in power), the strengthening of these liberties went through a peculiar process. When modern states, mainly as a consequence of the processes of industrialization and through victories of the working class, evolved from monoclass to pluriclass and the social basis of consensus spread to the lower classes, new civil liberties guarantees were claimed by the emerging classes. Liberties were proclaimed in constitutional documents and then interpreted in legislation characterized by mainly authoritative embodiments. The bourgeoisie, however, feared that every liberty could stir up social dissent, opening a door to other and more significant rights demanded by lower classes.

In Italy, social institutions and political parties struggling to obtain an expansion of these liberties had to lobby solely through legislation, since the judiciary did not perceive itself as empowered to develop civil liberties. Historically, class organizations took the shape of different parties at a political level and trade unions at a factory level. Parties and unions, in turn, provided the political mechanisms by which lower classes could improve their plight both in the workplace and in society in general. These institutions resorted to the courts and to litigation as a strategy to reach their goals only in periods of high social ferment.

However, currently in Italy, the notion of a strict separation between legislative and judicial power leads to an extreme oversimplification of the system. The dogma that only the legislature can make law is no longer acceptable. The power of the judiciary to review the constitutionality of laws weakens the traditional view of the legislature as the sole law-maker. The principle of the separation of powers was originally conceived of as an opposition between the legislature, elected by the people, and the executive, exercising the powers of the crown. In Italy, as well as in other continental European countries, such separation dictated a special jurisdiction for constitutional matters, different from the one pertaining to the court of last resort for ordinary matters. In this picture, the judiciary did not assume a political role, but was viewed simply as a body of executives with particular technical powers. Later on, as the opposition between legislature and executive disappeared, the expertise of judges was valued differently and special bodies were created with a political power of judicial review and formed by jurists chosen by political organs.

The 1948 Italian constitution[3] established the creation of a new body with a legal as well as a political nature, the Constitutional Court (Corte Costituzionale).[4] Most of the jurisdictional functions having a basic constitutional character were assigned to this court.[5] The goal of the constitutional framers was to concentrate all constitutional matters in one court with the power to abrogate *erga omnes* statutes deemed unconstitutional. Although it performs functions which are in substance judicial, the Court is not included in the judiciary. It is thus excluded from the classification of the three classical powers and considered as the supreme guarantor of constitutional norms. With its remarkable influence on the political life of the parliament and of the government, the Court essentially modified the functioning of the parliamentary form of government.

With its interpretative opinions,[6] the Court has added new norms and rules to the ones already operating in the legal system and has performed de facto legislative functions limiting the creation of dangerous legislative gaps. The normative competence obtained by the constitutional judges, justified on the grounds of the need for legal certainty, removes power from the legislature. The legislature has come to accept and employ the decisions of this Court. Moreover, the Court has often intervened at a legislative political level, formulating in its opinions guiding principles for future legislatures. These principles are intended to guarantee the constitutional consistency of legislative acts to fill in the gaps or to modify defective existing statutes (see Elia 1982; Pizzorusso 1980; Assini 1982: 1853).

Particularly since the beginning of the 1960s, the Court largely decided cases in such a way as to maintain the status quo, thereby appearing to exercise some self-restraint. But in the 1970s and 1980s, a series of political decisions taken by the Constitutional Court generated an extensive and evolutionary interpretation of the constitution, with an expansive nation-wide effect on civil liberties. This political trend continues even in the face of conflict with, or inertia by, the parliament. The power of the Court to determine the constitutionality of statutes is very important because it influences the political line of the government and the legislative action of the parliament which must necessarily fill in the gaps created by the frequent decisions finding legislation unconstitutional.[7]

The Constitutional Court thus frequently takes on a role of co-legislature (Capotosti 1993) and increasingly undertakes functions that mediate social interests and conflicts. The complexity of the present social stratification and the increasing heterogeneity of the parliamentary forces have made the task of the Constitutional Court increasingly difficult.[8] The Court not only operates in cases of legislative inaction, but also acts when the heterogeneous parliamentary forces create legislative text containing basic conflicts reflecting legislative political fractionalizing. In other words, the Court is a way to guarantee constitutional pluralism by solving such conflicts, as well as a means to accomplish a balance between political forces, social elements and jurisdictional power. The Court's action in such situations is not derived according to predetermined choices but, in essentially programmatic terms, stems mainly from a dynamic consideration of social interests.

Increasingly, the Court's work shows signs of cooperation and implicit dialogue with other courts. This has led at least some courts at certain levels to adopt provocative behaviour that stimulates the Court to favour, even if only indirectly, a democratic evolution of the system. All levels of the judiciary are now sensitive to constitutional values. In fact, ordinary judges, in their decisions, increasingly refer to constitutional norms when interpreting non-constitutional norms.

In this respect, the enactment of the 1948 constitution has distinctly changed the judiciary (see Bartole 1984: 749). Progressively, the hierarchical structure which characterized the judicial system during the fascist period has been overcome. During the fascist period, a judge's career was based on a series of promotions obtained by successive degrees going up the ladder of court jurisdiction (lower courts, courts of appeals, Corte di Cassazione). A judge could reach a higher level of the hierarchy with a promotion decided by superior judges. Therefore, judges of the appeals court and those of the Corte di Cassazione exerted direct power over the lower court judges, whose future careers they decided based on a scrutiny of the inferior court judges' decisions totally independent of the appeals procedure. Younger judges often tried to hasten career advances by uncritically adopting the mainstream trends of the Corte di Cassazione. The leading orientation of the superior judges was thus widely accepted not for any intrinsic validity, but mainly because innovations within the system were discouraged and the importance of the conservative components of the judiciary was stressed. The absence of a real independence of the judiciary and the cooperation between the executive and the highest levels linked the whole judiciary to the political trends of conservatism.[9]

Only with the creation of the Constitutional Court,[10] did ordinary judges gain the power to ask the new and independent body to decide all questions of the constitutional legitimacy of a law, upon the parties' request or the judge's own initiative. Judges of inferior courts took enormous advantage of this power and they became the main source of work for the Constitutional Court. Through their action, they allowed the Constitutional Court to overcome the distinction between normative and programmatic norms of the constitution – a distinction that had been used by the higher judges immediately after the end of the fascist period to render ineffective some of the most innovative parts of the constitution. By promoting the activity of the Constitutional Court, inferior judges have been participating indirectly in the formation of the political constitutional trend and in the interpretation of the programmatic norms.

Thus, in Italy, the Constitutional Court and, to a much lesser extent, courts in general have become a place where groups can address their claims after they have been unsuccessful in redressing their grievances at a jurisdictional level and thereby influence indirectly the legislative process. On the part of the Constitutional Court, there has been a willingness to exercise the power of judicial review to implement and safeguard the philosophy of democracy that underlies the present Italian constitution.

The United States: a common-law system

In common-law systems, civil liberties evolved within different historical events. The mediation between political authorities and the freedom of single individuals often took place through judicial decisions. As judges offered adequate guarantees to dominant elites, to whom judges were often connected, a wider and more flexible margin of tolerance towards social dissent and a greater protection of civil liberties were permitted. In the United States, in particular, the events surrounding the proclamation of civil liberties intermingled with the diffusive effects of the principles of religious tolerance and equal protection of the laws.

In United States' political ideology, legal pronouncements, especially those emanating from the highest courts, have important symbolic content. Indeed, 'law furnishes American politics with its most important symbols of legitimacy' (Scheingoll 1974; see also Bumiller 1988). The Supreme Court is often viewed as a stabilizing instrument of government that provides continuity and usually alters the direction of its judgments gradually. In contrast, the 'political' branches, the legislatures, are able, at least in theory, to make more sharp and sudden turns in law-making.

Some of the most important political questions are transformed into legal questions through the intervention of courts, especially regarding basic constitutional values of due process and equal protection of the laws. Although historically Americans have often resorted to courts to challenge the action of government and private persons, only since the late 1950s has the use of litigation as an instrument of social reform become so widespread as to be called a movement. Most notable in this field has been the work of civil rights groups which provide legal assistance and funding to support recourse to courts.

In the United States, constitutional justice originated as an aspect of ordinary jurisdiction. Albeit a highly contested issue in the early days of the Union, the constitution ultimately was declared the supreme law of the land. Of course, within the United States federalist structure, the decisions in which lower courts (federal or state) could hear constitutional issues evolved until 1875, with state courts having exclusive jurisdiction prior to that time and federal and state courts having concurrent jurisdiction subsequently. Following *Marbury v. Madison*[11] and its progeny, judges were required to consider, if raised by the parties, the constitutionality of a law as a normal task and, at least in principle, judges were compelled to adapt their decisions to constitutional norms. The principle of *stare decisis*, that is of considering decisions taken by higher courts as binding, confers on the Supreme Court's opinions an effectiveness that goes beyond any single case.[12] Moreover, the power of judicial review authorizes the Supreme Court to hold unconstitutional, and hence unenforceable, any law deemed to be in conflict with the constitution.

The importance of the role which courts have been viewed as playing in law-making and 'therefore in determining social and economic policy has varied in the United States throughout its history' (Gilmore 1977: 15). Prior to the Civil War, certain common-law courts took a surprisingly consequentialist view of their role (e.g. in addressing the challenges of the economic development of the new nation). Legislatures were not very active and therefore judges had to take over the task of answering questions they left unsolved. After the Civil War, during the reign of the so-called classical period of United States jurisprudence, the prevailing view was that law was a closed logical system: judges were not considered as law-makers, but their function was to declare and enforce the already existing law. The judicial function in theory had nothing to do with adapting existing law to changing social conditions. Towards the end of the nineteenth century, legislatures became more proactive and the first administrative agencies (sub-branches of the executive) were set up. In the early part of the twentieth century, this tradition continued: it was customary to draw a sharp distinction between the judicial function and the legislative function. Courts allegedly decided cases only in the light of pre-existing common law or statutory rules. Great deference was given to the legislature; when the legislature had spoken, the courts theoretically were bound to carry out the legislative command and only the legislature could change the rules. The coming of the New Deal marked a departure from this approach, as Gilmore points out: 'by the 1930s, with the prodigious legislative and regulatory efforts which marked the New Deal period, it became fashionable to say that judges had had their day, which would not come again. Nevertheless, since the end of World War II, we have witnessed an extraordinary resurgence of judicial activism' (Gilmore 1997: 15).

A leading and guiding principle was that judges must interpret the rules to reflect the changing conditions of life. Since the 1950s, particularly since *Brown v. Board of Education*,[13] civil litigation has been viewed as a means for reinterpreting the law. The strategy of the litigants is often called 'social advocacy' and the role of courts commonly called 'judicial activism'. The remedial mechanism is essentially twofold: change is sought in the substantive law through judicial decisions, and specific enforcement of legal obligation is sought through injunctions implemented under court supervision (Bickel 1962; Ely 1980; Brest 1981).

For example, the Warren Court was regarded as 'activist' because it issued decisions supporting equal treatment for society's habitual unequals: racial minorities, but also aliens, illegitimates and poor people. The Court's decisions in the field of political expression and association (Hall 1989: 309 ff., 323–4; Rostow 1952) have, for decades, been a matter of public praise or blame, even though judicial 'activism' has been an integral part of prior courts.[14]

So in practice the differences between the two systems tend to fade away. The role of the United States Supreme Court and that of the Italian Constitutional Court are somewhat similar: to be the conscience of the country and to guarantee change and yet continuity within a democratic process. The potential of the use of litigation as a tool to influence future cases is analogous in the two countries and constitutes an example of the convergence of civil law and common law. The judiciary is urged, or may be urged, to intervene, although with different modalities, in defence of civil rights.

To say that a civil-law system is lacking the binding character of judicial precedents is not always accurate. It is possible in such a system to carry out law reform through presenting typical cases in court and thus to move the courts beyond the interests of the parties involved in a single suit and to protect, indirectly, all members of a group. In fact, even in the Italian system, decisions in the constitutional area have normative power and therefore can give rise to a process of law reform. Similarly, the traditional description of common-law systems as characterized by the opposition between judicial and legislative sources of law-making is not always correct. In both countries, law reforms connected with the fight against poverty are grounded in constitutionally protected rights. The two systems also converge with respect to the law-making function of judicial action as the level of last resort.

SOCIAL ANTAGONISM

The relevance of litigation as a tool for combating poverty cannot be imputed only to the existence or to the lack of judicial review. The explanation of the different use and the target to which such litigation is directed must be sought at a distinct level: the social one. The protection of the poor can be conceived as the defence of the isolated litigant or can be targeted towards a group of people whose characteristics vary, in different systems, for historical reasons. This implies that, through a single case, the problems of an underprivileged group can be more broadly dealt with for the benefit of a group through a mobilization of forces able to modify the economic and social plight of the parties. Litigation can concern the problems of clients as individuals or the problems of clients as members of a social group. The protection of group interests (otherwise left unprotected or underprotected by political or economic power) is different in Italy and in the United States. In Italy, the increasing diffusion of forms of organized defence focused on the working class. In the United States, social group legitimation has mainly an ethnic and racial dimension and is focused on minorities. Whatever form it takes, social antagonism creates movements that are likely to appropriate the most effective ways to reach social and legal reforms and to use litigation as a tool to accomplish their political goals. The formation of these movements creates specific groups which are determined by the salient characteristic of the social history of the system. Therefore the historical context in which the group phenomenon evolves is extremely important.

Italy

Italian society remains an example of extreme class conflict and of a marked ideological fragmentation, reflected in the voting behaviour and political institutions of the country. A fairly rigid system of social stratification is still in place and recent economic developments have made it more fluid only to a minor extent. Class rigidities tend to be modified very slowly, because they mostly reflect situations that have evolved over several centuries.

The mobilization of underprivileged groups and the resulting social conflicts were directed against this class structure. The social antagonism resulting from a class system has been harnessed by some interest groups representing the working class. In a situation where the socialist and other left-wing parties were the main political forces opposed to the middle class, the various needs and expectations of weaker and oppressed classes were conflated into the political and socioeconomic perspective of the strongest section of workers. Slowly, with the development of the labour–management struggle, the problems of the poor and otherwise underprivileged tended to become secondary.

The concept of class is thus fundamental to understanding the extent of the protection offered to indigents. In particular, in the legal system, protection of the poor became equated with protection of the lower classes of workers (underemployed and unemployed), i.e. the underprivileged vis-à-vis their relation to the labour market. Protection was given to the weaker strata of society only as a by-product of the gains of the working class. The working class's common identification resides mainly in locating its members within the production process. However, the rest of the lower strata of society has no common element of identification with, perhaps, the controversial exception of characteristics of the culture, in the anthropological sense of the term, which they share.

This distinction evolved with the development of the industrialization process. Industrialization made a late appearance in Italy, compared with the rest of Europe. However, its implications were equally important. Mass parties built their political as well as electoral support primarily on the urban working class created by the industrialization process. Poverty came to be considered an extreme consequence of the class struggle that caused the exploitation of the weaker strata of society. The problem of poverty was absorbed into the wider issues of the dynamics of social classes, tending to disappear in the face of other interests of the working class. Poverty as such was neglected and the interests of the strongest components of this class were represented. On the other hand, from the industrial citizenship acquired by the working class, a network of social and civil rights radiated to other citizens, rights belonging mainly to higher classes. The working class was a sort of a buffer between the lower middle class which benefited, to a large extent, from its victories and the lowest classes, not connected with the labour market, which have only to a minor extent improved their plight as a reflection of the gains of the working class.

In general, the political system, in its highly fragmented form, plays a central role in Italian life. This political connotation is due to a characteristic of the Italian system known as the priority of politics (*primato della politica*) (Barcellona 1973; 1978: 21–33; 1984: ch. 1; Treu 1979: 39–53; Pizzorusso 1980b: 93–115). The ability to organize and the capacity for association are found mainly, if not uniquely, in those who made a precise political choice. The force and power for collective action can be gathered only when this action can be inserted into a certain well-defined political orientation. This happens not because of vetoes by political parties, but simply because, outside these parties, there is no energy, initiative or merely interest in collective action. The parties have rooted themselves deeply in society.[15] In fact, the organized work of voluntary associations of any kind is tied, in one way or another, to political parties. Their effectiveness as articulators and aggregators of certain interests is remarkable. In crucial moments of Italian history, politics took the place that religion holds in other countries, especially Protestant ones. The Italian identification with certain ideologies and social memberships was an answer to the needs of social and moral reforms that elsewhere were expressed within religious movements and struggles.

Political parties are not just the principal instruments of representation, but also the major institutions of policy-making and policy implementation. Many parties, not a single one, run the country. At the beginning of the 1970s, the monopoly of political parties on political action came to an end and a politicization of trade unions took place to represent the new interests of workers in the political system. Trade unions became more and more closely allied not only with political parties, but also with an increasing number of other public institutions. Italian unions have always articulated their demands beyond the immediate economic issues at stake and, as such, have become involved in larger social issues. With their politicization, trade unions' involvement became increasingly powerful. Later, their participation in the political arena increased.

Traditionally, class movement has meant a collective action implying the existence of a conflict concerning the appropriation of the resources of a society. That view contained two fundamental classes, opposed and antagonist: the capitalistic bourgeoisie and the working class. In recent times, the general effect of the antagonism of advanced capitalistic societies has given a different shape to the so-called class conflict that does not centre directly on the production process, but tends to move towards peripheral relations that connect the production to political regulation of the production cycle.

During traditional working-class struggles, forms of organization and struggle developed autonomously from the bargaining and conciliation procedures arranged and sanctioned by the state.[16] Certain demands for better living conditions in collective life are not addressed to the state to urge legislative intervention, but are addressed through initiatives of mutual aid, autonomously organized, in some cases even in illegal forms, or end up in a direct attack against opposite social interests. These collective phenomena which cross the social structure of an advanced capitalistic society like Italy represent the symptoms of new class movements. We are not dealing solely with the production of economic resources, but with the production of social relationships, of symbols and of identities. The control of social production has slowly shifted from mere property belonging to the bourgeoisie to huge apparatuses of economic and political decision-making. Capitalistic development can no longer be guaranteed through the simple control of natural resources, but rather it necessitates an increasing intervention in social relationships and symbolic systems of identity. It thus becomes impossible, or at least very difficult, to speak of a working class in the traditional sense of the term. The largest concentrations of employers are now found not in industries, but rather in other sectors such as public offices, universities, public transportation and other service sectors. The demands of unions reflect this new representational structure that does not necessarily coincide with the interests of the poor. However, one thing that has not changed is that the new movements are in the first place focused on the political system, which has become the only real target of collective demands.

Italian left-wing political parties and trade unions, whose purpose is the organization and the protection of the working classes, have a long tradition of strength and combativeness. Because of the ineffectiveness of the legal aid provided by the state, they, in large part, have filled the institutional gap in the legal aid system and appropriated the exclusive right to provide not only traditional union protection but also legal assistance within the framework of a strong political and social meaning. The main task of the legal aid offices of these organizations, which are formally directed towards the protection of single clients, has broadened and becomes a way to elaborate and coordinate broad-based legal issues.

In Italy, the role of litigation in combating poverty traditionally has been and continues to be in the background, both because of the perceived legal structure of the civil-law system and because social forces arising from the class conflict have not widely used and considered litigation as an important strategy to reach their political goals. But, of course, within civil-law societies, judges do create law through interpretation that reflects their own ideologies. However, when litigation has played a more important role in legal and social reforms, it has used the typical legal mechanisms developed within the social antagonism of its milieu and set forth by the most typical and strongest social forces expressing such social antagonism.

The United States

In the United States, there has been little political struggle and class consciousness in the sense seen in Italy. Private charity first and statutorily enacted governmental welfare programmes later were the tools used to deal with the problem of poverty. The poor have typically been acquiescent in their role and status and, in general, grateful for the charity and for the welfare benefits they receive. Less coercion has been necessary to maintain their acquiescence than has been true in other developed countries, even poor ones like Italy. The political rhetoric that America is the 'land of equal opportunities' pervades the system, legal and not, and the poor are inclined to attribute their unhappy condition to their own failings and inadequacies. Unlike Italy, where the principle is that of equality of wealth and income and of people ending up equal, in America the main assumption is that people start out 'equal', i.e. on a level playing field.

As racial minorities have increasingly mobilized to be heard in national politics, issues concerning underprivileged classes have been related to the concept of minority status, instead of one of class. But within a multiethnic and multiracial society such as the United States, effective voice often depends on the ability and willingness of various groups to mingle their overlapping interests and to bind themselves into a majority.

The lack of class antagonism can be related to the absence of a class-consciousness or solidarity of the kind seen in Italy. Nineteenth-century American society lacked inherited feudal institutions and class distinctions that in Europe had contributed to create social antagonism. A number of conditions prevented the full integration of the labour movement into American society. Lacking a unifying tradition, workers were sometimes identified with immigrants, also less integrated into American society. There was no centralized and consolidated state against which to turn for demands. The lower classes had no collective history or common traditions to share or to oppose.

Most importantly, in the United States, individualistic ethics prevailed over class solidarity. This was fuelled by the presence of economic opportunities, particular theories of social and political equality, and ethnic and partisan divisions. Universal white male suffrage existed in the United States long before it was instituted in most of Europe. There were immense territories, only partially exploited and controlled, which presented an alternative to factory work. The rapid exploitation of the continent's natural resources produced recurrent labour shortages and generally a rise in the level of real income. As a result, relatively few Americans believed that they or their children were going to be permanent members of the working class. The accelerated process of industrialization, accompanied by enormous technological changes, caused a strong social mobility of the labour force, already fragmented by immigration from overseas. Not only did American workers share no common grievance of exclusion from full citizenship, but they also developed strong loyalties towards both of the two major capitalist parties, a development that further reduced their sense of class unity.

Equally important, the ethnic and racial heterogeneity of American workers in the nineteenth and early twentieth centuries often overshadowed their common status as wage-earners, a fact that worked to the advantage of many employers. Ethnic and race prejudice divided and divides groups that have much in common (for instance, blacks and poor whites) and unites groups (for instance, whites, rich and poor) that have little in common except their antagonism for the racial minority. The degradation of blacks and of other minorities frequently served to bind together the white population and to create a sense of solidarity. Lower-class whites often support issues and conflicts advancing middle-class values, even to the detriment of their own economic interests. American blacks have thus been isolated from many potential allies (Bell 1980: 492).

Historically, ethnic groups were the first to coalesce and gain minority status, as well as, most importantly, a related consciousness (Braces 1872). Racial groups were the next to obtain this status and the related consciousness. Ethnic and racial movements in the United States focused largely on status and political gains. The rising demands among blacks first for civil rights, then for equality of opportunity and finally for equality of participation in the social, economic and political institutions of the country, resonated strongly within other ethnic groups. For historical reasons, the racial minority activities through which group consciousness was created were characterized by a strong political emphasis, which then extended to every underprivileged and marginalized group, whether based on ethnicity (first) or gender or sexual orientation (at a later stage).

In the second part of the twentieth century, a highly politicized consciousness of blacks as a group (poor and not poor) cut across economic class lines. Protests, boycotts and new-found social assertiveness were used to seek resolution of conflicts based on economic and political deprivation. These tactics aimed at transforming conflict into positive social change and into the creation of needed institutional alternatives.[17]

American blacks constituted a highly visible deprived minority, that had not as a whole shared in the affluence of the post-Second World War era. The exclusion of blacks from parts of the labour market and from electoral politics raised grave doubts, among both blacks and whites, about the authenticity and pervasiveness of the democratic process and of other basic freedoms. The oppression of religious minorities as well as of national ones (i.e. those connected with a foreign country, such as the Italian or the Irish immigrants), although involving forced assimilation through the state's control over education and xenophobic reactions to foreigners and their cultures, has usually not included exclusion from the political arena. Minorities other than blacks have not been as systematically victimized by an entrenched system of discrimination or by the politics that create and enforce it. Of course, Native Americans were confined by 1880 to reservations; their culture and traditions were not respected and treaties to which they were parties were easily broken. The government pursued a strategy of detribalization and concession of full citizenship. In the West and in California in particular, strong hatred of Asians existed, with ordinances and statutes providing for separated schools and discrimination in the laundry business. However, in contrast to the deep societal roots of governmental action against blacks, action against other minorities has often been sporadic, transitory and local.

The plight of blacks was different and much more dramatic. In the South, blacks were prevented from enjoying the advantages that would have come from full political participation. Terror was an omnipresent factor in southern regional politics (Myrdal 1944). Much of the internal history of the United States has concerned black and white relations and most major political and social issues have been affected by race relations. Despite the gains of the civil rights movement, the majority of black citizens still receive an inferior education, earn less and are underrepresented in government as compared to their white counterparts.

Expectations about social change in the area of racial and ethnic relations in the United States prevailed around the middle of the twentieth century among the liberal black and white leadership of the movement for racial equality. The outcome of this process was, in some quarters, an intensification of structural separatism and the emergence, generally unanticipated, of the black power movement. From the middle of the 1960s, an anti-white movement by the blacks has arisen with a marked transformation of black ethnicity into a political movement.

When the attention of American society has turned to underprivileged classes other than the ones that gained a group consciousness through ethnic and racial characteristics, interesting implications have emerged. The outcome of President Johnson's War on Poverty can be seen as evidence of the importance of group solidarity to social change and legal reform. The War on Poverty represented a bureaucratic effort, at a federal level, to work out a programme for the reduction of poverty. This effort turned out to be a fight among private and public agencies to gain resources and public support, as bureaucratic organizations were given funds by the government. The War on Poverty failed in its goal of eradicating or even substantially reducing poverty. Its failure, as a programme created bureaucratically, is even clearer if seen in comparison to the civil rights revolution, a movement created by social and political forces.

The intervention of the federal courts was critical to the civil rights revolution of the 1950s and 1960s. Blacks, who fought for their rights in many battlefields, used the Bill of Rights and the Fourteenth Amendment to the constitution to create case law on civil rights to an extent previously unknown. Civil rights organizations, first among them the National Association for the Advancement of Colored People (NAAPC), used litigation as a strategy to press for racial equality. During this period, blacks were by far the most vocal minority group looking at courts to obtain support.

The attitude of the Supreme Court towards black citizens changed markedly after the 1940s, although the reasons for the shift are quite complex. At first, the constitutional war on racism achieved only gradual results and indeed had major setbacks. The court declared that certain situations and practices were unconstitutional within individual cases, but although black plaintiffs won a number of particular cases, the larger issue of desegregation was avoided. But as it became clear that the oppression of a minority could raise significant political issues, often beyond the scope presented by a particular case, judicial intervention was considered justified to modify the constitutional structure itself. The Supreme Court, especially the Warren Court, took a stand on protecting unpopular minorities and furthering their interests. The Burger Court largely halted this development, but kept most of the law it inherited. The role of civil rights organizations and the importance of litigation for reaching reform-oriented objectives was articulated by the US Supreme Court:

> In the context of NAACP objectives, litigation is not a technique of resolving private differences; it is a means for achieving the lawful objectives of equality of treatment by all governments, federal, state and local, for the members of the Negro community in this country. It is thus a form of political expression. Groups which find themselves unable to achieve their objectives through the ballot frequently turn to the courts. Just as it was true of the opponents of New Deal legislation during the 1930's, for example, no less is it true of the Negro minority

today. And under the conditions of modern government, litigation may well be the sole practicable avenue open to a minority to petition for redress of grievances.[18]

The civil rights movement, although not initially, ultimately dealt with issues of poverty because so many blacks and other allies were poor and therefore in need of public support. It enlisted militant leaders who campaigned to improve the legal and then the socioeconomic situation of the poor, and trained a cadre of activists who informed poor people of their rights. Most importantly, the civil rights movement crystallized the sense of inequality and relative deprivation that affected all low-income people, regardless of race or ethnicity.

Most notably, wealth-based discrimination was left outside the core arena of judicial competence. The poor have not been considered a discrete group, as 'it is not clear that preferring a poor person confers a benefit on the poor conceived as a group, because in this instance the benefited individual merely leaves the group' (Fiss 1975: 163). Issues of economic inequality raise claims of competing groups, and courts are not considered competent to decide which group is worthier. Rather, the judgment has traditionally been left to the legislative branch,[19] because legislatures are believed to be the institutions that most accurately represent various groups' interests. On these assumptions, it is no wonder then that 'the crusade to extend special constitutional protection to the poor has turned into a rout' (Ely 1980: 148).

Despite this judicial marginalization of wealth-based discrimination, other groups attempted to replicate the judicial victories of blacks, envisioning litigation as a tool for social reform. Legal Services lawyers were committed to the poor and their cause, while other public interest lawyers were concerned with issues related to the environment, the protection of consumers' and women's rights. But the effectiveness of judicial reform is frequently tied to the consciousness of the group for which the legal reform is provided. The civil rights movement combined a traditional use of litigation with an increasing group consciousness, that of minorities, and a political context in order to achieve its victories.

CONCLUSIONS

The importance of litigation as a tool for combating poverty is, of course, connected to the role of the judiciary and of judicial review in a legal system. The roots of the perceived differences in using litigation to obtain social change and legal reform are on occasion traced to a contrast between a common-law and a civil-law system. However, this stereotypical vision does not have the clear-cut contours it was viewed as having in the past. Indeed, the role of the Italian judiciary has greatly changed within the past sixty years and the articulated differences between a civil-law and a common-law system have become less distinct.

In both Italy and the United States, legal reforms which can affect legal aid and leave a mark on the societal structure build mainly on rights protected and guaranteed at a constitutional level. The two systems do not have considerable differences with respect to the law-making function of courts of last resort, and, to a lesser extent, judicial action in general. Even in the Italian system, constitutional decisions have normative power and therefore can contribute to a process of law reform within the complex Italian technicalities. On a different level, the accepted doctrine and criteria in the two systems regarding the appropriate scope of political discretion in constitutional adjudication are analogous. In practice, the differences between the two systems tend to fade away. The role of the United States Supreme Court and the role of the Italian Constitutional Court is to be the conscience of the country and to guarantee change, and yet continuity, in the process of democracy. Also the criteria of political opportunity used in their jurisdictional activity are not different. The potential use of litigation as a tool to influence future cases is very similar in the two countries and constitutes an example of the convergence of civil law and common law. The judiciary is urged, or may be urged, to intervene, although with different modalities, in defence of civil rights, and, of course, organizations providing legal aid services may use these tools as a way to reach legal reforms.

The legal element cannot be detached from the social history of a country. Needs in general, and particularly access to justice, cannot be separated from the specific society's system of social relationships. In each societal system, tools and services provided by the system for the protection of fundamental rights have been and are long denied to various disfavoured and underprivileged groups. As a society evolves, new problems constantly appear and are left unsolved by the organizations of groups previously developed within social formations privileged by the legal system (from trade unions to political parties or civil rights organizations). New methods of dissent arise, which spontaneously create social alliances, on occasion exploiting new phenomena of underprotection. Often, such alliances try to use litigation as a tool of legal reform to accomplish their goals. In these instances, the protection of the poor is not necessarily viewed as the defence of the isolated litigant's case; but implicitly, through the single case, a mobilization of forces may be able to modify the economic and social plight of the underprivileged group. An individual request for assistance has, as an indirect beneficiary, a larger group of persons.

Yet the protection of marginalized groups' interests (otherwise left unprotected or under protected by political or economic power) is different in Italy and in the United States because of the identification of the group: the working class in Italy and minorities in the United States. As a consequence, the organized forms of strategic litigation that are increasingly diffused favour social class interests and the problems shared by their members have been solved, or efforts have been made to solve them, in terms of labour and class issues. In the United States, social group legitimation had an ethnic and racial dimension. The legal mechanisms created for implementation reflect this different structure, centred on discrimination and a concept of equal opportunity for all.

Both within Italy and the United States, these traditional forms of social antagonism have been made more complicated by the formation of new organizations representing e.g. women, children, the physically and mentally disabled, the elderly and so on. These groups have mobilized against a number of categorical injustices, including racial discrimination and equalities of wealth or income, and have assumed a variety of forms, e.g. environmental, consumer or welfare rights organizations. Based on the group, internal ties of solidarity and cohesion vary and the interests carried out may be related to the middle classes, more than to the lower classes. But as new groups struggle against oppression, they have often turned to litigation following the patterns of social antagonism that have evolved through the specific history of that particular society. Therefore, social forces arising from the conflicts within a system can use litigation as an important and successful strategy to reach their political goals.

NOTES

1. According to the most established historiographic doctrines, this way of conceiving the role of the judiciary goes back to the Romans and remained through the French Revolution; but a new historical interpretation points out the similarities among the role of the civil-law and common-law judges in the period preceding the French Revolution. See, for example, Merryman 1985: ch. VI; Gorla 1981: 547 ff.

2. The contribution of the Catholic movement was also essential at the beginning of this century.

3. The Italian constitution was ratified in December 1947 and came into effect on 1 January 1948. The Constituent Assembly, the body that drafted the document, completed its work in January 1947. The original text was extensively changed, often by a few votes, during the lengthy debate, first on the document in general and then on its single articles.

4. The Court was actually established only in December 1955. From the promulgation of the constitution in 1948 until 1955, ordinary courts could rule on the constitutionality of statutes, refusing to apply those they considered unconstitutional. The delay was due to the political climate immediately after the Second World War and to difficulties in selecting judges for this court.

5. The Court adjudicates the constitutionality of statutes, controversies regarding the division of powers among supreme organs of the state, among regions and between regions and the state as well as charges made against the president and ministers (Art. 134).

6. The interpretative decisions of the Court have been classified by the systematic civil-law doctrine into different kinds, according to their effects on the statute. First, there are interpretative decisions in which the question of constitutionality is rejected: in these decisions the Court usually enucleates from the statute a norm which is consistent with the constitutional command in order to save as much as possible of the statutory text. This sort of interpretation is not binding for ordinary judges, but is merely a reasonable presumption. Second, there are interpretative decisions in which the Court upholds the question of unconstitutionality: these decisions can be partial or reductive (i.e. where the declaration of the constitutional illegitimacy is limited only to a part of the statute), and additional (i.e. where the Court declares the constitutional legitimacy of the norm only in the part where the norm itself is silent and introduces in the place of the omission the discipline which was missing, obtaining it from other norms or from the general principles of the legal system). Finally, there are decisions in which the Court substitutes for a part of the text of the statute another part created by the Court as an interpretation of the norm in question. See Biscaretti di Ruffia 1983: 614ff.

7. The exceptional character of the effectiveness *erga omnes* of the decisions taken by the Constitutional Court affirming the constitutional illegitimacy of a norm implies *a contrario* that those decisions in which the question of constitutionality is believed to have no ground are binding only for the single case. It is therefore possible, in other trials, to raise the same question with respect to the same norm, for the same reason and by the same parties.

8. Elia, pointing out the composition of interests accomplished by the legislature in the part where this mediation can be submitted to a control according to the equal protection clause, states: 'It is clear that the Court must not superimpose its own choices on the ones adopted by the legislature. But it is also obvious that it cannot avoid exercising some control on that minimum of rationality necessary to give a foundation to those choices, in the absence of which we face real discriminations' (Elia 1984: 496).

9. However, this does not mean that, even during the fascist period, the judiciary did not express its autonomy of judgment in various ways.

10. The enactment of the constitution itself did not have the immediate effect of automatically subverting the existing judicial system.

11. *Marbury v. Madison*, 1 Cranch 137 (1803).

12. The trend to favour new social interests is facilitated by the fact that majority opinions can be accompanied by dissents or concurrences, with important reflections both on public opinion and on future cases.

13. *Brown v. Board of Education*, 374 US 483 (1954).

14. Example of earlier interventionist court: *Lochner v. New York*, 198 US 45.

15. For this reason, the terrorist attacks in the 1970s were turned not only against the state but also against political parties.

16. This is the case, for instance, of union law. Spontaneous strikes, occupations of factories and other forms of political mutual aid within working-class struggle in substance eliminate these very same assumptions on which wage autonomy regulated by the state is founded.

17. Function of control accomplished by the liberal ideology with the aim to protect the state from the excessive demands of the citizens.

18. *NAACP v. Button*, 371 US 415 (1963), 429–30.

19. A method, as opposed to test-case litigation, for obtaining legal reform is lobbying, which operates through the legislative branch. The lobbyist is a person who often stays with a key legislative committee or government agency for years, slowly and quietly building the relationship, supplying information and establishing confidence and mutual interest.

REFERENCES

Abraham (1982) *Freedom and the Court. Civil Rights and Liberties in the United States*, New York and Oxford: Oxford University Press.

Assini, N. (1982) 'Il Seguito (Legislativo) delle Sentenza della Corte Costituzionale in Parlamento', in *Giurisprudenza Costituzionale*, 27 (1).

Barcellona, P. (1978) 'Costituzione, Partiti e Democrazia', *Democrazia e Diritto*, XVIII.

— (1984) *I Soggetti e le Norme*, Milano: Giuffre.

— (ed.) (1973) *L'Uso Alternativo del Diritto*, 2 vols, Bari: Laterza.

Bartole (1984) 'Il Potere Giudiziario', in Amato and Barbera (eds), *Manuale di Diritto Pubblico*, Bologna: Il Mulino.

Bell, D. (1980) *Race, Racism and American Law*, Boston: Little, Brown.

Bickel (1962) *The Least Dangerous Branch*, New Haven, CT: Yale University Press.

— (1970) *The Supreme Court and the Idea of Progress*, New York: Harper and Row.

Biscaretti di Ruffia, P. (1983) *Diritto Costituzionale. Istituzioni di Diritto Pubblico*, 13th edn, Napoli: Jovene.

Braces, C. L. (1872) *The Dangerous Classes of New York*, New York.

Brest (1981) 'The Fundamental Rights Controversy: The Essential Contradiction of Normative Constitutional Scholarship', *Yale Law Journal* 90: 1063.

Bumiller, K. (1988) *The Civil Rights Society. The Social Construction of Victims*, Baltimore, MD, and London: Johns Hopkins University Press.

Calabresi (1982) *A Common Law for an Age of Statutes*, Cambridge, MA, and London: Harvard University Press.

Capotosti, P. (1983) 'Tendenze Attuali dei Rapporti fra Corte Costituzionale e Sistema Politico-Costituzionale', in *Giurisprudenza Costituzionale*, 28 (1): 1597–608.

Casavola (1995) 'I Principi Supremi nella Giurisprudenza della Corte Costituzionale', *Democrazia e Diritto*.

Delgado (1995) *Critical Race Theory. The Cutting Edge*, Philadelphia: Temple University Press.

Delgado and Stefancic (1997) *Critical White Studies. Looking Behind the Mirror*, Philadelphia: Temple University Press.

Elia, L. (1982) 'Conferenza Stampa 1981 del Presidente della Corte Costituzionale', *Giurisprudenza Costituzionale*, 27 (1).

— (1984) 'Conferenza Stampa del Presidente della Corte Costituzionale (La Giustizia Costituzionale nel 1983)', *Giurisprudenza Costituzionale*.

Ely (1980) *Democracy and Distrust*, Cambridge, MA: Harvard University Press.

Fiss (1975) 'Groups and the Equal Protection Clause', *Philosophy and Public Affairs*.

Friedman (1985) *A History of American Law*, New York: Simon and Schuster.

Gilmore, G. (1977) *The Ages of American Law*, New Haven, CT: Yale University Press.

Gorla (1981) *Diritto Comparato e Diritto Comune Europeo*, Milano: Giuffre.

Granata (1997) 'La Giustizia Costituzionale nel 1996 (Conferenza Stampa del Presidente)', *Giurisprudenza Costituzionale*.

— (1998) 'La Giustizia Costituzionale nel 1997 (Conferenza Stampa del Presidente)', *Giurisprudenza Costituzionale*.

Hall (1989) *The Magic Mirror. Law in American History*, New York and Oxford: Oxford University Press.

Merryman (1985) *The Civil Law Tradition*, 2nd edn, Stanford, CA: Stanford University Press.

Myrdal, G. (1944) *An American Dilemma: The Negro Problem and Modern Democracy*, New York: McGraw-Hill.

Pace (1986) 'Strumenti e tecniche di Giudizio della Corte Costituzionale nel Conflitto tra Poteri', *Giurisprudenza Costituzionale*.

Patterson (1981) *American Struggle against Poverty, 1900–1980*, Cambridge, MA: Harvard University Press.

Piven and Fox (1971) *Regulating the Poor. The Functions of Public Welfare*, New York: Vintage Books.

Pizzorusso, A. (1980a) 'La Corte Costituzionale tra Giurisdizione e Legislazione', *Foro Italiano*, V: 120.

— (1980b) 'Riformare la Costituzione?', *Democrazia e Diritto*, XX (1): 93–115.

Rostow (1952) 'The Democratic Character of Judicial Review', *Harvard Law Review*, 66.

Scheingoll, S. (1974) *The Politics of Rights: Lawyers, Public Policy and Political Change*, New Haven, CT: Yale University Press.

Sowell (1984) *Civil Rights: Rhetoric or Reality?*, New York: Quill/William Morrow.

Treu (1980) 'Sindacato e Sistema Politico', *Democrazia e Diritto*, XIX (1): 39–53.

Vassalli (2000) 'La Giustizia Costituzionale nel 1999 (Conferenza Stampa del Presidente)', *Giurisprudenza Costituzionale*.

EIGHT | Poverty and property – human rights and social security

ASBJØRN KJØNSTAD

§ In Western societies social security systems have gradually become a central source of income support. Contributions by citizens to collective systems have replaced individual savings for a substantial part of the population. As such, ensuring the legal protection of social security benefits becomes a critical agenda for poverty reduction and income redistribution.

One important test of the strength of legal rights is whether or not they are protected by principles held in constitutional law (Kjønstad 1994) and international human rights conventions. In most Western countries, traditional concepts of private property afford the best legal protection. One major question is whether social security rights can be protected in the same way as property. It is also important to consider whether social security rights can be protected in accordance with other human rights principles.

This chapter charts the historical use of these principles, primarily as reflected in Norwegian Supreme Court cases. First I address the different sources of income in a modern society and some of the main characteristics of social security systems. Thereafter follows a discussion of the social and civil human rights conventions protecting social security benefits, showing their potential, albeit unsuccessful, applicability to two early Norwegian Supreme Court cases. I then juxtapose three important cases regarding social security and property, one from the European Court of Human Rights interpreting human rights conventions, and two from the Norwegian Supreme Court interpreting Norwegian constitutional provisions. By exploring their different approaches, I discuss the importance of combining different fundamental legal principles and conclude with some remarks about social security as property.

There are four main sources of income used by people to cover their living expenses, such as food, clothing, housing, heating, electricity, telephone, television and newspapers:

1. Traditional concepts of property, such as property, private insurance or bank deposits and other savings.
2. Income that is earned through labour by self-employment, work for employers or freelance activities.
3. Family support by parents, spouses, children and other relatives.
4. Social protection, derived from social security and social insurance, social assistance and poverty relief, or charity and donations from private aid organizations.

Which of these sources of income is most important varies from time to time and from place to place. In Europe, income earned as employees has been most important in the twentieth century. In Norway presently, almost half of the population lives on income earned personally, and approximately one-quarter are children and young persons supported by their parents. However, more than one-quarter depend on pensions and other social protection benefits as their main source of income.

THE STRUCTURE OF SOCIAL SECURITY

The social security systems in the European countries provide financial support in the event of sickness, unemployment, disability, old age, death and loss of a supporter. These systems afford security to those who are not in a position to earn their own living. Social security has developed over the last century to become a cornerstone of the *welfare states*. Indeed, one-sixth of Norway's gross national product is allocated to social security purposes.

The Norwegian National Insurance Scheme (Kjønstad 1998) consists of many and varying social security benefits. Table 8.1 contains a survey of the social security benefits that are available under the Norwegian National Insurance Act. The categories, or life situations which can give rise to entitlement to benefits are listed in the left column, subsistence benefits are listed in the middle column, and benefits to cover special needs in the right hand column.

Unemployment benefit, sickness benefit, disability pension, old-age pension and other benefits that cover living expenses are *income-related*. The size of these benefits depends on previous income: the more you have earned, the more you have contributed to the social security sys-

TABLE 8.1 Social security benefits under the Norwegian National Insurance Act

Life situation	Subsistence benefit	Benefit to cover special meeds
Unemployment	Unemployment benefit	
Pregnancy and delivery	Maternity benefit and pregnancy benefit	Expenses in connection with family planning and birth
Adoption	Adoption benefit	
Single parenthood	Transitional benefit	Child-care benefit Education benefit
Own sickness	Sickness benefit	Medical assistance, important medicines and other medical benefits
Other's sickness	Care benefit	
Handicap	Rehabilitation benefit	Rehabilitation assistance
Temporary disability	Occupational benefit	Occupational assistance
Permanent disability	Disability pension	Basic grant and assistance benefit
Old age	Old-age pension	
Family caretaker	Pension/transitional benefit	Educational benefit
Death	Pension/transitional benefits to widow and widower	Educational benefit Child-care benefit Death grant

tem, and the more you receive in social security benefits. Therefore differences in income during working life (class differences) will continue in retirement and other situations when a person needs benefits.

The Norwegian pension system is build on a two-component model:

1. A *basic pension* which is equal for all insured persons. This component guarantees a minimum standard of living regardless of prior earnings and promotes the levelling of incomes.
2. A *supplementary pension* which is related to the insured person's previous income. This component attempts to allow a pensioner, as far as possible, to maintain the standard of living to which he or she is accustomed.

The pension system is therefore a combination of a socialistic model and a capitalistic model.

The social security pensions are *index-tied*, i.e. adjusted in line with changes in the general income level in Norway. This system ensures that the pensions' values are not decreased by inflation, and that pensioners receive a share of the general welfare growth in the country.

Since their introduction, the social security systems have been based upon a model of *legal rights* (Kjønstad and Syse 2001: 90–6). Conditions that entitle a person to receive benefits, and rules for the calculation of benefits, are laid down in laws and regulations. The funds that the social security systems collect as contributions from citizens, and those that the state grants, are distributed among those who have individual rights. The social security administrations do not take into consideration the economic situation of the applicant for a social security pension when they make decisions. On reaching retirement age, an individual has the legal right to receive an old-age pension based on prior earnings, irrespective of how many others are qualified to receive such a pension, or whether it results in a drain on social security funds.

An insured person who is dissatisfied with a decision from the social security administration can appeal to the Social Security Tribunal. This is an administrative body with many characteristics of a court of justice. A person who is dissatisfied with a Tribunal ruling may bring an action before the second level courts of justice.

Thus, given the centrality and pervasiveness of social security benefits as a source for ongoing social protection, it is critical to evaluate the legal character of social security and legal mechanisms, such as human rights provisions and private property concepts, that can protect the right to social security.

SOCIAL HUMAN RIGHTS CONVENTIONS

A number of social human rights conventions incorporate language that articulates a right to social welfare protections. First I will mention the Universal Declaration of Human Rights of 1948, Article 25:

(1) Everyone has the right to a standard of living adequate for the health and well-being of himself and of his family, including food, clothing, housing and medical care and necessary social services, and the right to security in the event of unemployment, sickness, disability, widowhood, old age or other lack of livelihood in circumstances beyond his control.

(2) Motherhood and childhood are entitled to special care and assistance. All children, whether born in or out of wedlock, shall enjoy the same social protection.

TABLE 8.2 Minimum amounts of social security benefits according to the International Labour Convention no. 102.

Contingency	Standard beneficiary	%
Sickness	Man with wife and two children	45
Unemployment	Man with wife and two children	45
Old age	Man with wife of pensionable age	40
Employment injury:		
Incapacity for work	Man with wife and two children	50
Invalidity	Man with wife and two children	50
Survivors	Widow with two children	40
Maternity	Woman	45
Invalidity	Man with wife and two children	40
Survivors	Widow with two children	40

This is followed up in international and regional conventions. The United Nations International Covenant on Economic, Social and Cultural Rights of 16 December 1966, Article 9, contains this short sentence: 'The State Parties to the present Covenant recognize the right of everyone to social security, including social insurance.'

According to the European Social Charter of 18 October 1961, Article 12, the Contracting Parties undertake 'to maintain the social security system at a satisfactory level at least equal to that required for ratification of International Labour Convention (no. 102) concerning Minimum Standards of Social Security'. This Convention contains a comprehensive system of rules and standards concerning the minimum amount of different social security benefits that usually cover 40–50 per cent of the loss of income. Table 8.2 provides a summary.

The social security systems in the Nordic, central and Western European countries have a higher level of benefits than shown in Table 8.2. In Norway, for example, sickness benefits for employees cover 100 per cent of lost income, limited to somewhat above the average income for industrial workers. Pensions and other social security benefits usually cover approximately 60 per cent of the loss.

While many cut-backs in benefits were undertaken in Europe during the 1980s and 1990s due to increasing social security expenditure and difficult economic situations, there is no reason to believe that cut-backs in the near future will bring social security benefits below the level contained in Convention no. 102.

However, for many other countries, this minimum income could prove very important in the struggle against poverty. Asbjørn Eide has stated: 'If the internationally recognized human rights in their entirety had been fully implemented, poverty would not have existed' (Eide 1997: 118).

CIVIL HUMAN RIGHTS PROTECTIONS

In addition to the protection of minimum income in the social human rights conventions, the civil human rights conventions can be significant in the creation and application of a social security system (Kjønstad 1996: 179–88). I will illustrate this with two cases from the Norwegian Supreme Court.

In the first case[1] a seaman was refused a pension for his service during the Second World War because he had been a member of the NS ('Nazi') party. Other seamen received a pension for service during the war. The plaintiff claimed that this provision in the Seamen Pension Act was a violation of the United Nations International Covenant on Civil and Political Rights, Articles 14 and 26.

Article 14 no. 7 states: 'No one shall be … punished again for an offence for which he has already been finally convicted.' The seaman had been punished for his crime (the NS membership) and felt that it would be double punishment if his pension were also reduced.

Article 26 states: 'All persons are equal before the law and are entitled without any discrimination to equal protection of the law.' The seaman felt that he was discriminated against, as compared to other seamen who had done the same work during the war but held another political opinion. The Supreme Court found that human rights were not violated in this case.

The second case[2] concerns the rights of an unmarried mother and her child. She received benefits as a single mother from the social security system, and the child received family support from his father. A section in the Social Security Act stated that the social security system had the right to repayment for the mother's benefit from the child's family support.

The mother and the child claimed that this provision was a violation of the European Convention for the Protection of Human Rights and Fundamental Freedoms, Articles 8 and 14.

Article 8 states: 'Everyone has the right to respect for his private and family life, his home and his correspondence.' The mother and the child claimed that the social security system confiscated the family support from the father, and that this was an interference with their right to a reasonable family economy.

Article 14 states: 'The enjoyment of the rights and freedoms set forth in this Convention shall be secured without discrimination on any ground such as ... birth or other status.' They claimed that they were discriminated against, as compared to other children. The Supreme Court found that the human rights were not violated in this case.

When these two judgments were issued, the two conventions mentioned were not legally binding as Norwegian law. However, since 1999 the European Convention for the Protection of Human Rights and Fundamental Freedoms, the United Nations International Covenant on Civil and Political Rights, and the United Nations International Covenant on Economic, Social and Cultural Rights, are parts of the Norwegian law and have a higher priority than an Act of Parliament. While the Norwegian Supreme Court ruled against the claimant in both these cases, they illustrate ways in which the provisions of human rights conventions were being raised in social security cases in the 1970s and 1980s and provide a framework in which to envision legal protections after 1999.

In light of the dismissive nature of the Norwegian Supreme Court in these two cases, it is instructive to juxtapose a ruling of the European Court of Human Rights with two recent Norwegian Supreme Court cases and to draw lessons therefrom.

INTERPRETATION OF THE HUMAN RIGHTS CONVENTION

In *Gaygusuz v. Austria*,[3] the European Court of Human Rights issued an important ruling protecting social security benefits as a human right. Social science law professors in Europe have followed this matter with close attention (Van Bogaert 1997; Pennings 1999: 181–201).

Mr Gaygusuz was born in Turkey in 1950, but lived and worked in Austria from 1973. He received unemployment and sickness benefits in Austria from October 1984 to July 1986. He then received an advance on his retirement pension in the form of unemployment benefits until April 1987. When his entitlement to unemployment benefits expired, he applied for an advance on his pension in the form of emergency assistance. His application was rejected in July 1987, and he subsequently moved to Turkey later that year.

Emergency assistance is paid to persons who are no longer entitled to unemployment benefits and are in urgent need (unable to provide for essential needs), in order to guarantee them a minimum income. The amount of unemployment benefits is calculated according to the recipient's prior income, and the emergency assistance amounts to 70–100 per cent of the unemployment benefits. Emergency assistance is financed partly from the unemployment insurance contributions that all employees must pay and partly from various governmental sources.

The Austrian Unemployment Insurance Act, section 33, no. 2, states: 'For a grant to be made, the unemployed person must (a) possess Austrian nationality.' There are eight exceptions from this condition in section 34 no. 3, but none of these was relevant in this case.

The Austrian authorities refused to grant emergency assistance to Mr Gaygusuz on the grounds that he did not have Austrian nationality. He argued that this was contrary to Article 14 of the European Convention for the Protection of Human Rights and Fundamental Freedoms (the Convention involved in the second case above) taken in conjunction with Article 1 of Protocol no. 1 of this convention.

Article 14 of the European Convention states: 'The enjoyment of the rights and freedoms set forth in this Convention shall be secured without discrimination on any ground such as ... national ... origin.' Article 1 of Protocol no. 1 to this Convention states: 'Every natural or legal person is entitled to the peaceful enjoyment of his possessions. No one shall be deprived of his possessions except in the public interest and subject to the conditions provided for by law and by the general principles of international law.'

The European Court of Human Rights came to the conclusion that Article 14 of the Convention taken in conjunction with Article 1 of Protocol no. 1 was applicable in this case. Entitlement to emergency assistance is

> linked to the payment of contributions to the unemployment insurance fund, which is a precondition for the payment of unemployment benefit ... It follows that there is no entitlement to emergency assistance where such contributions have not been made ... The court considers that the right to emergency assistance ... is a pecuniary right for the purpose of Article 1 of Protocol No. 1. That provision is therefore applicable without it being necessary to rely solely on the link between entitlement to emergency assistance and the obligation to pay taxes or other contributions.

Concerning compliance, the European Court of Human Rights expressed the following view: 'According to the Court's case-law, a difference of treatment is discriminatory, for the purpose of Article 14, if it "has no objective and reasonable justification", i.e., if it does not pursue a "legitimate aim" or if there is not a "reasonable relationship of proportionality between the means employed and the aim sought to be realized".'

Mr Gaygusuz 'maintained that the difference in treatment between Austrians and non-Austrians ... was not based on any objective and reasonable justification. He had paid contributions to the unemployment insurance fund on the same basis as Austrian employees.'

The Austrian government 'argued that the difference in treatment was based on the idea that the State has special responsibility for its own nationals and must take care of them and provide for their essential needs'. The European Court of Human Rights noted that

> Mr. Gaygusuz was legally resident in Austria and worked there at certain times ... paying contributions to the unemployment insurance fund in the same capacity and on the same basis as Austrian nationals.
>
> The Court ... finds the arguments put forward by the Austrian Government unpersuasive. It considers ... that the difference in treatment between Austrians and non-Austrians as regards entitlement to emergency assistance, of which Mr. Gaygusuz was a victim, is not based on any 'objective and reasonable justification' ... There has thereby been a contravention of Article 1 of Protocol No. 1.

The pecuniary character of emergency assistance and the contribution and property arguments were decisive in the Gaygusuz case. The protection of emergency assistance derived from a combination of the principle of non-discrimination and the principle of property, both contained within a Human Rights Convention.

We cannot be sure that Mr Gaygusuz would have been entitled to emergency assistance if the European Convention had contained an article relating to discrimination only, or if it had contained an article relating to property only.

It is also important to note that emergency assistance was protected in spite of the fact that it appears to be a type of social assistance, rather than ordinary social security insurance, which has traditionally received stronger legal protection. One could have expected that pensions and other social security benefits would be best protected by property principles in constitutions and human rights conventions. This seems to be the legal situation in Germany, where they have gone furthest in the treatment of social security as property (Zacher 1994: 107–34).

TWO NORWEGIAN CONSTITUTIONAL CASES

Constitutional protection of national insurance benefits was the issue in two important cases decided by the Norwegian Supreme Court in 1996 (Kjønstad 1997). The issue presented was whether new provisions in the Social Security Act violated Article 97 of the Norwegian constitution, which forbids retroactive legislation, and Article 105, which protects private property.

In the first matter, the *Borthen* case,[4] the issue was whether a new income limitation for the spousal supplement may be applied retroactively to an individual who, prior to the change in the law, received an old-age pension with a spousal supplement.

In the second matter, the *Thunheim* case,[5] the constitutionality of new legislation that reduced future pension points was challenged. This law affected the plaintiff's pension points and resulted in a lower supplementary (income-related) pension for Thunheim, who had been granted disability pension prior to the change of the law.

In the Borthen case, a majority of ten justices underlined that our 'pension system has been built up gradually through legislation for more than a hundred years'. The National Insurance System shall

> through basic pension … secure a minimum level for all and, through supplementary pension, a living standard at a reasonable level compared to what the pensioner had while working … Such security and safety has as a prerequisite that the insured can plan based on the assumption that the rights the law establishes – at least the most important part of them – are there when the pension situation is reached … The pension system … has replaced earlier systems with poverty and maintenance laws, and has – which is also the intention – to a great extent replaced earlier pension and insurance schemes. Through the system that has been built up, and the expectations that have been created, a position has been established which the legislator is not free to change.

In opposition to the argument for 'safety and expectations for the insured' stood the argument for

> freedom for the legislator to change the National Insurance rights … The National Insurance System constitutes a large portion of the state budget. National Insurance expenses are about ⅓ of the state's total expenses.
>
> Parliament, through Article 75 a and d of the Constitution is given control over the national budget – both income and expenses. An extensive limitation on the legislators' right to regulate national insurance benefits would be in conflict with the ideas behind Article 75 a and d, and this must have a considerable impact on the determination of the limitations Article 97 sets.

The Supreme Court's majority concluded that only 'clearly unreasonable and unjust' retroactive changes would be unconstitutional. The majority thereby gives more weight to Parliament's governing function than the individual's need for reliance.

In this case, six justices concluded that 'the Constitution basically does not give the pensioners any protection against changes in the National Insurance laws'. Only in 'extreme cases could changes in the National Insurance system – also when the supplementary pension is not taken into account – be of a character that would violate the Constitution'.

One justice dissented, stating that 'National Insurance benefits must have considerable protection under Article 97 in the Constitution'. He came to the conclusion that the challenged law in the Thunheim case was unconstitutional, but not the law in the Borthen case.

Under the Supreme Court's ruling in these two cases, National Insurance benefits are protected under the Norwegian constitution, but only in rare cases will the courts set aside new legislation that reduces granted or earned benefits.

The Supreme Court did not give the supplementary pension better protection than the basic pension and the spousal supplement; arguments linked to the 'earning' of national insurance benefits through payments of fees are given little or no weight. Finally, Article 105 in the constitution (protection of private property) was held not applicable to the protection of national insurance benefits in these two cases.

COMBINATION OF FUNDAMENTAL LEGAL PRINCIPLES

Constitutional and human rights are best safeguarded when we can combine two or more fundamental legal principles, such as non-discrimination, protection of property, protection of earned rights, legal expectancy, prohibition against retroactive legislation and the principle of proportionality.

A combination of two principles arose in the Thunheim case – the principle of prohibition against retroactive legislation and the principle of protection of property, in the context of whether or not to protect the supplementary pension to which Thunheim had paid contributions. In the Borthen case, it was a question of whether or not to protect the spousal supplement for which Borthen had not paid any special contribution, although it was a pecuniary right. But Borthen and Thunheim might have won their cases if the Norwegian Supreme Court had applied the pecuniary, contribution and property arguments in the same way as the European Court of Human Rights did in the Gaygusuz case.

One important difference between the Gaygusuz case and the Borthen and Thunheim cases is that Gaygusuz was refused any assistance, while Borthen's and Thunheim's pensions were only reduced, and for Thunheim by very little. Another distinction between these cases could be that the principle of prohibition against discrimination is considered as more important than the principle of prohibition against retroactive legislation, even within a property discourse.

It seems as if the Norwegian Supreme Court did not give the supplementary pension better protection than the basic pension and the spousal supplement. Arguments linked to the 'earning' of benefits through contributions were given little or no weight. Article 105 of the Norwegian constitution, which protects private property, was held not applicable to the protection of national insurance benefits in these two cases. One possible interpretation is that the property argument can be used only in combination with other main principles.

German law divides the systems of social benefits in which 'property' is acquired by the payment of contributions, and the systems of social benefits that are financed solely by taxes (Zacher 1994). This distinction was not applied in the two Norwegian cases, perhaps indicating that social assistance in some respects will be similarly protected as social security. The Gaygusuz case, as mentioned above, might also point in this direction.

SOME FINAL REMARKS ABOUT SOCIAL SECURITY AS PROPERTY

A hundred years ago, property and family support were the most important securities in Europe in the event of sickness, disability, old age and loss of provider. Now income from work and social security are most important.

If all of my possessions were taken from me, I would certainly be unhappy. It would, however, be a greater hazard to my well-being if I were to lose my job, my income, my earning capacity and the possibility of social security in case of lost income. In such a case property would be helpful but, for most of us, it would not last long. In a society where most people live on salaries or social security, these sources of income are more important than property and family support.

Social security has to a great extent replaced individual savings, capital investments and private insurance policies, which are undoubtedly protected as property in European constitutions and the European Convention of Human Rights. A similar function of social security benefits legitimizes the extension of the protection of property. This is especially the case when claims for benefits are based on contributions paid by the insured person and his employer.

NOTES

1. Rt. (*The Norwegian Supreme Court Case Reporter*) (1977), p. 1207.

2. Rt. (1987), p. 1004.

3. Court of Justice for Human Rights, 16 September 1996, no. 39/1995/545/ 631, Reports of Judgments and Decisions, 1996–IV p. 1129.

4. Rt. (1996), p. 1415.

5. Rt. (1996), p. 1430.

REFERENCES

Eide, A. (1997) 'Human Rights and the Elimination of Poverty', in A. Kjønstad and J. Veit Wilson (eds) *Law, Power and Poverty*, Bergen: CROP Publications.

Kjønstad, A. (1996) 'Gjennomføring av menneskerettighetene i norsk sosialrett' [Enforcement of Human Rights in Norwegian Social Law], in N. Høstmælingen (ed.), *Seminar in Memory of Torkel Opsahl*, Oslo: Juristforbundets forlag.

— (1997) 'Trygderettigheter, Grunnloven og Høyesterett' [Social Security Law, Constitutional Law and the Supreme Court], *Lov og Rett*, 1997: 243–92.

— (1998) *Innføring i trygderett* [Introduction to Social Security Law], Oslo: Tano Aschehoug.

Kjønstad, A. (ed.) (1994) *Trygderettighetenes grunnlovsvern* – Constitutional Protection of Social Security Benefits, Oslo: Ad notam Gyldendal.

Kjønstad, A. and A. Syse (2001) *Velferdsrett I* [Welfare Law I], Oslo: Gyldendal Akademisk.

Pennings, F. L. J. (1999) 'The Potential Consequences of the Gaygusuz Judgment', *European Journal of Social Security*: 181–201.

Van Bogaert, S. (ed.) (1997) *Social Security, Non-Discrimination and Property*, Antwerp–Apeldoora: MAKLU:

Zacher, H. F. (1994) 'Decisions by Constitutional Courts of Questions of Social Law – A European Survey', in A. Kjønstad (ed.), *Trygderettighetenes grunnlovsvern* – Constitutional Protection of Social Security Benefits, Oslo: Ad notam Gyldendal, pp. 107–34.

NINE | The effect of legal mechanisms on selective welfare strategies for needy persons: the Greek experience

GABRIEL AMITSIS

§ The Greek social security system provides an interesting case for the evaluation of the arrangements of laws affecting poor people within the general context of the European welfare model. The Greek model is a mixed system combining insurance, assistance and universal/contingency principles[1] to cover needy individuals or those faced with social risks. Despite the improvement of fundamental rights, including social security and citizenship rights, in Greece due to legislative changes during the 1980s and 1990s (see Petmesidou 1991; Papadopoulos 1996), shortcomings and gaps related to people without sufficient resources remain. Greece is the only European Union member-state without a general social safety-net for persons in need.[2]

The main concern of this chapter is to identify the effect of legal instruments on the promotion of the right to social citizenship in Greece. The theoretical establishment of citizenship rights is traced through the development of both civil/political and social components (see Plant 1992; Twine 1994), arguing that the influence that ideas of citizenship hold in systems of welfare provision should be examined according to the particularized legal framework of every country. The relationship between social citizenship and legal rights is used as a basic indicator to assess the validity of welfare strategies and state policies.

From a methodological point of view, three issues are critical:

1. Is there a social right to a safety-net within the Greek legal order?
2. Can this right be constituted as a basic element of citizenship?
3. Is this right properly enforceable?

Emphasis will be put on the normative establishments of citizenship through the application of defined rights; legislative rules and wider policies and principles are taken into account with a view to examining the development of welfare rights.[3]

Greece fails to provide an adequate social safety-net policy[4] for its poor, given that no minimum income guarantee scheme has been established.[5] This is an argument based both on legal and sociopolitical inquiries, taking into account domestic as well as international research in the field of social welfare.[6]

A distinction should be made between the lack of a national general minimum income scheme for every person without sufficient means and the design and implementation of broader anti-poverty strategies.[7] The Greek welfare state is based on the development of selective anti-poverty strategies, not directly related to public measures to combat poverty. This lack of unified state action is caused in part by the lack of any official poverty line (a legal definition of poverty; explained in Atkinson 1991; Nolan and Whelan 1996). Relevant anti-poverty strategies have been implemented in the fields of both social insurance and assistance, where universal principles are applied in relation to benefits for large families (family allowances); these benefits are paid without means tests on insured and uninsured persons. During recent debates, however, the main concern was whether social policy-makers have introduced legal instruments that affect the status of de facto poor persons or adopted specific mechanisms of income maintenance for certain target groups.

The 'peculiarities' of the Greek model are strongly influenced by the dominant role of social legislation as the principal means to enforce welfare rights. Irrespective of the theoretical debate on the enforceability of welfare rights (Scott 1984; Dean 1996), law is regarded as the most powerful instrument to satisfy basic needs that give rise to social rights. Does the legal machinery in Greece include mechanisms that support this argument?

Two key approaches could be developed here. A traditional legal approach distinguishes between the higher- and the lower-level legal institutions, providing a sound picture of a specific normative framework. An alternative approach focuses on policy implementation, distinguishing between 'normative declarations' and the effects of policies on persons.

Given that each approach embodies advantages and shortcomings, their multidisciplinary treatment provides interesting food for thought. However, the application of legally-oriented criteria remains crucial; benefits that guarantee a social safety-net need sound regulatory mechanisms that define entitlements and duties.

In order to identify legal mechanisms that construct a social safety-net (within the broader sense of the term) in Greece, we need to look at not only measures related to the coverage of need but also measures that supplement income earned through employment or gained through pensions. As such, the research discusses non-contributory benefits within social insurance schemes and cash or 'tied' benefits within social assistance schemes as part of the universe of Greek safety-net policies.

The social safety-net approach in social insurance

Greece does not have a single national insurance system as seen in the Danish and Netherlands models (Clasen 1997). Different funds for specific socio-professional groups provide coverage in case of the occurrence of certain insurance risks (Amitsis 1992b). Benefits from these funds are paid on the fulfilment of legally defined conditions, which include the establishment of contribution records and duration of employment.

For those employed full-time, all traditional risks are adequately covered through compulsory affiliation to relevant insurance funds, with the exception of unemployment protection that is limited to employees in the private sector. Benefits follow the contributory principle, based on a tripartite funding model (contributions of employers, employees and state participation in the case of private employees). However, additional benefits rules exist that 'violate' not only 'reciprocity' but also 'contributory' principles for the provision of social insurance benefits. These measures show the possibility of developing a social safety-net within the existing domestic legal regime.

Social benefits that violate reciprocity principles A pension scheme for farmers (persons working in the agricultural sector) was introduced in the 1960s and revised radically in 1997. According to the provisions in force till the end of 1996, farmers affiliated with the OGA Fund (a public body charged with the insurance coverage of farmers) were entitled to a non-contributory flat-rate pension, under three specific conditions: they should reach the age of sixty-five (both for men and women); they should have worked as farmers for at least twenty-five years; they should not be receiving a pension from any other social insurance fund.

The main objective of this system was to guarantee an adequate income for elderly farmers. However, the programme's internal shortcomings prohibited the fulfilment of such an ambitious task, the most important being the low level of benefits that failed to guarantee even subsistence standards. On the other hand, the universal character of the farmers' pension did diminish the stigmatizing effect or 'targeting side-effects' on farmers without sufficient means.

The former pensions scheme for farmers represents a typical example of the inadequacies of the 'Beveridgean approach' adopted in Southern countries, particularly in the 1960s and 1970s (Ferrera and Rhodes 2000). Marginal benefits were paid to a certain powerful socio-professional group, financed entirely from the public budget. The law was therefore used as a tool to satisfy an interest group through clientelistic policies, which led to serious moral and funding conflicts.

The pension scheme for farmers was a restrictive approach of a sound national pension scheme, which should not be regarded as part of a broader social safety-net system. It was neither oriented to the coverage of indigent farmers nor to the guarantee of sufficient resources for farmers in case of urgent need. The failure of farmers' pensions to assist in creating a safety-net was highlighted by the 1997 changes to the enabling legislation. According to the new provisions, pensions paid by the OGA Fund to insured farmers follow a traditional contributive principle, being financed by farmers' contributions and the state budget. Benefits are no longer flat rate; they depend on the contribution record of the beneficiary.

The abolition of the universal aspect of farmers' pensions did not give rise to any serious debate or protest. All interested parties agreed that the former scheme was neither satisfactory (in terms of coverage) nor acceptable (in terms of equity and social justice).

Social benefits that violate contributory principles Social insurance funds pay minimum pensions to those unable to establish a sufficient contribution record. This system was introduced in the early 1950s, subject to several legislative modifications and amendments that re-inforced its role as the basic 'solidarity' measure for pensioners in Greece.[8]

The development of the system was beneficial for many insured persons without entitlements to adequate benefits through their contribution records. Minimum pensions covered, therefore, gaps created by the strict implementation of the reciprocity principle to pensioners with career breaks or delayed entry into the domestic labour market.

According to a legislative amendment passed in 1992, the minimum pensions amount can be calculated in two ways. The first applies to persons insured till 31 December 1992; the second deals with new entrants in the labour market (after 1 January 1993).[9]

The existence of those two models reproduces inequalities between insured persons faced with the same risk, given that the amount of the second model is rather low and does not even guarantee basic subsistence needs. Minimum pensions can thus not automatically be seen as an integral part of ensuring equity within a broader social safety-net approach.

In order to determine whether minimum pensions constitute safety-net instruments, the programme's objectives and effects should be dealt with separately.

Objectives could be assessed according to the following typology:

- the improvement of earnings for insured persons unable to establish a sufficient contribution record
- the legal regulation of adequate living standards for needy pensioners (i.e. the establishment of a legal poverty level)

Relevant *effects* could be assessed according to the purchasing power of benefits and the index to which the programme's benefit level is tied.

Domestic research (Sissouras and Amitsis 1999) concludes that the role of minimum pensions is aimed mainly at the fulfilment of the first objective; universal benefits are therefore paid to insured persons, regardless of their ability to cover their inadequate contribution record through their own means. This universal benefit is associated with extremely high take-up rates; it is estimated that over 65 per cent of pensioners under the IKA Fund (the social insurance institution for private employees) receive minimum pensions (Amitsis 1997).

Given their effects on the living standards of pensioners, minimum pensions have received great attention from domestic social policy-makers as well as social partners.[10] Both the calculation of amounts and the selection of indexation instruments have been hotly debated: trade unions and pensioners' associations argue for the reform of the existing system through a more favourable calculation of pensions amounts and through their indexation according to the consumers' price index; while employers' organizations are in favour of the existing system, which links the amount of pensions to a specific formula (equal to the amount of a fifteen-year contribution record) and their adjustment to the increase in civil servants' pensions.

The state's approach has largely been to maintain the current system, although it is widely accepted that such a system cannot provide adequate support to low-income pensioners.

Mixed social benefits based on both social insurance and social assistance techniques In order to increase the purchasing power of minimum pensions, a new benefit was designed and introduced in 1996: the Social Solidarity Allowance for Pensioners. This allowance forms a mixed social security benefit, due to the application of both social insurance (coverage of pensioners) and social assistance principles (entitlement conditions include lack of resources). It is paid to pensioners faced with subsistence problems not met through personal or family sources.

The introduction of the allowance corresponds to a legal instrument directed towards basic sociopolitical ends: its objective is to supplement income resources of low-income pensioners through income-tested benefits.[11] It constitutes therefore a supplementary 'targeting' measure, adopted instead of the direct increase of the minimum amount of the pension and fiercely debated by trade unions and pensioners' associations.

The allowance was paid in 2001 to over 300,000 beneficiaries under the following conditions:

- recipients must be at least sixty years old (both men and women)
- their annual income from pensions and employment cannot exceed a fixed amount (1,806,000 Drs – about €5,473)
- their annual personal taxable income cannot exceed a fixed amount (2,107,000 Drs – about €6,385)
- their annual family taxable income cannot exceed a fixed amount (3,278,750 Drs – about €9,935)

The new benefits attempt to increase the resources of those receiving pensions, whose amount is inadequate to cover subsistence needs. This aim follows the tradition of Mediterranean countries, which have included additional benefits within contributory pension schemes for the supplementary coverage of low-benefit pensioners.[12]

The benefit amount of the Social Solidarity Allowance for Pensioners depends on the level of their basic pension (plus any income derived from employment). There are four levels of entitlement. The minimum amount equals 4,470 Drs – about €13 per month – and the maximum amount (for those with the lowest incomes) equals 17,850 Drs, about €54 per month. Benefits are financed by the public budget and adjusted according to the consumers' price index.

The socialist government in power since 1993 introduced the allowance on 1 July 1996, and described it as Greece's most important attempt to enhance solidarity principles within contributory pension schemes. Two short-term objectives could be identified: supplementary protection of low-income pensioners without sufficient private or family resources; and assessment of income-test techniques (in order to calculate the amount of social security benefits or even to evaluate entitlement conditions).

Despite the strong fear that no serious income-test would be effective in the current Greek framework due to lack of reliable mechanisms (Amitsis 1994), the second objective has been fulfilled, given that social security authorities take into account the sources of the claimants through strict assessment techniques. Applicants are obliged to supply their tax returns and cooperate with administrators in assessing taxable income sources.

This use of social security and taxation techniques constitutes a 'best practice' mechanism in Greece, which undoubtedly has diminished opposition to income-tested or means-tested benefits. The experience gained by the operation of the Allowance for Pensioners shows that 'targeting' goals depends on the application of relevant techniques to favour intended beneficiaries and not those inclined to abuse the system.

However, the allowance has perhaps not succeeded in fulfilling the first objective, i.e. the adequacy of benefits with respect to the supplementary protection of pensioners. There are two criteria for assessment.

1. The first concerns the 'social citizenship' approach within the design of the benefit's application. Equality goals demand that no low-income pensioner will be excluded.

Social policy-makers adopted a different approach. Eligible persons include any pensioner affiliated to social insurance funds, with the important exception of farmers who receive a pension from the OGA scheme.

Given that the former OGA pension is a flat-rate non-contributory benefit, it could be argued, therefore, that those who receive the lowest amount of pensions in Greece are currently excluded from the allowance. Their exclusion can hardly be defended on legal grounds, since it violates the equity principle to the disadvantage of de jure and de facto low-income pensioners.

2. The second is related to the purchasing power of the benefits in question. Their marginal amount (about 10 per cent of the minimum pension on average) can neither guarantee sufficient resources nor supplement low levels of income derived from employment and contributory pensions. This inadequacy was the main reason why the government increased the amount of benefits by up to 50 per cent after 1 January 1999.

Conclusions from the social insurance system The above analysis shows that 'solidarity' features, which violate *reciprocity* and *contributory* principles, are included within the current domestic social insurance system. Does this trend (already adopted by legislative mechanisms) lead to the development of a systemic social safety-net approach in social insurance coverage?

The answer is simply no. The allowance benefits do not fulfil the main objectives of a social safety-net (Atkinson 1992), because not every insured person receives benefits (equity aspect) and no legal definition of poverty is created that will address subsistence or exclusion problems (citizenship aspect). They rather constitute legally defined measures (given that they are based on enforceable legislative provisions), adopted for the satisfaction of interest-group-dominated sociopolitical wants without a direct impact on the development of new social citizenship rights for persons in need.[13]

The social safety-net approach in social assistance

The Greek social security system is characterized by the limited application of the welfare principle (promoted through the development of social assistance schemes) in comparison with the implementation of the insurance principle for the coverage of the working population.[14] There is no single social assistance scheme covering the whole population, but distinct programmes directed to specific target groups.

To evaluate the role and function of the Greek system as a cornerstone of the social safety-net, we have to adopt four basic categories internationally recognized as valid criteria by which to assess social assistance schemes:[15]

- objectives of benefits ('social assistance' versus 'selective' benefits)
- type of benefits (cash benefits for general use versus 'tied' benefits)
- scope of application ('universal' versus 'specified' coverage)
- legal establishment of benefits (enforceable rights versus discretionary claims)

According to the dominant welfare typology, the existing domestic social assistance programmes are distinguished as follows:

Emergency relief programmes These derived from an old legal instrument (Legislative Decree 57/1973)[16] that introduces welfare principles (need, subsidiarity) for the protection of persons without sufficient resources. The emergency programme is designed by the Ministry of Health and Welfare and implemented by the Social Welfare Departments of the Prefectures. In practice, it only covers persons affected by extraordinary events, not related to the consequences of poverty and social exclusion. Benefits under this programme consist of discretionary lump-sum payments, whose amount does not exceed 200,000 Drs (about €607); they are paid to individuals or households not covered by social insurance funds, unable to satisfy their subsistence needs by their own means.

Despite the introduction of welfare principles within the Greek social policy context, this particular programme should not be regarded as a general 'social assistance' scheme.[17] It is a traditional emergency relief programme for the short-term coverage of specific target groups, which does not guarantee even a subsistence minimum.

'Categorical' programmes that provide means-tested benefits These are not based on a single legal instrument but follow different rules laid out in presidential decrees and ministerial decisions (subordinate administrative acts). Their common feature is that they establish enforceable entitlements to benefits, which may be invoked through an administrative redress approach or before an administrative court.[18] The scope of such programmes is limited to the coverage of specific target groups, regarded as de facto groups in need of public support: unprotected children, pregnant women and the uninsured elderly.

The programme for unprotected children provides financial support to children who face severe problems due either to the absence of a parent or the father's inability to meet their needs. Entitlement to benefits depends on the presence of parents or relatives and the lack of sufficient family resources. Benefits are means-tested and paid till the children reach their sixteenth year; however, their limited amount (12,000 Drs per month – about €37) does not guarantee a subsistence minimum.

The programme for uninsured mothers provides income support to pregnant women without sufficient resources who are not affiliated with any social insurance fund or are not entitled to claim maternity benefits through social insurance schemes. Benefits are paid in the form of lump-sum allowances and their amount equals 150,000 Drs – about €455.

The programme for the uninsured elderly provides income support to persons over sixty-five who lack sufficient resources and are not affiliated with any social insurance fund. Benefits are means-tested and paid in the form of flat-rate monthly allowances; their amount equals €150.

Additional programmes that provide income-tested benefits This category should include the controversial scheme for mothers with three
or more children. It provides flat-rate benefits to mothers whose family
income falls below a specific level.[19] There are three different categories
of benefits:

- women receive on the birth of their third child a monthly benefit
  of 40,000 Drs, payable until the child is six years old
- women with three or more children receive a monthly allowance
  of 10,000 Drs per child, payable until the children are twenty-three
  years old
- women with many children over the age of twenty-three years receive
  a life welfare benefit of 23,000 Drs

*Specific 'categorical' programmes that provide non-contributory benefits
without the application of income or means tests*[20] Disabled persons
are supported through eight basic income-support programmes and
two supplementary progammes, covering over 100,000 beneficiaries.
Benefits are paid in the form of a monthly flat-rate allowance and their
amount varies according to the category and the rate of disability. The
most generous benefit equals 130,000 Drs – about €395 (programme
for paraplegics/tetraplegics) and the lowest equals 33,000 Drs – about
€100 (programme for deaf-mute persons). It should be noted that some
benefits are paid even to disabled persons who work or receive social
insurance pensions.

Programmes that provide 'tied' benefits to needy persons Under this
category we find:

- a programme for nursing and hospital treatment (including free
  medicine) for those unable to cover relevant expenses
- a programme providing a means-tested housing allowance to those
  over sixty-five who are not able to pay their rent. The benefit's
  amount is calculated on a flat-rate basis that takes into account the
  marital status of the applicants; 20,000 Drs (about €60) for a single
  person and 26,000 Drs (about €79) for a couple.

It seems from the above-mentioned analysis that domestic social
policy-makers have adopted the 'categorical' or 'specific target' approach
of the social assistance principle; there are several programmes directed
to different groups, covering people usually according to their sociopolitical status or power rather than according to their need.

The lack of a national general minimum income scheme (similar to the British Income Support or the German *Sozialhilfe*) is the basic shortcoming of the rudimentary Greek social assistance model, resulting in a system that discriminates against persons excluded from the scope of existing categorical measures.

Two broad target groups are significantly affected by the absence of a general scheme: unemployed persons who either have exhausted their entitlements to unemployment insurance or are not able to enter the labour market at all; and homeless persons not affiliated with any social insurance fund. Unemployed and homeless persons without sufficient resources have no right to social assistance benefits within the Greek context. Their only resources are family (if a family is available) or religious, charitable and voluntary organizations. The emergency relief programme provides only marginal support.

On the other hand, even the existing categorical programmes violate key welfare principles, given that benefits are hardly adequate to guarantee a decent standard of living or even promote the social integration of beneficiaries (Karantinos et al. 1992). This argument is valid not only for 'supplementary' benefits but also for the genuine 'means-tested' benefits; though different calculation models are applied, none provides more than a marginal amount.[21]

THE LEGAL ESTABLISHMENT OF SOCIAL SAFETY-NET POLICIES

Social safety-net elements have been identified through the analysis of social insurance and assistance policies. However, the question of the existence of a social right to a safety-net within the Greek legal order remains.

Much domestic (Kremalis 1991) and international[22] literature agrees that the right to a safety-net depends on the availability of legal mechanisms that guarantee sufficient resources to needy persons. The effect of relevant mechanisms is associated with the development of claims to benefits paid on the fulfilment of specific entitlement conditions.

The judicial construction of anti-poverty policies has the advantage of the distinction between the substantive and the procedural aspects of the social right to a safety-net. Substantive aspects are related to the establishment and the development of the right, while procedural aspects concern its enforcement through extra-judicial and judicial mechanisms, including legal aid.[23]

This chapter evaluates the development of the Greek legal framework within the context of substantive rights at the level of higher (constitution, international public law) and lower legal instruments (common legislation, administrative acts). Attention is paid both to the identification of provisions that embody concepts, as well as to norms that establish entitlements to benefits or define the settlement of disputes related to the proper enjoyment of benefits.[24]

The constitutional provisions

The Greek constitution of 1975 introduced for the first time social rights related to education, employment, health and social security. Although the text of the constitution does not mention the concept 'social security', two provisions are particularly relevant for the recognition of this right (see Amitsis 1997).

Section 21

- para 1: The family, as the basis for the preservation and progress of the nation, as well as marriage, maternity and childhood are under the protection of the State.
- para 2: Large families, war invalids and invalids of the peacetime, victims of war, war widows and orphans, as well as the incurable physically and mentally sick are entitled to special State care.
- para 3: The State will care for the health of its citizens and will adopt special measures for the protection of young people, the elderly, disabled as well as for assistance to the needy.
- para 4: For those without any or with insufficient accommodation, housing is subject to special State care.

Section 22

- para 5: The State will care for the social insurance of the working population, as specified by statute.

Section 21, para 3 forms the constitutional basis for the right to social assistance, while Section 22, para. 5 provides the right to social insurance. These rules have engendered two differing interpretations of Greek citizens' right to a safety-net: the lack of any direct reference to this particular right is proof of a lack of constitutional authority for its establishment; and the systemic interpretation of the spirit of the constitutional provisions and principles leads to the establishment of this right.

The second approach, strongly advocated by Kremalis (1991) and Amitsis (1996), incorporates other constitutional provisions that connect the right to welfare with the rights to human dignity and citizenship and the basic principle of the social state:

- The right to human dignity is established in section 2, para 1 of the constitution, which states that 'respect and protection of human dignity form the ultimate duty of the State'.
- The right to citizenship is established in section 5, para 1 of the constitution, which states that 'everybody has a right to develop freely his/her personality and to participate in the social, economic and political framework of the country, on the condition that he/she should not violate rights of other citizens, the Constitutional order and moral norms'.
- The social state principle, while not explicitly written in the constitution, was deduced through the interpretation of 'solidarity-oriented' provisions, including sections 2, 5, 21, 22 and 25 (promotion of national and social solidarity). After the constitutional reform in 2001, the principle of the 'Social State of Law' is established in section 25, para 1.

Section 21, para 3 ('the State will provide assistance to the needy') is regarded as the primary legal foundation for the establishment of the fundamental right to a social safety-net. However, according to dominant interpretations about the enforceability of social rights, the constitutional provisions have no direct applicability but, instead, require the interposition of the legislator to enact social legislation. On the other hand, this necessary intervention does not exclude the legal status of section 21, para 3; rather, the social right embodied in the constitution should be seen by the lower legal institutions as a mandate.

The legal effects of section 21, para 3 are without doubt limited. If the legislature fails to give full effect to the right through the enactment of safety-net schemes, citizens are not able to invoke the constitutional provision before a court in order to claim benefits. They can, however, take advantage of the sociopolitical value of the relevant provisions, as a basis for negotiations leading to a more fair allocation of resources.[25]

As far as the procedural aspects of the right to a social safety-net are concerned, the Greek constitution includes provisions to safeguard social rights, should such rights be enacted through the legislative process. Relevant provisions establish the following rights:

- the right to petition (stemming from section 10)
- the right to administrative redress (stemming from section 20, para 2) of social security disputes
- the right to the settlement of social security disputes through the intervention of competent, impartial and independent courts (stemming from section 20, para 1)

The results of the inquiry into the constitutional framework lead to the following conclusion: the social right to a safety-net forms an integral part of the constitutional legal order, although the provisions are not self-executing. It could therefore be argued that both substantive and procedural aspects of the right are 'transferred' to the legislative process for development and implementation.

International law instruments

The Greek constitution classifies international law as being among the sources of universally binding law for the Republic of Greece, under the condition that international instruments have to be ratified through the legislative process. Therefore, international agreements on freedoms, rights or obligations of citizens ratified by the parliament prevail over any contrary domestic legislative provision.

A detailed examination of the international instruments already ratified by Greece shows that mechanisms related to the right to a safety-net have been incorporated within the Greek legal order.[26] They include:

1. The International Covenant on Economic, Social and Cultural Rights adopted by the United Nations Assembly in 1966, ratified through Law 1532/85.[27] Section 11, para 1 recognizes 'the right of everyone to an adequate standard of living for himself and his family, including adequate food, clothing and housing, and to the continuous improvement of living conditions'.

2. The European Social Charter adopted by the Council of Europe in 1961, ratified through Law 1426/84 (see Harris 1984). This Charter is the only international treaty to establish the right to social and medical assistance in addition to the right to social security. These specific rights, as guaranteed in section 13 (also accepted by Greece), are supplemented by the new rights introduced in the Revised Charter (1996) in measures to combat poverty and social exclusion (Art. 30). Section 13, para 1 obliges Contracting States 'to ensure that any person who is without adequate resources and who is unable to secure such resources either by his own efforts or from other sources, in particular by benefits under a social security scheme, be granted adequate assistance, and, in case of sickness, the care necessitated by his condition'.

These two instruments establish the general right to a social safety-net within the international legal order. After their ratification by Greece, this right is also part of the domestic legal framework.

However, the enforceability of these instruments, like the Greek constitution, is limited by the scope of legislative action unless they are recognized as self-executing. According to the theory and practice of international public law (Jacobs and Roberts 1987; Jaspers and Betten 1988), a provision is considered as self-executing or 'directly applicable' when it defines the legal status of individuals in such a manner that no basic legislative or administrative implementation is necessary and subjective rights can be invoked directly before competent domestic courts.

Direct applicability effects are achieved with difficulty in the field of social welfare. International norms need to be elaborated by the domestic legislature in order to strengthen the claims of citizens. Contracting states are thus bound by these international norms, but citizens lack legal redress in the case of the state's inability or unwillingness to take into account its obligations.

The above-mentioned instruments have no monitoring or enforcement system to make legal rulings in case of infringements by the contracting states (i.e. the intervention of the European Court of Human Rights concerning the application of the Convention for the Protection of Human Rights and Fundamental Freedoms – Council of Europe).[28] Their implementation depends on the legislative activities of the states concerned, which are evaluated only by national courts. The Greek legal community (lawyers and judges), who seldom take advantage of ratified international norms for the establishment of the right to a safety-net, rarely discuss this topic.

The neglected use of legal instruments to impose obligations on states for the development of welfare rights policies has negative consequences for needy persons and intermediaries[29] who are interested in applying international social rights instruments in the struggle against poverty and social exclusion. Likewise, the lack of any judicial control over respect for international obligations concerning welfare rights is a vital shortcoming of the monitoring system adopted by international organizations. This shortcoming cannot be adequately addressed through internal monitoring mechanisms (like the periodic evaluation of national reports or the submission of individual recommendations to member-states that do not fulfil their obligations).

For example, following Article 20 of the European Social Charter, Greece has accepted sixty-seven out of the seventy-two provisions contained in the Charter, including Art. 13, para 1 (the right to social and medical assistance). Yet due to the lack of a general social safety-net, Greece is unable to comply with the requirements of Art. 13, para 1. This inadequacy gave rise to a strong intervention by the Charter's monitoring bodies (i.e. the Committee of Independent Experts and the Governmental Committee) resulting in the issuance of Recommendation no. R ChS (93)1, adopted by the Committee of Ministers on 7 September 1993 at the 487th meeting of the Ministers' Deputies. The substance of the Recommendation is very important, since it not only evaluates a national social security system according to internationally defined criteria, but also applies the 'rights approach' for the development of social safety-nets.[30]

The monitoring bodies came to the conclusion that the right to social assistance required the establishment of substantive and procedural safety-net mechanisms. Greece did not comply with this requirement and therefore breached the substance of Art. 13, para 1.

The following abstract of the Recommendation highlights the need to combine rights with enforcement mechanisms in the field of social welfare:

> Having noted also that in respect of article 13, paragraph 1 (social and medical assistance for those in need), the Committee of Independent Experts recalled that a state is obliged to ensure that persons in need are granted adequate assistance, which must be granted as of right, which can be invoked before an independent body of appeal, such as a court. It found that there was neither such as a right nor a right of appeal, the system of social assistance relying upon the provision of funds and services for the needy from a wide variety of bodies, including the church, private organizations and benefactors and the (extended) family, as well as the State.[31]

Yet the Recommendation attracted marginal attention in Greece. No serious legal measures were enacted in order to introduce a general social safety-net and those not affiliated with any categorical minimum income scheme remained unprotected.

The results of the inquiry into ratified international instruments led to the following conclusions:

- the social right to a safety-net is not available within the Greek legal order as a right applied for every person in need
- interested persons cannot invoke international provisions before any domestic court in order to claim specific social welfare benefits, due to the lack of direct applicability
- violation of this right does not produce legal effects, due to the absence of international legally binding sanctions
- inability to comply with international standards gives rise to socio-political debates or negotiations that may highlight gaps or shortcomings in the legal machinery to satisfy citizens' needs

The legislative approach

'Restrictive' social safety-net measures have been adopted in the fields of both social insurance and welfare. These limited measures fail to provide a substantive general social safety-net but do adequately promote procedural aspects of social welfare policies.

All benefits paid to eligible persons constitute enforceable rights, with the exception of the 'emergency relief' programme for needy persons which provides unenforceable discretionary benefits. Claimants may apply different legal mechanisms in order to implement their rights to benefits. These mechanisms are based on specific constitutional norms and principles as well as on instruments of international organizations that form an integral part of the Greek legal order after their ratification.

Procedural aspects of safety-net measures in Greece are advanced through the application of extra-judicial and judicial mechanisms. The following distinction should be made:

1. Application of extra-judicial instruments. These instruments include:

- Administrative redress of decisions taken by competent authorities through internal reviews and complaints. Complaints are submitted in principle to the body which has issued the decision in question and are assessed by administrative agencies.[32]
- Appeals submitted to the Ombudsman by those who claim that their social security rights are infringed by organs of public authority (a process introduced since 1997).

2. Application of internal judicial mechanisms. These mechanisms include:

- Appeals against decisions of social insurance funds and social welfare agencies before the ordinary courts. Given the existing jurisdiction of Greek courts (Kerameas and Kozyris 1996), claims on social insurance issues are litigated by civil and administrative courts and claims on welfare issues are litigated by administrative courts. The judgments of first instance courts can be appealed before courts of second instance, while cassation (determination on points of law) is also possible before the Supreme Court (for judgments of civil courts) and the Council of State (for judgments of administrative courts).
- Applications for judicial reviews submitted before administrative courts. This review is a particular legal remedy for social assistance and unemployment cases by which judges exercise control over the performance of public administration within specific legal bounds.

3. *Application of external judicial mechanisms.* These mechanisms correspond to the submission of a petition before the European Court of Human Rights by citizens who claim that their rights to social security or judicial protection (as defined in the European Convention for the Protection of Human Rights and Fundamental Freedoms) have been violated by the Greek authorities. Such a petition constitutes the final judicial means, given that all domestic remedies must be exhausted in order to apply this mechanism (according to the ratified Eleventh Protocol to the Convention and Article 6, para 1 of the Convention).

The adequacy and effectiveness of the resolution of social security disputes depend crucially on the fulfilment of specific tasks, strongly related to the sound implementation of the procedural and substantive dimensions of the right to judicial protection. Through the lens of traditional evaluation criteria, the current system is regarded as a satisfactory system for the legal protection of social security claimants. However, a few major inadequacies and shortcomings have been identified, leading to gaps in the entire process that bring into question the validity and adequacy of applied mechanisms. The most important shortcomings are:

- the limited access of claimants to social security agencies and courts due to lack of knowledge or inability to submit claims, reviews and appeals
- the lack of specialized bodies for the settlement of social security disputes through administrative redress procedures
- the lack of a statutory legal aid scheme
- the complexity of procedural rules for the judicial treatment of claimants
- the extensive duration of proceedings before a court that diminishes the application of rights of claimants who face serious problems due to insurance risks or welfare needs

THE IMPACT OF LEGAL INSTRUMENTS ON SAFETY-NET CLAIMS

The dualistic, almost 'polarized' function of the Greek income maintenance system (Ferrera 1996; Gough 1996) is a typical feature of the Southern model of welfare (Leibfried 1993) that discriminates against persons unable to enter the labour market. This is the principal indicator for classifying Greece among the Latin tax, medium de-commodification regime (including Italy and Portugal).[33]

The analysis of existing fragmented social safety-net measures leads to the conclusion that the so called 'southern syndrome' (an imbalance between insurance against risks, welfare safety-nets and income redistribution)[34] particularly affects Greece. A distinction could therefore be made between 'gainers' and 'losers'; insured persons who receive favourable treatment through the insurance schemes (Katrougalos 1996) and persons without adequate resources not covered by any dedicated social assistance scheme (Amitsis 1997).

It is clear that legal mechanisms provide no adequate protection to persons in need. The lack of a general minimum income scheme allows this situation to continue (Gough 1996).

Two further issues should be taken into account here: first, the legal consequences of the inability to enforce the right to a safety-net; second, the sociopolitical consequences of the marginal treatment of needy persons.

1. The right to a safety-net is established in the Greek constitution as a basic social citizenship right. Given that state institutions are charged with the task of promoting citizenship rights, their inaction over developing substantive and procedural aspects of safety-nets diminishes the ability of interested persons to implement their citizenship rights.[35] Legal interpretations of this argument should take into account the development of mechanisms that oblige state institutions to take specific actions in favour of needy persons. Due to the lack of relevant mechanisms in Greece, the legislator is free to decide about the establishment and the substance of anti-poverty measures for needy persons. Inaction does not give rise to legal remedies, due to the lack of direct applicability of constitutional or international law provisions.

The formal, rights-oriented, approach to citizenship (Taylor-Gooby 1991; Langan 1998) is violated by the lack of mechanisms to enforce the right to a social safety-net. Needy persons are discouraged from participating in the broader social and economic environment and in political processes; this brings the legitimacy of a political democracy into question (Twine 1994).

2. From a sociopolitical point of view, the inadequate coverage of needy persons in Greece puts at risk guarantees of human autonomy. In terms of political power, this leads to the development of 'nautonomy' features (i.e. the negation of autonomy), as discussed by Held (1994).

The lack of a systemic social safety-net endangers people's equal interest in the principle of autonomy. Asymmetries of life chances are not adequately addressed and sites of power are diminished.[36] The 'poor performance' of the existing selective welfare strategies not only fails to guarantee a decent standard of living, but also discourages social integration and participation.[37]

On the other hand, the restrictive application of the welfare technique violates the principle of social justice, as the interests of the weakest groups are hardly taken into account. Despite the conceptual debate on social justice theories (Campbell 1988), the hard-core substance of welfare policies is based on a 'fair treatment' of the most deprived citizens. Unfair treatment leads to breaks between welfare and justice.

Finally, the limited impact of social assistance leads to the inability of the welfare state machinery to promote social integration. This could be described as a significant factor for social exclusion, according to the typology discussed by social policy experts (Berghman 1997a: 18; Percy-Smith 2000), who suggest that social exclusion should be defined in terms of the failure of one or more of the following four systems:

• the democratic and legal system, which promotes civic integration
• the labour market, which promotes economic integration
• the welfare state system, promoting what may be called social integration
• the family and community system, which promotes interpersonal integration

An analysis of Greece's policies using normative and sociopolitical criteria shows that domestic legal institutions do not protect social citizenship rights but rather discriminate against persons faced with subsistence or unemployment problems. In spite of the obligations stemming from higher legal mechanisms (i.e. the constitution of 1975, ratified international conventions), the lower institutions fail to comply. Yet, the violation of key principles (social citizenship, autonomy, social participation, social justice) gives rise to no legal remedy, as it cannot be invoked before any domestic or international court.

THE USE OF LEGAL MACHINERY AS A MEANS TO PROMOTE SAFETY-NET POLICIES

The underdevelopment of safety-net policies in Greece could be explained through reference to the basic elements of the southern European model of welfare, as discussed by various scholars (see Ferrera 1996: 29; Gough 1996):

• the peculiar excesses in income maintenance (favourable social insurance treatment for 'labourers' versus marginal welfare coverage for needy persons)
• the low degree of state penetration of the welfare sphere

- the persistence of favoured groups and the formation of fairly elaborate 'patronage systems' for the selective distribution of cash subsidies

The persistence of poverty in Greece (Stathopoulos 1996) and the development of social exclusion trends (Karantinos et al. 1992; Katrougalos 1996) necessitate, on the other hand, the transformation of the existing fragmented measures towards coordinated systems with specific goals, objectives and techniques (Petmesidou 1996). What role could law play in this process?

Both a rights-based strategy and a selective welfare policy are again implicated.

1. The adoption of a rights-based strategy is strongly associated with the enforcement of social citizenship rights violated by the lack of a systemic safety-net. Emphasis is therefore paid to the introduction of measures that not only cover existing gaps but also promote social integration and participation, through the establishment of enforceable rights.

2. The adoption of a selective welfare policy is related to the fulfilment of cost containment objectives in the field of social policy. Attention is then given to the introduction of strict entitlement conditions or 'targeting' measures for the existing categorical programmes, which may lead to marginal benefits for specific target groups.

From a sociopolitical perspective, both approaches should be analysed not only within the traditional framework of social policy thinking (Spicker 1993) but also among postmodernist social policy analysts (Lewis et al. 2000). The main subject here is the function of minimum income schemes as an instrument to deal with 'new risks' (Berghman 1997b: 259) that are not covered by common welfare measures,[38] as a means to promote social integration and inclusion (Lister 1998: 217).

As far as the debate about legal rules is concerned, policy-makers are obliged to take into account the effect of legal instruments on the development of systemic safety-nets. Any departure from principles enshrined in the constitution or deduced by international obligations should be assessed both on legal and sociopolitical grounds, since legislative action (in comparison with legislative inaction) is evaluated according to basic principles and objectives (social state, social justice, citizenship, equality, equity, autonomy).

The primary task of the law to promote social citizenship is fulfilled only under the development of a 'social rights culture', related to the 'human rights culture' discussed by Rorty (1993). This approach will facilitate the adoption of rights-based strategies and highlight inadequacies of selective strategies that will strengthen gaps in the existing system, not adequately covered through family ties or informal networks, given that these networks are faced with serious performance problems (see Stathopoulos 1996; Symeonidou 1997; Rhodes 1997).

Two scenarios exemplify the establishment of the right to a social safety-net through legislative process:

1. Introduction of a general minimum income scheme that will guarantee citizenship rights through means-tested benefits. Income support benefits and personal social services (Schorr 1995) are an individual right for people whose resources are lower than a specific fixed amount at the individual or household level.

2. Coordination of the existing selective social safety-net measures (strict application of social insurance and welfare principles) through introduction of common entitlement conditions and development of an assistance-type scheme for the coverage of unemployed persons (including vocational training and employment promotion).

The influence of legal principles in systems of welfare provision is again crucial. The right to a social safety-net is best promoted through a proper combination of both scenarios, resulting in the establishment of a general scheme, supplemented by categorical measures for specific needs. Substantive rights gained through legislative action should be maximized by procedural features of welfare, including legal aid and advice, information services and user-friendly techniques to enforce relevant rights (Van Oorshot 1995).

A rights-based strategy will build on the power acquired by citizens through a welfare-oriented legal process. Disadvantages of means-tested benefits (stigma effects, limited take-up rates, poverty trap)[39] should be seriously considered during this legislative process, in order to increase welfare legitimacy (Peillon 1996). The successful implementation of any legal reform in the Greek welfare model must be closely linked to the enforcement of citizenship rights for every human being.

NOTES

1. The structure of the Greek model is discussed in Amitsis 1997.

2. Italy and Portugal have introduced general minimum income schemes and Spain provides relevant benefits through regional autonomous programmes.

3. Relevant criteria are drawn from Dean (1996: 3), who argues that 'entitlements to welfare benefits and services are both specifically defined and generally situated; they result both from particular legislative rules and regulations and from wider policies and principles'.

4. See Kremalis 1991; Schulte 1993; Eardley 1996; Gough 1996; Stathopoulos 1996.

5. The treatment of a minimum income guarantee scheme as the basic indicator for social safety net policies is explained by Atkinson (1991: 2).

6. See Sissouras and Amitsis 1999; Guibentif and Bouget 1997; Gough 2001.

7. From a methodological point of view, attention should be paid to the fundamental difference between anti-poverty strategies, minimum income standards and social assistance benefits, as discussed by Veit-Wilson (1998: vii):
- Poverty Measures are the findings of social science research about the minimum income levels at which whole populations show or state they can live adequately, whatever the political implications of the findings;
- Minimum Income Standards are political criteria of adequacy, whatever the findings of social science research;
- Social Assistance is based on political decisions regarding how much governments are prepared to pay.

8. Amitsis (1992a) argues that solidarity elements are strong due to the funding process of minimum pensions: the state budget guarantees a fixed amount, not equivalent to the contributions paid by the beneficiaries.

9. Critical comments on this different treatment are put forward by Robolis (1993: 59) through the evaluation of the legal framework that introduced the new calculation model.

10. The major social partners in Greece are represented through the General Confederation of Labour and the League of Hellenic Industrialists.

11. According to the definition of Eardley (1996: 63): 'income-tested or income-related benefits are taken to be those where the level of benefits to which a claimant is entitled is based only on an assessment of his or her earnings or other income (however defined) and where capital or other property and assets are not taken into account.'

12. Here, reference should be made to the French *Minimum Viellesse*, the Italian *Pensione Minimale*, the Portuguese *Minimum Pension* and the Spanish *Complemento por minimos*, as described in MISSOC 1999 and Eardley et al. 1996.

13. This issue has been discussed by Petmesidou (1991: 32), who claims that 'welfare policies in Greece hardly aim at a redistribution on the basis of social need and social citizenship rights'.

14. See Kremalis 1991; Amitsis 1992b; Papadopoulos 1996.

15. These criteria are elaborated by Schulte (1993: 40); Twine (1994: 157); Eardley (1996: 62); Ringen (1998: 44) and Hanesch (1999).

16. For a complete evaluation of this instrument see Amitsis 1996.

17. A different argument is put forward by Papadopoulos (1996: 185), who claims: 'although it is limited to a one-off, lump-sum payment, special assistance is as near to providing a generalized, non categorical safety net as exists in the Greek social security system.'

18. Judicial and extra-judicial techniques are discussed by Kremalis 1991.

19. Benefits have been means-tested since 1997. This has led to controversial debates, including legal rulings which found that the introduction of a means test violates the constitutional guarantees for large families. The government abolished means-testing in 2000.

20. Relevant benefits have been identified during the study of Eardley (1996:

62) and classified as a peculiar mode of social assistance, 'as there are countries where minimum income protection for some groups of people, particularly those over retirement age or disabled, comes through non-contributory "citizens" benefits or pensions awarded without a test of other resources'.

21. This general inadequacy is stressed by Veit-Wilson (1998: 8), in his major comparative research analysis on Minimum Income Standards: 'Though social assistance is by definition designed for the poor, its actual benefits may be demonstrably inadequate to meet minimum income or other needs for social participation. Not all the recipients of other minimum income benefits are categorised as poor, nor is government's aim necessarily to provide a sufficient income to combat poverty: it may be to help people maintain their previous levels of living, or to support their own efforts to get out of poverty.'

22. See Atkinson 1992; Schulte 1993; Twine 1994; Eardley et al. 1996.

23. See Brook 1979; Cappelletti 1981; Dean 1996; Kjønstad and Veit-Wilson 1997.

24. The enjoyment of welfare benefits depends crucially on the development of procedural principles in welfare, which should be included in the following framework according to Galligan (1992: 66):

- informing claimants of the services available
- getting claims before the providers and decision-makers
- ensuring expedition in deciding cases
- dealing with individual cases
- periodic review of the circumstances of claimants and the appropriateness of provision previously agreed
- providing for appeal against decisions made
- providing for complaints to be heard about the quality of services
- criteria for and modes of redress

25. Esping-Andersen (1990), Plant (1994) and Twine (1994) discuss the political function of social rights, while Eide et al. (1995) discuss their legal impact.

26. The findings of this examination are evaluated according to normative and sociopolitical criteria in Amitsis 1996.

27. The legal effect and the sociopolitical substance of this Covenant are scrutinized in Craven 1998.

28. Judicial machineries regarding the application of ECHR are examined in Gomien et al. 1997.

29. On this point, see the arguments raised in Kjønstad and Veit-Wilson 1997.

30. For the traditional distinction between 'as of right' and 'means-tested' benefits see Twine (1994: 96).

31. The full text of the Recommendation can be found in the publication of the Council of Europe, *European Social Charter – Collected Texts*, Strasbourg, 1996.

32. These agencies are high-level administrative bodies that function as intermediaries between the applicants and the pubic authorities.

33. For this typology see Twine 1994, based on previous studies by Esping-Andersen (1990) and Peters (1991). Recent typologies are presented in Pitruzello 1999.

34. See Rhodes (1997: 140), who argues that 'the distribution of costs and

benefits has often been dictated by the influence of pressure groups and political lobbies rather than principles of equality or equity'. This is exactly the case for the development of categorical minimum income programmes in Greece.

35. For the relationship between safety-net mechanisms and social citizenship see in particular King and Waldron (1988: 415).

36. This argument is strongly supported by Dean 1996.

37. This is due to their pure income transfer orientations, as explained by Karantinos et al. (1992) and Amitsis (1994).

38. This function is discussed by Ginsburg (1998: 268), who states that: 'None the less the postmodern perspective highlights the inappropriateness of modern social policy in managing the new risks. The idea of a citizens' income, a guaranteed minimum income for individuals under written by the state, addresses this issue directly and gathers considerable support from analysts embracing elements of a postmodern perspective.'

39. Relevant disadvantages are discussed by Twine (1994: 97), who brings the argument that 'a means-tested benefit cannot provide a social right of citizenship because it threatens the integrity of the self'. The proper application of legal techniques can provide a different picture, as debated by Eardley (1996: 60).

REFERENCES

Alcock, P. (1993) *Understanding Poverty*, Basingstoke: Macmillan.

Amitsis, G. (1992a) 'Legal Problems for the Regulation and Implementation of a Minimum Income Scheme in the Greek Social Security System', *Greek Justice*, 33 (3): 504–13 (in Greek).

—— (1992b) 'Social Security in Greece', *Basic Income Research Group Bulletin*, 15: 12–14.

—— (1994) *The Greek Social Assistance System – Main Dimensions and the Treatment of Specific Target Groups*, Report for the EC, Athens: Network on Minimum Income.

—— (1996) *The Normative Establishment of Social Security Minimum Standards*, PhD Thesis, Faculty of Law, University of Athens (in Greek).

—— (1997) 'The Greek Social Security System', in D. Pieters (ed.), *Social Security Law in the Fifteen Member States of the European Union*, Antwerpen: Maklu, pp. 147–69.

Atkinson, A. (1991) *The Social Safety-net*, Welfare State Programme Discussion Paper WSP/66, London: London School of Economics.

—— (1992) *The Western Experience with Social Safety Nets*, Welfare State Programme Discussion Paper WSP/80, London: London School of Economics.

Berghman, J. (1997a) 'Social Exclusion in Europe: Policy Context and Analytical Framework', in G. Room (ed.), *Beyond the Threshold – The Measurement and Analysis of Social Exclusion*, Bristol: Policy Press, pp. 10–28.

—— (1997) 'The New Social Risks – A Synthetic View', in J. Van Langendonck (ed.), *The New Social Risks*, The Hague: Kluwer Law International, pp. 251–61.

Brook, R. (1979) *Law, Justice and Social Policy*, London: Croom Helm.

Campbell, T. (1988) *Justice*, London: Macmillan.

Cappelletti, M. (ed.) (1981) *Access to Justice and the Welfare State*, Florence: Le Monnier.

Clasen, J. (ed.) (1997) *Social Insurance in Europe*, Bristol: Policy Press.

Craven, M. (1998) *The International Covenant on Economic, Social and Cultural Rights*, Oxford: Clarendon Press.

Dean, H. (1996) *Welfare Law and Citizenship*, Hemel Hempstead: Harvester Wheatsheaf.

Eardley, T. (1996) 'Means-testing for Social Assistance – U.K. Policy in an International Perspective', in N. Lunt and D. Coyle (eds), *Welfare and Policy – Research Agendas and Issues*, London: Taylor and Francis, pp. 58–77.

Eardley, T., J. Bradshaw, J. Ditch, I. Gough and P. Whiteford (1996) *Social Assistance in OECD Countries*, Department of Social Security Research Report no. 47, London: HMSO.

Eide, A., K. Krause and A. Rosas (eds) (1995) *Economic, Social and Cultural Rights*, Dordrecht: Martinus Nijhoff.

Esping-Andersen, G. (1990) *Three Worlds of Welfare Capitalism*, Cambridge: Polity Press.

Ferrera, M. (1996) 'The Southern Model of Welfare in Social Europe', *Journal of European Social Policy*, 6 (1): 17–37.

Ferrera, M. and M. Rhodes (eds) (2000) *Recasting European Welfare States*, London: Frank Cass.

Galligan, D. (1992) 'Procedural Rights in Social Welfare', in A. Coote (ed.), *The Welfare of Citizens*, London: Rivers Oram Press, pp. 55–68.

Ginsburg, N. (1998) 'Postmodernity and Social Europe', in J. Catter (ed.), *Postmodernity and the Fragmentation of Welfare*, London: Routledge, pp. 266–77.

Gomien, B., D. Harris and L. Zwaak (1997) *The European Conventions of Human Rights and the European Social Charter: Law and Practice*, Strasbourg: Council of Europe Publishing.

Gough, I. (1996) 'Social Assistance in Southern Europe', *South European Society and Politics*, 1 (1): 1–23.

— (2001) 'Social Assistance Regimes: A Cluster Analysis', *Journal of European Social Policy*, 11 (2): 165–70.

Guibentif, P. and D. Bouget (1997) *Minimum Incomes Policies in the European Union*, Lisbon: Uniao das Mutualidades Portugesas.

Hanesch, W. (1999) 'The Debate on Reforms of Social Assistance in Western Europe', in European Foundation for the Improvement of Living and Working Conditions, *Linking Welfare and Work*, Luxembourg, pp. 71–86.

Harris, D. (1984) *The European Social Charter*, Charlotteville: University Press of Virginia.

Held, D. (1994) 'Inequalities of power, problems of democracy', in D. Miliband (ed.), *Reinventing the Left*, Cambridge: Polity Press.

Jacobs, F. and S. Roberts (1987) *The Effect of Treaties in Domestic Law*, London: Sweet and Maxwell.

Jaspers, A. and L. Betten (eds) (1988) *25 Years of the European Social Charter*, Deventer: Kluwer.

Karantinos, D. et al. (1992) *Second National Report to the Greek Observatory on Policies to Combat Social Exclusion*, Athens: National Institute of Social Research.

Katrougalos, G. (1996) 'The South European Welfare Model: The Greek Welfare State, in Search of an Identity', *Journal of European Social Policy*, 6 (1): 39–60.

Kerameas, K. and P. Kozyris (1996) *Introduction to Greek Law*, Athens: A. N. Sakkoulas.

King, D. and J. Waldron (1988) 'Citizenship, Social Citizenship and the Defence of Welfare Provision', *British Journal of Political Science*, 18: 415–43.

Kjønstad, A. and J. Veit-Wilson (eds) (1997) *Law, Power and Poverty*, Bergen: CROP.

Kremalis, K. (1991) *The Right of the Individual to Social Welfare*. Athens: A. N. Sakkoulas (in Greek).

Langan, M. (ed.) (1998) *Welfare: Needs, Rights and Risks*, London: Routledge.

Leibfried, S. (1993) 'Towards a European Welfare State?', in C. Jones (ed.), *New Perspectives on the Welfare State in Europe*, London: Routledge, pp. 133–56.

Lewis, G., S. Gewirtz and J. Clarke (eds) (2000) *Rethinking Social Policy*, London: Sage Publications.

Lister, R. (1998) 'From Inequality to Social Inclusion', *Critical Social Policy*, 18: 217–29.

MISSOC (1999) *Social Protection in the Member States of the European Union*, Luxembourg: European Commission.

Nolan, B. and C. Whelan (1996) *Resources, Deprivation and Poverty*, Oxford: Clarendon Press.

Papadopoulos, P. (1996) 'Greece', in T. Eardley et al., *Social Assistance in OECD Countries*, Department of Social Security Research Report no. 47, London: HMSO, pp. 178–94.

Peillon, M. (1996) 'A Qualitative Comparative Analysis of Welfare Legitimacy', *Journal of European Social Policy*, 6 (3): 175–90.

Percy-Smith, J. (ed.) (2000) *Policy Responses to Social Exclusion*, Buckingham: Open University Press.

Peters, G. (1991) *The Politics of Taxation: A Comparative Perspective*, Oxford: Blackwell.

Petmesidou, M. (1991) 'Statism, Social Policy and the Middle Classes in Greece', *Journal of European Social Policy*, 1 (1): 31–48.

— (1996) 'Social Protection in Greece – A Brief Glimpse of a Welfare State', *Social Policy and Administration*, 30 (4): 324–47.

Pitruzello, S. (1999) *Decommodification and the Worlds of Welfare Capitalism: A Cluster Analysis*, Florence: European Forum.

Plant, R. (1992) 'Citizenship, Rights and Welfare', in A. Coote (ed.), *The Welfare of Citizens*, London: Rivers Oram Press, pp. 15–29.

Rhodes, M. (1997) 'Southern European Welfare States – Identity, Problems and Prospects for Reform', in M. Rhodes (ed.), *Southern European Welfare States – Between Crisis and Reform*, London: Frank Cass, pp. 1–22.

Ringen, S. (1998) 'Social Security, Social Reform and Social Assistance', in D. Pieters (ed.), *Social Protection of the Next Generation in Europe*, EISS Yearbook, The Hague: Kluwer, pp. 27–45.

Robolis, S. (1993) 'A View from the South – Reforms in Greece', *Journal of European Social Policy*, 3 (1): 56–9.

Rorty, R. (1993) 'Human Rights, Rationality and Sentimentality', in S. Shute and S. Hurley (eds), *On Human Rights*, New York: Basic Books, pp. 111–34.

Schorr, A. (1995) *The Personal Social Services – An Outside View*, York: Joseph Rowntree Foundation.

Schulte, B. (1993) 'Guaranteed Minimum Resources and the European Community', in R. Simpson. and R. Walker (eds), *Europe – For Richer or Poorer?*, London: Child Poverty Action Group, pp. 39–51.

Scott, J. (1994) *Poverty and Wealth – Citizenship, Deprivation and Privilege*, London: Longman.

Sissouras, A. and G. Amitsis (1998) 'The Social Safety Net and its Regulating Mechanisms within the Greek Social Protection System', in T. Sakellaropoulos (ed.), *Reform of the Social State*, Athens: Kritiki, pp. 537–66 (in Greek).

Spicker, P. (1993) *Poverty and Social Security: Concepts and Principles*, London: Routledge.

Stathopoulos, P. (1996) 'Greece: What Future for the Welfare State?', in V. George and P. Taylor–Gooby (eds), *European Welfare Policy – Squaring the Welfare Circle*, Oxford: Macmillan Press, pp. 136–54.

Symeonidou, H. (1997) 'Welfare State and Informal Networks in Contemporary Greece', in MIRE, *Comparing Social Welfare Systems in Southern Europe*, Paris: MIRE, pp. 337–62.

Taylor-Gooby, P. (1991) 'Welfare State Regimes and Welfare Citizenship', *Journal of European Social Policy*, 1(2): 93–105.

Twine, F. (1994) *Citizenship and Social Rights – The Interdependence of Self and Society*, London: Sage Publications.

Van Oorshot, W. (1995) *Realizing Rights – A Multi-level Approach to Non-take-up of Means-Tested Benefits*, Avebury: Aldershot.

Veit-Wilson, J. (1998) *Setting Adequacy Standards – How Governments Define Minimum Incomes*, Bristol: Policy Press.

PART IV

Legal Initiatives to Address Specific Aspects of Poverty

TEN | Gender mainstreaming as an instrument for combating poverty

SUE NOTT

§ The law plays a significant role in the creation, perpetuation and potential elimination of poverty. More particularly, the use of the law to create rights in favour of disadvantaged individuals, such as the right to social security or a living wage, sends an important message regarding the unacceptability of poverty. Legal rights can give individuals, as well as organizations seeking to eliminate poverty, a means by which they can exert political pressure for improved living standards. Furthermore, the binding nature of law offers the poor and those working on their behalf a way of vindicating their rights either through the courts or by administrative means. Legal rights can, in addition, be instrumental in securing change in society. They offer a way of eliminating or correcting those factors that maintain or exacerbate poverty. Discrimination on the grounds of race or sex, which has often been identified as a source of poverty, can be addressed by creating the right to equal treatment.

Examples of how legal rights have been employed in the struggle to combat poverty can be found at international and national levels. The International Covenant on Economic, Social and Cultural Rights is one instance of an international human rights convention that bears on poverty. It lists a variety of rights which are relevant to the alleviation of poverty, including the opportunity to gain one's living by work which one freely chooses or accepts (Article 6), the right to social security, including social insurance (Article 9) and the right to an adequate standard of living for oneself and one's family (Article 11).[1] Such international statements of rights have the advantage of universality. They represent the views of the international community and, once ratified, they impose a legal obligation on the states that adopt them to implement these rights.

At the national level, a state may have provisions in its constitution which commit it to combating poverty. For example, Article 58 of the Portuguese constitution guarantees the right to work and imposes on the state the duty to promote equal opportunities, full employment and training for workers. In addition, all workers, whatever their age, sex, race, nationality, place of origin, religion or political or ideological convictions, are given the right to fair remuneration, material assistance when they are involuntarily unemployed, compensation for accidents at work or industrial diseases, and a limit on the length of the working day and working week. In its turn, the state commits itself to setting a national minimum wage as well as maximum working hours and to protecting the working conditions of certain groups of workers such as pregnant workers (Article 59).[2] By guaranteeing these rights and imposing these duties, the economic position of workers (but not, of course, other groups in society) is, in principle, protected.[3]

However, although the law has considerable potential to combat poverty, via the creation of legal rights that redistribute power and income in favour of the poor, there are substantial barriers to this strategy's success. International guarantees of rights for the poor must be transformed from aspirations into practical reality. For example, Article 25 of the Universal Declaration of Human Rights (UDHR) provides: 'Everyone has the right to a standard of living adequate for the health and well-being of himself and his family, including food, clothing, housing and medical care and necessary social services, and the right to security in the event of unemployment, sickness, disability, widowhood, old age or other lack of livelihood in circumstances beyond his control.' Yet this statement of intent had then to undergo the lengthy process of being translated into legally binding commitments capable of producing a positive impact at a national level on the lives of those experiencing poverty. This process of translation requires the presence of two factors. The first is the will on the part of states and their governments to create binding legal obligations. Those with political power may well resist attempts at implementing human rights instruments at the national level, perceiving them as a threat to their own economic well-being (in the shape of higher taxes) or believing that the demands of the poor can be safely ignored because they are politically powerless. Others may argue that helping the poor by guaranteeing them social rights is beyond their country's financial capabilities. Secondly, the translation of international guarantees of rights into binding legal commitments may achieve very little if those commitments are not respected. It is vital that states possess a 'rights culture' if such commitments are to have a practical impact on the lives of the poor. A rights culture is one 'where individuals as well as politicians, administrators and security forces know and accept not only their own rights, but also their duties flowing from the rights of the other members of the community on a basis of equality' (Eide 1997: 125).

Once guarantees of rights for the poor are in place at a national level, there are other obstacles to the success of using the law to combat poverty. Laws may achieve very little if the means to enforce them, in the shape of legal remedies or financial aid for those wishing to bring legal actions, are not available. In addition, rights can and do conflict with one another. For example, Article 40.1 of the constitution of the Irish Republic provides that: 'All citizens shall, as human persons, be held equal before the law. This shall not be taken to mean that the State shall not in its enactments have due regard to differences of capacity, physical and moral and of social function.' In March 1996, the Irish Parliament agreed on an Employment Equality Bill which, among other provisions, placed a duty on employers to take 'reasonable steps' to accommodate the needs of persons with disabilities except where this would cause an employer undue hardship. Arguably, this provision, by making employers take account of the reasonable needs of the disabled, is giving substance to the notion that all persons are equal and has the potential to reduce poverty by increasing the numbers of disabled in employment. However, the Irish Constitutional Court ruled[4] that this provision was in violation of Article 40.3.1 of the Irish constitution.[5] This Article states: 'The State guarantees in its laws to respect, and, as far as practicable, by its laws to defend and vindicate the personal rights of the citizen.'

The obligation on employers to take account of the needs of the disabled was interpreted as an unjust limitation on an employer's right to carry on a business and earn a living. In addition, the Court ruled that such a duty constituted an attack on the property rights of employers protected by Article 43 of the constitution.[6] This demonstrates that, unless a constitutional right is regarded as absolute and subject to no qualification whatsoever, it will of necessity be interpreted to establish the boundaries between it and other constitutional rights. In such 'boundary disputes', the rights of disadvantaged groups may give way to those from more privileged sectors of society.

Thus, the 'traditional' approach of creating legal rights to combat poverty has numerous difficulties associated with it. In part these difficulties relate to the legal complications of establishing and enforcing rights. Of equal significance, however, is the fact that legal rights represent a blunt instrument for addressing the practicalities of why individuals are poor. The acknowledgement of this fact should not be seen as a wholesale rejection of the role that legal rights can play in the elimination of poverty. Legal rights have an educational and aspirational value. In times of crisis, the decision to ignore or expunge legal rights is one that cannot be performed covertly as may be the case with other less formal measures for eliminating poverty. Instead, an awareness of the shortcomings of legal rights should encourage those who wish to use the law in order to combat poverty to reflect on alternative legal strategies. In the first place attention should be paid to the reasons for poverty. X may be poor because she has no job. X may have no job because she is disabled and is, as a consequence, perceived by potential employers as unsuitable. Yet again X may be poor because she has a low-paid job. She may be low-paid because she is a woman. The existence of a right to work or a right to a fair wage would seem not to confront these specific causes of poverty. In order to combat poverty, the law has to address and eliminate (in so far as it is possible to do so) the reasons for poverty. Yet even this may not go far enough. Secondly, a means has to be devised of facing up to the fact that the law is as potent a tool for sustaining poverty as it is for eliminating it (Kjønstad and Veit-Wilson 1997). The creation of legal rights in favour of the poor will achieve very little if the policies which underpin other laws work against their interests. A state which is committed to eradicating poverty may (intentionally or unintentionally) make its laws to combat poverty less effective by pursuing policies in other spheres which ignore the needs of the poor. To take a simple example: a state which permits public transport operators to charge 'economic' fares will cause far more damage to the poor in society than to other income groups.[7]

This analysis of the law's current shortcomings in combating poverty leads irresistibly to the following conclusions. To achieve greater success, the law must address the causes of poverty and more generally there is a need for all proposed laws and policies to be audited for their potential impact on the lives of those who are disadvantaged. In order to put these assertions to the test this chapter will focus upon one specific cause of poverty: namely gender inequality. It will consider the link between poverty and gender inequality and the success of the law to date in breaking this link. It will then evaluate a new strategy for promoting equality between the sexes that goes by the name of 'gender mainstreaming'. Gender mainstreaming is a procedure that aims to take account of gender issues from 'the outset of policy development and throughout the process of implementation and review' (Spencer n.d.: 1). More recently, however, another procedure has emerged which, though linked with gender mainstreaming, is directly concerned with poverty and goes by the name of poverty proofing. Poverty proofing is designed to assess the effect of policy and legislative initiatives on poverty, or on the inequalities that lead to poverty. This chapter will consider whether poverty proofing is a more useful tool to combat poverty than gender mainstreaming.

THE RELATIONSHIP BETWEEN GENDER INEQUALITY AND POVERTY

Many explanations are offered for why individuals are poor. One reason is that they belong to a group in society that is the target of discrimination. If, for example, a community is divided into two religious or racial groups and one of those groups monopolizes political power, then the community's resources may be used to benefit one group and to exclude the other. Discrimination may, however, be neither as centralized nor as systematic as this. Indeed, many states condemn discrimination and their constitutions guarantee equal treatment to individuals whatever their sex, their marital status, their religious or political beliefs, their colour or their sexual orientation. Yet the inequality which is a product of discrimination is a complex phenomenon which is not eradicated by creating a legal right to equal treatment. This can be illustrated by considering the ways in which gender inequality manifests itself within society. Gender inequality is not simply a matter of rogue employers refusing to engage women or to promote female employees. Women are disadvantaged by cultural and social perceptions regarding their behaviour in society. These include the belief that, as caring individuals, women are particularly suited to certain occupations, such as nursing, and are unsuited to others that require physical strength, such as road mending. By way of contrast, men's values and preoccupations have, it is argued, come to dominate society while being presented as the (apparently) gender-neutral values and preoccupations of society as a whole (Mackinnon 1989). The very fact that society is dominated by male values works against women's interests in countless ways. For example, it allows male working patterns (full-time, permanent employment) to be put forward as the 'norm', while women's working patterns, if they deviate from this norm, are seen as exceptional or unorthodox.

The existence of gender inequality produces numerous disadvantages for women, including economic disadvantages. More particularly, there is a well-established link between gender inequality and poverty: 'There is a growing and compelling body of evidence that shows that not only do women bear the brunt of poverty, but also that women's empowerment is a central precondition for its elimination. Women's equality is an absolute necessity if the blight of poverty is to be removed and the nations of the world are to create a secure, sustainable and prosperous future' (Department for International Development 2000: 10).

The problem is that, despite efforts to combat sex discrimination and promote equal opportunities, women still remain some of the poorest individuals in society. For example, the United Kingdom has legislation outlawing discrimination on the grounds of sex (Sex Discrimination Act 1975), marital status (ibid., section 3), race (Race Relations Act 1976) and disability (Disability Discrimination Act 1995) and, in Northern Ireland, on the grounds of religious and political belief (Fair Employment Act 1989). Yet its legislation to secure equality between the sexes seems to have brought about only limited changes despite the fact that it has been in force for thirty years. In particular, the anti-discrimination legislation has not eradicated the financial disadvantages that individuals who are the object of discrimination may suffer. While over the decades women's economic activity rates have increased in the United Kingdom,[8] there still remains a substantial pay gap between the sexes. Full-time hourly earnings for male employees are £11 as compared with full-time hourly earnings for women of £8–9. This means that women's average full-time hourly earnings are 81 per cent of those of men. In the case of part-time workers, the pay gap is more pronounced with women in part-time employment earning, on average, 60 per cent of the average hourly pay of male full-time employees (Equal Pay Task Force 2001: 21).[9] This disparity is all the more serious when it is recalled that an estimated 4.9 million women in the United Kingdom work part-time as compared with one million men. Moreover, lower earnings over the course of a woman's working life result in smaller incomes during retirement.[10]

Nor is the situation of women in the United Kingdom unique. A similar situation exists across the European Union. Despite the Community's efforts to promote equal opportunities between the sexes, women remain financially disadvantaged. Full-time women employees in the member-states are paid 75 per cent of men's gross hourly wages (ibid.).

In the light of this evidence, two conclusions emerge. First, there is an undeniable link between gender inequality and poverty.[11] Secondly, the legal measures currently employed to combat gender inequality do not work satisfactorily with the result that this particular source of poverty remains uncorrected. This inevitably raises the question of why this is so.

In attempting to explain the failure of the law to promote equality
between the sexes reference will be made to the findings of an international research project financed by the European Commission and
involving an analysis of the equality strategies employed in Sweden,
Ireland, Spain, Portugal and the United Kingdom.[12] The project addressed the continued significance of gender as a factor in social
exclusion in the European Union, despite many decades of measures
to eliminate gender-based discrimination. One aspect of the project
consisted of an analysis of the effectiveness of measures that are
currently employed to tackle sex discrimination and promote equal
opportunities for women. Each of the countries that participated
in the project possesses a sophisticated system of laws, policies and
agencies designed to eradicate sex discrimination. In addition, all five
states are members of the European Union which itself is committed
to the pursuit of equal opportunities (Hervey and O'Keeffe 1996). The
data gathered during the course of the project enabled the following
conclusions to be drawn regarding the strengths and weaknesses of the
laws promoting equality.

Equality laws

Legislation outlawing discrimination on the grounds of sex is undoubtedly worthwhile, but it is limited in what it can achieve. How
such laws define discrimination, what areas of activity such measures
cover and the mechanisms for pursuing claims of sex discrimination
are vital in guaranteeing effectiveness. In Sweden, for example, the
Equal Opportunities Act 1991 is concerned with promoting equal opportunities for men and women in relation to employment, conditions
of employment and other conditions of work such as personal development. The 1991 Act obliges employers to adopt positive measures to
promote equality and also makes discrimination on the grounds of sex
unlawful. Commentaries on this legislation have noted that its scope is
limited to the workplace; that the obligation on employers to promote
equality is not adequately enforced and that the remedies in relation
to individual claims of discrimination are inadequate (Gillberg 1999:
section 2.2).

In some cases states have supplemented their anti-discrimination
legislation with provisions in their constitutions guaranteeing the right
to equal treatment. In the Spanish constitution, for example, there are

eight Articles with some bearing on equality (e.g. Articles 9.2 and 14). The effectiveness of such provisions in promoting equal opportunities depends on how easily these rights may be enforced. In some states, a law's constitutional validity can be challenged only by certain designated officials. Of course, the wording of such rights is also important, as is their relationship with other rights guaranteed by the constitution. Finally, the existence of such rights does not ensure that, in practice, life will improve for women. For example, giving women the right to vote does not mean that women will be well-represented in the national legislature.

Apart from anti-discrimination legislation, states may also make use of the strategies known as positive action or positive discrimination. The concept of positive action acknowledges that treating men and women equally will achieve very little if women face barriers to their progress in society that are not experienced by men. A state may therefore introduce a range of measures designed to 'compensate' women for these disadvantages. For example, positive action can address the discriminatory impact of pregnancy on women by offering pregnant workers additional rights, such as paid maternity leave. Alternatively, positive action may be used to confront gender stereotypes such as the belief that some forms of employment, such as nursing, are particularly appropriate for women while others, such as mining, are not. The state may authorize employers to train women for those occupations where traditionally they are underrepresented. Positive discrimination, however, takes this process a stage further by attempting to compensate women for past discrimination by awarding them preferential treatment in certain circumstances. In those occupations or activities where women are underrepresented, quotas or targets may be set. Quotas normally require the appointment of a woman even if her qualifications are inferior to those of a man. A target, however, represents a goal that may or may not be achieved. It does not require the appointment of a woman whatever the circumstances, though, if a man and a woman are equally well-qualified, the assumption is that the woman will be preferred.[13]

The project highlighted a number of examples where women were the target of positive action programmes. Portuguese Decree Law 392/79 (Article 3/2) specifies that: 'temporary provisions establishing a preference on the grounds of sex and imposed by the necessity to correct factual inequality, as well as measures that are intended to protect maternity as a social value shall not be considered discriminatory.'

However, the vagueness of this provision, coupled with the failure of the legislation to set goals to be achieved, has meant that this strategy has been seen as marginal in promoting equality between the sexes (Casqueira Cardoso 1999: 37). In the United Kingdom, the legality of positive discrimination has been questioned in certain situations. For example, the use of all-women short lists in order to increase the number of women candidates for election to Parliament was successfully challenged on the grounds that it was discriminatory (Beveridge et al. 1999: section 3).

Equality machinery

Each country involved in the project had one or more agencies which had been assigned the task of promoting equality between the sexes. These agencies, most of which were established by the state and financed with public money, perform a variety of functions. They might monitor the application of the anti-discrimination legislation, propose new legislative initiatives, investigate the actions of individual employers for evidence of discrimination, disseminate good practice information, conduct research and initiate litigation. The comments most frequently made regarding these bodies were that their performance was adversely affected by a lack of resources, by a restricted interpretation of their legal powers or by poor relationships with other government entities. For example, in Portugal the Commission on Equality and Women's Rights (CEWR) is given the task of scrutinizing policy or law-making initiatives for differential impact on men and women. Yet in assessing its effectiveness, it was concluded: 'CEWR is, however, prevented from effectively exercising this function because of a lack of co-operation by the Government and/or the Assembly'(Casqueira Cardoso 1999: 48).[14]

Many of the states in the project also possess a government minister with responsibility for women or for equal opportunities in general. The current government in the United Kingdom has recently appointed such a minister and has also set up a Women's Unit and a Cabinet Subcommittee on Women. These initiatives are meant to develop an effective cross-departmental approach to women's issues and involve women more directly with government. However, the problem with creating such structures is that they can establish 'a "waste-paper basket for women's problems" and an alibi for gender-blind policy in the rest of government' (Sawer 1998: 2). Based on the findings of the project, it appeared that the influence possessed by such a minister varies depending on the status accorded that minister/ministry within the government and the feminist credentials of the minister (Arranz et al. 1999: 33).

This research demonstrates the limited degree of success enjoyed by what is in any estimation a sophisticated array of legal and extra-legal devices designed to eliminate sex discrimination and promote gender equality. Factors such as complicated legislative provisions, lack of resources and the marginalization of equality agencies were all to blame. When considering the ways in which the law can be used to combat poverty, these findings have a particular significance. There is a significant link between poverty and gender inequality, and the law's failure to eradicate gender inequality means that this cause of poverty is unresolved. In addition, many of the mechanisms used to tackle gender inequality, such as laws promoting equality or authorizing the establishment of special agencies, are deployed in campaigns to eliminate discrimination against other groups in society. There is no reason to believe that these legal strategies will be more successful in these contexts, unless the flaws that have been identified herein are addressed.

Nor is it sufficient simply to tackle the weaknesses inherent in a particular legal strategy. There is considerable evidence to show that other laws or policy initiatives, which are apparently gender-neutral, can undermine the impact of measures to promote equality between the sexes. Hence the decision taken in the United Kingdom to privatize certain services, such as the provision of school meals, had the effect of reducing women's wages. Contracts were normally awarded to the cheapest bid, wages were driven down as a consequence and the majority of employees in these sectors were women (Equal Opportunities Commission 1995). Many of the strategies to combat gender inequality, or other forms of discrimination, are adversely affected by seemingly 'neutral' legislation. As a consequence a mechanism is required to audit legislation for its gender impact. In the context of promoting equality between the sexes, this procedure goes by the name of gender mainstreaming.

GENDER MAINSTREAMING

Gender mainstreaming[15] is a comparatively new strategy for promoting equal opportunities. It has been used by international organizations including the European Union (Hafner-Burton and Pollack 2000: 432) and at a national level by countries such as Canada, the Netherlands and New Zealand.[16] Gender mainstreaming is concerned with integrating an equality dimension into policy development, implementation and assessment. It requires that 'equality be seen as an integral part of all public policy making and implementation, not something that is separated off in a policy or institutional ghetto' (McCrudden 1999: 1704).[17]

As part of the research project under discussion, a number of processes were evaluated which apparently represented attempts at gender mainstreaming, although that was not necessarily the description used. In Portugal, for example, a Global Plan for Equal Opportunities had been adopted with the single objective of integrating the principle of equal opportunities between men and women into all economic, social and cultural policies, coupled with specific objectives in key areas. There was, however, an unwillingness among government bodies to take responsibility for implementation of the Plan (Casqueira Cardoso 2000). In the United Kingdom, two procedures known as PAFT (Policy Appraisal and Fair Treatment) and PAET (Policy Appraisal for Equal Treatment) had been in use from the 1980s onwards to assess policies for their impact on a range of target groups including women.[18] Both procedures came in time to be identified with mainstreaming, though arguably they lacked some of the procedure's essential features.[19] Latterly, however, the PAFT guidelines have assumed the status of a statutory duty[20] in Northern Ireland as part of the peace process in the Province (see McCrudden 1999) while the PAET guidelines have been updated.[21] At the same time, new regional assemblies in Wales and Scotland have adopted a form of mainstreaming as part of their working practice (Beveridge et al. 2000: 385). One feature of the United Kingdom's mainstreaming initiatives is the decision not to confine them to addressing inequality between the sexes. Instead, gender inequality is addressed alongside other inequalities such as race, disability and sexual orientation.[22]

An evaluation of these and other efforts at gender mainstreaming made it plain that the process is a cause for both optimism and cynicism. On the one hand, mainstreaming looks at the potential gender impact of *all* laws and policies before they are put into operation. No area of activity can, therefore, escape scrutiny. In this fashion, gender inequality becomes everyone's concern, not simply that of specialized agencies. Moreover, in assessing gender impact there is a need to accumulate evidence either in the shape of statistics or of views from the target group. Gender mainstreaming can thus be an inclusive process drawing groups into government whose views were previously unheard. On the other hand, a cynic might argue that gender mainstreaming is often little more than a bureaucratic procedure – not a real attempt to isolate the causes of gender inequality. Indeed, there is a danger that gender mainstreaming, with its notion that equality is everyone's business, will be used as an excuse for dismantling specialized equality machinery. Moreover, doubts have been expressed over the ability of gender mainstreaming to resist the pressures of the marketplace. While it is a strategy that may work well in the public sector, this may not be the case in the private sector when confronted by the pressures of profitability and deregulation.

In order to succeed, gender mainstreaming is a process that requires commitment at a number of levels. First, it requires political commitment, since without government support the strategy cannot succeed. Secondly, it requires officials who put this political commitment into practice by devising a procedure (impact assessment) that is capable of predicting the impact of new or existing policies or legislation on the target group. Third, it requires an effort to monitor those laws and policies that have been put into operation to determine whether their impact was as predicted. Finally, particular attention has to be paid to what constitutes 'adverse impact' in the context of gender mainstreaming. The classic definition of equality requires like cases to be treated alike. This, however, is a very narrow definition of equality since it merely requires men and women to receive the same treatment and ignores the biological and cultural differences between the sexes. Traditional jurisprudential theory is nevertheless very attached to the equal treatment concept of equality. Writers such as John Rawls (1972) construct individualistic theories of justice that take no notice of the special needs of discrete groups in society. Inequalities in the distribution of social goods, such as wealth and income, are justified provided the least advantaged gains. In the context of gender mainstreaming, if equality is defined as equal treatment, a law or policy would have an adverse impact only if it did not treat men and women identically. This, however, is not an acceptable notion of equality for the purposes of gender mainstreaming since it leaves untouched the majority of inequalities that exist between the sexes.[23] For this process to succeed, it must address inequality whenever it presents itself with a view to reducing its incidence within society.

Force is given to this argument by the fact that jurists, such as Ronald Dworkin (2000), have emphasized the central role which equality plays within society. In Dworkin's opinion, the weight he attaches to equality justifies restrictions on the liberty of some (hitherto advantaged) members of society in order that equality may prevail. In short, the promotion of equality can and does require that those who have been the target of discrimination should receive preferential treatment in the form of affirmative action. In the context of gender mainstreaming, this translates into a definition of adverse impact that takes account of how, in reality, men and women will be affected by a particular law or policy, including their access to wealth. Laws and policies will be preferred if they correct the cultural and social imbalance between the sexes and respond to the particular needs of women, even though some individuals who were hitherto in a privileged position suffer as a consequence.

The potential of mainstreaming to address gender inequality (or indeed other forms of inequality) offers a corrective to one of the major sources of poverty. Clearly a great deal of thought has to be given to making mainstreaming 'work' if it is to represent more than a paper exercise. Yet a cynic might argue that gender inequality is simply one of a range of reasons why individuals are poor. It would seem more sensible to use mainstreaming as a direct weapon in the fight against poverty. A few countries have done just this by introducing a process known as poverty proofing (Mullally et al. 2000).

POVERTY PROOFING

In a number of countries a conscious decision has been taken to reduce the incidence of poverty. In the Irish Republic, for example, a National Anti-Poverty Strategy (NAPS) has been developed. NAPS defines poverty as follows: 'People are living in poverty, if their income and resources (material, cultural and social) are so inadequate as to preclude them from having a standard of living which is regarded as acceptable by Irish society generally. As a result of inadequate income and resources people may be excluded and marginalised from participating in activities which are considered the norm for other people in society' (Mullally et al. 2000: 3).

NAPS's purpose is to reduce the percentage of individuals in Ireland identified as poor from between 9–15 per cent of the population to between 5–10 per cent over a ten-year period (1997–2007). The policy contains a number of specific targets relating to education, unemployment, income, disadvantaged urban areas and rural poverty. Other countries, including the Netherlands, have also put anti-poverty strategies in place.

There is no intention to use this occasion to analyse these anti-poverty strategies in depth. Their existence merely raises the general issue of how governments will ensure the effectiveness of any anti-poverty strategy. One device that has been utilized in the Irish Republic is 'poverty proofing'. This is seen as important because it will ensure 'that policies do not run counter to NAPS and more importantly policies are designed to substantially tackle poverty' (Johnston 1998: 5). In the context of NAPS, poverty proofing is defined in the following manner: 'Poverty proofing is the process by which government departments, local authorities and state agencies assess policies and programmes at design and review stages in relation to the likely impact that they will have or have had on poverty and on inequalities which are likely to lead to poverty, with a view to poverty reduction' (Department of Social Welfare 1988: 3).

Officials are instructed to undertake poverty proofing in a range of situations, including the preparation of legislation and budget recommendations, when designing policy proposals and in the preparation of the National Development Plan. In so doing, they are required to respond to the following questions:

- What is the primary objective of this proposal?
- Does it help to prevent people from falling into poverty?
- Does it reduce the level of poverty?
- Does it ameliorate the effects of poverty?
- Does it increase poverty?
- Does it contribute to the achievement of the NAPS targets?
- Does it address inequalities that might lead to poverty?
- Does it affect target groups?

Officials must respond to these questions on the basis of available data. They must then conclude whether the proposal increases, has no effect on or reduces poverty. In the first two instances, thought must be given to alternatives that might have a more positive effect on poverty.

The current verdict on poverty proofing is that it has had little effect on law and policy-making. Part of the reason for this has been a lack of resources as well as a failure to involve interested parties in such a process. Leaving aside any problems regarding the mechanics of poverty proofing, there is the separate issue of whether poverty proofing offers a better solution to eradicating poverty than gender mainstreaming. There is an argument that different groups in society experience poverty in different ways. A woman's experience of poverty is not necessarily the same as that of a man, while women from ethnic minorities may feel the effects of poverty very differently from white disabled men. If this is so, then asking what effect a proposed law has on 'the poor' may be a pointless question since it essentializes those who are poor into a homogeneous group, which they clearly are not. There is the added danger that the question (what effect does this particular law or policy have on 'the poor'?) may be answered wholly on the basis of the experiences of one section of those individuals (for example, white able-bodied males) who are judged to be poor.

CONCLUSIONS

What this chapter has set out to demonstrate is that if the law is successfully to combat poverty it is essential for the law to address the reasons for poverty, such as inequality between the sexes. In addition, it has advocated the need for all proposed laws and policies to be subject to mainstreaming. Whether mainstreaming should be targeted at the poor per se or at specific groups who are susceptible to poverty, such as women, the disabled or ethnic minorities, is harder to determine. If the latter course is taken, there could be a proliferation of impact assessments. As a consequence the decision-making process would become very lengthy and there would undoubtedly be financial and staffing implications for governments. It is also possible that a mainstreaming hierarchy would develop with perhaps the interests of one group (e.g. the disabled) being placed before others (e.g. ethnic minorities). Finally there is a danger that the flexibility that is a characteristic of mainstreaming could be undermined if disgruntled target groups began to seek judicial review when an impact assessment did not go 'in their favour'. While there is no denying these potential dangers, it does seem that a procedure, such as gender mainstreaming, designed to raise awareness of how exactly a proposed law or policy will affect gender inequality, offers a more subtle way of combating poverty than assessing a proposed law or policy for its effect on 'the poor'.

NOTES

This chapter is in part based on research carried out in the Feminist Legal Research Unit by Ms Fiona Beveridge, Dr Kylie Stephen and Miss Sue Nott in connection with the project Predicting the Impact of Policy: Gender-Auditing as a Means of Assessing the Probable Impact of Policy Initiatives on Women. Finance for this project was provided by the European Commission's Targeted Socio-Economic Research Fund.

1. Note that Articles 6 and 11 use the terms he/his, not gender-neutral language.

2. This English translation of the constitution of the Portuguese Republic is taken from the following website: <http://www.parlamento.pt/leis/constituicao_ingles/crp_uk.htm>.

3. Much, of course, depends on how these rights and duties operate in practice. A minimum wage would seem a very effective guarantee against poverty but that wage has to be set at a realistic level and employers must be made to respect it.

In addition, guaranteeing rights to workers may mean that a large portion of a country's population is not protected against economic disadvantage since they are not workers.

4. *In the Matter of Article 26 of the Constitution and In the Matter of the Employment Equality Bill, 1996*, 118/97 unreported, Supreme Court, 15 May 1997. This account of the case in taken from Mullally et al. (1999).

5. A version of the Employment Equality Bill, amended to take account of the Supreme Court's ruling, was eventually passed: the Employment Equality Act 1998. This requires employers to accommodate the needs of the disabled only when the costs involved are nominal.

6. For further comment on this case and other related issues see Mullally (2001: 99).

7. Higher fares will restrict the poor's ability to travel and hence to work or to purchase cheaper goods from out of town supermarkets.

8. In spring 2000 there were 12.5 million women in the labour market. This represents an increase of 843,000 as compared with the figure for 1990; *Equal Opportunities Review* (2001: 29).

9. This report can also be found at <http://www.bt.com/equalpaytask force/>. See also the Equal Pay Act 1970.

10. According to the Department of Social Security in Great Britain in 1996/97 the average independent income received by women in retired couples was around 40 per cent of men's; Cabinet Office (1999: 33).

11. It is, of course, incorrect to say that every member of a group that experiences discrimination will be poor. It simply renders this possibility more likely.

12. The project's full title is *Predicting the Impact of Policy: Gender-Auditing as a Means of Assessing the Probable Impact of Policy Initiatives on Women*; its abbreviated title is the PIP project. Details of this project may be obtained from Sue Nott and Fiona Beveridge, Feminist Legal Research Unit, Liverpool Law School, Liverpool University, Liverpool L69 3BX, UK. Alternatively, consult the project website: <http://www.liv.ac.uk/~scooper/pip.html>.

13. The problem with positive discrimination is that it has, in certain situations, been said to constitute sex discrimination. In *Kalanke v. Freie und Hansestadt Bremen*, Case 450/93 [1995] IRLR 660, the European Court of Justice held that a policy requiring the appointment of a woman when her qualifications matched those of any male candidates was contrary to the Equal Treatment Directive. Compare this decision with the European Court of Justice's decision in *Marschall v. Land Nordrhein-Westfalen*, Case 409/95 [1998] IRLR 39, where the scheme in question was acceptable because it permitted a certain level of discretion.

14. The assembly mentioned is the Assembly of the Republic which is the Portuguese national legislature.

15. For a more detailed account of mainstreaming see Nott (1999).

16. In those countries which have adopted mainstreaming the strategy has been used almost exclusively to promote equal opportunities for women.

17. In the same article McCrudden remarks that mainstreaming is an idea

whose time is come but whose meaning is uncertain and subject to varying interpretations.

18. PAFT was used exclusively by the Northern Ireland Office while PAET was employed by government departments in the rest of the United Kingdom.

19. For a more comprehensive analysis of PAFT see Osborne et al. (1996).

20. Section 75, Northern Ireland Act 1998.

21. The PAET guidelines were reviewed by the Women's Unit and relaunched; Cabinet Office (1998).

22. The wisdom of such an approach has however been questioned on the basis that the elements that contribute to gender inequality are not the same in the case of other inequalities such as race or disability; see Verloo (2000).

23. This point has been made on numerous occasions by feminist commentators. The dilemma is how to construct an alternative feminist definition of equality. On this point see Littleton (1987: 1279).

REFERENCES

Arranz, F., B. Quintanilla and C. Velaquez (1999) *Spanish Country Report on Behalf of the PIP Project*, Liverpool: Feminist Legal Research Unit.

Beveridge, F., S. Nott and K. Stephen (1999) *United Kingdom Country Report on Behalf of the PIP Project*, Liverpool: Feminist Legal Research Unit.

— (2000) 'Mainstreaming and the Engendering of Policy-Making: A Means to an End?', *Journal of European Public Policy*, 7(4): 385.

Cabinet Office (1998) *Policy Appraisal for Equal Treatment*, London: Cabinet Office.

— (1999) *Voices*, London: Cabinet Office.

Casqueira Cardoso, J. (1999) *Portuguese Country Report on Behalf of the PIP Project*, Liverpool: Feminist Legal Research Unit.

— (2000) 'Making Women Count in Portugal', in F. Beveridge, S. Nott and K. Stephen (eds), *Making Women Count: Integrating Gender into Law and Policy-Making*, Aldershot: Ashgate.

Department for International Development (2000) *Poverty Elimination and the Empowerment of Women*, London: Department for International Development.

Department of Social, Community and Family Affairs (1997) *Sharing in Progress – National Anti-Poverty Strategy*, Dublin: Department of Social, Community and Family Affairs.

Department of Social Welfare (1998) *Policy Proofing in the Context of the National Anti-Poverty Strategy*, Dublin: Department of Social Welfare.

Dworkin, R. (2000) *Sovereign Virtue: The Theory and Practice of Equality*, Cambridge, MA: Harvard University Press.

Eide, A. (1997) 'Human Rights and the Elimination of Poverty', in A. Kjønstad and J. H. Veit-Wilson (eds), *Law, Power and Poverty*, Bergen: CROP Publications.

Equal Opportunities Commission (1995) *The Gender Impact of Compulsory Com-*

petitive Tendering in Local Government, Manchester: Equal Opportunities Commission.

Equal Opportunities Review (2001), 96 (March/April).

Equal Pay Task Force (2001) *Just Pay*, Manchester: Equal Opportunities Commission.

Gillberg, M. (1999) *Swedish Country Report on Behalf of the PIP Project*, Liverpool: Feminist Legal Research Unit.

Hafner-Burton, E. and M. Pollack (2000) 'Mainstreaming Gender in the European Union', *Journal of European Public Policy*, 7(3): 432.

Hervey, T. and D. O'Keeffe (1996) *Sex Equality Law in the European Union*, Chichester: Wiley.

Johnston, H. (1998) 'One Year On – Assessing the Anti-Poverty Strategy', *Poverty Today*, 4.

Kjønstad, A. and J. H. Veit-Wilson (1997) *Law, Power and Poverty*, Bergen: CROP Publications.

Littleton, C. (1987) 'Reconstructing Sexual Equality', *California Law Review*, 75: 1279.

McCrudden, C. (1999) 'Mainstreaming Equality in the Governance of Northern Ireland', *Fordham International Law Journal*, 22: 1701.

MacKinnon, C. (1989) *Toward a Feminist Theory of the State*, Cambridge, MA: Harvard University Press.

Mullally, S. (2001) 'Mainstreaming Equality in Ireland: A Fair and Inclusive Accommodation?', *Legal Studies*, 21(1): 99.

Mullally, S., M. Donnelly and O. Smith (1999) *Irish Country Report on Behalf of the PIP Project*, Liverpool: Feminist Legal Research Unit.

— (2000) 'Making Women Count in Ireland', in F. Beveridge, S. Nott and K. Stephen (eds), *Making Women Count: Integrating Gender into Law and Policy-Making*, Aldershot: Ashgate.

Nott, S. (1999) 'Mainstreaming Equal Opportunities: Succeeding When All Else Has Failed', in A. E. Morris and T. O'Donnell (eds), *Feminist Perspectives on Employment Law*, London: Cavendish Press, ch. 10.

Osborne, R., A. Gallagher and R. Cormack with S. Shorthall (1996) 'The Implementation of the Policy Appraisal and Fair Treatment Guidelines in Northern Ireland', in E. McLaughlin and P. Quirk (eds), *Policy Aspects of Employment Equality in Northern Ireland*, Belfast: SACHR.

Rawls, J. (1972) *A Theory of Justice*, Oxford: Oxford University Press.

Sawer, M. (1998) *The Life and Times of Women's Policy Machinery: Lessons from Australia*, Paper prepared for the UN Expert Group meeting on National Machineries for Gender Equality, Santiago, Chile, 30 August–4 September 1998.

Spencer, F. (n.d.) *Briefing on Mainstreaming*, Manchester: Equal Opportunities Commission.

Verloo, M. (2000) 'Making Women Count in the Netherlands', in F. Beveridge, S. Nott and K. Stephen (eds), *Making Women Count: Integrating Gender into Law and Policy-Making*, Aldershot: Ashgate.

ELEVEN | Does alcohol and tobacco legislation help reduce poverty? The evidence from Sri Lanka

KALINGA TUDOR SILVA

§ Substance use is a worldwide phenomenon affecting all income groups. However, in many countries its adverse consequences are most acute among the socially disadvantaged, including large sections of the poor. Many governments have enacted legislation to regulate the production, sale and consumption of alcohol and tobacco. These laws have dual and often conflicting motivations and purposes: to generate revenue for the state from sale of these substances and, at the same time, to minimize the adverse social, economic and health consequences of the widespread use of these addictive substances. Such legislation can thus, in theory, affect poverty in two contrasting ways depending on one's perspective and how far the unintended consequences of the relevant legislation may offset the intended ones. To the extent such legislation serves to reduce substance use and related deprivation among the poorer sections of a population in particular, it can be expected to contribute to poverty alleviation by discouraging habits and lifestyles leading to perpetuation and reproduction of poverty. On the other hand, if alcohol and tobacco legislation merely becomes a legal instrument employed by the dominant classes in society against the poor, leading to their frequent criminalization and to a heightened 'gaze' directed at the powerless and the poor on the part of law enforcement agencies (Foucault 1977), the legislation can contribute to discrimination and perpetuate both poverty and marginality. This chapter explores these two contrasting hypotheses relating to the possible impact of alcohol and tobacco legislation on poverty, using data from the small island nation of Sri Lanka.

MULTIPLE LINKAGES BETWEEN POVERTY AND SUBSTANCE ABUSE

Research indicates that there is varied and diverse interaction between substance abuse and poverty. While substance abuse is by no means restricted to poor communities, often there is a two-way relationship between substance abuse and poverty, addictions serving to perpetuate and at times intensify poverty and becoming part of the coping mechanism in dealing with the stresses and strains arising from poverty and poverty-related deprivations (Nastasi and DeZolt 1994; Kleinman 1988; Townsend 1979). Production of and trafficking in substances can be important informal sector activities in certain low-income communities (Reuter et al. 1990; Bourdieu 1993). This, in turn, suggests that legislation dealing with substance abuse must carefully assess its possible complex interactions with poverty.

The role of substance abuse in the social reproduction of poverty

The factors involved in the social reproduction of poverty, including intergenerational transfer of poverty, perpetuation of poverty through cultural mechanisms, and practices and subjectivities of the poor themselves as well as linkages between poverty and social exclusion, have been explored by social scientists for many decades (Bourdieu 1993; Lewis 1965). However, the role of substance abuse in the social reproduction of poverty remains a relatively underexplored topic.

Substance abuse is by no means limited to the poor and it is possible that any excessive and distinctive pattern of substance abuse among the poor may be a reaction against their poverty and social marginality rather than an underlying cause of their condition. However, there is considerable evidence to support the view that excessive, persistent and widespread collective use of tobacco, alcohol and drugs is not merely a manifestation of poverty and deprivation. On the contrary, substance abuse can be expected to contribute to processes of impoverishment, perpetuation of poverty and social marginalization in a number of important ways.

First, compulsive expenditure on substances constitutes a heavy and frequently unstoppable drain on the scarce resources of the poor. Often such families are left with inadequate funds for essential needs like food, healthcare, education and recreation. Second, substance abuse continued over a long period of time can lead to loss of productivity, ill-health, domestic violence and problems with law enforcement agencies. This, in turn, can lead to an irreversible process of impoverishment and cumulative deprivation. Finally, those affected by addiction may experience a process of social marginalization whereby their effective social universe becomes gradually and progressively restricted to those sharing similar lifestyles. This, in turn, can set off social exclusion where the affected populations are socially cut off from the mainstream, preventing access to services and, at the same time, reinforcing prejudices and discriminatory practices on the part of those representing the social mainstream. The tendency among vulnerable people to progress from use of less harmful to more harmful substances can further aggravate the socioeconomic consequences. Thus patterns of substance abuse in selected populations can generate an expenditure pattern and an alienated lifestyle, setting off mutually reinforcing processes of increased addiction, impoverishment, marginalization and social exclusion.

It must also be noted here that poverty, particularly when associated with social marginality, may increase one's vulnerability towards substance abuse. For the poor and the socially marginal, the euphoria (the 'kick' or '*arthal*' in local usage) derived from addictive substances may be an important means of coping with the intolerable conditions associated with their day-to-day existence.

Legislative means of regulating substance use and their potential impact on poverty

Legislation aimed at preventing substance abuse is generally based on one of two models: prohibition or legalization of the substances at issue. In the prohibition model, typically inspired by puritanical and moralistic views, the legislation totally bans production, sale or use of specific substances. For instance, during the period from 1920 to 1934, when a national alcohol prohibition was enforced in the United States, alcohol consumption reportedly dropped by 30 to 50 per cent and the incidence of cirrhosis correspondingly dropped. On the other hand, the same period saw a marked growth in organized crime and violence, as well as a rise in death and disease caused by the consumption of illegal alcohol (UNICDP 1997). Similarly a ban on drugs can encourage users to go underground, establish their own exclusive social networks supportive of drugs and resort to more harmful practices such as intravenous drug use. Under the circumstances, as stated by Bourdieu (1993: 176), 'from being a tool in the struggle against poverty, the public authority is transformed into a weapon in the war against the poor'.

While the prohibition model forbids any acknowledged use of banned substances, the legalization model seeks to regulate substance use and bring it under social and institutional (usually medical) control while also granting a degree of choice to the individual. Legislation facilitating regulated drug use has been introduced in countries like the United States, the Netherlands, Australia and Switzerland with corresponding improvements in harm reduction associated with drug use. In the modern world, a version of the legalization model exists in relation to alcohol use in almost all countries with the exception of some Islamic countries. For tobacco, the legalization model seems to be universal.

The likely consequences of prohibition or legalization of substances on poverty, however, have not been systematically explored in any country. In the present chapter we are unable to examine this issue in full as we concentrate on one country and limit ourselves to exploring the implications of regulations relating to two substances subject to legalization, namely tobacco and alcohol.[1]

In the present chapter we attempt to examine the implications of the variation in legal status of various substances for poverty and the lifestyles of the poor. The issues addressed here are as follows:

- Does legalization of substances make them more accessible or less accessible to the poor?
- As the prices of legal substances increase, do the poor turn more towards illegal substances which are less costly but potentially more harmful?
- Which legislation is more likely to prevent substance abuse by the poor and which legislation is more likely to criminalize and socially marginalize the poor?
- What effects do economic liberalization policies have on alcohol and tobacco industries and what implications do they have for the lifestyles of the poor?
- What lessons can we learn from the experience of one country regarding possibilities for reduction of poverty through modification of alcohol and tobacco legislation?
- What type of alcohol and tobacco legislation would best serve the objective of preventing or minimizing social reproduction of poverty via substance abuse and related practices?

SUBSTANCE ABUSE AND ITS RELATION TO POVERTY IN SRI LANKA

Our aim here is to establish linkages between poverty and substance abuse in Sri Lanka, using a range of available information. Section A deals with Sri Lanka's country context relevant for understanding the issues at hand. Sections B and C review data relating to patterns and trends of substance use, focusing on alcohol and tobacco use respectively. Section D addresses the issue of linkages between substance abuse and poverty.

A. Sri Lanka: the country context

When examining the socioeconomic impact of alcohol and tobacco legislation in Sri Lanka, we have to bear in mind several distinctive features in the country. First, as an island nation of about 18 million people inhabiting a total of 65,454 sq. km, Sri Lanka provides a compact setting within which the impact of various country-specific policies can be assessed without much concern about potential cross-border influences.

Second, consumption of intoxicating substances is discouraged on religious grounds in Buddhism, Hinduism and Islamism, accounting for 70, 15.5 and 7.5 per cent of the total population in the country respectively.[2] While domestically produced toddy (an alcoholic beverage extracted from palm trees) has been consumed in Sri Lanka since ancient times, large-scale commercial production of alcohol and tobacco was initiated by colonial rulers, who utilized the industry for extracting revenue for the state. One of the lasting means of resistance against colonial rule and Western domination took the form of temperance movements led by the Buddhist elite (Fernando 1971). Because of this historical context, legislation against alcohol and possibly other addictive substances is unlikely to evoke any adverse reactions from within indigenous cultures.

Third, Sri Lanka has a history of enlightened welfare policies. Since national independence from the British in 1948, Sri Lanka has been acclaimed as a 'successful welfare state' in the Third World, with heavy public investments in education, health and rural infrastructure. As a result, Sri Lanka has much experience in using state policies and legislation as a tool for social development affecting a wide spectrum of the country's population. Sri Lanka's notable achievements in quality of life – female life expectancy of seventy-four years (1991), female literacy of 88 per cent (1994) and infant mortality rate of 18.2 per 1,000 births (1992) – attest to the impact of a series of enlightened welfare policies and legal measures.

Fourth, Sri Lanka is moving away from the socialist-type closed economic policies fashionable during the 1956–77 era, and, since 1977, has increasingly turned towards a model of economic liberalization and pro-Western strategies of capitalist development. Among other industries, the alcohol and tobacco industries have profited from policies favouring foreign investments over the past two decades.

Finally, since 1983, the threat of civil war has affected the stability of the country. The Liberation Tigers of Tamil Eelam (LTTE), a secessionist movement seeking to establish an independent state guaranteeing sovereignty to Sri Lanka Tamils, the largest minority ethnic group in Sri Lanka, is engaged in an armed struggle with the Sri Lankan state. Conflict between the LTTE and the Sri Lankan government threatens the territorial integrity of the country as well as its law and order situation. Equally significantly, however, the LTTE is widely reported to be engaged in transnational 'narco-terrorism', with serious implications for the illicit drug trade in Sri Lanka and various other countries throughout the world (NDDCB 1986).

B. Patterns and trends of alcohol consumption in Sri Lanka

The type of alcohol consumed in Sri Lanka varies significantly on the basis of the social class background of its consumers. Variations in purchasing power, shared tastes signifying social class specific 'distinctions' (Bourdieu 1979) and accessibility and availability all play a role in determining variation in alcohol consumption. The broad pattern is outlined in Table 11.1.

With a few exceptions, alcohol consumption in Sri Lanka is largely restricted to men. Imported exclusive drinks like whisky and brandy are primarily consumed by the elite. The middle classes (mainly government servants and private sector workers) consume industrially manufactured arrack (a highly intoxicating drink introduced to Sri Lanka by the Portuguese and made either from spirit distilled from toddy or from molasses) or beer. Liquor consumption among the poorer sections of the population is dominated by *kasippu*, a highly potent illegal alcoholic drink made from spirit extracted from local fruits combined with sugar, yeast and various other unknown ingredients. The poor also consume arrack and toddy, an indigenous wine extracted from palm trees.

Typically, the poorer man's alcoholic preferences are shaped by a

TABLE 11.1 Variation in alcohol consumption in Sri Lanka by social class

Category of alcohol	Type	Legal status	Social class of consumers
Imported spirits	spirit	Licit	Elite
Imported wines	wine	Licit	Elite
Beer and stout	malt	Licit	Elite/middle/poor?
Arrack	spirit or molasses-based	Licit	Middle/poor
Toddy	wine	Licit or illicit	Poor
Kasippu	spirit	Illicit	Poor

TABLE 11.2 Total and per capita consumption of alcohol per annum in Sri Lanka 1989–95

Year	Arrack million litres	Toddy million litres	Malt liquor (beer, etc) million litres	Wine million litres	Other spirits* million litres	Total per annum million litres	Per capita consumption litres	Population >000
1989	29.511	9.809	7.894	0.240	0.738	48.192	2.864	16,825
1990	37.244	11.466	9.116	0.302	1.120	59.248	3.487	16,993
1991	46.322	10.722	9.563	0.240	1.627	68.474	3.970	17.247
1992	51.953	11.752	10.563	0.032	1.706	76.006	4.367	17,405
1993	48.976	13.286	10.847	0.027	1.680	74.816	4.246	17,619
1994	55.000	11.899	10.975	0.223	2.552	80.649	4.514	17,865
1995	66.520	4.888	12.608	0.359	2.776	87.151	4.812	48.112
% change 1990–95	78.6	-57.4	38.3	18.9	147.9	47.1	38.0	6.6

* Other spirits include whisky, brandy, gin, rum and vodka.

Source: Sri Lanka Excise Department

need to get high intoxication at the lowest possible cost. *Kasippu* (price of a bottle Rs. 75–100) is considerably cheaper than its competitor arrack (price of a bottle Rs. 150–250). Moreover, *kasippu* is readily available in remote areas where industrially manufactured legal alcohol is not readily available, particularly at times of the day and during days of the month when outlets of legal alcohol are closed due to legal requirements. Beer has traditionally been popular among higher income groups in Sri Lanka, but lately its popularity has increased to a wider cross-section of the population, due to changes in taxation making beer cheaper than some of the other legal drinks.

Macro level data relating to consumption of licensed alcohol reveal that per capita alcohol consumption in Sri Lanka steadily increased between 1989 and 1995 (see Table 11.2).

The reasons for this marked increase in alcohol consumption may include:

• expanded production resulting from the establishment of several new local subsidiaries of multinational alcohol producers encouraged to invest in Sri Lanka under the programme of economic liberalization
• aggressive promotion of alcohol
• greater availability through recent expansion of licensed outlets
• increased purchasing power of the population at large
• increased emotional and social stress associated with ongoing social and economic processes in the country

Arrack accounts for the highest increase in per capita consumption, followed by malt liquors. The consumption of toddy, a poor man's drink, shows a downward trend, perhaps due to a switch of poor consumers to illicit toddy and *kasippu* (because of the rapid increase in the price of legal alcohol) rather than due to a genuine decrease in alcohol consumption among the poor. It must be noted that the published data on alcohol consumption exclude illicit alcohol, which is widely consumed by the poor in the rural, estate and urban sectors of Sri Lankan society. According to one estimate, nearly 90 per cent of liquor consumption in certain dry zone districts in remote areas of Sri Lanka is illicit (Sober Sri Lanka 1997: 28). Further, in assessing per capita consumption, we must remember that alcohol consumption is not common among females in Sri Lanka.[3] If we leave out the female segment of the population, the actual per capita consumption among male consumers would be much higher than is reported in Table 11.2.

Data on alcohol-related morbidity and mortality in Sri Lanka reveal a parallel increase in the 1985–95 period (see Table 11.3).

TABLE 11.3 Morbidity and mortality caused by chronic liver disease in Sri Lanka, 1975–95

| Year | Number of cases | | Per 100,000 | |
	Morbidity	Deaths	Morbidity	Deaths
1975	5,700	508	42.2	3.8
1976	4,523	355	33.0	2.6
1977	4,269	333	30.6	2.4
1978	4,265	334	30.1	2.4
1979	5,757	473	39.8	3.3
1980	4,766	491	32.3	3.3
1981	4,742	502	31.9	3.4
1982	4,691	526	30.9	3.5
1983	5,489	586	35.6	3.8
1984	6,477	606	41.5	30.9
1985	7,134	623	45.0	3.9
1986	7,575	781	47.0	408
1987	7,832	580	47.9	5.2
1988	9,211	1,025	55.5	6.2
1989	10,063	1,069	59.9	6.4
1990	9,330	929	54.9	5.5
1991	8,663	956	50.2	5.5
1992	8,077	793	46.4	4.6
1993	9,423	1,068	53.5	6.1
1994	8,894	999	49.8	5.6
1995	9,955	1,345	55.0	7.4

Source: Sober Sri Lanka 1997

Alcohol-related offences also show an upward trend (see Table 11.4).

TABLE 11.4 Alcohol-related offences in Sri Lanka, 1990–93; rate per 100,000 population

Year	Drunk driving	Manufacture	Unlicensed liquor Possession	Sale	Transport
1990	8.86	115.8	598.4	92.0	4.7
1991	12.72	167.0	553.7	99.1	4.3
1992	15.62	164.3	737.8	65.8	7.9
1993	20.75	135.9	662.1	71.5	7.1

Source: Sober Sri Lanka 1997

C. Patterns and trends of tobacco smoking in Sri Lanka

Tobacco, like Western-style alcohol, was introduced to Sri Lanka by the Portuguese. Today the preferred form of tobacco smoking, particularly among the middle and upper classes, is cigarettes. Among the poor, hand-rolled *beedi*s (cheap local cigarettes made from inferior tobacco) and *suruttu* (cigars) are popular. Most of the *beedi* and cigar manufacture is done in unlicensed cottage industries typically found in economically depressed areas in the country. Primarily because no centralized agency is responsible for monitoring the tobacco industry, no reliable macrolevel information regarding trends in tobacco smoking in Sri Lanka exists. Periodic surveys published in the medical literature indicate that the prevalence of smoking among men increased in Sri Lanka until the early 1990s. In 1969, 48 per cent of adult men and 1.6 per cent of adult women were found to smoke, while in 1987, 55 per cent of adult males smoked regularly. The World Bank reported in 1992 that adult per capita consumption of tobacco in Sri Lanka was the highest in South Asia, although levels of smoking among Sri Lankan women remained negligible.

Since this time, however, studies have documented that Sri Lanka has achieved an impressive reduction in smoking, with prevalence among adult males declining as low as 12 per cent as of 1995 (Mehl 1996). On the other hand, some empirical studies in low-income populations reveal that prevalence of tobacco smoking continues to be as high as 80 per cent of the adult male population, suggesting that while tobacco smoking may be on the decline among the rich and middle income groups, those from lower socioeconomic backgrounds may be an exception to this pattern.

D. Poverty, marginality and addictive behaviours

Numerous studies in Sri Lanka indicate that both the prevalence of and problems related to addictive behaviours are quite high among low-income groups. A survey conducted in the remote Hambantota District in the South by Sober Sri Lanka, an anti-alcohol NGO, found that 60 per cent of families supported by the Janashakti programme[4] had at least one member addicted to alcohol or smoking (Gunasekera and Perera 1997). In another survey it was found that 43 per cent of shanty dwellers in Colombo were alcohol users, a majority of them being daily users (ADDIC 1994). In labour barracks in the estate sector,[5] prevalence of alcohol use was found to be 65 per cent among adult males and 42 per cent among adult females (ADDIC 1995). A study covering six districts found that the male prevalence rate was considerably higher in the dry zone districts of Monaragala (66 per cent), Hambantota (55 per cent)

Sector	% of per capita expenditure
Urban	2.4
Rural	4.1
Estate	8.5
All island	3.8

Source: Department of Census and Statistics 1993

and Polonnaruwa (55 per cent) (ADDIC 1995). In a representative sample of 2,445 households in Mahaweli System H contacted in a study conducted by the NDDCB, 37 per cent of the households had at least one regular consumer of alcohol (Pereira 1992). The same study found that 85 per cent of the households had at least one member who had consumed indigenous medicines containing alcohol (*tharalasaraya*) or marijuana (*madanamodakaya*). In an intensive ethnographic study of one settlement unit in Mahaweli System H, De Soyza (1995: 346) reported: 'The rough climatic conditions and physical terrain, economic strife, depression and sheer boredom have meant that with closure of the frontier poor male settlers are prone to temporarily escape their misfortune by turning to drink.'

National-level data on per capita or household expenditure on alcohol and tobacco smoking are somewhat misleading due to the possible underreporting of alcohol expenditure. In the first round of the Household Income and Expenditure Survey (HIES) of 1993 carried out by the Department of Census and Statistics, per capita expenditure on alcohol and tobacco was found to be 3.8 per cent, with the estate sector reporting the highest percentage of per capita expenditure on substance use (see Table 11.5).

A comparison of expenditure on alcohol and tobacco among various income deciles indicates that the percentage of income spent on substance use tends to be higher in lower-income deciles, with the lowest-income decile reporting 12.25 per cent of income diverting to substance use as compared to 1.6 per cent for the highest income decile. These data suggest that the impact of substance use on the expenditure pattern in general is greater in lower-income groups, where a substantial share of limited incomes appears to be diverted to maintaining the addictive behaviours of one or more adult household members (usually the male head of the household).

Various microstudies indicate that the actual expenditure on alcohol in low-income households may be substantially higher than those reported in HIES. Samarasinghe (1995) points out that a daily consumption of four cigarettes and two units of alcohol by one member of a household can amount to 40 per cent of the earnings of the family in the lowest income quartile in Sri Lanka. In a study of urban shanty households, ADDIC found that those studied spent nearly 30 per cent of their monthly expenditure on alcohol alone (ADDIC 1995; Amarasuriya and Salgado 1998). Hettige (1993) found a similar pattern among new settlers in irrigation schemes.[6]

In assessing the impact of tobacco and alcohol on poverty, it would be misleading to consider only their negative impacts. It is important to note here that the tobacco and alcohol industries are an important source of employment for a cross-section of society, including the poor. Although there are insufficient data regarding the significance of these industries as a source of employment for the poor, it is known that (in addition to the numbers employed in licensed industries) illicit alcohol and illicit tobacco manufacturing and distribution provide employment to a reasonable number of persons from lower socioeconomic backgrounds. For instance, the *beedi* industry has evolved as a cottage industry absorbing excess labour in several poverty-stricken areas (Hewavitharana 1992). Similarly, tobacco farming provides a somewhat lucrative, but precarious and environmentally hazardous, livelihood to farmers in certain areas of Sri Lanka.

The information available suggests that the illicit liquor industry is largely controlled by some powerful individuals with the backing of politicians and law enforcement personnel in more remote areas (De Soyza 1995; NDDCB 1986). However, it appears to be the case that dealers of illicit liquors, as well as many of the consumers, typically come from lower socioeconomic backgrounds (De Soyza 1995; Hettige 1993). Retail sale of illicit liquor, drugs and, to some extent, even tobacco products remains within the purview of the informal sector that provides income-earning opportunities for the poor (Silva and Athukorala 1993; Marga Institute 1979). It is, however, important to note that some poor people earn their living producing or as employees of those who produce unlicensed products. This, in turn, makes them susceptible to criminalization by law-enforcement agencies.

In order to explore the role of addictions in the social reproduction of poverty and marginality, focus group discussions were conducted by a team of researchers headed by the author of this chapter in six estates covering upcountry, mid-country and low-country. These studies revealed that the expenditure on alcohol among the estate residents may be much higher than those reported in the 1993 HIES. The estate residents, most of whom are of Indian Tamil origin, have remained in separate ethnic enclaves in tea and rubber plantations established during the British period. Only recently have they received full citizenship rights due to their history of migration from South India and the unwillingness of the politically powerful Sinhala ruling elite to recognize them as citizens of the country. The estate residents are cut off from mainstream society because of their language (Tamil), lower educational achievement, working-class history, lack of skills needed for alternative employment, their long-term residence in 'labour lines',[7] and lack of contacts outside the plantations. Not having identity cards and other documentation to prove their citizenship status, many of them also encounter legal and security problems in southern parts of Sri Lanka where Tamil identity can evoke suspicion and occasional harassment from those responsible for maintaining law and order.

According to our data, those consuming alcohol daily or at least weekly ranged from 50 to 75 per cent of working men and 10 to 20 per cent of working women in the estates (CARE Sri Lanka 1998). Alcohol consumption (most often *kasippu*, followed by arrack, beer and toddy) was part of the daily routine of many male estate labourers, accounting for 25 to 50 per cent of daily income. We did not come across any instances where *kasippu* was manufactured within the estates. Typically *kasippu* and toddy were manufactured in nearby villages by Sinhalese entrepreneurs and supplied to the estate residents through dealers in and around the estates. The estate-dwellers' socially and ethnically marginal position has resulted in limited bargaining power vis-à-vis those outside the estates. While some estate residents visited legal outlets situated in the vicinity of the estates, in some instances there were unofficial dealers operating in collaboration with liquor outlets in nearby towns.

Many regular consumers tended to see alcohol as the only pleasurable experience in a world full of deprivation, discrimination, subhuman experiences and hostility (see also Samarasinghe 1995). In some estates, alcohol was the adult males' primary motivation for earning extra income from estate incentive payments or off-estate employment opportunities. Thus living conditions remained unchanged or even worsened despite improved income. Estate workers generally perceived alcohol as a 'pain killer' and a coping strategy for dealing with the physically demanding work schedule more strictly enforced by the new management companies in the estates, particularly in tasks assigned to men such as pruning or uprooting of tea bushes. In the focus group discussions, the estate residents also mentioned that alcohol helped them forget their daily share of worries and deplorable working conditions and cold, damp and even more deplorable living conditions associated with the labour lines. Women were routinely given a dose of alcohol after child delivery, extending the notion of alcohol as a remedy for all kinds of body pains, including labour pains. On the other hand, a range of evils were attributed to alcohol, including the drain on household income, the diversion of funds from basic needs, absenteeism from work, indebtedness, domestic violence, adverse health effects such as ulcers in the bowel and cirrhosis and problems with police and supervisory staff.

The findings reported in the preceding paragraphs indicate that addictions may be an important factor in the perpetuation and intensification of poverty in certain subpopulations in Sri Lanka. Substance abuse seems to be a common feature of a range of communities, including urban low-income communities, 'colonies' and estates, where widespread poverty exists side by side with social marginality. Research in the estates points to the manner in which addictions and related outcomes like domestic violence and problems with worker supervisors and law enforcement agencies contribute to the process of social marginalization. In the case of estate residents, addictions, while contributing to low self-esteem, also tend to reinforce negative ethnic stereotypes held by outsiders.

THE LEGAL FRAMEWORK FOR REGULATING ALCOHOL AND TOBACCO USE

The laws for dealing with substance use in Sri Lanka are drawn from:

1. the Excise Ordinance
2. the Tobacco Ordinance
3. the Poisons, Narcotics and Dangerous Drugs Ordinance

All three ordinances have evolved from the British colonial era. The Excise Ordinance, which originated around 1840, mainly covers alcoholic drinks. The Tobacco Ordinance, which is in many ways less comprehensive than the Excise Ordinance, regulates the tobacco industry. The third ordinance, which is outside the scope of the present chapter, mainly deals with cannabis, opium and psychotropic drugs made available through approved channels.

The key goals in enacting the Excise and Tobacco Ordinances were twofold: generating revenue for the state by taxing the alcohol and tobacco industries and reducing consumption of the relevant substances.

As leaders of the temperance movement in the nineteenth century readily pointed out, these two goals were often contradictory (Fernando 1971). The first objective called for an expansion of the alcohol and tobacco industries, including generating an increased demand for these substances. In contrast, the second objective required a contraction of these industries and a corresponding reduction in availability and consumption of their products.

Since the time of British colonial rule, the alcohol and tobacco industries have been an important source of revenue for the Sri Lankan state. However, the relative failure of ordinances as instruments for regulating addictive behaviours and alleviating negative economic, social and health consequences has become more evident in recent years in the wake of the visible increase in alcoholism, crime and violence, social disturbances and various other manifestations of stress such as a sharp rise in youth suicide[8] (Silva and Pushpakumara 1996). Evidence of users' graduation from less harmful substances (e.g. cigarettes) to more harmful ones (e.g. heroin) as well as simultaneous involvement in multiple addictions has made it necessary to re-examine the choice of legislation based on prohibition vis-à-vis legalization.

The Excise Department, which implements the Excise Ordinance in collaboration with the police, regulates the supply of alcohol by controlling the import and export of alcohol and licensed manufacture of alcohol, limiting the number and location of legal outlets, taking action against illegal suppliers, regulating business hours in legal outlets, requiring closure on days of religious significance (e.g. Buddhist poya days) and on days of potential mass mobilization and street violence (e.g. election days), ensuring that legal outlets supply alcohol to approved customers only (women and children under eighteen are not allowed to purchase alcohol), enforcing the volume sold per customer and the volume retail customers are permitted to transport and stock, and conducting periodic checks in legal outlets to ensure that they do not stock adulterated or illegal substances.

The Excise Ordinance makes provision for the Excise Commissioner and the minister in charge to introduce any additional regulatory mechanisms needed for maintaining law and order by issuing gazette notifications periodically. Many of the regulatory mechanisms noted above have been introduced through gazette notifications, rather than through amendment of the ordinance itself.

The Police Department implements excise laws by raiding illegal outlets and by checking legal outlets for conformity with regulations. In addition, the police are responsible for taking action against all alcohol-related offences, including drunk driving, disorderly conduct and any other offences committed under the influence of alcohol.

The Tobacco Ordinance is implemented by the Excise Department, primarily through measures designed to prevent the illicit manufacture of tobacco products. A gazette notification made under the Tobacco Ordinance mandates a warning about the adverse health consequences of tobacco smoking on the external labels of all packets containing commercially manufactured tobacco products. Additionally, there are several clauses in the Tobacco Ordinance intended to prevent tobacco smoking by children, but they have not been implemented due to a variety of constraints in the Excise Department, including staff shortages, lower priority assigned to tobacco matters relative to alcohol matters[9] and non-cooperation by the public.

Successive governments have gradually increased already heavy taxes and levies on alcohol and tobacco products. Subsequent increases in prices of legal products have made it increasingly difficult for the poor to afford them. This, in turn, has compelled them to turn to less costly, but potentially more hazardous, illicit products.

Anti-alcohol and anti-smoking lobbies in Sri Lanka have identified several weaknesses in the existing laws and institutional mechanisms for dealing with alcohol and tobacco industries:

1. There is neither a coherent policy nor a well-coordinated programme for regulating the use and preventing the misuse of substances. A presidential committee appointed to investigate the relevant issues has prepared a draft policy document relating to alcohol, tobacco and dangerous drugs, which is yet to be implemented (Government of Sri Lanka 1997). The overall aim of this policy is to 'reduce and finally eliminate use of all harmful substances, enhance health, well-being and productivity of and eliminate poverty among all Sri Lankans'.

2. The anti-alcohol and anti-tobacco lobbies have campaigned for banning all alcohol and cigarette advertisements in the media and public places. They have had a measure of success with regard to advertisements in the electronic media, banning since 1995 TV and radio advertisements of commercial brands of alcohol or cigarettes. These bans have been imposed using public security legislation,[10] as the existing Excise and Tobacco Ordinances do not provide for such a ban. However, the available legal measures are inadequate to address this situation. In some instances the companies have successfully bypassed this ban by resorting to indirect but highly

effective advertisements in the electronic media. For instance, TV advertisements about a local brand of beer named after a particular animal, which is also of symbolic significance to the majority ethnic group in the country, simply highlight the needs and urges of the animal.

3. The tobacco industry uses sponsorship of sporting events as a major strategy for enhancing their public image. At present there are no legal provisions for banning such sponsorships.

4. There are no satisfactory legal provisions for protecting the non-smoking and/or non-drinking public from the adverse effects of tobacco smoking or alcohol consumption by others in public places, on public transport and in private homes.

5. Aggrieved parties face many obstacles in pursuing litigation against alcohol and tobacco companies. Whenever their interests are threatened, the companies use whatever social contacts they have with intermediaries, law-makers and administrators of the law. Legislation that removes these constraints, as well as legal aid for the aggrieved parties, is necessary to promote the use of litigation.

6. Many politicians and those holding public office are stakeholders in the alcohol and tobacco industries. A recent move to issue licences for opening liquor shops through local politicians affiliated with the ruling party has highlighted the level of influence the industries exert over the government, rendering many of the existing controls over the industries and mechanisms for distribution of legal as well as illegal alcohol ineffective.

THE IMPACT OF ALCOHOL AND TOBACCO LEGISLATION ON POVERTY

Alcohol and tobacco legislation in Sri Lanka has had a limited impact on trends in substance use in the country. Alcohol consumption appears to be on the increase. While much of the legislation aimed at reducing alcohol consumption has had a limited impact in terms of regulating consumption of licensed liquors, such legislation may have paradoxically pushed the poor towards increased use of illicit liquor.

In contrast, tobacco smoking tends to be on the decrease, but no evidence indicates if this decrease is applicable to the lower income groups. The reported reduction in tobacco smoking may be attributed to multiple factors including public health campaigns, rising literacy in the population as well as the mandatory warnings.

Even though Sri Lankan alcohol and tobacco legislation is based on

TABLE 11.6 Direct admission of convicted prisoners in Sri Lanka by type of offence 1990–95

Year	Narcotic drugs		Excise		Other		Total	
	no.	%	no.	%	no.	%	no.	%
1990	6,654	47.1	2,248	15.9	5,226	37.0	14,128	100.0
1991	7,642	40.2	5,723	30.1	5,654	29.7	19,019	100.0
1992	5,915	32.4	4,928	27.0	7,408	26.1	18,251	100.0
1993	6,656	35.7	4,873	26.1	7,115	38.2	18,644	100.0
1994	5,660	34.9	4,002	24.6	6,579	40.5	16,271	100.0
1995	5,181	32.6	4,162	26.2	6,550	41.2	15,893	100.0

Source: Prison Statistics of Sri Lanka

a legalization model, there are several ways in which it approximates a prohibition model when it comes to dealings with the poor. First, the poor man's alcoholic drinks (*kasippu* and toddy) and tobacco smoking (*beedi* and *suruttu*) are more often treated as illicit, with the result that much of the gaze and legal action under the relevant ordinances has been directed against the manufacturers, dealers and transporters of these products, who often come from poorer social backgrounds. Second, due to the taxing policies, many of the licensed liquors and commercially manufactured cigarettes have become too costly for the poor, encouraging them to turn to potentially more harmful illegal products easily accessible at cheaper prices and on easy terms (e.g. on credit) through local outlets. Third, mafia-like bodies in rural and urban areas increasingly control the production and distribution of illicit alcohol and drugs, with considerable backing from local politicians and law-enforcement agencies. These unlawful social formations tend to play an important role in organized crime and patterns of violence in areas outside the war-zone in northern and eastern parts of Sri Lanka. Some of the gang rivalries and political conflict are related to the struggle for achieving monopolistic control over illicit alcohol and illicit drug trades.

The processes examined here are important for understanding trends in prison admissions in Sri Lanka.

As Table 11.6 shows, over 50 per cent of new admissions to prisons in Sri Lanka in the 1991 to 1995 period are convicted of offences under the Excise Ordinance and Poisons, Narcotics and Dangerous Drugs Ordinance. As a result, Sri Lankan prisons are filled with those convicted of excise and drug-related offences. Nearly 40 per cent of those newly admitted have previous convictions, suggesting that prisons perhaps serve more as a breeding ground of criminal behaviour rather than as an effective place of rehabilitation. The majority of the prisoners come from unemployed or casual employment backgrounds, indicating a lower class social origin. The actions of the law-enforcement agencies entrusted with the task of implementing the relevant legislation often involve some kind of 'a war against the poor'. Certain types of neighbourhoods (e.g. urban slums and shanties, crowded village expansion colonies in the rural areas and certain plantation enclaves) are constantly under scrutiny for illicit alcohol and drugs. These data confirm that the Excise and Poisons, Narcotic and Dangerous Drugs Ordinances serve to criminalize people from poorer socioeconomic backgrounds, rather than to wean them from addictions. The legislation thus fails to pull them out of poverty as expected. Moreover, in their actual operation these laws tend to contribute to impoverishment and marginalization of the poor.

POSSIBILITIES FOR IMPROVING THE IMPACT OF ALCOHOL AND TOBACCO LEGISLATION ON THE ALLEVIATION OF POVERTY

Making existing alcohol and tobacco legislation more responsive to the needs of the poor is difficult because of structural constraints within the laws: their colonial origin, the appropriation and manipulation by dominant classes in society, and the laws' historical evolution as instruments utilized against the poor. However, this does not mean that alcohol and tobacco legislation cannot be an instrument for poverty reduction. Considering the importance of addiction as a factor in the perpetuation and reproduction of poverty and social marginality as discussed earlier in this essay, legal measures for regulating substance use must play an important role in any successful anti-poverty effort, particularly in Third World settings.

We make the following suggestions for improving the impact of the relevant legislation on the alleviation of poverty.

1. Possibilities for expanding legalization to cover illicit alcohols and unlicensed tobacco products must be explored. In the Sri Lankan context, this might include the legalization and standardization of production, distribution and consumption of *kasippu*, toddy, *beedi* and other substances consumed primarily by the lower classes. Positive effects could include a reduction of adverse health effects by making producers conform to certain standards stipulated by authorities (e.g.

mandatory warnings), removal of the current practice of criminalizing the poor because they are producing, transporting or consuming the substances in question, mainstreaming a range of economic activities which are currently associated with the underworld and elimination or at least reduction of the social marginalization and exclusion processes currently associated with the substances in question. On the negative side, some would resist legalization of these products on moral grounds, believing that legalization would clash with the overall objective of reducing substance use. In addition, if the newly licensed substances increase in price, poor people may shift to even more dangerous, but cheaper, substitutes.

It is important to ensure that the legalization of these products does not increase their costs beyond the reach of the poor.[11] Moreover, the same regulations applicable to the existing licensed products, such as mandatory health warnings, times and days of availability, and distribution through approved outlets to approved customers, should be applied to the newly legalized products with required modifications. Finally, the impact of legalization should be closely monitored so as to identify any further changes needed in policy and legislation.

2. The scope of the relevant legislation must be enhanced by the formulation of a coherent national policy on substances, along the lines suggested by the anti-alcohol and anti-tobacco lobbies.[12] Legal provisions banning tobacco and alcohol advertisements in the media and in public places must be included in the revised alcohol and tobacco legislation.

3. Opportunities for public action litigation against alcohol and tobacco manufacturers must be enhanced. So far in Sri Lanka such litigation has been conspicuous by its absence. Legal aid for consumer groups to help them protect their rights vis-à-vis alcohol and tobacco producers needs to be provided. Legal aid may also have a place in efforts to ensure the rights of private individuals charged with excise or tobacco-related offences. Appropriate government and non-government agencies may provide such legal aid.

4. Efforts must be made to remove any existing discrimination in the relevant ordinances against poorer consumers. For instance, the number of alcohol bottles a person can legally have in his possession varies between two bottles (in the case of toddy) and ten bottles (in the case of all other licensed alcohols). This distinction is presumably aimed at discouraging the illicit manufacture and sale of locally-made alcohol. However, this regulation discriminates against the poorer classes of consumers who are, thereby, more easily arrested and punished under

the relevant ordinances. There is an urgent need to review carefully these ordinances so as identify and rectify anti-poor provisions.

5. Narco-terrorism, including the rise of drug and alcohol cartels in rural and urban areas, must be legally confronted. Legal measures enacted to address this phenomenon must deal with the reality that many cartels operate in concert with politicians and those in law-enforcement agencies. Such unlawful social formations must be dealt with under more powerful legislation such as public security acts, rather than alcohol or drug ordinances.

6. Opportunities for encouraging poorer consumers to shift from more harmful to less harmful substances must be explored. As is evident from the recent popularity of beer, taxing policies and related legislation may be strategically used to encourage poorer consumers to move away from harmful substances with their negative consequences on health, productivity and family well-being.

CONCLUSION

The existing alcohol and tobacco legislation in Sri Lanka has had only a limited success in controlling substance abuse. While tobacco smoking has been on the decline, the reasons for this decline have had more to do with increasing awareness of the adverse health consequences of smoking rather than any important shifts in legislation. On the other hand, consumption of alcohol, of both the legal and illegal varieties, has increased in response to a range of factors. The existing legislation tends to work against the poor and poverty reduction by criminalizing the poor and contributing to the social marginalization and exclusion processes. The challenge for advocates of alcohol and tobacco legislation is, on the one hand, to identify ways in which multiple linkages between substance abuse and social reproduction of poverty can be broken, and, on the other, ensure that the law does not merely become an instrument against the poor. This chapter contends that legalization rather than prohibition of substances widely consumed by the poor has the best prospects for mobilizing legal measures for regulating substance use (e.g. a system of mandatory warning) and, at the same time, reducing the adverse social consequences of substance use, including the resulting impoverishment and marginalization of substance abusers.

NOTES

1. While we use concepts of prohibition and legalization as polar opposites, we acknowledge that alcohol and tobacco legislation can be placed along a

prohibition–legalization continuum (as suggested in the World Drug Report of 1997 prepared by the United Nations International Drug Control Programme).

2. The remaining 7 per cent of the country's population belong to various Christian denominations.

3. To the extent any alcohol consumption by females is reported in Sri Lanka, it is confined to high society women who have adopted a Western lifestyle and women in socially marginalized estate worker and urban poor communities.

4. Janashakti Programme, conducted by an NGO active in southern Sri Lanka, aims at social mobilization of the poor and improving their access to credit.

5. The labour population in the estate sector of Sri Lanka mostly belong to the Indian Tamil ethnic group. To a large extent they are a marginalized social group with poor linkages with mainstream Sri Lanka society. They live in barracks-like labour quarters provided by the estates and their physical and social mobility is restricted due to historical and structural constraints.

6. From the 1940s Sri Lanka has implemented an extensive human resettlement programme whereby the excess population in the wet zone of Sri Lanka was resettled in newly developed irrigated farm land located in the dry zone of Sri Lanka. These newly established 'colonies' are often characterized by social disintegration and spatial marginality.

7. 'Labour lines' are barracks-like labour quarters which serve as a means of segregating manual workers from other residents in the estates, including the owners, managers and other 'staff' categories. Each labour family was typically accommodated in a one-room unit within a row of labour lines made of brick walls and corrugated-iron roofs.

8. In many male suicides alcoholism and heavy alcohol consumption have been important immediate precursors to the suicide event (Silva and Pushpakumara 1996).

9. One of the main reasons for higher priority being assigned to regulation of alcohol use as against tobacco use is that alcohol is often seen as a factor in violence and social disruption, in addition to being a health hazard.

10. This is legislation aimed at preventing unlawful acts threatening public security, including riots, insurrections and provocation of the masses for violence and disorderly conduct.

11. Licences for manufacturing the relevant products can be given to small producers in order to maintain current price levels and prevent loss of employment to low-income populations. This will not deviate substantially from the current patterns of production and distribution with the exception of mandatory licensing.

12. Anti-tobacco and anti-alcohol lobbies in Sri Lanka consist mainly of medical professionals, religious activists and non-government organizations involved in social development. Among their proposals are banning relevant advertisements, particularly in printed and electronic media, streamlining of mandatory health warnings and banning of smoking in public places.

REFERENCES

ADDIC (1994) *Impact of Alcoholism on Family Well-being*, Colombo: ADDIC.

— (1995) *Community Survey on Substance Abuse*, Colombo: ADDIC.

Amarasuriya, K. and M. Salgado (1998) *Impact of Alcohol Use on Family Well-being*, Paper presented at the sixth national Convention on Women's Studies, 19–21 March 1998.

Bourdieu, P. (1979) *Distinctions: A Social Critique of the Judgement of the Taste*, London: Routledge.

— (1993) *La Misère du Monde*, Paris: Seuil.

CARE Sri Lanka (1998) *Rapid Food and Livelihood Security Assessment for Estate Sector in Sri Lanka*, Colombo: CARE (unpublished report).

Department of Census and Statistics (1993) *Household Income and Expenditure Survey*, Colombo: DCS.

De Soyza, D. A., (1995) *The Great Sandy River: Gender Transformation among Pioneer Settlers in Sri Lanka's Frontier*, Amsterdam: University of Amsterdam Press.

Fernando, P. T. M. (1971) 'Arrack, Toddy and Ceylonese Nationalism', *Modern Ceylon Studies*, 2 (2): 123-50.

Foucault, M. (1977) *Discipline and Punish: the Birth of the Prison*, London: Allen Lane.

Government of Sri Lanka (1997) *The Draft Policy on Tobacco, Alcohol and Drug Abuse*, Colombo: Government of Sri Lanka.

Gunasekera, O. and M. R. C. Perera (1997) *Survey on Assessing the Impact of Drug Use for Programmes for Alleviation of Poverty*, Colombo: Sober Sri Lanka.

Hettige, S. (1993) 'Alcoholism, Poverty and Health in Rural Sri Lanka', *Sri Lanka Journal of Agrarian Studies*, 8 (1 and 2): 27–44.

Hewavitharana, B. (1992) *Rural Non-farm Employment: Problems, Issues and Strategies*, Colombo: IFS.

Kleinman, A. (1988) *Rethinking Psychiatry*, New York: Free Press.

Lewis, O. (1965) *La Vida*, New York: Panther Modern Society.

Marga Institute (1979) *The Informal Sector of Colombo City*, Colombo: Marga Institute.

Mehl, T. N. (1996) *Trends in Smoking in Sri Lanka*, Colombo: ADDIC.

Nastasi, B. K. and D. M. DeZolt (1994) *School Interventions for Children of Alcoholics*, New York: Guilford Press.

NDDCB (National Dangerous Drugs Control Board) (1986) *Illicit Drug Trafficking and Drug Abuse in Sri Lanka*, Colombo: NDDCB.

Pereira, A. S. (1992) *Alcoholism and Poverty in a Mahaweli New Settlement*, Colombo: NDDCB.

Reuter, P., R. MacCoun and P. Murphy (1990) *Money from Crime: A Study of Economics of Drug Dealing in Washington, D.C.*, Santa Monica, CA: Rand Corporation.

Samarasinghe, D. (1995) *Tobacco Smoking in an Urban Sri Lanka Sample*, Colombo: ADDIC.

Silva, K. T. and K. Athukorala (1993) *Watte-dwellers: A Sociological Study of Selected Urban Low-income Communities in Sri Lanka*, Lanham, MD: University Press of America.

— (1996) 'A State of the Art Review on Recent Poverty Research in South Asia', in E. Øyen, Miller and Samad (eds), *Poverty: A Global Review*, Oslo: Scandinavian University Press, pp. 65–85.

Silva, K. T. and W. D. N. R. Pushpakumara (1996) 'Love, Hate and Upsurge in Youth Suicide in Sri Lanka: Suicide Trends in a Mahaweli New Settlement', *SJSS*, 19 (1 and 2): 73–92.

Sober Sri Lanka (1997) *Profile of Alcohol and Tobacco Use in Sri Lanka*, Colombo: Sober Sri Lanka.

Townsend, P. (1979) *Poverty in the United Kingdom*, Harmondsworth: Penguin.

UNIDCP (United Nations International Drug Control Programme) (1997) *World Drug Report*, Oxford: Oxford University Press.

TWELVE | Child labour – a threat to the survival of civilization

AMITA AGARWAL

§ The child, an important component of any society, socially and physically represents the weakest part of human society. This situation favours a child's exploitation in different areas: labour, sex, integrity, etc. Child victimization in its different expressions is a constant feature of practically every society, and more so of developing societies like India.

In 1950, the Indian constitution made provisions for the protection of the rights of the child, e.g. laws preventing child labour, bonded labour and child abuse. In spite of all constitutional arrangements, though, India continues to use child labour even after half a century of planned development. The reason for this is the state of abject poverty in which many people have to live in India. In such a situation, when the very survival of so many is threatened, who is in a position to demand rights specifically for the development, protection and participation of children? But it should be remembered that children are the future of our country and whatever problems the country as a whole is facing, they cannot wait.

The Supreme Court of India has adopted a more active and positive role – 'judicial activism' – to protect the rights of the citizens of India. In this regard, Public Interest Litigation (PIL) is a very important development and may become an essential instrument in protecting the human rights of the poor, ignorant and deprived classes of Indian society.

This chapter will study and analyse the rights of the child as enumerated in the constitution of India, and as compared to international human rights legislation; it investigates why we still find ourselves unable to halt the violation of the human rights of the child in India; and it discusses the changing role of the judiciary in protecting the human rights of children. Finally, we suggest steps to be taken to ensure the rights of the child in India at national, international, governmental and NGO levels.

> If a child lives with criticism,
>   he learns to condemn.
> If a child lives with hostility,
>   he learns to fight.
> If a child lives with ridicule,
>   he learns to be shy.
> If a child lives with shame,
>   he learns to feel guilty.
> If a child lives with tolerance,
>   he learns to be patient.
> If a child lives with encouragement,
>   he learns confidence.
> If a child lives with praise,
>   he learns to appreciate.
> If a child lives with fairness,
>   he learns justice.
> If a child lives with security,
>   he learns to have faith.
> If a child lives with approval,
>   he learns to like himself.
> If a child lives with acceptance and friendship,
>   he learns to find love in the world.

Nothing illustrates the environment a child should grow in better than this poem of Dorothe Law Notle, 'Children Learn What They Live By' (Desta 1994: 403). To develop a better world of the future, children must grow up in a positive environment that provides a sense of 'justice' in all spheres of life: social, cultural, political and especially economic.

> Law is a means to an end, i.e., justice. If this end is to be achieved, law cannot stand still. It must change with the changing needs of the society. If the bark that protects the tree fails to grow and expand along with the growing tree, it will shed the bark and grow a new living bark for itself. Similarly, if the law fails to respond to the needs of changing society, then either it will stifle the growth of the society and choke its progress or if the society is vigorous enough, it will cast away the law which stands in the way of its growth. Law must therefore constantly be on the move adapting itself to the fast changing society and not lag behind. (Bajwa 1985: 253).

The importance of development is heightened by the growing poverty of most nations of the world. While political colonization has collapsed, it is being increasingly replaced by economic colonization. Twenty per cent of the world's population lives on 80 per cent of its resources. 'The equal world is only growing grossly unequal' (Bhandare 1998). Breaking down trade barriers often has the deleterious effect of breaking the financial backbones of the weaker nations. It is imperative that the concept of 'free' market yields to human democracy. In human democracy, development does not compromise programmes for the alleviation of poverty, equity and social justice. The first priority in achieving 'social justice must be children because unless the tender plant is properly tended and nourished, it has little chance of growing into a strong and useful tree' (Rao 1974: 64).

While for a long time many have felt that children should be treated humanely, they were restricted because 'the societies considered children to be mere possessions and believed that those who "own" them, parents and relatives, had a right to do whatever they felt with them. With the advent of the human rights era after the Second World War, it was assumed that all human rights applied automatically to children' (Subramaniam 1997: 115). In reality, delineated human rights were denied to children and the discourse of human rights failed to address their particular needs.

'In traditional societies, the child was integrated into the society through its family. The parents' principle duties were to monitor, protect and educate the child but there was no question of rights as understood now-a-days' (Desta 1994: 408). 'The juristic concept that the child is a legal person entitled to the protection of law has developed during the last two centuries following industrialistion' (Raina 1995: 183). The advent of the industrial revolution brought about the enactment of child labour laws, which have gradually given way to the rights of the child.

CHILDREN UNDER INTERNATIONAL LAW

The first international conventions that protected children began in the late nineteenth and early twentieth centuries. 'Geneva convention IV and the additional protocols incorporated and expanded many of the principles contained in the Hague conventions and specifically provided for the protection of children' (Raina 1995: 183).

The Forced Labour Convention of 1930 and the Abolition of Forced Labour Convention of 1957 required state parties to suppress and abolish forced child labour imposed by either the state or by private individuals and organizations.

In 1959 the UN General Assembly adopted 'The Declaration of the Rights of the Child, recognizing the need for social safeguards for children including appropriate legal protection within the rubric of human rights' (Goswami 1994: 108). This 'soft law'[1] declaration enunciates general principles and entitlements for the care and protection of children. It is mainly concerned with economic, social and cultural rights.

> It was because of the widespread plight of children that in December 1976, the United Nations adopted a resolution which proclaimed 1979 as International Year of the Child. The resolution declared that this was to provide a framework for advocacy on behalf of the children. It also declared that there was need to promote children's programmes to form an integral part of the economic and social development plans with a view to achieving sustained activities for the benefit of children at national and international levels. (Raina 1995: 184).

Children as a class constitute the weakest, most vulnerable and defenceless section of human society. Recognizing that 'children are vulnerable to various forms of abuse, malnutrition, exploitation, diseases etc. and based on the broad consensus on the rights to which children are entitled, the UN committee on the rights (1989) of the child brought forth an all encompassing document (Convention on the Rights of the Child – CRC 1989) which has been ratified by the overwhelming number of member states of the UN' (Desta 1994: 404). This document (Article 35) also requires that all states recognizing it must take all appropriate measures to prevent abduction, sale or traffic in children for any purpose or in any form.

This Convention (1989) was based on the basic principles of the UN charter which recognizes the equal and inalienable rights of the human family. The Convention stressed the role of the international community in securing children's rights and needs through legal and other protections while on the other hand emphasizing the primary responsibility of the family for children's care. The convention consists of thirty-five Articles which apply in four main areas of children's rights: survival, development, protection and participation.

The right to survival includes provision of adequate food, shelter, clean water and primary healthcare. The development right includes access to information, education, cultural activities, opportunities for rest, play and leisure and freedom of thought, conscience and religion.

The right to protection includes the stipulation that a child must be assured of protection not only from the violation of these rights but also from all kinds of exploitation, cruelty, arbitrary separation from the family and abuses in the justice and penal systems. The right to participation includes the right to express opinions and to have these opinions taken into account in matters affecting the child's own life, and the right to play an active role in the community and society through freedom of association.

These rights are based on three principles;

1. Children need special safeguards beyond those provided to adults.
2. A protective and nurturing family setting is the best environment for a child's survival and development.
3. The adult world in general could be committed to acting in the best interests of children. (Subramaniam 1997: 111)

This Convention for the first time brought together in one document a statement of children's rights, which had previously been scattered throughout many human rights instruments. It also broke new ground and focused on issues of justice, adoption and prevention of exploitative practices.

The Vienna Declaration of Human Rights 1993, while fully supporting the convention urged the nations to:

1. Combat exploitation and abuse of children by addressing their root causes,
2. Devise effective measures against female infanticide, harmful child labour and sale of children, child prostitution, child pornography and other forms of sexual abuse and to organize means of improving the protection of children during armed conflicts and difficult situations and for the after care and rehabilitation of children in war zones and affected areas. (Goswami 1994: 109)

'A resolution adopted unanimously at the Geneva UN Human Rights Conference on March 9, 1995 shows the heightened awareness on the part of the world community of the need to save the deprived child' (Subramaniam 1997: 115–16).

RIGHTS OF THE CHILD UNDER THE INDIAN CONSTITUTION AND STATUTES

The constitutional law of India cannot be an exception to the general law of change but rather must be interpreted to obliterate the outdated norms and endorse, recognize and indeed construct new norms to protect the human rights of its people.

When the constitution of India was being drafted, the Constituent Assembly had before it the Universal Declaration of Human Rights and other ILO (International Labour Organization) conventions and the work-in-progress on Covenants on Human Rights (both ICESCR and ICCPR) which was before the Commission on Human Rights. Since India was a party to the Universal Declaration of Human Rights, the Constituent Assembly tried to shape the Indian constitution in light of international human rights documents.

A comparison of the human rights provisions of the Indian constitution and those of the Universal Declaration of Human Rights and the Covenants on Human Rights indicates that most international provisions are contained in the Indian constitution. In the constitution of India, fundamental rights and the Directive Principles of State Policy reflect the country's serious commitment to the well-being and protection of children with the objective of ensuring that they are 'self reliant and responsible citizens of the country' (Gupta 1995: 271).

Some of the provisions directly dealing with children are:

- Article 24: 'No child below the age of 14 years shall be employed to work in any factory or mine or engaged in any other hazardous employment.'
- Article 39:[2] the state shall, in particular, direct its policy towards securing '(e) that the health and strength of workers, men, women and tender age of children are not abused and that citizens are not forced by economic needs to enter avocations unsuited to their age or strength (f) … that children are given opportunities to develop in a healthy manner and in conditions of freedom and dignity and that childhood and youth are protected against moral and material abandonment.'
- Article 45: 'The state shall endeavour to provide within a period of ten years from the commencement of this constitution for free and compulsory education for all children until they complete the age of 14 years'. (Sarma 1994: 98)

In addition the Child Labour (Prohibition and Regulation) Act of 1986 elaborates on the rights of child workers vis-à-vis employers. In this Act, 'child' is defined as a person who has not reached the age of fourteen years. This now seems to be the uniform meaning of the term 'child' under all Indian labour statutes. In fact, some statutes that defined a child as a person who had not reached the age of fifteen years have now been amended to lower the age to fourteen years (Dewan and Dewan 1996: 416).

The schedule to the Child Labour Act in Part A lists certain 'occupations' and in Part B lists certain job processes where the employment of children is prohibited.

The 'occupations' listed in Part A are:

1. Transporting of passengers, goods or mails by railway.
2. Picking cinder, clearing an ash pit or construction work in the railway premises.
3. Working in a catering establishment at a railway station, that involves the movement of a vendor or any other employee of the establishment from one platform to another or into or out of a moving train.
4. Working on the construction of a railway station or any other work in close proximity to or between railway lines.
5. Working for a port authority within limits of any port. (This work is also considered hazardous for children's safety, health and overall development of their personality.)

The job processes listed as Part B are:

1. bidi-making
2. carpet weaving
3. cement manufacturing, including bagging of cement
4. cloth printing, dyeing and weaving
5. manufacturing of matches, explosives and fireworks
6. mica-cutting and splitting
7. shellac manufacturing
8. soap manufacturing,
9. tanning
10. wool-cleaning
11. working in the building and construction industry

The above list does not apply to any work situation where any job process is carried on by 'the occupier' with the aid of his family or to any school establishment run by or receiving assistance or recognition from the government. The term 'occupier' means the person who has the ultimate control over the affairs of the establishment or workshop. The term 'family' in the present context means the individual, the wife or husband of such individual and their children, and the brothers and sisters of such individual.[3]

The central government has the power to include any other occupation or job process in the schedule. This can be done by issuing a notice in the *Official Gazette* of the government's intention to do so three months prior to the effective date. Thereafter the government may issue the notification listing other occupations and job processes in the schedule.

Child labour is completely prohibited in the occupations and job processes listed in the schedule. In other occupations and job processes, child labour is not banned but is regulated. Even before the Child Labour Act was enacted a number of statutes set forth protections for child workers, namely:

1. Employment of Children Act, 1938
2. Children (Pledging of Labour) Act, 1933
3. Child Marriage Restraint Act, 1929
4. Children Act, 1960
5. Factories Acts, 1881, 1891, 1911, 1934 and 1948
6. Plantation Labour Act, 1951
7. Mines Act, 1952
8. Merchant Shipping Act, 1956
9. Motor Transport Workers Act, 1961
10. Juvenile Justice Act, 1986

THE INDIAN SCENARIO

The extent of child labour

Despite the Indian constitutional and statutory commitment, a majority of children in India are deprived from birth of minimum fundamental human rights, such as the proper environment needed to encourage them to become useful citizens of the country.

Child labour is not considered to be wrong in India and thus, in spite of all the legal provisions, it is a widespread phenomenon and children continue to suffer. The magnitude of the child labour force is often an indicator of the economic development, political maturity and social order of a region or country. A larger child workforce indicates symptoms of an underdeveloped economy and an unjust social order. Children in India are involved at an early age in household work and family occupations as part of their training and work. A decade after the 'International Year of the Child' they still work in precarious conditions detrimental to their health and development. Children not only perform diverse economic activities but also form a sizable part of the workforce, as shown in the Table 12.1. However, the table is underinclusive.

The extent of child labour in India is not accurately documented through government statistics because full information does not flow to government channels, particularly in the case of the informal labour sector.

TABLE 12.1 Projection of child labour (workers) in India to 2000 (millions)

Year	Projection of child labour 5–14 years
1981*	13.64
1983	17.36
1985	17.58
1990	18.18
2000	20.25

* 1981 figures exclude Assam as there was no census in Assam.
Source: Sanjaba (1994)[4]

Table 12.2 throws some light on the distribution and pattern of work among male and female child workers.

TABLE 12.2 Percentage of child workers in the 5–14 age group, 1981

Category of work	Rural	Rural Male/Female	Urban	Urban Male/Female
Cultivators	43.9	36.8	6.1	5.3
Agricultural labourers	39.9	51.6	12.2	23.2
Livestock forestry	7.81	3.3	3.7	1.8
Mining and quarrying	0.2	0.2	0.3	0.4
Manufacture	4.9	0.2	3.7	1.8
Construction	0.4	0.5	3.3	3.2
Trade and commerce	1.3	0.4	19.0	2.9
Transport and communication	0.1	0.0	3.0	0.4
Service	1.5	1.3	13.0	24.6

Source: Census of India 1981 (all figures are percentage of total)

Children who are not in school take care of cattle, tend younger children, collect firewood and work in the fields. Some of them are bonded labourers, other children are employed in tea stalls and restaurants or as household workers in middle-class homes. Some become prostitutes or live on the streets begging or picking rags and bottles from rubbish for resale. Large numbers work in cottage industries, producing carpets, matches, fire-crackers, cigarettes, brassware, diamonds, glass, hosiery, handloom cloth, embroidery, bangles and traditional handicrafts. Such work undoubtedly improves their family's income, but it deprives the children of their basic human rights. Child labour has many repercussions on children's well-being and personality development. For example, working children are denied educational opportunities and their mental growth is thereby stunted. Cooped up in work places for long hours, usually away from their families, they are totally deprived of the joys of childhood, having no time for recreation, rest or emotional sustenance normally provided by family members.

Child labour and neglect have been defined as the portion of harm to the child that results from human action or inaction. Whatever may be the exact figure, there is no doubt that the problem is grave and the number of children affected is staggering. War, poverty and social disruption, all sharing the common denominator of being related to economic conditions, are the three root causes of child suffering. Poverty surpasses the other two and is the direct cause of child labour, i.e. child slavery.

According to official estimates: 'Twenty million child workers (though unofficially 100 million) are working in farms, quarries, mines, carpets, glass factories and other hazardous small scale industries' (Goswami 1994: 110). Another study found that there are 'more than seventeen million child labourers in India which includes two million working in hazardous industries' (ibid.); according to the ILO, this figure is 44 million (Raina 1995: 184). There are also hundreds of thousands of children working as domestic servants in almost bonded-like conditions, where they are exploited by their employers. What else can be expected of a country where despite all the programmes, efforts and planned development in over fifty years since independence, even now 40 per cent of the population is poor and living below the poverty line? In this sorry state of affairs and abject poverty, 'the future of mankind' has not only to live but to fight for its very survival.

The nature of child labour in India is complex and its magnitude is vast: 'It is most prevalent in the unorganized sector which as recognized and accepted by the National Commission on Labour (1969) is almost limit-less employing nearly 90 percent of the Indian work force. The industries include manufactures of fireworks, watches, bangles, pottery, brass ware as well as diamond polishers and gem cutters. Girl children are to be found mostly in the bidi, carpet and garment industries' (Ganguly 1995: 11).

The employers in these industries find it far cheaper to employ children, quite often without wages or for payment in kind. Trapped in debt bondage, there are several million child bonded labourers for whom going to school remains a distant dream because, according to their parents, schools are too costly.[5]

Children exposed to stark poverty are the most exploited section of the Indian working class. Parents, themselves working, are forced to send their children to work to augment the family income. The vast majority assert that the family needs the children's wages. When the very survival of the family is at stake everyone (including the child) has to lend a hand. This phenomenon is common not only in India but in any society where extreme wealth coexists with extreme poverty.

The National Policy on Child Labour 1987 (NPCL – it is not a statute but a policy adopted by the government; it has no legal structure nor is it binding) is a model document, but in the absence of implementation it has not been able to help children forced into labour. Provisions in the NPCL, drawn from the constitution, spell out measures for the elimination of child labour through employment generation (the government tries to provide employment to at least one member of a family by starting new works such as road construction and other building operations), poverty alleviation, the general development of rural and urban areas, extension of adequate facilities for both formal and informal education, free and compulsory education of children, free tiffin (in schools run by the government in remote tribal areas, the government provides free lunch to encourage children to go to school), textbooks, exercise books, etc., and an extension of the coverage of social security, health and welfare schemes.

In spite of all these provisions (not legal but voluntary), little has been achieved by way of protecting children's rights due to widespread corruption and lack of political will. Recently the government has announced the establishment of a separate Human Rights Commission for Children. In addition, the National Human Rights Commission has set up a Central Action Group to explore various aspects of bonded labour and the Supreme Court of India has asked the Commission to supervise the implementation of bonded labour laws. These initiatives may help not only adult bonded labourers but also child labourers. The Commission has already started working towards eradication of child labour in specified fields and has recommended immediate implementation of effective remedial measures in the Child Labour Act, while pointing out the Act's shortcomings.

The role of the judiciary

'Law is for men, for society, for the advancement towards the fundamental goals expressed in the Preamble to the Constitution of India by "we the people of India"' (Ganguly 1995: 11).[6] The corner-stone of the edifice of justice under the law is a people-oriented legal profession imbued with a sense of social justice and an urge to fight perpetually to fulfil 'the first task of constituent assembly' (of India, as Nehru told its members) which was to 'free India through a new constitution, feed the starving people and to clothe the naked masses and to give every Indian the fullest opportunity to develop himself according to his capacity' (Iyer 1987: 140).

Salus Populi est Suprema Lex (Regard for public welfare is the highest law) is one of the oldest maxims of Civil Law. The constitution of India made justice the first promise of the republic, which means that state power will execute the pledge of justice in favour of the millions who are the republic. Public Interest Litigation (PIL) is a modern reflection of this maxim.

Through recent actions of the Supreme Court of India, as the guardian of the law, 'dynamically interpreting fundamental rights and introducing "Public Interest Litigation" (PIL) the enforcement of human rights has increased' (ibid.: 140). In fact, much of the development of human rights jurisprudence in India, particularly in favour of the weaker sections of Indian humanity, has taken place as a result of PIL. Supreme Court judges, particularly Justice P. N. Bhagwati and Justice V. R. Krishna Iyer, have taken particular initiatives in this endeavour.

'Judicial activism has made an endeavour to extend the jurisdiction of courts in cases of public interest litigation. The court has even treated a telegram sent to one of the judges as a writ petition even though the sender of the telegram complained of a violation of the rights of some other person. Similarly, petitions filed on the basis of newspaper reports have also been considered by the Supreme Court' (Kernunja 1994: 217). The highest judiciary allowed public-spirited persons to come forward and become guardians for the protection of the human rights of the poor and those ignorant of their legal rights. Under the system of Public Interest Litigation any public-spirited citizen can invoke the courts to secure redress for those who cannot litigate or where the law is being flouted to public detriment. Due to the efforts of such concerned persons, with the active assistance of social activists and public interest litigators, the judiciary in India is promising innovative remedial attention to vindicate the government's commitment to the welfare and relief of the oppressed and to protecting and promoting human rights.

Public interest litigation can be seen as a partial answer to the problem of the state's failure to protect and promote the human rights of its people and to make it accountable for its actions, inactions, misperformance and non-performance of its duties towards its people.

This does not mean that the judiciary is anxious to take the executive's or legislature's role; the constitution of India has provided for the separation of the three arms of government in order to keep a balance.

Traditionally, the judiciary has sought to do justice according to the law but sometimes the question arises of how you balance law and justice. When you see justice on one side and law sort of midway, you tend to stretch the law towards justice, because injustice is what hurts the most. To a great extent the courts are much more aware now of the injustices going on in society and they try to provide people-oriented justice.

To ensure justice for the poor, uneducated and deprived, the forty-second amendment to the constitution of India introduced Article 30(A) for free legal aid to the poor. Though, in pursuance of this article, a massive legal aid programme for the poor and legally ignorant was started, it could not do much in the desired direction.

The most serious stumbling block in the advancement of social justice to the underprivileged in India was the requirement of *locus standi* (*J. M. Desai v. Roshan Kumar*, AIR, 1979, SC 578). The traditional doctrine of *locus standi* had its root in the adversorial litigation which was of ancient vintage and insisted on direct injury to the aggrieved who alone had a right to bring an action. The state was regarded as the sole guardian of public interest and the individual had no role to play in overseeing the administration.

The restrictive rule of *locus standi* insisted that only an aggrieved person could go to the court for relief and other members of the public had no access to the court unless they also suffered injury. Due to the efforts of Justice Krishna Iyer and Mr Justice Bhagwati, a liberal interpretation of *locus standi* was started which brightened the future of PIL in India.

To provide social justice to the deprived, courts started using absolute powers under Article 226 (and inherent powers under CPC 151) of the constitution of India, liberally interpreting it, as was done by Justice Bhagwati in a case (*S. P. Gupta v. Union of India*, AIR, 1982, SC 149) in which he had observed,

where a legal wrong or legal injury has caused or threatened a person or class of persons and such person or class of person is by reason of poverty, helplessness or disability, or socially or economically disadvantaged position, unable to approach the court for relief, any member of the public can maintain an application for an appropriate direction, order or writ in the High Court under article 226 and in case of breach of any fundamental right of such person or determinate class of persons, in this court under article 32 seeking judicial redress for the legal wrong or injury caused to such person or class of persons.

The Indian judiciary which was hitherto enforcing only the rights of the rich and affluent sections of society has now become the rescuer of the poor through PIL. The Indian judiciary is becoming more and more active in providing social justice and in entering newer and wider fields to do so by liberally interpreting the constitution of India for the benefit of the poor, legally ignorant and deprived people. This is essential to provide people-oriented justice and ensure human happiness and well-being.

SUGGESTIONS

Laying down rules and regulations governing children's rights is no doubt important, but it is equally important that there is a mechanism at the national and international levels to ensure that the rights of the child are respected and observed.

International level

The rights of the child in any one country cannot be protected until and unless the overall situation in this regard is improved globally. If human rights of adults are not protected and they have to keep on fighting for protection of their rights, they will not be able to concentrate on protecting the rights of children. They can pass on to their children only what they themselves have. To attain this objective:

*1. New rights should be acknowledged.*The developing International Law of Human Rights should strive to implement certain new emerging human rights, e.g.

- the right to peace
- the right to development
- the right to enjoy the common heritage of mankind
- the right to resistance
- the right to humanitarian assistance
- the right to a healthy environment

2. *Assembly on human rights*. Human rights have rapidly evolved from the first to the third generation.[7] Now the need is to establish an assembly on human rights in which the different constituencies of the United Nations should be directly represented, i.e. women, children and other less empowered groups, always with an understanding of the multiple perspectives represented within each group. This assembly should concern itself only with the promotion, protection and implementation of human rights and make recommendations directly to the General Assembly of the United Nations.

3. *International Court of Human Rights*. In some regions, i.e. Europe and Africa, citizens can appeal to regional courts following decisions of their highest national court, while other regions have no such legal arrangement. An International Court of Human Rights should be established.

4. *High Commissioner on Human Rights*. The issue of the appointment of a High Commissioner on Human Rights is already pending before the UN General Assembly. The High Commissioner, if appointed, would assist in promoting and encouraging universal respect for human rights. The High Commissioner can maintain close relationships with other agencies concerned with the protection of human rights. The appointee would also render assistance and services to states at their request and, with the consent of the states concerned, submit a report of such assistance and service. These functions assigned to the Commissioner would be of an advisory nature.

5. *Public awareness*. The most important task in the implementation of a Human Rights Programme is raising of world public consciousness. This can be done by making people aware of the minimum standards of treatment to which they are entitled and raising awareness of human rights violations. Mass media should be used to bring the message to the public.

6. *Limited interpretation of the domestic jurisdiction clause*. The trend in developing countries of narrowly defining the domestic jurisdiction clause should be continued and strengthened in order to enable the UN to take effective steps when implementing the UN Charter's human rights provisions. Violations of human rights within a state should not be treated as a matter essentially within the domestic jurisdiction of that state, but rather should be a matter of international concern.

7. *Addition of Article 99 (A)* (Kernunja 1994: 217). As suggested by U Thant, a new Article 99 (A) should be incorporated in the UN Charter conferring power on the Secretary General of the UN to advise the Security Council, or other appropriate branch, of serious human

rights violations so that effective measures to check their violations should be adopted without delay.

8. *Universal accountability.* The principle of universal responsibility for the trial of persons guilty of gross violations of human rights should be developed so that, even if such persons are pardoned by their national governments for the atrocious crimes which they have committed, they may be, if caught outside their countries, be subject to international proceedings.

9. *Naming the violators.* In order to make violations of human rights an international criminal responsibility, the specialized agencies under the UN should register, at the General Assembly or the International Court of Justice, all serious crimes against humanity, including the names of both governments and persons allegedly involved in violations of human rights.

10. *A greater role for NGOs* (Sait 1999). The UN legitimized the theatre of the absurd by extending a partnership role through a limited bilateral dialogue only to state governments rather than to international civil society. NGOs, particularly non-Western ones, have no right to present evidence before UN bodies; their reports are not officially on record or referred to in the proceedings. They sit as members of the public and their interaction with committee members is restricted to lunchtime encounters or the like, ignoring the growing role of NGOs as evident from their participation at World Conferences such as Stockholm, Rio, Beijing and Vienna.

Yet nothing concrete can be achieved until and unless the basic causes that deny human rights are removed. The primary underlying reason for the violation of human rights is economic, i.e. poverty, at least in the developing countries. To help eradicate poverty, the developed nations of the world will have to pitch in; the affluent sector of the world cannot remain a quiet island in the midst of a stormy ocean, an oasis of prosperity in a desert of desperate poverty. The affirmation of children's rights, which would greatly contribute to the world's prosperous future, can be achieved only through international cooperation and sound implementation of the rights to development, for children.

To create a proper focus and coordination of activities of voluntary organizations in the human rights field, an International Monitoring Committee has been set up. Operators of the committee closely monitor the performance of nations and provide guidance and assistance in implementing various international instruments regarding the rights of the child.

National level

We have not inherited the future, we have merely borrowed it from our children to whom the future belongs. Hence it is our primary duty as trustees to act truthfully and honestly, so that the future of our progeny is not imperilled. We should take the following action at the national level:

1. *Provide human rights education.* Illiteracy and poverty are two basic reasons for human rights violations. People should be made aware of their rights by providing human rights education at the elementary level. This can be done by incorporating courses on human rights in the syllabi of schools.

2. *Develop an integral understanding of rights.* It is necessary not only to publicize violations of human rights but also to study, in the light of judicial decisions, various expanding dimensions of the right to life v. the right to realize full life expectancy, the right to a safe and healthy environment, the right to peace, the right to development, the right to a livelihood and the right against unwarranted deprivation of life, among other factors in our socioeconomic fabric.

3. *Create public opinion.* Human rights organizations can play an important role in building public opinion against violations of human rights and can help awaken social awareness against the crime of child labour.

4. *Establish an inspection process for human rights organizations.* Governments should allow human rights organizations to inspect in all cases where there is a charge of violation of human rights. Investigation of rights by such agencies will enable the public to know their country's position on the protection of various human rights.

5. *Make the National Commission on Human Rights an independent body.* India's central government has established a National Human Rights Commission which has been followed by Independent State Human Rights Commissions and Independent Commissions for women and children to inquire into alleged violations of human rights. These Commissions should be independent bodies (like the judiciary), so that the government may not directly influence their deliberations. These Commissions should also try to coordinate the work done by human rights organizations in India, should be given their own independent investigating machinery with punitive powers, and should be empowered to grant compensation or even immediate interim relief to victims or members of victims' families.

6. *Strengthen public interest litigation.* The public interest litigation

system introduced by the Supreme Court is an interesting and encouraging trend through which an individual can seek judicial redress for the benefit of poor, illiterate or socially and economically disadvantaged people. As a right step in the right direction for the protection of human rights, this system should be incorporated into the Indian constitution itself to make it more wide-ranging and give it more authority for enforcement.

7. *Withdraw reservations to the International Covenants on human rights.* The Indian constitution should be amended to guarantee these rights which were left out to make it strictly parallel with the Universal Declaration of Human Rights and the International Covenants. The government should withdraw its reservations, accede to the International Covenants on Human Rights, thereby setting an important example for the world community.

8. *Create a Department of Human Rights.* The creation of a separate department for the implementation of human rights at the central and state government level would help the government to discharge its various duties relating to human rights more effectively.

9. *Make people's representatives more responsible.* Members of Legislative Assemblies (MLAs) and Members of Parliament (MPs) should be obligated to go to their respective constituencies before the beginning of each session, so that genuine problems of the people may be gathered and presented before the house to be dealt with immediately (Sing and Garg 1995: 103).

10. *Give statutory recognition to the right to know.* For democracy to survive in India and the constitution of India to remain valid, the public must remain well informed about the administration of the state. Hence, the right to know should be given a statutory recognition. The right to know is the right to seek information from government departments and offices about their public activities and decisions. Under this right, the people of India can demand photocopies of government records and plans of concern to the public.

The role of NGOs

The NGO community has emerged as a potent force in catalysing various actions through the mobilization of social forces and pressure on governments to take needed actions in all spheres of activity (Desta 1994: 409). The NGO community dealing with children's issues is no exception. Third World NGOs in particular have a number of roles and tasks in the years ahead. As many NGOs have participated in the process of drafting the Convention on the Rights of the Child (CRC 1989), they should involve themselves in the implementation process too.

NGOs have many roles to play. They will need to lobby governments to ratify the Convention at the national level and they should lobby for and monitor steps undertaken by governments to incorporate the provisions of the Convention into national laws. At regional and international levels, NGOs must identify specific areas for cooperation. Socially committed people must come forward and help poor children out of their miserable conditions.

To provide greater incentives to NGOs government can give them tax benefits to start night shelters and night schools for child labourers. The Indian government can also work in coordination with the International Programme for Elimination of Child Labour (IPECL) and Child Labour Action and Support Project (CLASP). Similarly, a national task force can be set up for the eradication of child labour.

It is time for the Indian government, the largest democracy in the world, to take active steps to abolish child labour. All that is needed is political will combined with effective administrative support.

CONCLUSIONS

The various rights enshrined in the constitution of India are yet to be implemented and they have yet to serve useful purposes for the protection of human rights. In order to wipe the tears from the eyes of the millions, the government will have to take necessary steps for the protection of human rights. Though the Indian constitution has given many rights to children, 'it has entered substantial reservations to CRC (Convention on the Rights of the Child)' (Sait 1999). While human rights as a mainstream concern are an essential part of good governance, India has a long way to go in this direction.[8]

The issue before us today is to find the ways and means to eradicate the multiple forms of child abuse and neglect suffered by child labourers. The problem, however, has to be discussed at various levels. Any attempt to eliminate this disorder and injustice only by the magic wand of a legal ban is unworkable; rather, it must be carried out through the removal of economic injustices, restoration of justice, reorientation of social perspectives and switching value systems over to the needs of the poor.

No country has successfully ended child labour ('as the ILO reports millions of children labour in the western advanced capitalist countries also'; Ganguly 1995: 12), without first educating its children. In India the free and compulsory primary education envisaged in the constitution still remains a distant dream. Mere enactment of laws will not serve the purpose. Society at large has to be sensitized and, like the Supreme Court of India, other wings of government should be actively concerned to ensure the welfare of the child.

The Indian government has made a commitment to improve work conditions for the welfare of children. A national authority for the elimination of child labour was formed to coordinate education, rural development, women and child development and health and labour programmes, with the goal of progressively withdrawing children from the workplace and placing them in schools. The violation of human rights is a global phenomenon, not one limited to a single country such as India. The difference between nation-states is only one of degree. Where a majority of the people (as in India) are legally ignorant, poor and exploited, violations of human rights are bound to be more frequent, but where people are educated, aware and advanced they are likely to be less prone (albeit not immune) to inhumane treatment and exploitation.

India urgently needs to mobilize public opinion and make people aware of their rights and the dangers associated with violations of these rights, and this is especially true in the case of children upon whose upbringing the future of the nation depends.

The child of today is the future of our country, so the investment made in children will be an investment in the future of our country.

> We are guilty of many errors and faults,
> But our worst crime is abandoning the children,
> Neglecting the foundation of life,
> Many of the things we need can wait,
> The child cannot,
> Right now is the time his bones are being formed,
> His blood is being made,
> And his senses are being developed,
> To him we cannot answer,
> 'Tomorrow'
> His name is Today ...
> Dare we answer 'Tomorrow'? (Desta 1994: 414)

NOTES

1. In international law, 'soft law' instruments are those whose execution and implementation are exclusively within the domestic domain, whereas 'hard law'

instruments are externally binding upon the states parties that by ratifying them have formally undertaken an obligation to their execution.

2. This is an article of the Indian constitution. Children over the age of fourteen years have the human rights of men so they are not covered by the special human rights given to minors/children.

3. For this one has to understand the Indian family and cottage industry system as well as the education system. Families have complete control over their cottage industry. A child learns special skills like weaving etc. under the able guidance of its parents; sometimes the trade is so specialized that it is not known outside the family. Children working in such industries are taken care of by their parents and brothers and sisters, so the question of their exploitation does not arise. We have three types of schools: (1) those completely run by the 'government'; (2) those recognized by the government and receiving financial assistance; and (3) those which are recognized by the government but receiving no financial assistance. The first two types of schools are governed by a different set of rules which make the authorities fully responsible and leave no chance for exploitation. Private schools (the third category) are also checked and controlled by the government but they have a certain latitude.

4. See, the Factories Act, 1948; the Plantation Labour Act, 1951; the Merchant Shipping Act, 1956; and·the Motor Transport Workers Act, 1961.

5. Bonded labourers are different from other labourers. Though the practice of bonded labour is banned by the Indian constitution it still continues in some remote rural areas. Such labourers are treated as slaves by their masters and have no free will whatsoever. They cannot leave their present masters and work at other places of their choice.

6. Preamble to the Indian constitution: 'we, the people of India, having solemnly resolved to constitute India into a sovereign socialist secular democratic republic and to secure to all its citizens: justice, social, economic and political; liberty, of thought, expression, belief, faith and worship; equality, of status and opportunity; and to promote among them all fraternity assuming the dignity of the individual and the unity and integrity of the Nation; in our constituent assembly this twenty-sixth day of November, 1949 do hereby adopt, enact and give to ourselves the constitution.'

7. It is common in current discourse to distinguish three notions of rights. First-generation rights are the classic political rights associated with liberal Western regimes, e.g. the rights of freedom of speech, assembly and association. Second-generation rights concern economic and social issues and involve notions such as rights to an adequate standard of living or the right to education. Third-generation rights include the right of the peoples to preserve their culture or the rights of a community to protect its environment.

8. Though India has enacted the Indian Protection of Human Rights Act 1993, which contains both constitutional safeguards and international obligations that can be enforced, Indians do not have recourse to any regional court (as none exists for Asia) and India has not accepted the individual petition system under the ICCPR (International Covenant on Civil and Political Rights).

REFERENCES

Bajwa, G. S. (1985) *Human Rights in India: Implementation and Violations*, Delhi: Anmol Publications.

Bhandare, M. C. (1998) 'Making Human Rights a Way of Life', *Times of India* (New Delhi), 10 December 1998, p. 10.

Desta, M. (1994) 'Rights of the Child', in K. P. Saxena (ed.), *Human Rights Perspectives and Challenges*, New Delhi: Lancer.

Dewan, P. and P. Dewan (1996) *Human Rights and the Law: Universal and Indian*, New Delhi: Deep and Deep.

Ganguly, P. K. (1995) 'The Scourge of Child Labour', *Popular Jurist*, 7(2).

Goswami, S. (1994) 'Child Labour and Human Rights in India (A Politico-Social Analysis)', in N. Sanjaoba (ed.), *Human Rights*, New Delhi: Omsons.

Gupta, R. K. (1995) 'Implementation of Human Rights: A Realistic Approach Needed to be Adopted', in B. P. Singh Sehgal (ed.), *Human Rights in India*, New Delhi: Deep and Deep.

Iyer, Justice V. R. Krishna (1987) *Social Justice: Sunset or Dawn*, Lucknow: Eastern Book Co.

Kernunja, S. (1994) 'Public Interest Litigation in Human Rights', in N. Sanjaba (ed.), *Human Rights*, New Delhi: Omsons.

Raina, B. K. (1995) 'Child Labour and Human Rights. An Insight', in B. P. Singh Sehgal (ed.), *Human Rights in India*, New Delhi: Deep and Deep.

Rao, Subha K. (1974) *Social Justice and Social Law*, Delhi: Institute of Constitutional and Parliamentary Studies.

Sait, Siraj M. (1999) 'International Human Rights', *The Hindu* (Delhi), 17 January 1999, p. 5.

Sanjaba, N. (ed.) (1994) *Human Rights*, New Delhi: Omsons.

Sarma, M. (1994) 'Human Rights of the Child', in N. Sanjaba (ed.), *Human Rights*, New Delhi: Omsons.

Singh, S. and M. R. Garg (1995) 'Human Rights as the Base Component of the Democratic State', in B. P. Singh Sehgal (ed.), *Human Rights in India*, New Delhi: Deep and Deep.

Subramaniam, S. (1997) *Human Rights: International Challenges*, New Delhi: Manas.

THIRTEEN | Labour organization and labour relations law in India: implications for poverty alleviation

DEBI S. SAINI

§ Poverty alleviation measures often involve the distribution of bounties to the poor. But a more effective measure in this regard is the provision of instrumentalities and arrangements so as to enable people to raise their living standards themselves. Thus, providing a fishing rod rather than the fish itself to the needy is known to be a more viable measure. In a market-dominated economic framework, working people, especially at lower levels, are often likely to receive lower wages and employment benefits, particularly in labour-surplus developing countries. Most of these countries suffer from the problem of overpopulation and a high rate of unemployment and underemployment. They also suffer from related problems such as poverty, illiteracy, lower standard of living, lack of the latest technology, acute inequalities in incomes, corruption, etc. All these features exacerbate and perpetuate labour poverty.

Contemporary social policy in most advanced democracies is founded on the premise that economic gains from productivity cannot be equitably distributed unless society permits and fosters the accumulation of the countervailing power of workers to match the superior economic power of employers. The state therefore owes an obligation to working people to allow them to unite, form associations, and enact a labour-relations law which permits labour to use its association rights for improving its economic conditions. In Third World countries – and especially in a country like India – these aspects take on added significance where a large percentage of the population lives below the poverty line,[1] receives low or even starvation wages, and is subjected to unfair labour practices (ULPs) by employers. A mere 8.3 per cent of the Indian labour force is actually organized, the majority of which is in the public sector. A mere 2 to 3 per cent of the labour force in India is able to participate in the collective bargaining process. Collective bargaining is an accepted mechanism for improving the contract of employment and thus empowering labour. As Otto Kahn-Freund rightly puts it:

> Typically the worker as individual has to accept the condition which the employer offers. On the labour side, power is collective power ... the relation between an employer and an isolated employee or worker is typically a relation between a bearer of power and one who is not a bearer of power. In its inception it is an act of submission, in its operation it is a condition of subordination, however much concealed by that indispensable figment of the legal mind known as the contract of employment. (Kahn-Freund 1977: 17)

The problem of disrespect for labour rights, including the right to organize, in the developing world is quite different from that in the developed world. In the former, enforcement of labour rights can be seen as a major device for poverty alleviation in general. A large part of the working population in the developing world does not get minimum wages. Laws relating to wage-fixing are also violated with impunity. In these societies, key labour relations issues are not issues of the equitable sharing of the gains of industry, but of mere survival so far as labour is concerned. Therefore, the state in these societies has to be heavily involved in helping to foster a just and egalitarian social order – not necessarily by becoming a custodian of substantive labour rights, but by providing an even floor where labour and management can negotiate the terms of employment and work cooperatively. The concept of the gold-collar worker has emerged in the advanced world, especially in sunrise and knowledge organizations. A gold-collar worker is one who offers valuable skills in high demand, but does not desire to join a union. They wish to bargain their wage levels by individual contracting, based on their skills and performance. Much of the advanced world follows high-wage policies within the framework of globalization to cater to the needs of gold-collar workers, with the intention of transferring low-wage employment to factories and establishments based in the developing world. In the developing economies, gold-collar workers are few and far between. In this world, the collective power of labour is further diluted by bureaucratic indifference, corruption and non-enforcement of laws. Eventually, rights often become mere symbols. Therefore, developing world lawyers must continue to search for more efficacious legal instruments to cope with these realities. In a country like India, with a population of more than one billion, more than a quarter of whom are estimated to be living below the poverty line, labour organizational rights assume special significance.

This chapter attempts to explain the importance of the right to labour organization as a significant human right in the Indian context. In this regard, it develops a contextual framework for the right to labour organization in India and examines the provisions of the Indian constitution and those of the statutes comprising Indian industrial relations (IR) laws. It then attempts to understand the working of labour relations law as it relates to labour organization, and labour dispute processing as it stands in relation to the Indian political economy. It addresses the following questions, among others: how the labour relations law actually works; what legal processes lead to the neutralization of labour organization; what role the state and its agencies play in the securing or denial of collective labour justice; who makes a more beneficial use of the legal framework; and what concrete manifestations of injustice to labour as individuals and as collectives are visible. It suggests what can be done to attempt a better realization of labour organizational rights. Many answers to these questions are based on findings in larger research (Saini forthcoming), which involved a reconstruction of thirty-three collective labour disputes (see Table 13.1)[2] belonging to the private sector; of these, four cases were live conciliation cases (30 to 33) in which the author participated as an observer. Most of these related to smaller and medium-sized establishments where workers were organized or semi-organized. This research represents the first comprehensive analysis of the workings of the Indian labour adjudication model.

LABOUR ORGANIZATION AS A HUMAN RIGHT

Individual workers enjoy little effective power when seeking a just and fair arrangement of the distribution of industrial gains. This gives rise to the need to allow labour to unite, form collectives, and thus struggle to alleviate its poverty on its own through unionization and collective bargaining. Interestingly, Article 23 of the Universal Declaration of Human Rights, adopted by the United Nations as a common standard of achievement for all people in all nations, recognizes the legitimacy of union rights, providing for everyone 'the right to form and to join trade unions, for the protection of his interests'. This issue has been raised in discussions regarding the threats of globalization to the basic human rights of working people. Even though the International Labour Organization (ILO) has sought to redefine what constitutes basic rights, the right to organize continues to attract the attention of international institutions. The World Summit for Social Development in Copenhagen in 1995 adopted a programme of action based on allegiance to 'basic workers' rights'. These rights, among others, include the freedom of association and the right to organize and bargain collectively. In addition, the ILO Declaration on Fundamental Principles and Rights at Work and its follow-up adopted in the ILO meeting in 1998 consider 'freedom of association and the effective recognition of the right to collective bargaining' as a basic right.

Labour organization is considered as an important human right and a basic condition for building an enlightened society. In regard to raising the conditions of the poorer sections of society, the Indian constitution contemplates law-making in the model not of 'politics of production' but of 'production of politics' (Burawoy 1985) and a programme of action for empowering these sections, including labour. Ironically, however, studies of social justice and 'poverty studies' are still a 'nascent enterprise' in India (Baxi 1988: x). In terms of rhetoric, the Indian labour law (including IR law) system proposes that labour laws will work as important instrumentalities for empowering the powerless and the downtrodden so as to realize the cherished goals of the constitution. All branches of the state are enjoined to facilitate the realization of these goals. A large number of labour laws were enacted in independent India to operationalize the constitutional vision, and the labour bureaucracy was entrusted with the role of ensuring compliance with these laws.

Understanding labour relations law as a tool for poverty alleviation necessitates examination of the working of the law relating to labour organization and processes of labour (dis)empowerment. In this regard, it is important to ask how far this law has actually gone towards the realization of its projected goals of uplifting the powerless by securing labour and social justice for them. Ironically, most labour law research in India is doctrinal; hardly any empirical accounts of labour law in action are available. Even law-and-society research is underdeveloped and has not adequately addressed this issue (Baxi 1982; Dhavan 1989). Also, most labour law scholars often use hortatory and instrumentalist arguments, failing to distinguish between symptoms and causal roots. In order to make law an effective tool of poverty alleviation, it is necessary that lawyers study law in conjunction with social sciences. Indeed, Justice Brandeis went so far as to say that a lawyer who has not studied economics and sociology is very apt to become a public enemy (Clark and Wedderburn 1983: 30). The working of the legal system is often presumed by law scholars, without demonstrating it. We need to understand the concrete dynamics and processes through which vested-interest groups conspire and intervene to maintain the impoverished state of labour. Very few studies in India have focused on labour law sociology (Saini forthcoming; Ramaswamy 1984).

No understanding of the working of the law is possible 'without a consideration of where power lies' (Kjønstad and Veit-Wilson 1997: iii) and without appreciating that implementation of law is a process in which dominant political values are subtly absorbed. Sociologists of law have emphasized that most disputes in societies and organizations 'arise out of power differential' (Edelman et al. 1993). Baxi (1995 and 1994) charges the Indian state with being a saboteur of labour laws. Technically, though, unorganized labour can use the protective framework, but the legal system works in such a way that it does not command enough political power to preserve its basic human right, i.e. the right to association and collective bargaining. It is not suggested that effective legal action has no limits; but the important question is, can these limits be moderated to enhance the political power of labour, especially unorganized and semi-organized. It is important, therefore, that we develop a legal framework conducive to producing respect for labour organization and labour struggle.

THE CONTEXTUAL FRAMEWORK OF LABOUR ORGANIZATION

The framework of all legislative, executive and judicial actions in India is contained in the constitution of India. In its Preamble, the constitution seeks to secure to the people, among other things, 'justice, social, economic and political ... and liberty of thought, expression'. Article 19(1)(c) of this *grundnorm* guarantees to all citizens a fundamental freedom 'to form associations and unions'. Part IV of the constitution is titled 'Directive Principles of State Policy', and contains directions to the state to operationalize a scheme of social justice and upliftment of the downtrodden guided by the basic postulates of the welfare state (see Articles 38(1), 39, 41, 42, 43 and 43A of the Indian constitution). The Directive Principles are considered so important that they have been described as the 'soul of the Constitution' (Dhavan 1989: xxii).

Premised in the framework of the Directive Principles, the four main branches of labour laws in the country provide a large number of central (federal) labour statutes. India has a comprehensive labour law framework, but the instances of labour law violation are immense; so much so that, when one sees the working conditions of many unorganized labourers, it appears as if no labour law exists for them (Saini 1998 and forthcoming; Patel and Desai 1995).

The most crucial aspect of the labour laws in any country is the labour relations law. This branch of law enables labour to organize and struggle to free itself from poverty and secure social justice by striving for a just sharing of organizational gains. In this regard, the Trade Unions Act 1926 (TUA) and the Industrial Disputes Act 1947 (IDA) are the key labour relations laws in India enacted by the central legislature. These are over and above the guarantee provided by Article 19(1)(c) of the constitution, which envisages provision of union rights in general. The TUA is an important legal document that provides for union formation in industries. Its provisions relate to conferring corporate status on unions, registration of unions, and unions' rights and obligations. Strangely, however, union recognition was not provided for in the TUA until a 1947 amendment, but this provision has not been enforced. Today, recognition can be gained by a union only through a show of its strength.

Like the TUA, the IDA applies to the whole country. It provides a model of conciliation, arbitration and adjudication of both rights (individual as well as collective) and interest disputes. This is a colonial law, which was enacted by the British Indian legislature in April 1947.[3] The IDA envisages compulsory adjudication (also known as compulsory arbitration in some countries) of industrial disputes when parties fail to agree and the government so decides. Even though compulsory adjudication was initially intended to be only a war measure in 1942, the government subsequently formalized it in a more comprehensive form, by enacting the IDA. Leaders such as V. V. Giri (later President of India) wanted the IDA to be replaced by a law that would promote voluntarism based on bipartism and strengthen unions. Being the ruling party, the Congress Party, however, found the IDA a useful instrument for containing or suppressing conflict. The IDA has now been in place for more than half a century and has promoted state paternalism in IR, leaving unions weak and susceptible to bureaucratic inertia and manipulation.

A dispute prevention and resolution machinery is envisaged by the IDA, which mainly consists of joint committees of labour and management (works committees); conciliation officers who are government officers (without autonomy from the government framework); and labour courts and tribunals, which are adjudicatory bodies. Unlike most labour courts and labour tribunals in Western countries which are well staffed,[4] adjudicatory bodies under the IDA are comprised of one judicial person only. Labour courts mainly adjudicate rights questions such as dismissal and propriety of an order given by the employer, whereas tribunals adjudicate primarily interest questions such as terms of employment including wages and allowances. Labour courts and tribunals deliver decrees (called awards under the IDA) that are binding on parties.

The jurisdiction of the adjudicatory bodies cannot be activated by the disputant parties at their will; the appropriate government – both the central (federal) and state governments in their respective jurisdictions – has the discretion of referring or not referring industrial disputes to these bodies. They cannot resort to strikes/lockouts when a dispute is pending before an adjudicatory body or during the period in which awards of these bodies are in operation. In fact, there are scarcely any situations when parties have the freedom to strike/lockout. It is rightly commented that the law of industrial disputes in India is so framed that a legal strike is nearly impossible (Ramaswamy 1984), especially if the state so desires. The government in its discretion also has the power to prohibit strikes/lockouts that are in existence when disputes related to these have been referred for adjudication. The enforcement of the awards of the adjudicatory bodies as well as settlements, if not implemented by the party concerned, is the duty of the labour department staffed by labour officers and inspectors. Labour departments have been created by the central as well as state governments in their respective jurisdictions.

The representation of parties at the conciliation level through practising lawyers is prohibited by the IDA; however, lawyers are allowed to appear before the adjudicatory bodies with the consent of the parties and the leave of the labour court/tribunal. In fact, a large number of labour lawyers, union leaders and management consultants represent parties before adjudicatory fora. This culture has promoted 'legalism, consultationism, and government unions' (Bhattacherjee 1988: 212). The IDA has a widespread presence in the dispute process, as a result of which a large number of trade union leaders are running consultancy services for workers by representing them before these bodies; in actuality, they have become briefcase union leaders (Saini 1995b) and hardly involve themselves in the labour organizational process.

If a dispute is settled during the course of conciliation proceedings, the conciliation officer (CO) is obliged to register that result if he considers it to be 'fair' and 'amicable' under section 12(3) of the IDA. Such settlements are popularly known as 12(3) settlements. They have wide-ranging application and even bind those employees who are not party to them, and also those who join the organization later, during the period such settlement is in force. A voluntary settlement under section 18(1) of the IDA, however, binds only the signatories to such a settlement. Hence both parties desire to go in for conciliated settlements – the management because of the undisputed applicability of such settlements, and workers because they think that 12(3) settlements are more proper and legal. If a conciliation exercise results in failure, the CO writes a failure report in which he states his own assessment of the dispute and sends it to the appropriate government. The CO is also supposed to write a confidential report suggesting whether, in his opinion, the demands of some or all of the workers should be referred for adjudication. The government often bases its reference[5] decision on the recommendation of the CO, though it is not bound to do so. Thus, the conciliation system is intimately intertwined with the adjudication system.

On paper, the powers of the COs appear small as they cannot impose their own views on the disputant parties. But the actual working of the IDA shows that these powers have often been misused for corrupt or ulterior motives, many times guided by the personal financial interests of the CO or at the instance of the political executives under whose overall direction the COs work (Saini forthcoming). The COs also act as labour officers with duties to enforce the awards and settlements under the IDA and the employers' obligations under other labour laws. This, of course, happens in other non-Western situations as well (Hanami 1980). The IDA provides that the parties are free to choose voluntary arbitration of their industrial dispute, both rights and interests, but they can do so only before the dispute is referred by the government for adjudication. Collective bargaining, as well as arbitration of industrial disputes, takes place in the dense shadows of the adjudication system. The IDA provides certain protection for union members against dismissal and change in their service conditions during the pendency of disputes before any of the authorities, but this protection is grossly violated by employers. The time taken in adjudication of collective-demand cases, on average, is between thirty-seven and forty-nine months, which tremendously disappoints workers (Saini 1992; Upadhyay 1995).

STATE AND LABOUR DISORGANIZATIONAL PROCESS

The discussion in the above section shows that conciliation and adjudication are the two key sub-systems provided in Indian labour relations law. Both these mechanisms have been charged with promoting the just and fair resolution of industrial disputes when voluntary efforts fail. It is interesting to note that the capacity of the labour organization to alleviate the poverty of workers depends on how these two systems actually work. These two are deeply intertwined. The former is the invisible stage of the latter, because the government's decision as to which labour cases are to be referred for adjudication usually has its genesis in the outcome of the conciliation proceedings. Saini's (forthcoming) study, however, locates alternative structures, operating at the covert level, which explain the actual working of the conciliation system. The key assumption in a conciliation process is that a conciliator is a neutral third party to ensure a 'fair' and 'amicable' settlement. However, Saini finds that this power is variously exercised: merely symbolically (Case no. 31, FIL); or fraudulently (Case no. 32, KGK, and Case no. 22, HPL); or even involving tyranny on labour (Case no. 33, PSL). All these cases involved unions of fragile strength, some wanting to remain in power with the help of collusion with the employer and others wanting to represent the genuine voice of the hapless, semi-organized worker. Those in the former category mostly had the patronage of the ruling political party (see Table 13.1 and Table 13.2). In KGK (Case no. 32), the case involved two unions, the recognized one having a tacit understanding with management. The rival union's support rose to 90 per cent of the workforce. It sought recognition through asking for negotiation of its demand charter. The CO, however, used his 12(3) power to see that the settlement was signed with the minority union. The CO neither investigated the dispute nor ensured the 'fairness' of the settlement (which he was obliged to do under the IDA). One stroke of his pen helped the corrupt union to survive with the support of barely 10 per cent of the workers. The daring and cavalier way in which the CO signed the 12(3) settlement with the knowledge of his entire staff demonstrates the impunity and frequency with which such frauds can be practised due to the bureaucratization of industrial conflict. The CO undertook administrative manoeuvring to project a façade of adherence to legal form. His action resulted in keeping the majority union at bay to watch its demise in fraudulent conciliation and bureaucratic indifference. The CO had been bribed and was favouring an illegitimate workgroup. But more importantly, the recognized minority union was an ally of the political party in power. In the case of smaller and medium-sized unions, COs are often found favouring unions affiliated to ruling parties.

In PSL (33), the CO concerned was acting on behalf of the State Chief Minister. This case file provided evidence of horrendous repression of the union by the state. The employer fired forty activist workers of the majority union which had mass support and had demanded recognition. The conciliation and labour administration power in this case was exercised tyrannically, which shifted the union agenda from recognition to protecting the dismissed workers. This happens in most situations of nascent labour struggle. Similarly, in HPL (22), the fraud committed on a majority union at the behest of the CO led to disastrous consequences for the labour movement in the whole region (i.e. Faridabad Industrial Complex in the State of Haryana), in which police fired on workers assembled to protest against the corrupt exercise of bureaucratic power by state officials and eight workers died. The workers of HPL have not yet recovered from the shock of the firing incident that led their colleagues to sacrifice their lives in the furtherance of the labour struggle. They saw with their own eyes the naked repression by state power and its debilitating impact on labour organization. Even though HPL employs 800 workers, it did not have a union until very recently. The spectre of the graveyard hovered over the workplace for more than a decade.

A reading of the confidential files also showed that COs had recommended reference of cases to the adjudicatory body on extraneous considerations in many situations (Saini forthcoming). Since these recommendations are confidential, they have remained an untapped source for labour researchers. In fact, it is felt that it is impossible to gather hard evidence on the abuse of the adjudication system (Ramaswamy 1984: 166). In nearly a quarter of the thirty-three cases, COs admittedly rejected reference for corrupt motives (as admitted by management).

Thus, we see that the government-appointed conciliators have not done their duty to ensure that parties enter into 'fair' settlements. Rather, they have allowed themselves to be used to disguise a corrupt alliance between vested-interest groups. Labour, therefore, cannot hope for fairness in settlements from just the favourable attitudes of the COs. The alliance is too integral to the system to be disturbed. Whenever spontaneous protests against injustice emerge, the alliance works to silence them through the institutionalized channels covertly designed as a part of the IDA (peace) model. Instead of administering social justice, these systems help the alliance to carry out its vested interests, which mainly relate to the disempowerment of labour by diluting the efficacy of labour struggle through the misuse of legal structures and procedures. Thus, over the years, the Indian state has been directly or indirectly privatized for the benefit of some sectors of the political economy and to the exclusion, or partial exclusion, of other sectors (Dhavan 1989). Therefore, one doubts whether a bureaucratic model like the IDA can change the fate of the Indian labouring masses in their struggle for redefinition of the norms of workplace justice dispensation.

Indeed, bureaucratic models may suffer from a serious lack of potential as instruments of social justice dispensation in developed as well as developing nations. Bureaucratic systems may reflect: 'Over-devotion of officials to precedent, remoteness from the rest of the community, inaccessibility, arrogance in dealing with the general public, ineffective organization, waste of manpower, procrastination, an excessive sense of self-importance, indifference to the feelings of inconvenience of citizens, an obsession with the binding authority of departmental decision, inflexibility, abuse of power, and a reluctance to admit error' (*Encyclopaedia Britannica* 1987: 342).

The Indian labour relations model gives an important place to bureaucratic power in several ways: ensuring enforcement of awards of tribunals and settlements, recommending reference, prohibition of strikes under section 10(3) of the IDA, and use of the police force in containing workers' protests against unfair exercise of this power. If one looks at the actual reference decisions, it is noticeable that, in nearly 90 per cent of the cases, the decisions favoured the unions affiliated with the ruling-party federations (Saini forthcoming). This is, of course, not to deny the merits of these cases. The same did not, however, happen in the case of the labour wings of the opposition parties. Seemingly biased exercise of discretionary power was also noticeable in the case of strike prohibition power under section 10(3) of the IDA. In six out of the thirty disputes that involved reference, the 10(3) power was exercised. Strangely, in all six cases, 10(3) was used where the unions involved were union-wings of the opposition parties. In many similar cases, where ruling-party unions were involved, this power was not exercised, even though worse circumstances prevailed.

It has been observed that the state is pro-management in matters of determination of capacity to pay, but is pro-worker in matters relating to termination (Ramaswamy 1984). Saini (forthcoming), however, shows that this is not really so. As shown in Table 13.2, in eighteen cases out of those that involved termination, the workers concerned were not taken back, even in some cases where the workers concerned won at the Supreme Court level.

Saini's study shows that the state and management alliance is stronger than that between the state and ruling-party-affiliated unions. Wherever a union tried to show its independent status in a labour struggle, it had to undergo the wrath of the management, resulting in substantial weakening or even wiping out of the union concerned. The state has endorsed the disciplining process used by management, both by remaining a mute witness and even by actively abetting lawless behaviour. It never enforced even the symbolic protection available to unions by prosecuting management for unfair labour practices (ULPs) as envisaged in the Fifth Schedule of the IDA. Not a single case of such prosecution was found, regardless of whether the unions involved were allies of the party in power. Many complaints were made by the workers/union concerned relating to commission of ULPs by the employer but the state agencies opined that they were frivolous or baseless.

Labour bureaucracy has also been charged by the IDA with ensuring the reinstatement of dismissed workers if so provided in an award of a labour court or an industrial tribunal. Most such cases in small and medium organizations are settled for money; despite awards providing for reinstatement in workers' favour, not even in 1 per cent of reinstatement awards is the worker concerned actually taken back. In Saini's study, in the case of AMT (5), the worker was not reinstated even after the Supreme Court's judgment in the worker's favour. When asked about the reason for it, a clerk in the state labour department revealed that, in such cases, the labour inspector concerned becomes a consultant to the employer as to how not to implement the award. The role of labour bureaucracy in perpetuating ULPs by employers and in eventually smashing the unions is too deeply ingrained to be questioned. Those who are involved in union activity must know through the narration of these cases what it means to actively involve oneself in labour organizing. That is why India has an extremely low unionization rate in the private sector despite the constitution and a trade union law giving people the freedom of association.

DILUTING LABOUR ORGANIZATION THROUGH JURIDIFICATION

Labour–management relations are continuing relations; the parties concerned must desire to sustain this relationship, accepting the legitimacy of the respective adversarial interests of the two sides. Labour relations scholars often caution against giving a dominant role to law or lawyers, so as to prevent labour relations from being absorbed into legalism or juridification, thus restricting the rule-creating potential of the actors involved in the exercise. The IDA's restrictions on professional lawyers representing the disputant parties at the conciliation and tribunal levels reflect this concern. Juridification implies a process by which legal intervention produces a tendency to distinguish between lawful and unlawful, and attempts to categorize all actions into these two possibilities (Clark and Wedderburn 1983: 188; Saini 1991). The Indian labour relations model works in such a way that it produces tangible manifestations of these very apprehensions. Despite experiencing disappointment, workers and even management believe in the inevitability of the IDA, and the possibility of developing alternative structures appears to them as something utopian. Juridification conditions parties' behaviour when workplace issues are debated and negotiated. Employers may not disapprove of this happening, as it is to their advantage. It helps them to prevent powerless labour to unite and carry on its struggle. At least in so far as it does not directly produce deep worker alienation and thus inefficiency, juridification is a powerful weapon in employers' distributive conflict with workers. Bargaining in the shadow of dilatory and impersonal adjudication, labour is prone to acquiesce in settlements on management's terms.

The Indian system of consultation through lawyers and briefcase union leaders in the Indian labour relations context further reinforces juridification. Saini's (forthcoming) study reveals that 90 per cent of disputes at the conciliation stage and 86 per cent at the tribunal stage involved representation of workers by external leaders. In addition, 45 per cent of management representatives at the conciliation stage and 97 per cent at the tribunal stage were outside management consultants or practising labour lawyers. The working of the IDA model cannot be thought of without significant lawyer involvement, in that the propriety of parties' action is determined through the adversarial process. Given the fact that 'the ingenuity of lawyers is endless' (Wedderburn 1971: 8), lawyers influence the attitudes of employers and unions towards labour law and law-administering institutions, and eventually workplace labour relations. Because of the presence of professionals, the system thus creates the impression that justice can be administered exclusively through state-created formal bodies. This image is based not only on the fact that these bodies make authoritative proclamations, but also because professionals' personal pecuniary interests are promoted by this approach. This has the result of blunting the teeth of labour collectives in their struggle for labour justice.

Most lawyers have their own interests and stakes in dispute outcomes and have been described as 'traditional elites' (Abel 1973) and 'repeat players' (Munger 1990: 604). They exert significant influence on shaping the development of disputes. In the labour relations context, their interests are often antithetical to those of the disputant parties, especially the weaker ones. For this reason, union leaders enter into alliances with employers and the state to serve their interests. Saini's disputes reconstruction demonstrates lawyers' dubious role in the union-smashing or weakening tactics of management. Union-avoidance has become a flourishing industry. Professional manipulation has become accepted business practice in the never-ending labour-juridification process. The above study also reveals that in a small industrial town, the INTUC (Indian National Trade Union Congress) union federation has eleven factions, each with a leader practising labour law in the name of INTUC. Many of these leaders are not even on speaking terms due to the exigencies of business competition. One such leader remarked: 'Our role as pleaders is so absorbing that there is no time for organizational work.'

The high incidence of unfair labour practices (ULPs) by employers, terminations by them for trade union activities, and the inability of the labour relations system to get workers reinstated further reinforce the weakening of the labour struggle (see Table 13.2). The use of legal channels to process industrial conflict has resulted in labour power being directed into thousands of individual cases and questions. Presently, 447,195 labour cases are pending before various labour courts and tribunals in the country,[6] most of which are individual termination cases, including those for participating in union activities (for state details, see Table 13.3).

Instead of empowering labour, the IDA 'peace model' strengthens already dominant employers, allowing them to intimidate labour and exclude workers from political processes relevant to industrial justice. Nader (1975: 168), a legal anthropologist, referring to such a use of law, remarks as follows: 'In industrialized nation states, the wealthier members of a society override and superimpose their views on the poorer, less powerful sectors by means of the law. In the developing nations, law will play a great part in this determination because the law is fashioned to legitimate the status quo.'

Thus labour relations law, in practice, produces juridification, which, in the Indian context, results in diluting the efficacy of labour organizations. Therefore, any discourse on the use of law to combat poverty and powerlessness in India has to begin from this starting point; otherwise it is likely to be merely platitudinous.

JUDICIALIZATION OF THE LABOUR (DIS)ORGANIZATIONAL PROCESS

As originally conceived, the IDA was expected to provide a forum for resolving labour relations issues peacefully and minimizing industrial conflict. Theoretically, unions were expected to derive countervailing power from the awards delivered, thereby enabling them to resolve political disputes such as interest questions in labour relations.

The established quasi-judicial bodies were expected to provide greater accessibility to the weaker side, a more informal atmosphere than that created by the civil court culture, the use of the special skills of labour adjudicators, and expeditious dispute resolution by minimizing delay. These objectives are particularly relevant to the resolution of interest-disputes, such as those related to wage and benefit levels, but similar objectives have also been embraced in relation to the resolution of rights disputes, for example in UK tribunal adjudications (Olney 1997). A tribunal framework that promotes these objectives would surely aid labour organizations in securing a more equitable share of organizational gains. Ironically, however, even the report of the British experience is not too encouraging in this regard (Dickens et al. 1985). The Indian scenario is much worse, almost totally denying any of these goals.

Parties to labour adjudication often perceive labour tribunals as accessible. In doing so, however, they narrowly define 'accessibility'. So as to be labelled as accessible, adjudicatory bodies must demonstrate and promote the following expectations: the knowledge that a forum for dispute processing exists, the perception that there are reasonable chances of success by accessing that forum, bearable costs for processing the dispute in terms of time and money, a convenient geographical location of the forum, availability of competent representatives to plead the case of the party concerned, a perception that the weaker party (usually the workers) will not be victimized for pursuing a dispute, and, in the Indian context of the IDA, obtaining a successful outcome of the dispute.

Judges are usually not interested in being nominated to labour tribunals. Thus, a large number of vacancies are routinely present in almost all the states in India. This, of course, reduces accessibility. In addition, Table 13.2 shows that the system does not ensure that union leaders pursuing disputes will not be victimized for doing so. Likewise, Table 13.2 shows that management withdrew the dismissal action in only three of twenty-one cases. Interestingly, in two of the eighteen cases, the workers were not reinstated even after the Supreme Court of India found their dismissal wrongful and decided in the workers' favour. The employers in these cases indulged in ULPs to ensure that the reinstatement decrees remained unimplemented. A high incidence of dispute abandonment by powerless workers is also evidence of accessibility restriction. In Saini's (forthcoming) study, 40 per cent of all cases were dropped. Even though the dispute statistics log these cases as peacefully resolved, no information is recorded regarding the circumstances that led to such a conclusion. In fact, some of these cases involved the complete smashing of unions, yet the tribunal put its seal of approval on their demise, issuing a 'no-dispute' award when nobody appeared before the tribunal on the appointed date. In this study, 35 per cent of cases resulted in 'settlement awards' by the tribunal. A large number of such cases also tell the story of the vulnerability of the downtrodden in the labour relations process, where labour submitted to the wishes of powerful employers after it felt humiliated by the commission of ULPs and the inability of the tribunal to protect it. Can we then say that the tribunals have demonstrated accessibility?

Under the IDA, tribunals are allowed to develop their own procedures for processing disputes. They are not guided by the normal laws of civil procedure and evidence. Thus, they have been expected to minimize the use of jargon and promote an inquisitorial rather than an adversarial style of dispute investigation. They also do not have to wear a judge's dress, perceived as promoting formalism. Compared to civil courts, tribunals are somewhat informal in their approach. Because those adjudicating are trained as judges, however, they are substantially following the civil procedure and evidence law. More importantly, interest-dispute processing is a matter of political decision-making; formalism becomes a hindrance in this process. Though the IDA provided that the tribunals could make use of two experts for facilitating a dispute, evidently to promote expert investigation and to minimize legalistic interpretations, such expert assessors have rarely been sought or appointed.

For workers, especially the downtrodden and powerless, seeking justice from tribunals, the most important expectation is expeditious handling of disputes. As noted earlier, however, the lengthy delay, mainly caused by the juridifying atmosphere in which the tribunal functions, virtually renders void any benefit from the tribunal adjudication.

The central government has shown indifference to restructuring the labour relations model so as to facilitate the above-mentioned goals. Baxi (1982 and 1994) looks at this problem as a wider crisis in the Indian legal system. He charges that, within the state agenda, the dispensation of justice is a low national priority. Consequently, the labour adjudication system is used by powerful actors to defeat their adversaries in conciliation proceedings and adjudication procedures. Surely, the delay impoverishes labour struggles. Union leaders who become victims of management's power to fire cannot wait for years for justice, to see the tribunal confirm the dismissal order on a technical interpretation or deliver an award that the labour bureaucracy cannot implement.

Tribunals have failed to live up to their projected goals; but their legitimating role is substantial, and so is their role as a source of power. Saini disputes reconstruction has documented that major gains rarely come to labour through the tribunal system. In the one case (PML, 8) that did provide a significant victory for labour, the employer appealed to the Supreme Court and managed to extract an out-of-court settlement from the worn-out workers with less beneficial terms than those awarded by the tribunal. Due to the impact of the above messages, workers in general avoid the tribunal. In most cases where new unions are involved, management colludes with outsider union representatives at some stage of the dispute processing, resulting in the dismissal of the internal union activists. Sometimes, the latter are also taken into the alliance. The labour collective is thus wiped out or becomes very weak, and the will to revive the labour struggle gets dampened or even extinguished. Most cases of dispute abandonment at the tribunal or their settlement at some stage of the tribunal proceedings experience this conscious labour disempowerment process.

Thus, in India, the structure of labour adjudication adversely affects collective bargaining and labour organization and, consequently, labour power. The adjudication system is fully entrenched in Indian labour relations, and has integrated labour collectives into the state apparatus. The responsible trade unionism preached through the IDA thus results in unions being wiped out or virtually crippled. A large number of those who use the tribunal system are the first-timers who experience defeat in this model and rarely decide to use it again. Thus, the grist in the tribunal mill is a new union that has yet to see its nemesis in adjudication. Strangely, however, even militant national union federations like the CITU (Centre for Indian Trade Unions), which is the trade-union wing of the CPI-M (Communist Party of India-Marxist), have become so accustomed over time to the system that they do not put forward any major challenge to its existence. It is rightly remarked that a bird born in the cage cries for the cage. In fact, the National Commission on Labour (NCL) 1969 had recommended conferring autonomy on the labour dispute processing fora (which it called Industrial Relations Commissions) from the state apparatus. It also wanted these fora to be multi-member bodies with experts supporting the judicial members. However, a meeting of the state labour ministers called by the central government to debate the NCL's recommendations vehemently opposed any autonomy for these bodies, as it considered labour relations to be matters of law and order. Thus, they put a seal of approval on the status quo, a tribunal (including labour court) system that substantially dilutes the potential of labour struggle and labour organizing.

Within the context of India, over-legalization of labour relations has weakened labour power. A legalized labour relations system can be beneficial to those who can develop institutional skills to use it to their advantage. But a legalized framework promotes bureaucratization, and thus enables the Indian government to prevent labour from organizing and promoting industrial equity and democracy. The government's first concern is production and peace, at whatever social cost. A focus on consultation and adjudication, inherent in the IDA in the Indian context, produces management consultants and briefcase union leaders. They help strengthen opportunistic alliances between various power centres and, thus, help to make the legal labyrinth more convoluted. The individualization of labour relations exacerbated by them further dilutes the labour struggle. The Dunlop Commission on Labour Relations, which was appointed to examine the state of industrial relations in the USA in the post-Reaganomics era, also revealed a rise in the above tendencies in the US context. The Commission estimated that 70 per cent of US employers used outside consultants, and 40 per cent of the workplaces were not able to secure a collective bargaining agreement after winning certification (US Department of Labor 1994). Especially, employers owning small and medium businesses showed a greater tendency to commit ULPs. Thus, the legal structure becomes an instrument for preserving the status quo rather than serving as an instrument to change the condition of labourers. Such an institutionalization of legalism prevents the dispensation of substantive justice to the poor; the law becomes merely a symbolic protection.

Redistribution of power cannot come about without struggle and conflict. In India, employers have used the structural contradiction of the IDA framework as a resource for their own dominance. They have used IR law to legitimize their low wage strategies through the practice of authoritarianism, fraud, and even tyranny against workers seeking redefinition of labour relations through labour organizing and struggle. They have also used it to forge alliances to legitimate the structures and processes of power distribution under the existing IR law framework.

Nonet and Selznick (1978) argue that legal development can be divided into three stages. In the first stage, the law is repressive and is passively and opportunistically in the service of the predominant social and political forces as an instrument of coercion. In the second stage of its development, the legal system attains 'formal rationality', which they describe as autonomous law. In this stage, they claim that the law seeks to establish and preserve institutional integrity. In furtherance of this goal, the law 'insulates itself, narrows its responsibilities, and accepts a blind formalism as the price of integrity'. In the third stage, law again responds to the exigencies of the social environment as it had done in the repressive stage, but this time geared to meet societal needs. According to this analysis, the Indian labour relations law as it is implemented is in the first stage of Nonet and Selznick's legal development. Labour relations law in practice cannot be used as an instrument of poverty alleviation unless the opportunistic alliances that dilute its efficacy are exposed and made dysfunctional.

An important prerequisite of labour empowerment is allowing the development of strong labour collectives which can prove to be a countervailing power to management's unilateral operation of private industrial governments and thus promote fairness in processes of industrial relations rather than their juridification. Legalism creates a labyrinth that empowers labour at one moment and disempowers it at the next. Kjønstad and Veit-Wilson (1997: vii) note seven prerequisites for achieving the goal of breaking the vicious circle that links poverty and powerlessness. These are (1) a conducive national constitution; (2) the opportunity of struggle provided by tribunals; (3) treating human rights as also a discourse on poverty; (4) the possibility of mobilizing the poor; (5) the perception of danger by power wielders if they deny rights to the poor; (6) mobilizing altruism by the powerful; and (7) encouraging the non-poor to participate in the struggle against poverty. So far as the labour struggle in India is concerned, only the conditions laid down by prerequisites numbers 1, 6 and 7 are fulfilled. Others are fulfilled partially or not at all.

In view of the above, the following concrete issues (also see Saini 1998) can be identified as reforms for alleviating poverty in the context of Indian labour:

1. The IDA with its resulting legal structure has weakened labour in its fight for the enforcement of labour rights. A large part of Indian labour does not receive the minimum wage. We need a programme of social action for the requisite sensitization of all concerned in this regard. Intellectuals, NGOs and an international trade union movement can play useful roles.
2. Any programme of action for enhancing labour power needs to involve better enforcement mechanisms. Labour needs to be given representation in carving out such an enforcement mechanism.

3. There is a need for constant monitoring of the implementation mechanism by rights groups at national and international levels.
4. There is a need for simplification of the labour laws, and internalization of such simplicity as a social value. In India, the National Labour Law Association (NLLA) has come out with such a code which can be a good starting point for facilitating people's understanding of a complete labour law framework (NLLA 1994).
5. It is absolutely necessary to ensure autonomy of tribunals and conciliators from the state apparatus. This is perhaps the most difficult task in the Indian context as the analysis in this chapter reveals.
6. Public interest litigation can be a useful instrument for enforcing labour standards, especially in the Indian context, but we need to involve in it those people (such as lawyers and case presenters) who are genuinely interested in poverty alleviation and fairness in industrial relations.

In the globalization euphoria, the values of unionism and collective bargaining as well as the values of the welfare state and welfare economics themselves are in a deep crisis. Researchers in the UK reveal that pluralism has survived there, despite Thatcherism and the fall in the unionization rate (Storey 1992). We need a wider popularization of the perspectives that unions are not fundamentally antithetical to globalization philosophy and can well be accommodated in this thinking to provide a more humane face to it. In view of a high incidence of labour poverty in general, India especially needs to check the declining labour power and the new managerial unitarianism that is developing in IR. Based on the analysis of the working of the IR law framework in India in the present chapter, this will require state action at several levels – legislative and judicial as well as administrative. The rights groups and non-governmental organizations (NGOs) also need to play a significant role in compelling the Indian state to take such actions.

TABLE 13.1 List of reconstructed disputes

Case	Abbreviated name of the dispute	Name of the organization**	No. of workers
1	HSL*	Highclass Sheets Ltd	1,400
2	GRIL	Giant Rubber India Ltd	1,600
3	ECL*	Essac Cotton Mills Ltd	700
4	AML	Aman Meters Ltd	210
5	AMT*	Ardit Machine Tools	150
6	JSF*	Jazz Steel Fastners Pvt. Ltd	150
7	TCC	Technique Consultation	140
8	PML	Print Machines Ltd	45
9	APL*	Avis Production Pvt. Ltd	52
10	ASL*	Ashok Synthetics Pvt. Ltd	420
11	BIL	Bask India Ltd	1,250
12	BCM	Bhushan Carbon Mfg. Co. Ltd	530
13	HVG*	Himalaya Vikas Glass Pvt. Ltd	695
14	EL*	Equipments Ltd	450
15	PHL	Partap House Ltd	155
16	UMM	Union Machinery Mills Ltd	75
17	SEC	Swastik Engineering Co. Ltd	220
18	RVL*	Robin Vikas Ltd	125
19	OEW*	Om Engineering Works	110
20	SKW*	Swan Knitting Works	250
21	UAL	Uma Automobile Ltd	70
22	HPL*	Hammer Private Ltd.	800
23	UCB*	Unique Conveyer Belts	140
24	ARL	Asish Rubber Ltd	80
25	CEW*	Cast Engineering Works	45
26	OS*	Oshima Steel	350
27	FRF*	Frontal Rubber Factory Pvt. Ltd	90
28	SEW*	Sidhu Engineering Works	45
29	FAP*	Ferguson and Allied Products	
30	SL*	Sahnis Ltd	110
31	FIL	Fenning India Ltd	480
32	KGK*	Kanwar G. Khemka Ltd	950
33	PSL*	Parikshit Steels Mills Ltd	700

* Cases in which the services of union leaders were terminated in relation to the labour dispute
** The real names of the employers have been changed and pseudonyms are being used, to follow the policy of concealing their identity, as promised
Source: Saini (forthcoming)

TABLE 13.2 Cases involving termination of workers due to pursuit of union activities

Name and case no.	No. of workers whose services terminated	Whether union is ally of party in power	Reasons for termination (real)	Whether taken back	Remarks
(1)	(2)	(3)	(4)	(5)	(6)
HSL (1)	2 union activists dismissed	Yes	Violence during strike	No	Lost at tribunal
ECL (3)	6 union activists dismissed	Yes	Basically for inciting strike	No	In a settlement treated retrenched without notice pay
AMT (5)	47 union activists dismissed	Yes	Basically for inciting strike	No	In a settlement treated retrenched without notice pay
JSF (6)	8 union activists dismissed	Yes	For espousing the dispute	No	Were paid money to leave the concern
APL (9)	3 workers dismissed including 2 union activists	No	For union activities – under the false pretext of closing a section where they worked	No	One settled and left. Two fought up to the Supreme Court and won, but were made to resign after receiving compensation
ASL (10)	8 union activists dismissed	Yes	For union activities, on frivolous charges of beating a worker 1 km outside the factory	No	Managing director initially promised to take them back, but later on backed out. Case referred for tribunal adjudication. Lost due to no proof of proper espousal
HVG (13)	6 union office-bearers suspended	No	For inciting go-slow	Yes	Taken back as per a settlement
EL (14)	2 union office-bearers suspended	Yes	For espousing demands	No	Referred to Tribunal. They settled and left
RVL (18)	3 union office-bearers suspended	No	For inciting workers to participate in *bandh* against IR Bill, 1978	No	Two settled and left. One went to tribunal and lost

OEW (19)	5 union activists suspended after reference, later dismissed	No	For espousing the dispute	No	Settled their account and made to leave
SKW (20)	17 union activists suspended	No	For inciting the strike	Yes	After the dispute was referred and strike prohibited, workers came back to work; and in the package suspended workers were taken back
HPL (22)	46 activists dismissed	No	Union activities	No	After nearly one year of strike, treated retrenched without notice pay; 330 more strikers treated similarly
UCB (23)	8 union leaders dismissed	No	Union activities	No	Settled their dues and were dismissed
CEW (25)	4 union activists	No	Union activities	No	Settled their dues and were made to leave
OS (26)	2 union leaders dismissed	No	Union activities	No	All workers resorted to 103 days' strike. Strike prohibited, cases referred. Lost at tribunal
FRF (27)	3 union leaders dismissed	Yes	Union activities, but charges of theft levelled	No	Made to leave and take dues
SEW (28)	2 union leaders dismissed	Yes	Union activities	No	Made to leave and take dues
FAP (29)	6 union leaders told to leave	Yes	Union activities	No	Management paid Rs. 2,000 to each, for leaving
KGK (32)	80 HMS activists suspended, 23 dismissed	No	Union activities	Yes	Suspension of 80 revoked. Five had left; 18 who were contesting at tribunal taken back on condition that they support the INTUC union
SL (30)	6 workers suspended	Yes	Union activities	No	As a package deal made to leave and settle dues
PSL (33)	40 workers suspended	No	Union activities	No	Four settled and left, 36 contested at tribunal

Source: Saini (forthcoming)

TABLE 13.3 Labour cases pending before labour courts/industrial tribunals and those cleared during 1996–97

Sl. No.	Name of state/UT	No. of cases pending on 31.03.1997	No. of cases cleared during 1996–97
1	Uttar Pradesh	21,386	9,194
2	Assam	167	25
3	Punjab	13,105	6,663
4	Tripura	3	NIL
5	Gujarat	120,968	23,721
6	Maharashtra	83,360	17,292
7	Chandigarh	931	263
8	Haryana	8,432	3,045
9	Andaman and Nicobar	12	2
10	Manipur	4	NIL
11	Nagaland	NIL	20
12	Pondicherry	135	19
13	Karnataka	15,451	3,099
14	Madhya Pradesh	83,665	20,701
15	West Bengal	2,336	519
16	Tamil Nadu	*18,922	7,192
17	Goa	106	28
18	Daman & Diu	7	1
19	Orissa	4,866	623
20	Himachal Pradesh	598	1,047
21	Delhi	*40,214	5,821
22	Kerala	4,021	1,658
23	Rajasthan	16,001	3,039
24	Andhra Pradesh	5,402	3,952
25	Bihar	7,008	696
26	Jammu and Kashmir	95	11
	Total	447,195	

* Includes cases under Sections 33, 33A and 33C of the IDA

Note: In the states/UTs of Lakshadweep, Dadra Nagar Haveli, Mizoram, Meghalaya, Arunachal Pradesh and Sikkim, no industrial dispute is pending

Source: Unpublished data collected from the latest records of the Ministry of Labour, Government of India, New Delhi

NOTES

1. The *Economic Survey 1998–99* of the government of India shows that the Planning Commission has estimated the population below the poverty line (for the year 1993–94, which is the latest available) to be 320 million, which is 36 per cent of the total population of the country. The percentages for some other

developing countries are: China, 22.2; Philippines, 35.7; Indonesia, 11.4; Malaysia, 17.4; Thailand, 8.1.

2. The author participated in conciliation proceedings in four of these thirty-three disputes. The remaining twenty-nine were sampled from the total of 195 interest disputes handled by the industrial tribunal in a five-year period.

3. India become independent on 15 August 1947.

4. See, for example, Olney (1997) for details on the constitution and structure of labour adjudicatory bodies in European countries.

5. The term 'reference' denotes the act of the appropriate government to send a dispute to a tribunal/labour court for adjudication. A party cannot approach these bodies directly. The government has the discretion to refer or not to refer a dispute for adjudication (see 10, IDA).

6. As on 31 March 1997. This number also includes cases under section 33, 33A and 33C of the IDA. This figure was obtained from the unpublished records of the Ministry of Labour, Government of India, New Delhi.

REFERENCES

Abel, R. (1973) 'A Comparative Theory of Dispute Institutions in Society', *Law and Society Review*, 8: 298.

Baxi, U. (1982) *Crisis of the Indian Legal System*, Delhi: Vikas.

— (1994) 'Industrial Justice Dispensation: The Dynamics of Delay', in D. S. Saini (ed.), *Labour Judiciary, Adjudication and Industrial Justice*, New Delhi: Oxford and IBH.

— (1995) 'Unorganized Labour? Unorganized Law?', in D. S. Saini (ed.), *Labour Law, Work and Development*, New Delhi: Westwill.

Baxi, U. (ed.) (1988) *Law and Poverty – Critical Essays*, Bombay: N. M. Tripathi.

Bhattacherjee, D. (1988) 'Unions, State and Capital in Western India: Structural Determinants of the 1982 Bombay Textile Strike', in R. Southall (ed.), *Labour and Unions in Asia and Africa – Contemporary Issues*, London: Macmillan.

Burawoy, M. (1985) *The Politics of Production*, London: Verso.

Clark, J. and Lord K. W. Wedderburn (1983) 'Modern Labour Law: Problems, Functions and Politics', in Lord K. W. Wedderburn et al. (eds), *Labour Law and Industrial Relations: Building on Kahn-Freund*, Oxford: Clarendon Press.

Dhavan, R. (1989) 'Introduction', in M. Galanter (ed.), *Law and Society in Modern India*, Delhi: Oxford University Press.

Dickens, L. et al. (1985) *Dismissed – A Study of Unfair Dismissal and the Industrial Tribunal System*, Oxford: Basil Blackwell.

Edelman, L. B., Howard S. Erlanger and J. Lande (1993) 'Internal Dispute Resolution: The Transformation of Civil Rights in the Workplace', *Law and Society Review*, 27(3): 497.

Encyclopaedia Britannica (1987) Vol. 26, Chicago: University of Chicago Press.

Hanami, T. (1980) 'The Settlement of Labour Disputes in Worldwide Perspective', *International Social Science Journal*, XXXII: 490.

Kahn-Freund, O. (1977) *Labour and the Law*, London: Stevens.

Kjønstad, A. and J. H. Veit-Wilson (eds) (1997) *Law, Power and Poverty*, Bergen: CROP Publications.

Munger, F. (1990) 'Trial Courts and Social Change: The Evolution of a Field Study', *Law and Society Review*, 24: 217.

Nader, L. (1975) 'Forums for Justice: A Cross-cultural Perspective', *Journal of Social Issues*, 31: 151.

NLLA (National Labour Law Association) (1994) *Indian Labour Code* (Draft), New Delhi: National Labour Law Association.

Nonet, P. and P. Selznick (1978) *Law and Society in Transition*, New York: Harper and Row.

Olney, S. (1997) 'European Labour Court Experiences', in ILO (ed.), *Labour Adjudication in India*, New Delhi: ILO-SAAT.

Patel, A. and K. Desai (1995) 'Rural Migrant Labour and Labour Laws', in D. S. Saini (ed.), *Labour Law, Work and Development*, New Delhi: Westwill.

Ramaswamy, E. A. (1984) *Power and Justice*, Delhi: Oxford University Press.

Saini, D. S. (1991) 'Compulsory Adjudication of Industrial Disputes: Juridificaton of Industrial Relations,' *Indian Journal of Industrial Relations*, 27: 1.

— (1992) 'Delay in Industrial Adjudication: Crisis of the Tribunal System,' *Cochin University Law Review*, XXI: 209.

— (1995a) 'Compulsory Adjudication Syndrome: Some Implications for Workplace Relations in India', in D. S. Saini (ed.), *Labour Law, Work and Development*, New Delhi: Westwill.

— (1995b) 'Leaders or Pleaders: Dynamics of Briefcase Trade Unionism Under the Existing Legal Framework', *Journal of Indian Law Institute*, 37: 73.

— (1997) 'Labour Court Administration in India', in ILO (ed.), *Labour Adjudication in India*, New Delhi: ILO-SAAT.

— (1998) 'Liberalization, Human Face and the Labour Justice System', in P. Singh (ed.), *Legal Dimensions of Market Economy*, University of Delhi: Faculty of Law, and New Delhi: Universal Book Traders.

— (forthcoming) *Industrial Relations in India: Law in Action*.

Saini, D. S. (ed.) (1994) *Labour Judiciary, Adjudication and Industrial Justice*, New Delhi: Oxford and IBH.

Storey, J. (1992) *Developments in the Management of Human Resources*, Oxford: Blackwell.

US Department of Labor (1994) *Fact-Finding Report – Commission on the Future of Worker–Management Relations* (John T. Dunlop Commission Report), Washington, DC: Department of Labor.

Upadhyay, S. (1995) *Delay in Industrial Adjudication: A Case Study of Central Government Industrial Tribunal* (mimeo), Noida, India: V. V. Giri National Labour Institute.

Waterman, P. (1975) 'The Labour Aristrocracy in Africa: Introduction to a Debate', *Development and Change*, 6: 3.

Wedderburn, K. W. (Lord) (1971) *The Worker and the Law*, 2nd edn, Harmondsworth: Penguin Books.

Index

Dworkin, Ronald, 216
Dyzenhaus, David, 77

Economic and Social Council
    (ECOSOC), 21; Resolution 1503, 23
Eichmann, Adolf, case, 77
Eide, Asbjørn, 166–7
elderly, uninsured, programme for, 183
emergency relief programmes, in
    Greece, 182–3
Employment Equality Bill (Ireland),
    207
empowerment, 116; of labour, 272, 287;
    of women, 115, 210
energy crisis, 18
Equal Opportunities Act (Sweden), 211
equal opportunities, in USA, 151
equal rights, 2
equal treatment concept of equality, 216
Ethics of Liberation, 74
ethnic movements, in USA, 152
European Commission, 133; document
    on exclusion, 125–6
European Convention for the
    Protection of Human Rights and
    Fundamental Freedoms, 167–70,
    189
European Convention of Human
    Rights, 173
European Court of Human Rights, 162,
    172, 189, 192
European Social Charter, 188, 189
European Union (EU), 124, 132, 175,
    214; gender equality strategies in,
    211; Recommendation no. R ChS
    (93)1, 189–90
Excise Ordinance (Sri Lanka), 236, 241
exclusion: and rights, 124–36; definition
    of, 124–8; of black people in USA,
    152; relationship to poverty, 125,
    126, 127, 128

Falk, Richard, 56–8, 71
Family Credit, 93
famine, causes of, 131
Federal Office of Child Support
    Enforcement (USA), 87
female infanticide, 251
Finland, 131

Finnish Free Mission, 111
Food and Agriculture Organization
    (FAO), 27
food stamps, 38
Forced Labour Convention (1930), 249
Foxley, Alexander, 66, 70
France, social security system in, 124–8
Frei Ruiz-Tagle, Eduardo, 64
French Revolution, 140
Friedman, Milton, 63, 71

Gano Shahajyo Sangstha (GSS)
    (Bangladesh), 111
Garreton, Manuel Antonio, 58
Garzón, Baltasar, 54, 58, 59, 60, 72, 75
Gaygusuz v. Austria case, 168, 172–3
gender equality machinery, 213–14
gender inequality, relation to poverty,
    209–10
gender mainstreaming, 205–22; as new
    strategy, 214
genocide, 60
Germany, social benefits in, 173
Gilmore, G., 145
Giri, V.V., 274
Global Plan for Equal Opportunities
    (Portugal), 215
globalization, 17, 18, 21
gold-collar workers, 270
Graham v. Richardson case, 38
Greece, 5–6; constitution of, 186–8;
    welfare strategies in, 175–202

Harberger, Arnold, 63
von Hayek, Friedrich, 71
homelessness, 125, 126, 185
Honduras, 70
human rights, 18, 162–74, 249, 287;
    education in, 263; new, 260; relation
    to right to development, 14–17;
    violations of, 23, 24, 25, 26, 54–79
Human Rights Commission for
    Children (India), 257

Idealist school, 56
IKA Fund (Greece), 179
immigration, 31; regulation of, 32, 33,
    34, 39, 43 (in US welfare policy,
    36–9); undocumented, 41

poverty proofing, 6, 208–9, 217–19
Princeton Principles of Universal
  Jurisdiction, 60
prison, commitment to, in relation to
  child support, 98
prisoners, rights of, 132
privatization: in Chile, 66, 68; in India,
  278; in UK, 214
property: definition of, 3; in relation to
  poverty, in Norway, 162–74
PROSHIKA organization
  (Bangladesh), 112–13
Public Interest Legislation, 247, 258–60
public interest litigation, strengthening
  of, 263
public–private distinction, 4, 7

racial minorities, mobilization of, 151
racial prejudice, in USA, 152
racism, 125
Rattray, K.O., 62
Rawls, John, 216
Reagan, Ronald, 63
Realist school, 56
reciprocity, principle of, 177–8, 182
redistribution, cross-border strategy
  for, 44
remittances of migrant workers, 43, 44
Revenu Minimum d'Insertion (RMI)
  France), 124–5, 128–9; weakness
  of, 132–3
right to know, 264
right to work, 132; in Portugal, 205–6
rights: civil and political, 56, 57, 72,
  129–31; cultural, 56, 72; developing
  understanding of, 263; economic,
  129–31, 132–3; exclusion and,
  124–36; legal see legal rights;
  of children, 247–68, 260–4 (in
  India, 251–4); of citizenship, 196;
  of labour organization, 271–3; of
  strike action, 275; of the excluded,
  131–4; political, 72; poverty of, 59;
  social, 56, 57, 72, 129–31, 133–4,
  187, 188, 195, 205; to citizenship,
  186–7; to human dignity, 186–7; to
  peace, 260; to security, 206; to social
  security, 165; to standard of living,
  165, 206 see also administrative

redress; human rights; legal rights;
  petition, right to; right to know *and*
  welfare rights
rights-based strategy, 195, 196
rights culture, 195, 206
Rorty, R., 195
Rushdie, Salman, 24

safety-net, right to, 193; policies; use
  of legal machinery as means to
  promote, 194–6 *see also* social
  safety-net
Saini, D.S., 279, 280, 281, 283, 285
Salvation Army, 111
Savar Ganosastha Kendro (GK)
  (Bangladesh), 113
Scottish Executive, 129
Selznick, P., 286–7
Sen, Amartya, 71, 76, 127, 131
sewage treatment, 68
Sheba Shongho organization
  (Bangladesh), 111
sickness benefits, 131, 166
single mothers, 37, 43, 84, 167; US
  welfare policy for, 35–6
single-parent families: poverty of, 5; on
  income support, cost to economy,
  87; US policy on, 31
Smith, Adam, 71
Sober Sri Lanko organization, 232
social advocacy, 145
social genocide, 59, 72–6; definition
  of, 74
Social Inclusion Partnerships
  (Scotland), 129
social safety-net approach, 177, 182;
  claims, impact of legal instruments
  on, 192–4; legal establishment of,
  185–92
social security: as property, 162; in
  Norway, 162–74 (structure of,
  163–5); right to, 205
Social Security Act (1935) (USA), 35
Social Security Committee (UK), 90–1
Social Solidarity Allowance for
  Pensioners (Greece), 180, 181
social state principle, 187
solidarity, 5, 124, 133, 135, 151, 157, 180,
  182

United States of America (USA), 4, 5; attitude to right to development, 24; child support in, 86, 94; civil rights groups in, 144; class issues in, 150–5; cross-border poverty relationship in, 31–53; legal system in, 139, 144–6, 156–7; low wages economy in, 31; workfare in, 128

universal accountability, 262

Universal Declaration of Human Rights (UDHR), 15, 16, 55, 57, 72, 130, 165, 206, 252, 264, 271

universal jurisdiction, 54, 60, 72

universality, 205

Uruguay, 75

Vienna Declaration (1986), 11, 12–13, 15, 26

Vienna Declaration and Programme of Action (1993), 16, 55, 60, 251

'voluntary activity', definition of term, 109

voluntary societies, rules for, 112

wages: low, 69 (in Chile, 70; in Mexico, 34; in US, 36; in USA, 36–9); minimum, 206, 270, 287

war against the poor, 241

War on Poverty (USA), 153–4

Warren Court (USA), 146, 154

water, access to, 68–9

welfare: right to, 129; selective, 195; Southern model of, 192

welfare rights, development of, 175

welfare state, 130, 163, 227

White Paper on Social Policy (EU), 132

Weit-Wilson, J.H., 287

women: disadvantaged, 209–10; empowerment programmes for, 115; experience of poverty, 218; Muslim, going out to work, 116; part-time work of, 210; reduced social security access of, 91; right to vote, 212; traditional dependent role of, 94; working patterns of, 209

women-and-children-only towns, 43, 44

Women's Unit (UK), 213

workfare, 37, 128

working class, 150; consciousness of, in USA, 150–5; identification with immigrants, 151; in Italy, 148; in USA, 152; struggles of, 149

working hours, maximum, 206

World Bank, 20, 27, 59, 61, 67, 110, 232

World Conference on Human Rights (1993), 15, 55

World Summit for Social Development (1995), 16, 271–2

World Trade Organization (WTO), 59